Valley Vets II

★ ★ ★ ★ ★ ★ ★ ★ ★ ★

Korean and Vietnam Veterans
of the Lower Rio Grande Valley

William L. Adams

EAKIN PRESS Fort Worth, Texas
www.EakinPress.com

The Korean conflict map on page 2 and the Southeast Asia map on page 74 were taken from the 1988 revised edition of the U.S. Army Center of Military History's *American Military History* and reproduced with the kind consent of Gen. John S. Brown, the center's chief historian.

Copyright © 2004
By William L. Adams
Published By Eakin Press
An Imprint of Wild Horse Media Group
P.O. Box 331779
Fort Worth, Texas 76163
1-817-344-7036
www.EakinPress.com
ALL RIGHTS RESERVED
1 2 3 4 5 6 7 8 9
ISBN-10: 1571688587
ISBN-13: 978-1571688583
Library of Congress Control Number 2004109758

To

Russell Paul Adams—

my beloved son.

Contents

Preface vii

Korean War Overview 1

The Valley's Fighting Men 13
    Alfredo Hernandez, Jr. / 13
    Jesus Hernandez / 17
    David Barrera / 21
    Fernando Rodriguez / 24
    E. E. "Gene" Cockrill / 27
    Herman Wise / 32
    Juan Guerra / 38
    Harold L. Adams / 41
    Lorenzo Ramos, Jr. / 45
    Jesus F. Rodriguez, Sr. / 48
    Juan Lopez / 00
    Raul J. Leal / 00

The Enemy 61
    Jin Dinghan / 00
    Lin Qingshan / 00
    Lu Yunkui / 00
    Hao Ru / 00

Vietnam War Overview 73

The Valley's Fighting Men 94
    Luis Lucio / 94
    Raymond L. Simonsen / 99

Ben Cortez / 101
   Richard Ghionzoli / 103
   James Franceschi / 105
   Feliciano Saldivar / 109
   Willie F. Canant, Jr. / 114
   Reynaldo Aguinaga / 116
   Edward Moore / 118
   Luis Martinez / 124
   Richard Wilson / 127
   Jose Gonzalez / 131
   Juan Torres / 133
   Epitacio Lopez / 137
   Jose Ibarra / 139
   Manuel Torres / 142
   Raul Saavedra / 146
   Garrett Tyra / 150
   Joe Serrano / 152
   Roberto Garcia / 154
   James A. Scanlan / 156
   Catarino Murillo / 158
   Jose G. Leal, Jr. / 163
   Doss Kornegay, Jr. / 167
   Roberto Miguel Rodriguez / 170
   Alonso "Tiny" Barrientes, Jr. / 172
   Ralph J. White, Jr. / 176
   Leonardo Villarreal / 181
   Joe Castillo / 184
   Ricardo Ortiz / 190
   Leonel Casanova / 192
   Ricardo Zapata / 194
   Roberto Pina, Sr. / 197

The Enemy 200
   Nguyen Duc Huy / 202
   Nguyen Van Khien / 207
   Dang Thi Phuong / 209
   Nguyen Duc Hanh / 211

Reflections 214
Endnotes 233
Bibliography 237
Index 239

Preface

In 1999 I published *Valley Vets: An Oral History of World War II Veterans of the Lower Rio Grande Valley*. Even while that book was in preparation I began to feel that, in all fairness, I was obligated to write a sequel that would chronicle the experiences of the Valley's Korean and Vietnam veterans. Accordingly, over the past couple of years, I have required senior and graduate students enrolled in either my American Military History or Cold War courses at the University of Texas at Brownsville to seek out and interview local Korean and Vietnam veterans as a part of the writing component of those two courses.

In most cases the students sought out their subjects among their personal circle of friends, relatives and neighbors, or, alternatively, were directed to likely subjects by local chapters of the American Legion and Veterans of Foreign Wars. The veterans who participated therefore represent the same locales the university draws upon for most of its student body—principally Brownsville, but also Harlingen, San Benito, Port Isabel, South Padre Island, Los Fresnos, and other Valley communities.

As the book gradually took shape, it occurred to me that greater depth and balance would be obtained if some of the enemy soldiers' voices were also heard. In the heat and hatred of battle our Asian adversaries were usually dismissed as mere "gooks"—so they were seen and so they were called. This dehumanization of the enemy is necessary for soldiers. It is difficult to kill a man. The sane mind revolts at the prospect, and yet that is precisely what is expected and demanded of American servicemen in battle. If, however, that man in the cross-hairs can by a sleight of the mind be transformed into a "gook," no more human than a cut-out silhouette used for target practice, killing him becomes, if not easy, at least tolerable. Of course, every reader of this book and certainly every veteran represented in this book recognizes that those "gooks" were real people. They had names, they had faces, they had families, and they had dreams. In order to hear their voices and to see the wars from their eyes, I traveled to northern China in May 2003 and interviewed several combat veterans of China's People's Liberation Army who fought in Korea, and in

December 2003 I flew to Vietnam and interviewed Viet Cong and North Vietnamese Army veterans in Hanoi and in the typical farming village of Thanh Ha in Nam Ha Province.

Compiling an oral history such as this one necessarily involves the help of numerous people, and as a result I have many people to thank. First of all I thank my senior and graduate students for conducting the bulk of the interviews. I thank the brave veterans who agreed to recount their experiences—sometimes painfully. I am indebted to my dear friend Yang Hua-jing ("Jane"), a star reporter for *International Talent Monthly*, who served as my faithful guide and interpreter while in China. Professor Jin Dinghan of Peking University kindly located and arranged interviews with suitable Chinese veterans of the Korean War. In Vietnam I have to thank my two interpreters and guides—friends—Nguyen Viet Bac ("Quân") and Nguyen Van Loi ("Nam"), and also Gen. Nguyen Duc Huy of the Vietnam People's Army. Here at home in Brownsville, Lorena Estrada efficiently prepared the computer disks and the typed manuscript, while my dear wife proofread that same manuscript. Juan Miguel Gonzalez of UT-Brownsville Media Center sized and enhanced the book's photographs. Friend and artist Kisti Beckwith designed and painted the book's arresting cover.

Finally, I thank once again my friend, patron, and brother-veteran Dr. Bennie Walthall. Bennie, a retired geologist of the Arabian-American Oil Corporation, asked to underwrite the costs of preparing this book, my fourth, just as he has done all the others.

WILLIAM L. ADAMS
Brownsville, 2004

Korean War Overview

The Korean War is only understandable within the context of the Cold War. As World War II drew to a close, fractures in the winning U.S.-British-Soviet alliance were already appearing. This was not surprising, considering that the alliance had been forged solely out of necessity—the threat the Axis Powers, and principally Nazi Germany, posed to all three of the Alliance members. Nothing other than the precept "the enemy of my enemy is my friend" could have forced the capitalist, Christian democracies of Britain and America to align themselves with communist, atheistic, dictatorial Russia. But as that war drew to a close, the prospect of continued cooperation of the Allies in the postwar world grew increasingly unlikely. Numerous resentments had grown up. For one thing, the Soviet Union blamed its staggering war losses—27 million lives[1]—on British and American tardiness in opening the second front. The fact that the Soviets were forced to bear the brunt of the German onslaught from June 1941 until June 6, 1944, when the Anglo-American D-Day landings took place and opened a second front, a western front, left an indelible impression on the Soviet psyche. The Russians asked themselves why the landings could not have been made in 1942 or 1943 and thereby have relieved the pressure on the Red Army and saved millions of Russian lives. Protestations by President Franklin Roosevelt and Prime Minister Winston Churchill that the D-Day landings could not have been successfully undertaken any earlier than June 1944, due to shortages of landing craft and the need to first "soften up" Germany with a strategic bombing campaign, were dismissed out of hand. Stalin and the Russians believed the long delay was intentional—a perfidious scheme of Roosevelt and Churchill to promote German-Russian attrition—let them "bleed each other white"—and so ensure Anglo-American dominance of the postwar world.

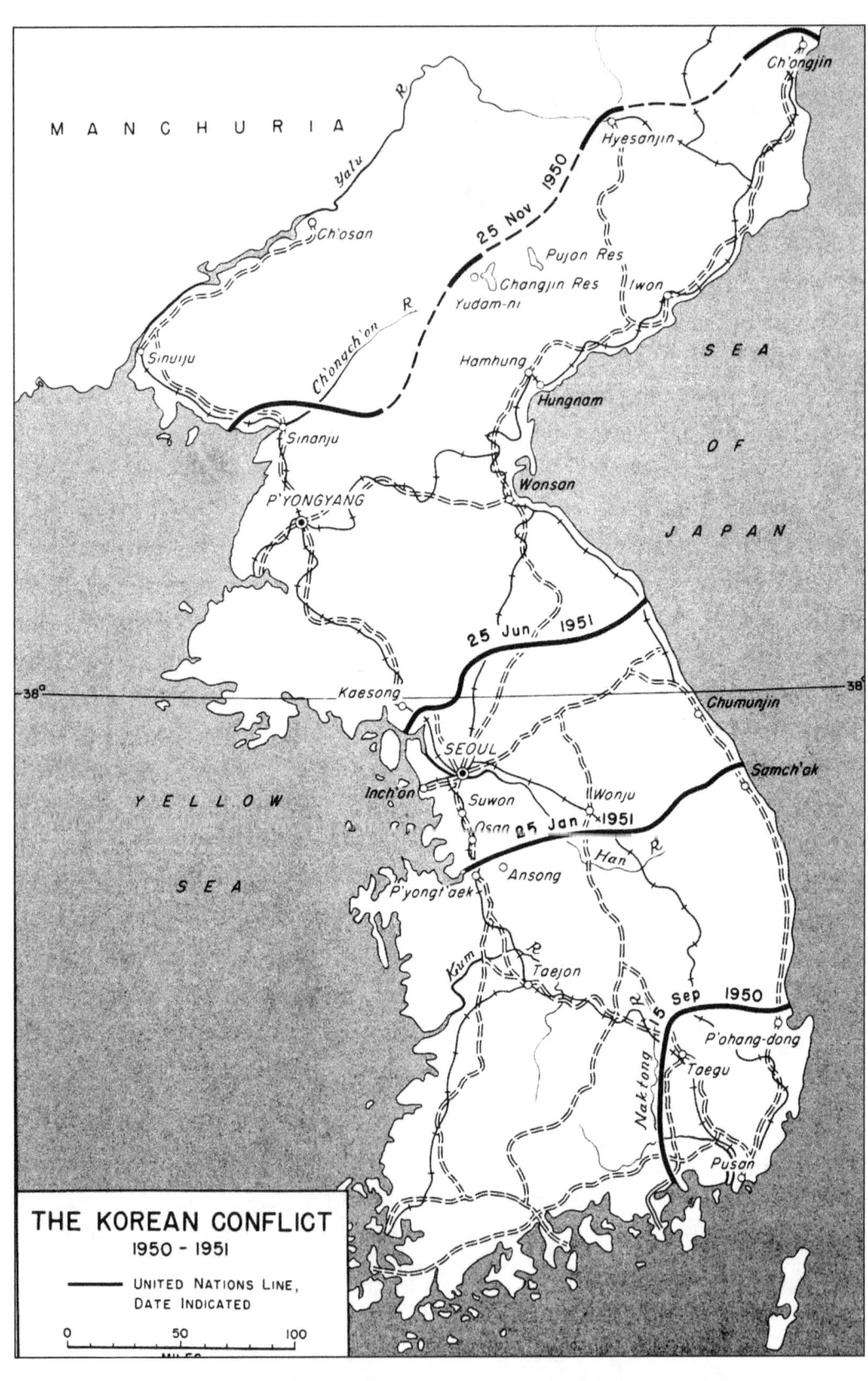

Equally galling to the Soviets was the fact that they were not made privy to the Manhattan Project—the Anglo-American project to develop atomic weapons—until the day after the first atomic bomb was test exploded near Alamogordo in the New Mexican desert. Why had they not been included? Why had Soviet scientists not been invited to participate in the project? The Soviets concluded that the only possible answer could be, once again, that the Anglo-Americans were intent on achieving a postwar hegemony.

For their part, the British and American mistrust of their Soviet counterpart was solidified by the Russians' failure to live up to the agreements reached at the Yalta (February 1945) and Potsdam (July-August 1945) conferences. Those conferences had called for British and American forces to sweep across Western Europe and the western part of Germany as far as the Elbe River and then, having disarmed Nazi forces and achieved pacification, to sponsor United Nations supervised elections in the liberated nations and allow them to choose their own governments. Nazi Germany, of course, was to be partitioned into occupation zones, with Britain assuming control of northwestern Germany and the U.S. assuming control of southern Germany. Simultaneously, the Red Army was to sweep across Eastern Europe and eastern Germany to the Elbe, and, while the Soviets would be permitted to occupy eastern Germany indefinitely, they agreed to allow the liberated nations of Eastern Europe to hold free elections under United Nations auspices. After the war, though, they reneged on this agreement. United Nations officials were not allowed into Eastern European nations to conduct elections—rather, Soviet officials conducted sham elections and installed communist puppet regimes in each of the subject countries. By 1946, at Fulton, Missouri, ex-Prime Minister Churchill would speak of an "Iron Curtain" having descended on Europe from the Baltic to the Adriatic, separating the world into two halves.

That same division was mirrored half a world away in Korea. Yalta and Potsdam had called for the 38th Parallel to serve as a temporary dividing line in the Korean Peninsula (as the Elbe had done in Europe), where the Japanese held sway from 1910 until the final days of the Pacific War. On August 8, 1945, two days after the Hiroshima blast and just six days before the Japanese capitulation, Soviet forces, which had been massing along the Russian-Chinese border, swept into Japanese-occupied Manchuria and thence on into Korea. The Russians were to disarm (and eventually repatriate) the Japanese occupiers north of the 38th Parallel while American forces did the same south of that line—all as a prelude to conducting Korean-wide national elections under a United Nations authority. But once again, the Soviet Union dismissed the agreement, barred UN election officials from entering northern Korea, and instead installed a communist stooge they had been preparing for that task for several years: Kim Il Sung. In southern Korea, where the UN elections did take place, Syngman Rhee was elected president. Now Korea was two nations: a communist North Korea (the Democratic People's Republic of Korea), and a democratic, at least ostensibly, South Korea (Republic of Korea). By mid-1949 both the Soviet Union and the United States had withdrawn their occupation forces, although the U.S. did leave behind a small advisory group to help train the South Korean armed forces.

4 Korean War Overview

Nineteen forty-nine proved to be a seminal year—a crystallizing year—in the emergence of the Cold War and a bi-polar world. In that year the Soviet Union successfully exploded an atomic bomb, ending the American monopoly on nuclear weapons. Also in that year Mao Zedong's communist forces emerged triumphant in their long struggle with Chiang Kai-shek's Kuomintang army, and Chiang and remnants of his forces and their families fled to Taiwan. The new People's Republic of China was proclaimed on the mainland and quickly concluded a treaty of mutual assistance with the Soviet Union. The recommendations of George Kennan, U.S. ambassador in Moscow, to treat the expanding communist bloc like a cancerous tumor and to prevent it from spreading by ringing it with U.S. bases and an American alliance system was adopted in 1949 as the U.S.'s postwar foreign policy—the "containment policy"—and in April of that year the cornerstone of that alliance system was laid with the creation of NATO (North Atlantic Treaty Organization). Other alliances would follow: CENTO (Central Treaty Organization); SEATO (Southeast Asian Treaty Organization); ANZUS (Australia-New Zealand-United States Treaty); and a number of bilateral treaties between the U.S. and individual nations, until a reasonably solid barrier to communist expansion was erected.

In the case of Korea, however, there was some cause for apprehension. In the first month of 1950 the U.S. publicly announced an Asian defense perimeter that would run from Alaska's Aleutian Islands down through Japan and south to the Philippines. Korea was left outside the line. Did this mean it was considered strategically expendable, and might be forcefully annexed into the communist sphere without fear of American retaliation?[2]

North Korea's Kim Il Sung apparently thought so, or at least thought the risk worth hazarding, for with strong Moscow encouragement—and armed with Soviet weaponry—he launched a dawn attack Sunday, June 25, 1950. The North Korean army crossed the western sector of the 38th Parallel, under cover of an artillery barrage, with the South Korean capital of Seoul, a scant thirty-five miles south of the Parallel, as their initial objective.

The North Koreans advanced rapidly against light ROK (Republic of Korea) resistance for, in truth, the North Korean army was clearly the superior force. The North's army numbered 135,000 to the South's 95,000. But far more important than the slight numerical advantage was the North's qualitative advantage. A significant portion of North Korean troops had combat experience in fighting the Japanese while serving in Korean volunteer units attached to either the Soviet Red Army or China's People's Liberation Army during World War II.[3] Moreover, the North Koreans had been much better equipped by their Soviet ally than the South Koreans had been by the Americans. The North had 120 T-34 tanks, abundant artillery, and 180 Soviet aircraft. The ROK army had almost no combat experience, no tanks, and only a handful of training and reconnaissance aircraft.[4] Seoul fell to the invaders in just three days. Meanwhile, the North Korean strategy began to unfold. In addition to the main thrust to Seoul in the western part of the peninsula, a second North Korean force was advancing south along the east coast and still a third force down the central spine. They were pushing all before them in an effort to clear the whole of the peninsula.

America moved swiftly to thwart this possibility. Within twenty-four hours of the invasion's commencement, the UN Security Council, at America's behest, passed a resolution calling for North Korea's immediate withdrawal from the South, and when this failed to produce any result, on June 27 the Security Council asked member nations to provide forces to assist South Korea in repelling the invasion. Eventually fifteen nations would provide ground combat forces in roughly this order of strength: U.S., Great Britain, Australia, New Zealand, Canada, Turkey, Greece, France, Belgium, Luxemburg, the Netherlands, Thailand, the Philippines, Columbia, and Ethiopia.[5] Another nine nations offered naval forces, air forces, or medical units. America's legendary Gen. Douglas MacArthur, who was then commanding U.S. occupation forces in Japan, was appointed to lead the coalition forces.

But whereas sizable UN forces were pledged, it would in most cases be months before those forces arrived in the theater. So the immediate question MacArthur faced was whether he was going to be able to stop the rapid North Korean advance before they had secured the entire peninsula and presented the world with a fait accompli. To answer that question MacArthur visited South Korea and personally assessed ROK prospects of halting, or at least slowing, the North Korean drive. Those prospects, he determined, were not good—so he sought and received President Truman's permission to introduce immediately American forces from the only units to hand, i.e., U.S. occupying forces in Japan and Okinawa. About 60,000 troops in total could be scratched together, but these troops had become more comfortable in their constabulary role as occupation troops, and most would be combat novices. Moreover, aside from light arms, they were shamefully under-equipped: there were virtually no American tanks to be found anywhere in Asia, and precious few ground support aircraft. To make matters worse, transport was short and the whole 60,000 could not be committed at once to at least achieve the advantage of mass. They would have to be introduced piecemeal to try to halt the North Korean advance. It was Lt. Gen. Walton H. Walker who was given this unenviable task as commander of all American, ROK and, when they arrived, UN forces.

Because of the rugged nature of the Korean terrain and the underdeveloped transportation system—the bulk of the peninsula was composed of hills, and relatively few roads and railroads traversed the country—Walker could surmise the likely routes of advance of the three North Korean forces as they moved southward, obviously intended to converge on Pusan, the main southeastern port where American and, eventually, UN forces and supplies were landed. In July, Walker committed his first "piecemeal" unit. This was a 540-man force of riflemen known, after its commander, as Task Force Smith. Its orders were to set up a roadblock to the main North Korean force—the western force—advancing on the line Seoul-Suwon-Osan-Taejon-Taegu-Pusan. Near Osan, Task Force Smith dug in astride the road, hoping to halt the North Korean force spearheaded by thirty-three tanks and a full division. The result of this first face-to-face meeting of American and North Korean troops was not auspicious. The Koreans attacked Task Force Smith head on while simultaneously swarming around both flanks to envelop the unit. The Americans abandoned their equipment and fled with heavy casualties. As the weeks unfolded, this same scenario played out time and again as other blocking units were committed to slowing the relentless North Korean advance. By early August the Americans had already suffered 6,000 casualties and their ROK allies a stunning 70,000 and had been pushed into a small corner of southeastern Korea.[6] But here General Walker ordered a final stand: "There must be no further yielding under pressure from the enemy. From now on let every man stand or die."[7]

The defense of the "Pusan Perimeter" was the first successful operation of the Americans and their allies in the Korean War. The perimeter stretched in a broad arc from sea to sea at a distance ranging from twenty to fifty miles from the port of Pusan—a toehold on the peninsula that had to be held at all costs for reinforcements and supplies to arrive. Here, with his frontal area minimized and both his flanks anchored on seacoasts, Walker had short interior lines of communications and could quickly move forces around to shore up any breaches in the perimeter. Futhermore, the North Korean Army was now at maximum disadvantage. They were over 300 miles from their main supply bases in North Korea, and their supply lines were increasingly vulnerable to attack. U.S. warships brought up from the Seventh Fleet could bombard the roads and railroads that ran along both the east and west coasts, while land-based and carrier-based aircraft could interdict rail and vehicular traffic in the interior—beyond the range of naval guns. Strafing and bombing—including napalm bombing—of North Korean troops pressing on the perimeter were also taking a heavy toll. And, meanwhile, coalition reinforcements were finally arriving: army and marine units from Hawaii and the States, a British infantry brigade from Hong Kong, and, most importantly, 500 medium tanks. The North Korean drive was dead in its tracks. And now MacArthur could move over to the offensive.[8]

In MacArthur's long and illustrious career, a career that featured many superb operations—his World War II New Guinea campaign, his retaking of the Philippines—no operation ranks higher than his Inchon Landing. This operation was brilliantly conceived and brilliantly conducted. And it was daring, so daring that many of his superiors in Washington were reluctant to permit it.[9] The plan was to make an amphibious landing with two divisions (the Army's 7th Division and the Marine's 1st Division) in the built-up port area of Inchon, twenty-five miles west of Seoul. The port itself presented special difficulties, including extreme tidal variations and high sea-walls to scale. But, once taken, the divisions could proceed east, retake Seoul, cross the narrow waist of the peninsula, and cut many of the road and rail lines supplying the North Korean forces massed at the Pusan Perimeter. The plan was carried out to perfection; Inchon was taken on September 15, 1950, and Seoul was liberated on September 29. From thence the Americans proceeded east and established themselves as a blocking force to intercept any North Koreans trying to flee from the south, and fleeing they were. Simultaneous with the Inchon Landing, General Walker launched an offensive all along the Pusan Perimeter. At first the North Koreans resisted stubbornly, but as news reached them of events in the North and the impending certainty of finding themselves entirely cut off, they broke and fled. About 30,000 eventually succeeded in reaching the north, but many thousands more were captured or forced to hide out in the mountains of South Korea. The North Korean invasion army had ceased to exist.[10]

At this point MacArthur could have concluded the Korean War. He had driven out the invading force, restored the country's borders and reinstalled President Syngman Rhee in Seoul's Blue House. He had, in fact, fulfilled all the tasks of his UN mandate. And yet, with the North Korean army now in tatters and a UN coalition army assembled and on the ground in South Korea, it would seem almost foolish not to march north, destroy the North Korean army's remnants, and restore Korea as one unified nation. There were warnings emanating from the Soviet Union and China that UN forces must not cross the 38th Parallel, but these warnings were regarded mainly as bluff. MacArthur, and both the American and South Korean governments, favored crossing the Parallel and reunifying the nation, and on October 9, 1950, the UN sanctioned it.

The coalition's northern advance was rapid; the North Koreans could put up no more than token resistance. The North's capital, Pyongyang, fell on October 19. Meanwhile, UN forces streamed up both coastlines and through the central region in a reverse image of the North Koreans' rapid southerly advance of the previous summer. MacArthur had every intention of his ground forces reaching the northern border—the Yalu River—and completing the conquest of the North before the onset of the harsh Korean winter.[11]

What MacArthur had failed to detect, however, was that in the latter half of October, China had in fact decided to enter the war and had successfully, and completely undetected, inserted 200,000-300,000 Chinese soldiers into the hills and ravines of Korea's far north.[12] Most of these Chinese troops were battle-hardened veterans of the war with Japan or the "liberation" campaigns against the Kuomintang. Their stealth was exceptional: they marched only at night and camouflaged themselves by day. They completely outfoxed coalition aerial reconnaissance. And their numbers were growing.[13]

In the final week of October and throughout the month of November, as successive columns of UN forces entered the far northern region, they, by turns, were engaged and mauled by these capable Chinese troops. On November 28, 1950, MacArthur messaged Washington: "We face an entirely new war."[14]

And, indeed, it was. The Chinese now mounted a major attack all along their lines that sent American and coalition forces reeling. General Walker, the ground force commander, was forced to order a general retreat. Pyongyang was abandoned on December 5, and by December 15 the coalition had withdrawn all the way back to the 38th Parallel, where Walker hoped to dig in and solidify a coast-to-coast defensive line, and at least preserve South Korea from a second invasion. Alas, General Walker was himself killed in a vehicular accident near the front on December 23, 1950, and the task of preserving the South and rallying the demoralized coalition forces fell to Lt. Gen. Matthew B. Ridgway (who had won World War II fame in the heroic defense of encircled Bastogne), hastily flown out from Washington on December 26.[15]

But, as matters proved, UN forces were not strong enough to prevent a second communist invasion of the South. Chinese forces assisted by a rapidly reconstituted North Korean army launched a major new offensive on New Year's Eve. United Nations lines crumbled and on January 4, 1951, Seoul fell for the second time to communist forces. Indeed, Chinese and North Korean troops surged southward as much as forty to fifty miles below the Parallel before their offensive power was spent.

Potentially the loss of Seoul for a second time, coupled with the prospect of the coalition having to combat a powerful new opponent in a war of indeterminate duration, could have had a debilitating effect on his troops' morale, but Ridgway effectively scotched such thinking. He correctly prognosed that although his opponent could muster sufficient strength to mount periodic offensives, these offensives would have to be of very limited duration—perhaps no more than two weeks. The North's supply system was simply too primitive and too vulnerable to coalition naval and air forces to enable the enemy to sustain an attack. Accordingly, Ridgway evolved a simple strategy to foil the enemy. When attacked, coalition forces were instructed to give ground (albeit stubbornly so as to inflict maximum casualties), and then, when the enemy paused to resupply, to counterattack and pursue—again with the aim of inflicting maximum casualties on enemy forces. This strategy worked.[16] The communists were pushed back out of South Korea. Coalition forces recovered Seoul in March, and by April 1951 they stood once again at the 38th Parallel.

But while the lines see-sawed back and forth on the Korean front, a momentous debate was underway at the highest levels of the American government. The UN's commanding general, Douglas MacArthur, could see that while his ground commander might be able to hold South Korea, American and UN forces in the theater were insufficient to totally defeat the Chinese and restore Korea as a unified nation. Only such an outcome would satisfy MacArthur's conception of victory.

Frustrated by the strictures imposed upon him and by Washington's and the United Nations' apparent willingness to countenance a "limited victory" in a "limited war," MacArthur instead called for a dramatic expansion of the war—immediate escalation of force levels and direct retaliation against the Chinese mainland including: (1) blockading China's coastline; (2) destroying China's war industries by naval and air attack; (3) introducing Nationalist Chinese army units to fight alongside UN forces in Korea; and (4) "unleashing" Chiang Kai-shek and allowing Nationalist forces from Taiwan to make diversionary attacks on the mainland.[17]

However, MacArthur's bold proposal was welcomed neither by the Truman administration nor by most of the general's superiors at the Pentagon. Any escalation of force levels in Asia would necessarily cause a concomitant reduction of American and NATO force levels in Europe, and this was not acceptable. Aside from protecting the American homeland itself, protecting the highly developed, highly industrialized democratic societies of Western Europe from Soviet expansion was seen as the first principle of U.S. foreign and defense policy.

Quite simply, MacArthur was told he had to make do with the forces already assigned to him. There would be no substantial reinforcement. If he had the strength to regain the North with these forces, well and good. If he only had the strength to hold his ground and salvage South Korea, that was well and good also. And, if he had insufficient strength to hold the South, so be it: he was to evacuate American and UN forces, and Korea would be sacrificed.[18]

For a general of MacArthur's ego and aggressive spirit this was too much to accept. When he learned that President Truman was planning to signal China and North Korea of U.S. willingness to open peace negotiations premised on restoring the status quo antebellum, i.e., the acceptance of the 38th Parallel as a permanent dividing line, MacArthur brazenly pre-empted the president by sending what amounted to his own personal ultimatum to his Chinese and North Korean military counterparts. The wording of his message was designed to effectively sabotage any peace efforts:

> The enemy must by now be painfully aware that a decision of the United Nations to depart from its tolerant effort to contain the war to the area of Korea, through an expansion of our military operations to its coastal areas and interior bases, would doom Red China to the risk of imminent military collapse.[19]

This act of insubordination, committed in March 1951, was followed a month later by another. In this instance MacArthur used House Republican Leader Joseph W. Martin as his mouthpiece to deliver these words to the House: "If we lose this war to communism in Asia the fall of Europe is inevitable." There could be "no substitute for Victory" in Korea.[20] This was going beyond insubordination; now MacArthur was attempting to dictate foreign policy.

Clearly a crisis was at hand. No president, no commander-in-chief, could have or should have tolerated such a blatant violation of a basic tenet of American government—that uniformed members of the military accept the orders of their civilian masters. President Truman did what he had to do: on April 11, 1951, he "relieved" MacArthur of his command and elevated Matthew B. Ridgway to replace him. Lt. Gen. James A. Van Fleet was in turn appointed to take over from Ridgway as commander of UN ground forces.

From this point (April 1951) onward, until an armistice was finally concluded (July 27, 1953), the nature of Korean hostilities changed. The sweeping, see-sawing rounds of offensives, retreats, and counteroffensives that had marked the earlier phase of the war and in which virtually the whole length of the peninsula might be incorporated into the battlefield had ended. Instead, the opposing forces now fought for relatively tiny increments of territory for the twin purposes of demonstrating their force's resolve and of strengthening their side's hand at the negotiating table.

For educated soldiers such as those fielded by America and the coalition open admission by their governments and military superiors that their lives were being risked for limited objectives in a limited war (which, prima facie, it was not strategically crucial for their nation to win) was extremely taxing on morale. Nonetheless, the overwhelming majority of Korean War troops stoically accepted their lot, fought valiantly, and sacrificed themselves when necessary. Their fate was nothing so grand as to help win a war or even to liberate a city. No, their fate was to help maintain a static line on a map ("Line Kansas," "Line Wyoming," "No Name Line") or to take or hold a hill, ridge or valley in order to "straighten the line" and keep the frontal area exposed to the enemy at an absolute minimum. The grueling ferocity expended in taking or holding such hills, ridges and valleys is evidenced in the tragic nicknames they earned: "Hamburger Hill," "Bloody Ridge," "Heartbreak Ridge," "The Punch Bowl." Perhaps even more poignant were battles referenced only by a number—a metrical elevation cited on a topographical map: "Hill 235," "Hill 504," "Hill 914"—scraps of terrain meaningless and anonymous to all but those who fought and died there.

Meanwhile, the four-way negotiations which pitted North Korean and Chinese delegates against South Korean and American representatives and which had begun in July 1951 dragged interminably on at the small, no man's land village of Panmunjon. There were frequent breakdowns in the talks due to one perceived slight or another. Clearly the communist delegates were stalling for time, hoping that some slightly improved tactical situation on the battlefield might by parlayed into better terms at the negotiating table. The communists were in no hurry. They were very mindful that the voting public in both America and the democratic nations of the coalition were growing restive with the slow pace of the negotiations and that this might force the American and South Korean delegation to ease their bargaining position in hopes of hastening an agreement.

The issue of prisoner of war repatriation served as the principal bone of contention—or excuse—in delaying an agreement. The U.S., South Korea, and the United Nations coalition partners all insisted that the provisions of the 1949 Geneva Convention regulating warfare be abided by: that is, individual prisoners of war should each have the right to choose between repatriation or being set at liberty in the land where they are held captive. China and North Korea quite correctly could foresee this would prove an international public opinion disaster for their dictatorial and impoverished societies. They therefore insisted upon the forced repatriation of all prisoners of war.

Ultimately two events solved the impasse. In February 1953, Dwight D. Eisenhower was sworn in as the new Republican president, and he let it be known to the communist regimes in North Korea, China, and the Soviet Union that if an armistice were not quickly forthcoming, "We intended to move decisively without inhibition in our use of weapons, and would no longer be responsible for confining hostilities to the Korean peninsula."[21] A few months before, America had successfully test exploded a hydrogen bomb, and these blunt words, coming from a retired five-star general, had to have had a sobering effect on Pyongyang, Beijing, and Moscow.

The second event that helped break the logjam was the death of Soviet Premier Josef Stalin in March 1953. A Politburo power struggle had ensued, and consolidation rather than adventurism seemed the wiser course for Soviet foreign policy, at least for the time being. And, when all was said and done, it was the Soviet Union—the only first-rate power within the communist bloc—that served as military guarantor for its Chinese and North Korean allies.

At any rate, before the end of March the impasse was breached. The repatriation issue was turned over to a Neutral Nations Supervisory Commission and the problem was expeditiously solved. The armistice itself called for hostilities to cease at 8:00

A.M., July 28, 1953, and for the combatants to withdraw two kilometers from the cease-fire line, creating a four-kilometer-wide demilitarized zone (DMZ) that serves to this day as the national border between North and South Korea. The armistice—the truce—still remains in effect, but a permanent peace treaty has remained elusive, and technically the two sides remain at war.

American casualties in Korea included 33,629 killed, 103,284 wounded, and 5,178 missing or captured. Total UN casualties were over 550,000 including 95,000 dead—the bulk of these being ROK soldiers. It is believed North Korean casualties numbered about 600,000 in total and Chinese casualties about 900,000.[22]

America had concluded its first limited war of the Cold War era.

The Valley's Fighting Men

Alfredo Hernandez, Jr.
INTERVIEWED BY RODOLFO R. FLORES

I interviewed Mr. Hernandez at his home in Olmito, where I found him outside his house repairing his weedeater. He is a man of gentle demeanor and looks younger than his years.

MR. FLORES: I THANK YOU FOR YOUR TIME, AND IT IS MY PRIVILEGE TO HEAR YOUR STORY. WHEN THE WAR BROKE OUT, WERE YOU ALREADY IN THE SERVICE OR DID YOU JOIN?

Mr. Hernandez: I was already in the army—the 2nd Infantry Division, 38th Field Artillery Battalion, B Battery. We were stationed at Fort Lewis in Seattle, Washington, and the whole division got shipped straight to Korea.

MR. FLORES: HOW LONG WERE YOU IN KOREA?

Mr. Hernandez: I was there almost a year. We were stationed at the Pusan Perimeter, where we stayed almost a month. We didn't move or nothing. We just fired at the enemy, and finally, when they made the invasion in Inchon, we started pushing forward. We went seventy-five miles one day north; we were still in South Korea and finally stopped at Yung Dun Poo to rest. We put up tents. We had not slept good for days. The first night we were going to sleep, one truck from service battery caught on fire and the ammunition started blowing up, and we had to take off running to the hills to get away from the explosions. Somebody left a cigarette that caught a sleeping bag or something on fire and destroyed all of our trucks. Down at the Pusan Perimeter, they killed a friend of mine from Iowa, I. D. Johnson. They shot him right in the forehead. [Mr.

14 Korean War

Alfredo Hernandez at home in Olmito, Texas, with his medals.
—Courtesy of Alfredo Hernandez

Hernandez points his index finger just above his eyes.]

We were packing the ammo. We were coming home for Christmas. Our trucks were going on the "Red Ball Express" that carries supplies for the infantry, but after a few days, they said we're not going [home]. We're going to the front and we had to pack everything up and load it. We had those 105 howitzers that we hooked to the truck. We went up north; we were supporting the infantry. We went up and up [northward] and the last position where we were, around the 28th of November, a Chinese patrol hit us, and they killed about four or five of our people. Finally, a "half track" with four machine guns and a battery of 155s of black soldiers fired point blank at them and there were fragments flying all over the place.

MR. FLORES: DO YOU MEAN THAT THE GROUP OF BLACK SOLDIERS WERE SEGREGATED?

Mr. Hernandez: Yes, later on, in '52, they integrated. After that attack, we pulled back about the 30th [of the month], supporting our infantry, and began to fire to the south, the opposite way. We reached a roadblock of damaged vehicles when it was getting almost dark. We had another battalion, the 15th Field Artillery, fired all their ammo and left their guns there. The 23rd Infantry Regiment loaded their trucks, went east, and got out. It got dark and the shooting began. I was the only one of my crew of fourteen that got out. A grenade landed by my feet and I still carry a fragment right here in my leg. [He lifts his pant's leg and points to his wound.] Our commanding officer told us everybody is on his own. We fired one round and they poured machine gun fire at us. I got between the doors of the truck to shield myself; finally, we just took off. They [the enemy] were all over the place, hundreds of them, but we couldn't see them. It was night. One of my friends named Blankenship from Tennessee hit one with the butt of his carbine. We ran until we got to a railroad. My friends that went to the north got captured. Only four or five from our group that went south got out. We just kept going and going, walking all of the next day until we got to the 1st Cavalry Division.

MR. FLORES: YOU WERE OVERRUN?

Mr. Hernandez: Well, we were trapped. They said it was a strategic withdrawal, but [laughs].

MR. FLORES: DID YOU REMEMBER THE WORDS OF YOUR COMMANDING OFFICER, "EVERYONE FOR HIMSELF"?

Mr. Hernandez: He got captured, too.

MR. FLORES: WOULD YOU SAY THAT WAS THE WORST ENCOUNTER?

Mr. Hernandez: If they [enemy] would have been more orderly and more organized, we could not have gotten out. The road was blocked by tanks taken out, and they kept killing people. Men were wounded and were run over by our own vehicles. Nobody came to help us. When we got to the 1st Cavalry that night, we were packed in a truck like matches. I almost fell off a couple of times. We went to the North Korean capital, Pyongyang, and stayed a couple of days. Then I went with the infantry, all the way to Pusan. All the way to the end. Then we finally pulled back with the 37th Field Artillery, I think, and we had to wait to get replacements and train them. By the end of December, we were already on the line again. There were big battles in February, April, and May of '51.

MR. FLORES: HOW WAS YOUR MORALE?

Mr. Hernandez: We were trying to get out ... My friends, they were 33-month POWs, a lot of them didn't die. I called one last night from Paul's Valley, Oklahoma. I talked until 3:00. I have some in North Carolina, Illinois, New York, all over. I go to the POW reunions. I was there [Korea] from August of '50 till July of '51.

MR. FLORES: DID THEY SHIP YOU BACK TO THE UNITED STATES WHEN YOU WERE WOUNDED?

Mr. Hernandez: They wouldn't even give me a Band Aid! They said as long as you can walk, you're okay 'cause there were a lot of wounded and dead and everything—I think about it all the time.

MR. FLORES: HOW LONG BEFORE THEY SHIPPED YOU BACK?

Mr. Hernandez: They rotate us, about a year. They give us points. My cousin was there. He was in the 9th Infantry, lost a finger and had fragments all over his head.

MR. FLORES: BY A MORTAR?

Mr. Hernandez: By a mortar or artillery. One day we broke a record. We fired

10,000 rounds in one day. We had eighteen 105 howitzers: A, B and C Battery. Our battalion commander got shot five times! And they left him for dead. Finally, somebody came and saw him move and got him out and he lived. It's in this book. [He points to a book that he had brought out for me to see before my arrival.]

MR. FLORES: WHAT WAS YOUR FARTHEST TREK NORTH?

Mr. Hernandez: We were about thirty-five miles [south] from the Yalu River.

MR. FLORES: WE LEARNED IN CLASS THAT THE AMERICAN MILITARY CONFRONTED CHINESE-SPEAKING SOLDIERS NEAR THE YALU RIVER AREA.

Mr. Hernandez: MacArthur wanted to go to the Yalu River and we'd be home by Christmas, but there were thousands and thousands of Chinese. They were attacking everybody. A marine division and the 7th Infantry Division got to the Yalu River, and they had to fight their way back; some regiments got trapped and wiped out.

MR. FLORES: YOU WERE THERE IN THE WINTER. HOW DID THE COLD WEATHER AFFECT YOU?

Mr. Hernandez: When we got trapped, it was 30 below zero and we had summer clothes. We hadn't gotten winter clothes yet. It was a disaster. It was pretty bad.

MR. FLORES: NOT ONLY DID YOU HAVE TO FIGHT THE ENEMY, BUT YOU HAD TO CONTEND WITH THE WEATHER ALSO?

Mr. Hernandez: They couldn't get them [winter clothes] up there. The cold was bad, and we had to fire and be there in the open.

MR. FLORES: DID YOU CARRY A RIFLE?

Mr. Hernandez: I carried an M-2 carbine. There was no M-14s. They had the 30-caliber that you had to load every time.

MR. FLORES: DID YOU GET THE PURPLE HEART?

Mr. Hernandez: Yes, I was in six major battles. One silver star and one bronze star. They didn't have as much artillery as we did when we were there, until later on in '53. But they would get two or three divisions and they would keep firing. We would overpower them by the artillery, but they kept coming and coming. There were piles of enemy dead. We were at the back, the infantry was at the front. Our forward observers (our lieutenant with a radio operator) would call back with coordinates to tell us which way to fire, elevation, and deflection.

MR. FLORES: THE HOWITZER WAS A 155?

Mr. Hernandez: A 105. It was a little projectile [extending his hands]. It had seven powder bags. Depending on the distance, they tell us how many powder bags to take off. The 155, two guys had to carry the shell, push it in and put the powder bags behind it.

MR. FLORES: ANYTHING ELSE YOU REMEMBER THAT STOOD OUT?

Mr. Hernandez: In February and around May, there were battles that we fired for days without stopping. They said "keep firing until we tell you to stop." That's how some forward observers got killed, because they were out there with the infantry. They had a rough time. Sometimes we fired short rounds because something went wrong. We [would] hit them. They were real upset—maybe they had the wrong coordinates or something.

MR. FLORES: WHERE WERE YOU STATIONED WHEN YOU RETURNED TO THE STATES?

Mr. Hernandez: We left from Seattle, Washington, and returned through Seattle, Washington. They sent me back to Fort Lewis, Washington, with the 195th Field Artillery. I went to class to train those that were going to Korea on active reserve.

[Mr. Hernandez proceeds to bring out and show me more of his war mementos and, of course, his medals, neatly displayed in a glass and wood frame crafted by one of his close friends.]

Jesus Hernandez
INTERVIEWED BY RODOLFO R. FLORES

I interviewed Mr. Hernandez at his home in Harlingen, Texas. He is a friendly, hospitable man, having walked out of his house to greet me as I was parking my vehicle.

MR. FLORES: I THANK YOU FOR YOUR TIME AND HOSPITALITY, AND IT'S MY PRIVILEGE TO HEAR YOUR STORY. WHEN THE WAR BROKE OUT, WERE YOU ALREADY IN THE SERVICE?

Mr. Hernandez: I joined in 1948, before the conflict started in 1950. I took training in Camp Chaffee, Arkansas, and then they sent me to Guam, the island, in the area of Saipan and Las Marianas Islands. I stayed there for about eighteen months and then came back with two weeks' leave; then I had to report to Seattle, Washington. I went in an ordnance company and then the war broke out, so they started asking for volunteers. I had a friend from San Benito, named Cavazos, who said let's get together and sign up for the Korean War. I signed up, but he didn't. In July 1950 they shipped us to Korea. We arrived in Pusan, I believe.

Jesus Hernandez at home in Harlingen, Texas, with his medals.
—Courtesy of Jesus Hernandez

MR. FLORES: HOW LONG WERE YOU THERE?

Mr. Hernandez: We stayed there for about a day and a night and then they took us out to the front. I remember, like right now, that first night. They made us dig about five holes, and that dirt there is not dirt, it's like rock. We started one foxhole going about six, eight inches and we moved forward. I remember we had a Sergeant Blum who had a company here [he motions his hand on the table] and a company on the left-hand side. The next day we moved forward. To tell you the truth, I was scared. I was young, nineteen years old. I remember the first day they attacked us. Most of the fighting was early in the morning, three or four o'clock in the morning, sometimes daylight. I lost a lot of acquaintances, friends. I was new with that outfit, with that company. We went to a place they used to call "Cloverleaf Hill."

MR. FLORES: WERE YOU A RIFLEMAN?

Mr. Hernandez: At that time I was a private first class, in charge of a squad. The reason, I don't know. I had a corporal under my command. I think I learned quite a bit during the war.

MR. FLORES: WERE THERE A LOT OF FIREFIGHTS AS OPPOSED TO ARTILLERY?

Mr. Hernandez: We had both. We had artillery and we had a lot of mortars coming in. I remember one night we moved a hundred, two hundred yards at that place, "Cloverleaf Hill"; we were overrun. We had fourteen men left out of 180. Everybody ran; many were killed. They overran us. It was about ten to one. I ran. If you [were outnumbered] ten to one, you have to look for help or run for your life. We stayed about twenty-four hours behind enemy lines, trying to cross over to the American side. I had a sergeant who was wounded on the side, and I had a young man who was wounded on the hands. We walked about ten to fifteen miles that night until we got to an American company, and they sent us back and we got some reinforcements. It was the worst. It was the worst. It was in the middle of my nine months [time served in Korea]. The be-

Jesus Hernandez (left) with his cousin Alfredo Hernandez at Fort Lewis, Washington, 1950.

—Courtesy of Jesus Hernandez

ginning, like I say, I can't remember a lot of things. You can't remember things from fifty years ago. Every day for me, I had to pay attention to what was going on here, what was going on there, take care of your friends because your life is in their hands and their life in your hands. We lost people. I don't say that I cried but that man [killed] up over there [motions up toward heaven] could have been me, and I was too young. I remember little things, you know, that happened. Like I told you, I cannot give you specific details, but we were up and down [in reference to advancing and retreating]. I was nine months in the combat zone.

MR. FLORES: YOU DID NOT RECEIVE "R&R" (REST AND RECUPERATION)?

Mr. Hernandez: I did receive R&R, in other words, not R&R. I was wounded, and they sent me to Japan and then to the United States. I got wounded near a river, "Cong Cong," or something like that, and if you don't mind, I'll get the DD 214 to know exactly the place where I was wounded. [Mr. Hernandez stands, goes to another room, and brings back and shows me a document.] Amral, A-M-R-A-L, Korea. I was wounded left elbow, left hand, right wrist, neck and shoulder. I was hit with a mortar. [His hands quiver as he holds the paper then points to several areas of his body.] My hand here [shows me two missing fingers on his left hand], I have shrapnel here. I have shrapnel in my head, my shoulder; they took out a big chunk of shrapnel. That's as much as I can remember. I know I joined the United States Army in 1948 and I was discharged from Camp Aliberry, Indiana, in 1952.

MR. FLORES: YOU WERE IN COMBAT FOR THE NINE MONTHS THAT YOU WERE THERE?

Mr. Hernandez: Yes, except one time that I went to Japan because we turned over in a truck. After that is when I got hurt. [Again he says in Spanish that he doesn't remember much, that he feels bad, as if to apologize for not giving more information. His breathing is deeper and he seems to be stressed.] I thank God that I came back home. Many of my friends didn't come back home, sergeants, and lieutenants. Most of the time when we were moving, we lost three or four men. I, I can't say more, sorry sir. I wish I could help you more. [Mr. Hernandez appears more stressed.] We went to hell in that Korean conflict. It wasn't a war, [has] been forgotten, and we like to forget what we went through. Sorry if I can't help you anymore.

MR. FLORES: WHEN YOU RETURNED, HOW DID THE PEOPLE OF SAN BENITO TREAT YOU?

Mr. Hernandez: They were glad to see me. I got married in Sarita and went to work at the Kenedy Ranch near Sarita. Then I went to work at King Ranch, stayed about twelve years and came back home.

MR. FLORES: WHAT KIND OF RELATIONSHIP DID YOU HAVE WITH THE SOUTH KOREANS, AND DID YOU SERVE TOGETHER WITH THEM?

Mr. Hernandez: We had some with us as guides, but some of those gentlemen wanted to be free, but at the same time, they used to go to sleep at night on guard duty. I used to get up and make rounds. It's pretty hard to sleep when you're in combat. It was easier to sleep in daytime than nighttime. We used to make nights like days, two, three o'clock in the morning, you could hear the cannons or the whistling of the mortars going by overhead. But if you don't hear the whistling, you'd better duck, because they're coming in.

MR. FLORES: WHEN YOU LANDED IN KOREA, DID YOU HAVE ANY IDEA OF WHAT YOU WERE GOING TO EXPERIENCE?

Mr. Hernandez: No, no, no. I was very young, inexperienced. I knew we were going to war. Let me put it this way, the eighteen months that I was in Guam and Saipan, it was all right, for practice [training]. When they shipped me to Korea, we practiced shooting at balloons, to get the feel of the weapon. Now, when you get in combat, it's a very different story, because there you have to fight for your life.

MR. FLORES: DID YOU FEEL LIKE THE ARMY DID NOT GIVE YOU ENOUGH TRAINING?

Mr. Hernandez: Well, in a way they did, but eighteen months without using a weapon is hard, to start practicing on a ship, where you go up and down on the waves...

[At this moment, Mr. Hernandez' wife, Antonia, arrives and introduces herself.]

Mr. Hernandez: Flores, I don't know what to say, I remember little things here, little things there, but I wish I could... is there something else that I can help you with? I'll try. I remember a lot of things, but it hurts. It hurts because of the acquaintances that I met when I was going to Korea. We lost about fifteen Mexican friends. When we were on the ship, we'd get to know each other and ended up in the same company, some in the same squad.

MR. FLORES: DID YOU HAVE BLACK SOLDIERS IN YOUR GROUP?

Mr. Hernandez: We had some, we were mixed. I had one as a companion and he did not want to sleep at night. He was scared. I talked to him and he realized that he had to rest, to sleep. I used to take care of him, and he would take care of me. One time we went up a hill that took about one and a half hours to get up to the top. About ten or eleven o'clock that night, they [the enemy] started attacking. They were already there. I scattered the men out in a line [gestures with his finger on the table]. I remember someone running in front of me and I fired a couple of shots and he ran like a deer. It turned out to be my black friend. We started running; we couldn't hold them, the hill, there were too many, North Koreans and Chinese. In fifteen minutes, we were down the hill.

MR. FLORES: DID YOU LOSE SOME MEN?

Mr. Hernandez: Yes, we lost some men. I can't give you names. That colored boy that I fired a couple of shots at, he came back. I saw him at the hospital where I was at [recuperating from injuries] and he resented that I had fired shots at him, but I didn't mean to. He had left the position that I had put him in.

MR. FLORES: DID HE SAY WHY HE LEFT HIS POSITION?

Mr. Hernandez: They were pushing us [back], there were too many. We ran, and I ran, too. I fell at one time and hit my back on a rock, maybe. We ended up behind the 23rd Division; how we got there, behind them, I don't know. They didn't see us; it was at night.

MR. FLORES: DID YOU HAVE ANY PROBLEMS KEEPING YOUR MORALE UP?

Mr. Hernandez: Well, one time, yes. I remember that we were making an advance, and for some reason or other, my legs gave out on me; the reason, I don't know. From that day I felt that I wasn't going to come back home. I thank God that He gave me the opportunity to see my family again. [Pauses and takes a deep breath.] I remember when Mr. Bob Hope came to see us and made us happy. He is one of those men who always thought about the troops. Mr. Flores, I don't think I can help you anymore. [Mr. Hernandez having said this for the third time, I decide to end the interview.] I'm sorry, and I hope that I was of some help to you.

MR. FLORES: YES, SIR, YOU MOST CERTAINLY WERE.

[We continue speaking as I put my recorder and notes away. He shows me pictures of family and of his younger years working as a cowboy on the King Ranch. I bid farewell, and he is kind enough to escort me with his vehicle to the freeway for my trip back.]

David Barrera
INTERVIEWED BY LEO VILLARREAL

Mr. David Barrera is an owner of Sandy's Restaurant on the corner of Levee and 10th Street in downtown Brownsville. I called Mr. Barrera and that same day he invited me down to his place of business around 2:15 P.M. to do the interview. I had met Mr. Barrera at the Veterans of Foreign Wars post at the veterans' monthly meeting.

MR. VILLARREAL: WHAT MILITARY BRANCH DID YOU SERVE IN AND WHAT WAS YOUR RANK?

Mr. Barrera: I served in the army. I enlisted in the army in July 1948. I entered as a private, moved up in rank to corporal, and when I was discharged I was a staff sergeant. Let me tell you how I became a corporal. The commander in charge asked me if I wanted to go on a trip. I asked him what it was about. He told me, "Trust me. You'll have fun." So I said I would do it. The trip was a special assignment to pick up a deserter from Stillwater, Minnesota. We had to sign for two firearms. My partner and I headed for Stillwater, picked up the prisoner who was an army deserter, and returned the next day. Well, when I got back they told me I did a good job, handed me a paper, and told me to sew them on: corporal.

MR. VILLARREAL: WHY DID YOU VOLUTARILY ENLIST IN THE ARMY?

Mr. Barrera: Well, let me tell you, I have a story for you. I enlisted because at that time I did not have a job and I did not know what I was going to do. The reason why I joined the army was because of the advertisement of Uncle Sam and the phrase, "I want you." If they would have had the phrase, "be all you can be," like they do now, I would have probably made a career out of it or done something more, but I did not know. Also, right before we were going to boot camp they called my name out and five others. They asked us if we wanted to go to OCS (Officer Candidate School) since

David Barrera

our scores on the military exam were high. I declined. A big mistake. If I would have known better I could have been an officer, stayed in for thirty years, and I would be receiving a pension check right now.

MR. VILLARREAL: WHAT WAS BOOT CAMP LIKE?

Mr. Barrera: You know, let me tell you how I took the army. I did my job the best I could. Did not complain. Some guys I knew would complain, "Why did we join the army?" We were sent to Fort Lewis in Washington, which is between Olympia and Tacoma, and that is where I was stationed until they sent me to Korea. But while I was there, I just did what they told me. The captain would come in and check my living quarters and I had everything neat. My bed was perfect. They could bounce a quarter on it. One time the captain turned to the sergeant and said that if all the soldiers were as neat as this man I wouldn't need to do inspections. This is why I got promoted quicker than others who just complained about being in the army. I would tell them, "Hey, you're here. Just make the most of it." Some of them would never get out of PFC (Private First Class).

MR. VILLARREAL: WHAT WAS YOUR FUNCTION IN THE ARMY BEFORE AND DURING THE KOREAN WAR?

Mr. Barrera: In Fort Lewis I was with the Corps of Engineers. I was a parts clerk and I liked it, but when they sent me over to Korea I was assigned to the Signal Corps. It's like communications. I would have to relay information from the front line to the back. Why they put me there I do not know, but I did not question anyone. They asked me to do it.

MR. VILLARREAL: WHEN DID YOU GET SENT TO KOREA AND WHAT WAS YOUR EXPERIENCE THERE?

Mr. Barrera: Let's see. I was sent in September 1950. I was attached to a "bastard unit," which is what we called a bigger unit, and we entered Korea through the port city of Inchon. Before we arrived in Inchon there was only three infantries from Japan: the 1st Cavalry, the 24th and the 25th Infantries, and those were not enough to stop the North Koreans. They were pushed back to Pusan and did not advance until we arrived in Inchon. I never really fought in actual combat. They would tell us that if the line would fall to hide in a hole that is created by the bombs and don't shoot because there were too many of them. Your life was always in danger being in Korea at that time, and being an American soldier you had to be careful. If I would have been in combat I can tell you this, I would not be here right now, and every one of us knew that if we would have had to fight, we die. Because we saw the soldiers dying and the bodies lying on the ground and there were just too many of them. We were right behind enemy lines, like four to five miles from the fighting. I would have to move in a way where they could not see me because if the enemy spotted me I could be shot. So it was dangerous even though I did not fight the enemy. By returning gunfire I could still be killed.

Let me tell you one thing about the war. When those Chinese entered the war (because we went all the way up to the Yalu River and MacArthur wanted to bomb those bridges), President Truman pulled him back. Our military jets would get in dog fights with Russian Migs, and when the enemy was getting their butts kicked they would fly into Manchuria and our planes could not follow them and finish them off. That was bad. What kind of war was that? We could not use our artillery; we could not bomb them, and take out the bridges; so the Chinese had everything. They came right in and pushed us back to the 38th Parallel. Those Chinese only had rifles. They did not have any major artillery, but they had numbers. We would kill a good number of them, but they kept coming. They were like a bunch of ants.

Another thing that is tough is how do you know who is a North Korean and who is a South Korean? We did not know who to shoot at. You don't know, the enemy could be right there next to you. It was dangerous. Sometimes you could not sleep because you were afraid. I mean they all look the same. But that is what happens when you go fight a war like in Korea, and I imagine Vietnam was the same, because the people were the same. It was between North and South.

MR. VILLARREAL: HOW DID YOU FEEL ABOUT THE KOREANS?

Mr. Barrera: No, I did not hate them. We knew some because we also fought with them and sometimes we would joke around when we had the chance, but the problem was how to tell them apart. A North Korean can sneak in and pretend to be a South Korean soldier and kill as many of us as he could. It was scary, but I really did not hate them back then or now. I even know a few because some of them have businesses around the area and we talk about it. In fact one of them wants me to gather the Korean War veterans so he can buy us dinner and thank us for what we did for them.

MR. VILLARREAL: IS THERE ANY OTHER EXPERIENCE FROM KOREA—MAYBE SOMETHING OTHER THAN COMBAT?

Mr. Barrera: Yes, let me tell you the weather in Korea is bad. I mean below zero weather. It was bad. People would get frostbite and a lot of people lost toes and fingers because we were wet and cold. I almost lost my toes, but I was lucky. I did not have feeling in my toes. It was scary. On top of fighting a war we were also worried about freezing to death, but seriously I have never experienced any weather like in Korea. It was bad.

MR. VILLARREAL: WHEN DID THE WAR END FOR YOU?

Mr. Barrera: Well, we were on a rotation in Korea. You go for one year and then return and get replaced by new soldiers coming from the States. But I did not get to leave. My replacement was three months late, so I was there for a total of fifteen months. I ended up coming home in December 1952, and I returned to the U.S. I had only signed up for three years but there was a congressional order extending the service for all military people for one more year because of the Korean War and tensions in Europe, I guess. Anyways, I only served nine months out of the year because they let those that had fought in the Korean War leave early. So I was discharged from the army in April of 1952.

MR. VILLARREAL: DID THE KOREAN WAR AFFECT YOU IN ANY WAY?

Mr. Barrera: You know, what really makes me angry is when I read an article like in this magazine [he shows me a veteran's magazine he receives monthly]—or a television show—saying the Korean War is the "Forgotten War." How could you call it a "forgotten war"? People died. Families lost sons, husbands, and fathers. Are you going to tell them that the war is forgotten? This really bothers me. I saw men buried. They would dig a big hole, stack the bodies in the grave, and stick a cross for each one of the soldiers. The military would not send your body home. They were fighting a war. The only way the body would come home is if you died in the hospital in Japan, because that is where you went if you were injured.

Fernando Rodriguez
INTERVIEWED BY H. JAIME CRUZ

I interviewed Mr. Rodriguez at his home. I have known him all of my life and I have been friends with his children all that time. Our families have always been close ever since his family moved in across the street from us around 1953, and my parents are godparents to his children. When I approached him about this interview, he seemed quite pleased to be asked. We met in the family home in the dining room. I had given him a list of sample questions a few days previous and he was prepared with dates and locations of his service.

MR. CRUZ: WHEN DID YOU ENTER THE ARMY?

Mr. Rodriguez: The first time was on April 4, 1945, and then again in 1948. I was supposed to go in 1941, but I was sick. The way it was, I was sick in bed with the flu and a doctor came to see me. I lived with my aunt and uncle on 13th Street. I was too sick to draft so they made me 4-F. Later I was afraid I'd be nothing, so I tried to volunteer and they accepted me. I was supposed to be in, in 1942. My younger brother was in CCC and went into the army in the infantry and then tank destroyers. He went to England, France and Germany, then Austria and Czechoslovakia.

MR. CRUZ: WHERE DID YOU GO FOR YOUR BASIC TRAINING?

Mr. Rodriguez: I went to Fort Hood for seventeen weeks of basic training. It was thirteen weeks and then they added four weeks. You could not even miss one minute. Once I lost two hours and I had to make them up in another company. I was supposed to be a paratrooper because the pay was higher, but the war ended. We were in the last week of basic when they dropped the atomic bomb on Japan. We got a lecture on what an atom was. [For much of the next three years Mr. Rodriguez served as a tower guard at a military prison in Puerto Rico guarding Puerto Rican military prisoners.]

MR. CRUZ: YOU RE-ENLISTED, DIDN'T YOU? WHERE DID YOU GO AND WITH WHAT UNIT?

Mr. Rodriguez: I re-enlisted in 1948 and went to somewhere in Washington. I was in the 532nd Engineering Special Brigade. All they did was build and tear down bridges for practice. I was in a weapons platoon; I was a .30-caliber machine gunner. We had .30-caliber, .50-caliber and 37mm machine guns. When you fire 600-plus rounds a minute, you burned out the barrel. We had to change them all the time. Everyone wanted to be a machine gunner. The average lifespan of a machine gunner in battle was five minutes, but everyone wanted to do it.

MR. CRUZ: WHERE WERE YOU WHEN THE KOREAN WAR BEGAN?

Mr. Rodriguez: I was in Washington State as a fireman for the army. In July 1950 I went back to my company to prepare for Korea.

MR. CRUZ: WHEN DID YOU ARRIVE IN KOREA?

Mr. Rodriguez: We arrived in Korea three weeks after the invasion. We were at Pusan before we went to Inchon. The army and the Koreans were trapped in a very little bit of land.

Fernando Rodriguez

MR. CRUZ: DID YOU PARTICIPATE IN ANY BATTLES?

Mr. Rodriguez: We arrived at Inchon on September 15, 1950, at 2:30 P.M. We were supposed to land at 5:00 A.M. but the tide stranded our boats. We were five miles offshore and had to come ashore in small boats. We spent six weeks in Inchon then at Iwon; we slept six weeks on the ground.

We worked as longshoremen in Inchon. Once I worked for sixty-four hours straight. We went to Hamhung in North Korea. When the Chinese came over we pulled back in December 1951. We pulled out at 11:00 P.M. and dynamited the docks at Hamhung and went back to Inchon to Wolmi-do Island then to Ulsan and built a road from the beach to the town.

MR. CRUZ: WHAT WERE CONDITIONS LIKE IN KOREA?

Mr. Rodriguez: Unsafe food and water; we had to carry our own. There were people holding their stomachs, lying in the streets dying of hunger. The weather was very hot in the summer and -35 degrees in the winter. We could hardly walk because we had so many clothes on; we had three pairs of wool socks on in oversize boots.

MR. CRUZ: WHAT WAS THE WORST SITUATION YOU WERE IN?

Mr. Rodriguez: Lack of food. Korean food was off limits and army food was bad. We were in a machine gun nest and we had to live in it. We made a stove from a piece of steel and used diesel as fuel. We got someone to bring us some bread and toast. That and butter was the best food we ever had. We cooked in billy cans made from bread cans. I cooked spaghetti and meatballs with a little water and it was better food than they fed us in the barracks.

MR. CRUZ: FOR WHAT REASON DID YOU THINK YOU WERE THERE?

Mr. Rodriguez: We were there as a "police force." It was the Korean "conflict," because we were not at war.

MR. CRUZ: HOW DID YOU FEEL ABOUT THE WAR ENDING ALMOST AT THE SAME PLACE IT BEGAN?

Mr. Rodriguez: I was happy the war was over.

MR. CRUZ: DID YOU SERVE WITH OTHER SOLDIERS FROM THE VALLEY?

Mr. Rodriguez: Only with my cousin. I was in Company E and he was in Company B boat platoon for river crossings. His company transported Ridgway when he replaced MacArthur. We were there a year, but I never saw my cousin there.

MR. CRUZ: HOW WERE HISPANICS TREATED IN THE SERVICE? DID YOU EXPERIENCE ANY UNFAIR TREATMENT?

Mr. Rodriguez: We were very few and had no problems. I had a friend from Hondo, Texas. We went to visit him on the bus. We stopped in a bar for a beer before calling our friend. When we told him what bar we were in, he was surprised that we had been served.

MR. CRUZ: HAVE YOU EVER SPOKEN WITH ANYONE ABOUT YOUR WAR EXPERIENCE BEFORE?

Mr. Rodriguez: A lot of people lie. If they say they were never afraid, they are lying. Everyone is scared all the time.

E. E. "Gene" Cockrill
INTERVIEWED BY EDITH LIZBETH CANO

I had the pleasure of meeting Mr. Cockrill at his home on Friday, June 6, 2003. I was looking for Korean War veterans and decided to go to the National Guard by the University of Texas at Brownsville. There I noticed that the building was closed, but there was a man there who wanted to know what I needed. I told him that I was wondering if somebody from the National Guard would know any Korean War veterans. He told me that the reserves were stationed at Weslaco at the moment, but that he knew somebody, his father. He gave me his father's card and I called him later that night.

I arrived at Mr. Cockrill's house at noon and began interviewing him in his living room. His house felt very comfortable, and I was at ease from the start. I met his wife, Pat, and his two dogs.

MS. CANO: WHEN AND WHERE WERE YOU BORN?

Mr. Cockrill: I was born in Harlingen, Texas, in 1930. I lived most of my life in Brownsville, Texas.

MS. CANO: WHEN DID YOU HEAR THAT THE UNITED STATES WAS GOING TO GO TO KOREA? WHERE WERE YOU AT THAT TIME?

Mr. Cockrill: I was in the marines at the time in Great Lakes, Illinois, working in electronics.

MS. CANO: HOW DID YOU FEEL ABOUT THE UNITED STATES GOING TO WAR WITH NORTH KOREA?

Mr. Cockrill: I didn't like electronic school. I had enough pre-engineering courses from TSC. They figured they were going to make an electronics technician out of you, and I'm scared of 110 watts. There was a program the Marine Corps had between World War II and the Korean War, marine reserves. You enlisted, served one year on active duty and six years in the inactive reserve. That's how I was in there. In the electronics school at Great Lakes there were twenty-two or twenty-three of us, all the same age. I was nineteen and had two years of college. My year would have been up on July 9, 1950, and almost all of us that were there about the same time as well. Then when the Korean War started, the 25th of June, all but one of us went back to the main site, marine barracks, and told Captain Highland who was there that we didn't want out. The federal government was going to release us on the 30th of June at the COG, "Convenience of the Government." That is when the fiscal year ended in those years. Highland said, "Don't worry about it. All your records are being processed. You're going home. But take a nice leave, and I'll see you in Camp Pendleton." I was out eighty-one days, spent seventy-nine days in Matamoros, Tamaulipas, Mexico, and one night in the hospital in Brownsville, Texas. Then I left to Camp Pendleton. There were a lot of us, marine reserves. I went to Korea with four other guys from Brownsville. They were all marine reserves and had been in World War II: John R. "Rob" Hesseling, Tommy Thompson, Dick Wright, and Castille.

MS. CANO: DID YOU VOLUNTEER TO BE IN THE MARINES?

Mr. Cockrill: I volunteered in 1949. I had a problem. I have had these fingers off ever since I was thirteen years old. [One of his hands is missing some fingers.] I didn't know if they would take me. They wouldn't draft me. I went to Harlingen (there was no recruiter in Brownsville) in the summer of 1949. I asked the recruiter if I could get in the marines with these fingers off. He said, "*Quien sabe,* sir. We will find out." He wrote a letter to the headquarters in the marine offices in Washington, D.C. He told me to come back within a week. So a week or so passed and I was in Harlingen and I asked what they told him. "They said they will take you." I asked when I leave. He said, "Tonight." Hell, I gotta go tell my folks I've enlisted! So I went back to Brownsville and I had never told my mom and dad that I had thought about enlisting. They had known that I wanted to be a marine since I was a kid. I got to San Diego as a recruit. There were so few guys joining that it took a couple of weeks to get seventy-five men together to make a boot platoon. When they finally did, we started training. We finished sometime in September. I came home for eight days' leave and then went back to San Diego and then they sent me to Great Lakes. When they called me back in, it was the 19th of September, 1950.

MS. CANO: WHAT WERE THE MARINES LOOKING FOR IN A SOLDIER FOR THE KOREAN WAR?

Mr. Cockrill: They were looking for artillery men and tankers. Well, I had studied all the way to calculus, and what better way to be than artillery? So I volunteered for the artillery and trained at Camp Del Mar right down the ocean. We got on a ship transport on the 16th of November, 1950. On our way over the Chinese got into the fight and the 1st Marine Division lost so many infantrymen and lost so many people that they went down the roster and there was a tank company with no tanks, artillery batteries with no guns and a lot of infantry. So I ended up in the infantry with guys that I had trained in the artillery with. I never minded the infantry. [He laughs.] I think in the infantry you find out who your friends are.

MS. CANO: SO YOU WOULD SAY THAT WAS YOUR SPECIALTY IN THE MARINES?

Mr. Cockrill: Infantry was my final occupational specialty, MOS (Military Occupational Specialty). First, I had electronics technician, then artillery, and I ended up in the infantry.

MS. CANO: ON WHAT DATE DID THEY TELL YOU THAT YOU WERE GOING TO KOREA?

Mr. Cockrill: I don't remember. I think it was the 1st of December. By that time they were already bringing in marines out of the Changjin Reservoir. So instead of going up north, we landed in Pusan, right off the ship and onto the dock. An army band was there and those "mariachis" were playing "If we had known you were coming, we would have baked a cake." [Starts laughing.] I have Scotch blood and German blood, and I thought "My God! My ancestors will think I'm crazy going to war to that kind of music." [Laughs again.] In those years I knew a lot of Mexican revolutionary songs. It would have been better going to war with, "La Cucaracha," (The Cockroach) or "Cuando vienen los Mexicanos con Cartuches y Cañones"

(When the Mexicans Come with Guns and Cannons). It is better than with what they greeted us with.

MS. CANO: WHEN YOU FIRST ARRIVED IN PUSAN, WHAT WAS YOUR REACTION TO WHAT YOU SAW?

Mr. Cockrill: Pusan was full of refugees. Koreans were coming down to get away from the communists.

MS. CANO: WHERE DID THEY SEND YOU AFTER YOU ARRIVED IN PUSAN?

Mr. Cockrill: They put us on a train. We traveled all night going about thirty-five miles to Masan. At Masan, they started rebuilding the 1st Marine Division. I don't know what percent of the division were reserves at that time. Those from Brownsville were inactive. I wasn't out long enough to make any weekend meetings, summer camps or anything like that. There were marine reserves organized that were called back as early as July of 1950 to form the 1st Marine Brigade. The marines were ready to move on, the first to fight. They placed the 1st Marine Brigade over there and used them like a fire brigade. The marines always headed in before the army. One of the Korean areas over there the marines fought for about a week for a whole big chunk of land. Then we turned it over to the army and the army lost all of that in six hours.

MS. CANO: DO YOU REMEMBER WHO WAS THE GENERAL IN CHARGE OF THE MARINES' FIRST DIVISION?

Mr. Cockrill: It was General Shepard. [Lt. Gen. Lemuel C. Shepard.]

MS. CANO: WHEN WAS YOUR FIRST ENCOUNTER WITH THE NORTH KOREANS?

Mr. Cockrill: After Christmas they moved us from Masan. From there we went out on what is referred to as "The Great P'ohang Guerrilla Hunt." It appeared that we would chase the North Korean soldiers that had been bypassed. I think by the 1st Cavalry.

Those brutes were moving from village to village, roughing up the civilians, killing the oxen, eating the rice and chasing the girls. Then we go in and they shoot us up a bit and they leave. We would chase them till we got caught up again.

MS. CANO: WHAT WAS THE NAME OF YOUR PLATOON?

Mr. Cockrill: Easy Company, 2nd Battalion, 7th Marine Regiment of the 1st Marine Division.

MS. CANO: HOW DID YOU GET WOUNDED?

Mr. Cockrill: They told us when we were out on patrol that there were three North Korean snipers on a ridge. If they had rifles it was no big deal, we were sixty-four. But we got right in the middle of an S-curve and they were shooting down the road and across the road. They were trying to drop grenades. It turned out the next day that they didn't have three rifles, but at least three machine guns and we had no idea of how many they were. I was with the machine gun section. The section leader was in front of me and the gunner was right behind me. So the North Koreans started shooting and the leader fell in front of me and the gunner fell behind me. They were both lying face down. I got hit the first time as I was getting to go down on my knees.

I got hit once. It wasn't so bad. It was a pretty good-sized wound, but I didn't know how bad I was hit. I got down to my knees. I would hear the leader in front of me saying, "I got hit again." When they picked him up, he looked like lace. He had so many holes.

MS. CANO: HOW DID YOU PASS THE HOLIDAYS?

Mr. Cockrill: We had gotten there shortly before the holidays and I hadn't gotten any mail. I would go down to mail call and on Christmas Eve I went to the mail call. No mail. I headed back to the tent, that's where we lived. As I headed back I heard my name, so I went back down there. My mother had packed a little box and inside there were date loaves my mother had made. My dad had sent me a couple of pens and slipper socks, with leather on the soles. It was cold in Korea. Imagine a little skinny *gringo* of South Texas in Korea. My brother sent a pocketbook. That was the best mail of my life. All the rest of the packets from Christmas I received when I was in the hospital in Japan. I received cookie crumbs and melted chocolate that looked like marble. My younger sister and her husband, he had been in World War II and they were in Guam, sent me a comb, handkerchiefs, toilet paper and things like that, things he remembered and had a use for in World War II.

MS. CANO: COULD YOU DESCRIBE THE WEATHER IN KOREA?

Mr. Cockrill: Cold. When we moved from Masan to P'ohang, Bob Hesseling found out that the temperature was 20 below zero. Marines didn't fight in any cold weather, except for some marines that were in Iceland in World War II. Island fighting was not anything like the cold weather in Korea. The boots we had were shoe packs, rubber bottoms, and leather tops. The leather socks my father gave me I wore inside my boots. Being rubber, if you stood by the fire your feet would sweat. You walked ten feet away from the fire and your feet would freeze. There were a lot of guys with frostbite. A lot of people think that's what happened to my fingers.

E. E. Cockrill, January 1951.
—Courtesy of
E. E. Cockrill

MS. CANO: COULD YOU TELL ME ONE INTERESTING EXPERIENCE FROM KOREA?

Mr. Cockrill: There was a guy named Espinosa from California. They sent my outfit up one time, my platoon, to cover some wounded that were coming back out of Fox Company. We set up a Korean cemetery and they buried them sitting up, placing large amounts of dirt on top of them. So I had my automatic rifle on top of one grave and Espinosa has a machine gun with his people in the next grave. The troops were chasing these wounded guys trying to shoot again. Then they started shooting at us. I heard Espinosa laughing. I thought he was crazy. The next day this soldier came by and told me that Espinosa has said that I was the craziest *gringo* he had ever seen! "I'm crazy?" I said. I didn't see anything funny. Espinosa doesn't speak Spanish. He said we were using words that he had only heard in the gutter. [Starts laughing.] He said he didn't know what some of them meant. So I met Espinosa later and asked him if he knew Spanish, and he said "no." His parents had come from Mexico to San Francisco, and when they were kids they told them they were Americans and you don't speak Spanish. His folks did speak Spanish, but they didn't want the kids to know what was going on. He had a lot of friends that did. He said some of the language I was saying was bad. He had heard it. I didn't realize that I was saying those things. Man, it was bad! He told me, I was *"echando grocerías at todos."* [Yelling obscenities at everyone.] There was another instance where two guys I had gone to school with were in Masan living in tents. Just about Christmas time they got in the company street and played ping-pong. No ping-pong table, no ping-pong balls, and no ping-pong rackets. Both of them could snap their fingers real loud. No equipment and they kept score. Everybody would watch those two idiots play.

MS. CANO: WHAT WOULD YOU SAY WAS THE WORST THING ABOUT KOREA?

Mr. Cockrill: The first marine I ever saw get killed. He had gone to Korea with the reserve outfit. He got shot through the left leg. It had cut one of the main arteries and it didn't break his leg. They asked him if he could get up and run and, he said, "yeah." He

E. E. Cockrill

ran to the back side of the ridge. When he got there he was whiter than my shirt. He had bled to death. He was just a kid and freckled-faced. He never voted, never bought a glass of whiskey. He was too young. He was eighteen years old. They pulled out all the guys that were younger than eighteen years old and sent them to Japan, and as soon as they were eighteen they sent them back.

[Mr. Cockrill left the marines after he was shot in the leg. Later he attended Mexico City University and graduated in June of 1954. He was telling me that there were a lot of Korean War veterans in Mexico due to its accessibility. Mr. Cockrill later got married and worked at the Port of Brownsville. Years later he accidentally met the South Korean ambassador to Mexico (whom he had known in Korea as an interpreter for the 1st Marine Division) at the Port. Mr. Cockrill meets with veterans from previous wars every year. He is truly an inspiration.]

Herman Wise
Interviewed by Santiago Salazar, Jr.

This interview with Mr. Herman Wise was conducted at his place of business in Harlingen. Mr. Wise owns and operates a used car dealership and has numerous clients who enter and exit frequently.

My focus in this interview was centered on the consequences of war on the individual rather than battles. Yes, the battles are important, but we fail to realize the changes that occur to the human body after heavy amounts of stress.

MR. SALAZAR: HOW DID YOU ENTER THE MILITARY?

Mr. Wise: I was drafted November 2, 1950, immediately after the Korean War started. I turned twenty in June.

MR. SALAZAR: SO WHAT DIVISION WERE YOU IN WHILE YOU WERE IN THE ARMY?

Mr. Wise: I was in the 224th Infantry Regiment, 40th Infantry Division.

MR. SALAZAR: HOW DID YOUR FAMILY FEEL ABOUT YOU BEING DRAFTED?

Mr. Wise: Fathers and mothers did not like this. In our family, it was worse. My older brother served in World War II. Miguel was drafted first, I was drafted months later, and we served in the same outfit. I caught up with him in Camp Cook, California. And then my little brother volunteered to enter the air force. So my mom had three children in the Korean War. It was rough on her.

MR. SALAZAR: WHEN YOU WERE DRAFTED, IN WHAT CITY WERE YOU LIVING?

Mr. Wise: San Benito.

MR. SALAZAR: SO WERE THE CITIZENS OF SAN BENITO ANTI- OR PRO-WAR?

Mr. Wise: I don't remember. Kids like me wanted to enter the military and low-income families like ours never saw the world. Going to Corpus Christi was a vacation. This is the reason I wanted to go. In fact I tried to volunteer, but my friends wouldn't sign. So when I got drafted, they said okay and advanced my drafting status. I wanted to volunteer.

MR. SALAZAR: DID YOU KNOW THAT A WAR WAS ABOUT TO START?
Mr. Wise: No.
MR. SALAZAR: WHERE DID YOU TRAIN?
Mr. Wise: I was sent to Fort Sam Houston [Texas] first. They sent us on a troop train. Nothing but troops. Then they sent me to California to a place called Camp Cook. They reopened this camp after World War II. There was sand all over. That's what you saw. I was there for two-and-a-half months before they sent us to Oakland. While in Oakland they put us on a boat for Japan named *General Breckenridge*. It had about 4,000-5,000 troops on it, but blacks were not allowed on the boat. It took us about fifteen to seventeen days to get there. Race mixing was not allowed.
MR. SALAZAR: WHY WERE BLACKS NOT ALLOWED TO INTERMINGLE WITH THE OTHER SOLDIERS?
Mr. Wise: That's the way things were. We were considered white, not Mexicans, so the *gringos* accepted us as different. We were white people. In my company, a heavy mortar company, we dropped shells on the enemy. We dropped bombs on the enemy. I had the biggest mortars. They called me "mortar man."
MR. SALAZAR: WHILE YOU WERE IN TRAINING, DID YOUR COMMANDERS TRAIN YOU ADEQUATELY FOR THE TYPE OF WAR YOU WERE GOING TO EXPERIENCE?
Mr. Wise: We had several commanders who served during World War II. They trained us good. Very, very good. We went to Japan and continued with advanced training. That's what they called it, "advanced training." We went to Japan and trained at the base of Mt. Fujiyama, the highest volcano in Japan. We then built tents at Camp McNair. Tent city. It was so big that it looked like a city. We trained there, but then we were hit by a typhoon and it tore up all the tents. It was nothing but nature. On Sunday we would hike up the mountain.
MR. SALAZAR: HOW DID THE CITIZENS OF JAPAN TREAT THE AMERICAN SOLDIER?
Mr. Wise: Very good. We can't complain. They were extra nice to us. We did not take advantage of them. They were intimidated by us. We were very civil with each other, especially the girls or the women. There was a few that hated us, but most of the citizens treated us good. I went to one of the homes of one of my girlfriends and they did not want me there. I kind of forced myself into their home because I knew they wouldn't do anything to me. But my girlfriend told me they did not want me there, because of World War II. Maybe they had a son that died in the war. I was twenty years old and didn't give a shit.
MR. SALAZAR: DID YOU EVER FEEL THAT ANYTHING WAS GOING TO HAPPEN TO YOU?
Mr. Wise: I knew that nothing was going to happen. I was kind of crazy and volunteered for many things I was not supposed to volunteer for. But we dared each

other. We were stupid, but that's the way we were. In training, we trained hard. We trained five days out of the week and were off for the weekend unless you misbehaved; then they wouldn't give you a pass. Most of the time we were off half a day Saturday and all day Sunday.

MR. SALAZAR: HOW LONG DID YOU TRAIN IN JAPAN?

Mr. Wise: From April 1951 through December 1951. Live ammunition. You had to crawl about 100 yards. They would tell us not to stand up or you would be hit. They also had live artillery. The Koreans knew we were training, but they did not know when we would go over.

MR. SALAZAR: DO YOU REMEMBER THE CITY YOU WERE STATIONED IN KOREA?

Mr. Wise: By all means. Early 1952, the whole outfit was going to the front lines. From Camp McNair they sent us to Camp Hogan. We continued the training there. At night we would hike thirty- to forty-mile hikes. Hard training. From there, the whole army was going to Korea. In January we left Japan and trained to get off the ships with the nets. There was no port. So we had to unload onto the loading barges. When we got there it was 18 below zero. Very cold. We were not prepared for the cold. We did not have the right clothes. They gave us coffee and doughnuts, but the coffee froze up before we could drink it. When we would take a leak, the piss would freeze before hitting the ground.

MR. SALAZAR: WERE YOU AND YOUR FELLOW SOLDIERS EXCITED ABOUT THE ORDER TO GO TO THE FRONT LINES?

Mr. Wise: I'm pretty sure we were concerned. But none of us were scared. The enemy knew that we were coming and that we were trained well. The Koreans told over the radio that they were going to wipe us out, but we knew they were scared. We were not scared. They were trying to intimidate us. We got there and my sergeant volunteered my squad to go to the front lines.

[At this point, Mr. Wise broke down and started to cry. We then took a ten-minute break so that he could compose himself.]

MR. SALAZAR: HOW WAS THE MORALE OF THE SQUAD WHEN YOUR SERGEANT VOLUNTEERED YOU GUYS FOR THAT MISSION?

Mr. Wise: I never saw fear. We were young. We were ready. We were friends. Half of the squad was Mexican. We went straight for the front lines and set up our mortar. It was so cold. We had special gauges for the cold. We had barriers with sandbags so that if the gun blew up it would not kill us. We did not take a bath for a good two months. Sometimes we had to thaw out snow for water. They would feed us twice a day; early in the morning, for breakfast, and at night. We had MRE's called C-rations and K-rations. We would eat that at noon. They had beans and ham. In one can they had all the goodies, gum, toothpaste. We ate good. I think the enemy had it worse. Cigarettes were available everywhere.

MR. SALAZAR: BEFORE YOU WENT TO KOREA DID THEY INJECT YOU WITH VACCINES?

Mr. Wise: Oh yes, we got tetanus shots. Vaccination for measles, but the tetanus shot was a must.

MR. SALAZAR: CAN YOU DESCRIBE YOUR FIRST NIGHT IN KOREA?

Mr. Wise: The bombings stayed on all day and all night. When you were on guard duty, eight to ten people depended on you to stay alive. You could not fall asleep. You think about your friends, your girlfriend, and your family.

MR. SALAZAR: DID YOU KNOW WHERE YOUR BROTHER WAS?

Mr. Wise: He was about a mile behind me. He had a jeep and he would visit me. He wanted to fire the mortar, and we let him. We were not supposed to be together. They were supposed to send one of us away from the front lines but they never did. That was Miguel. He has passed away already.

MR. SALAZAR: DID YOUR COMMANDER EVER TELL YOU THAT THIS WOULD BE THE DAY YOU WOULD SEE BATTLE?

Mr. Wise: Sometimes, we were playing ball. We had to wait. When they said "fire mission," we went straight to our gun. They would give us our instructions; we would use aiming sticks to fire the gun. Once they gave us the elevation and measurements we would fire. We had a soldier who would tell the command post where the enemy was and we would fire at it. After one round, we would make the correction and fire another round. If we were on target the commander would say "Fire for effect."

[Mr. Wise, at this point, begins to cry and tells me he needs a break.]

MR. SALAZAR: WERE YOU CONSTANTLY HEARING BOMBS AND GUNFIRE WHERE YOU WERE?

Mr. Wise: Artillery yes, but not gunfire. You hear it when it comes in.

MR. SALAZAR: CAN YOU DESCRIBE THE DIFFERENCE BETWEEN SOUTH KOREAN SOLDIERS AND AMERICAN SOLDIERS?

Mr. Wise: Let me tell you, you cannot trust the South Koreans. If you had them on your flank they would run away. They would not cover the flank. We could not trust them. In a way they hated us. Why? I don't know why. They don't appreciate us.

MR. SALAZAR: WHY DID THEY HATE THE AMERICAN SOLDIERS?

Mr. Wise: I don't know. Maybe because they were jealous. They did not appreciate us. They were worse. The Japanese were nicer. When I was there, they put five Koreans in our outfit. They wanted to learn. My company was sent to deal with POWs. I was in charge of 400 POWs. The Koreans were very mean to them. They would kick them and push them. Most of the soldiers were Chinese. When I got there, that's who we were fighting, mostly Chinese. The Koreans were mean. They hated the Chinese.

MR. SALAZAR: HOW DID THE NORTH KOREANS REACT TO AMERICANS BEING ON THEIR SOIL?

Mr. Wise: I was not there when the Americans invaded North Korea. I got there when the Chinese had entered the war and I was at the 38th Parallel. Nineteen fifty-one was when they came to the 38th Parallel. That's where the fighting took place. We would fight for hills and then come back. February 18, 1952, we went out to take out some hills. They sent my company, and we set up at night. They took the first hill without problems. Not even one shot was fired. When we got to the valley, all hell broke loose. They started firing and we lost twenty soldiers. We got orders to fire "smoke screen" to help the soldiers get out of there. I don't remember how many rounds we fired, but we knew that there was no way we could get the second hill. The wounded started coming in. They forgot about us. We loaded up the gun and took off. We forgot some things, but, what the hell, we lived.

MR. SALAZAR: DID YOU GET THE OPPORTUNITY TO WRITE OR CALL HOME?

Mr. Wise: Yes, I called home only once. I spoke to my dad and mom. I talked to both of them. They found out I was injured. I told them I was okay and not to worry. It had been a few weeks and they had no idea that I was okay.

[Mr. Wise once again asks for a break from the conversation. I again ask him if he can continue with the conversation, and he says that he can.]

MR. SALAZAR: WHAT WAS YOUR WORST EXPERIENCE IN KOREA?

Mr. Wise: I didn't even know I was injured. We were firing our guns. They had counter mortar, and when we fired they had imaginary lines to pinpoint us. I got hit with shrapnel.

MR. SALAZAR: WAS THERE ANY MAJOR DAMAGE TO YOUR BODY?

Mr. Wise: Not so much. I was so pissed off when it happened. I would get on top of the sandbags and curse them out. I was stupid and crazy. I did it to get courage and show the others not to be afraid. I was crazy and stupid.

MR. SALAZAR: CAN YOU DESCRIBE YOUR BEST EXPERIENCE IN KOREA?

Mr. Wise: In Korea, no there was no "best experience." I had a lot of good times in Japan. But in Korea, not really. I just had a date or two with a Korean girl. But when you're in the front lines there were no good times.

MR. SALAZAR: AFTER PUSAN, DID YOU GO BACK TO THE FRONT LINES?

Mr. Wise: No, after my injury I got enough points to get sent home.

MR. SALAZAR: AFTER THE WAR, DID YOU REMAIN IN CONTACT WITH YOUR FELLOW SOLDIERS?

Mr. Wise: Yes, here in the Valley there are not very many left. About ten years ago my fellow soldiers started to have a reunion in California. From the Purple Heart magazine a fellow soldier advertised about a reunion. I called him up and his wife answered. We had a good time and I am glad that we did get together. This was in 1990. Every year we got together to remember.

MR. SALAZAR: HOW DOES WAR DIFFER FROM WHAT YOU SEE ON TV AND THE REAL LIFE EXPERIENCE?

Mr. Wise: Let me tell you, the movies and TV are worse in some cases. They are not the same as what I went through. Movies like John Wayne pulling the grenade with his teeth are not true. You have a hard time pulling it with your fingers. They make movies to make money. Like I was telling you, sometimes we were playing ball and you never see that on the movies. We lost quite a few people but not as many as the movies tell you.

MR. SALAZAR: HOW DO YOU FEEL ABOUT MOST HISTORY BOOKS REFERRING TO THE KOREAN WAR AS THE "FORGOTTEN WAR"?

Mr. Wise: You can tell, like right now, that emphasis is placed on the Iraq War.

We had very little killed or injured compared to the Korean War. In the Korean War we were called heroes but I think that we were mostly victims. Even our captain would tell us that death teaches lessons on how to live. Do not become a POW. If you do find a way to, escape and get out. If you're a POW, you can't help getting hurt or getting killed. Very few people know that the Korean War happened. Korea was not on the map. The world was too big, and now we know about Korea. We are more educated.

MR. SALAZAR: HOW DO YOU FEEL ABOUT THE CHINESE SOLDIERS?

Mr. Wise: You hate your enemy. Right now I will not go eat Chinese food. I hate the word Chinese. Especially when we fought them. When the Chinese fought they would send out the first wave with sticks, the second wave had small arms, and the third wave had good guns. They would use humans to waste ammunition. When they came in, we would have no weapons because we would waste them on the first two waves. It was hard for the marines. The Chinese would sacrifice their army.

MR. SALAZAR: WHEN YOU CAME HOME, HOW DID THE AMERICAN PUBLIC TREAT YOU?

Mr. Wise: Very nice. They had parties for us. We were all invited. When we got home we visited a family whose son was killed in the battle. That was hard, but we had to do it. He was killed "a brother," so we loved his family, too.

MR. SALAZAR: DID YOUR BROTHERS COME HOME SAFELY ALSO?

Mr. Wise: Yes, we all came home safely. My mother made a *promesa* that if we made it back safely, we had to go to Mexico and celebrate there.

MR. SALAZAR: DO YOU THINK THAT YOU SUFFER FROM ANY PHYSICAL OR MENTAL DISABILITIES BECAUSE OF THE WAR?

Mr. Wise: Yes, I guess you can tell. I have battle fatigue, or Post Traumatic Stress Disorder. I have a good business, and I have made a good life for my family and myself.

MR. SALAZAR: WHAT MEDALS WERE YOU AWARDED DURING THE KOREAN WAR?

Mr. Wise: I was awarded the Purple Heart, Combat Infantry Badge, Japanese Occupation, Korean Conflict Medal, and Korean Battle Citation with two major battles.

MR. SALAZAR: HOW DO YOU FEEL TODAY ABOUT NORTH KOREA?

Mr. Wise: I see that people are suffering, but their military is being built up. But there is not a country that can stand up against the United States. We are the aggressors for any war. Look at Iraq, we destroyed them and we are wasting money. We have to respect this country and what they want to do. It is not right to go in there and fight.

MR. SALAZAR: HOW DO YOU FEEL ABOUT GENERAL MACARTHUR?

Mr. Wise: He was a great man. He wanted to fight and win the war. Every time we go to war it is to avoid a depression.

MR. SALAZAR: WHAT ADVICE WOULD YOU GIVE TO NEW RECRUITS JOINING THE ARMED FORCES?

Mr. Wise: Don't do it. If I was your age and another war started, if they invaded us, then I would fight. But if we attack another country I will do what President Clinton did and go to another country. It is not my war, so why should I worry about it? Why fight it? It doesn't concern us. If we are so concerned about liberation, why don't we liberate Cuba? They need the help more than Iraq.

Juan Guerra
Interviewed by William L. Adams

I was introduced to Mr. Guerra, literally "Mr. War," through my friend Joe Ibarra. One evening in December we met at the San Benito McDonalds on Sam Houston, then drove in Joe's truck to the trailer park where Mr. Guerra lives with his wife. This was not a fancy mobile home park of double-wides for retired folks and winter Texans, but a trailer park for working people. The Guerra trailer had a chain-link fence around it and a no-trespassing sign on the gate. We went in.

The interior of the trailer is kept neat as a pin by Mrs. Guerra—Carmen—and hand-knitted antimacassars in Mexican hues are draped on every sofa and chair. The walls of the living room are covered with framed photographs of Juan and Carmen's family: children, grandchildren, nephews, and nieces. The males of the family are usually photographed in their military uniforms or in colorful, dress western wear with cowboy hats and string ties. The girls are shown in *quinciñera* or wedding gowns.

Some of the wall space is taken up with framed newspaper clippings of Juan Guerra's military deeds and, make no mistake about it, we are in the presence of one of the Valley's most decorated military heroes, a man who earned five bronze stars during World War II fighting in such hell holes as Guadalcanal, New Guinea and Leyte, and then, when recalled to service during the Korean conflict, demonstrated such valor that he was plucked from the front line by a helicopter, flown to Tokyo, and personally presented with the army's Distinguished Service Cross by theater commander Matthew B. Ridgway. One framed 1952 *Valley Morning Star* clipping reads: "Battle-Hardened Veteran Returns."

But the focal point of the living room is not the framed clippings nor is it the family photographs, it is the man himself, Juan Guerra. He is an arresting sight. A lean eight-four with hair still worn in a stiff, martial crew cut, he has demonic eyes. The irises are brilliant white. It looks like someone took liquid paper and went around each iris and carefully daubed out all the color. Juan has been blind with glaucoma the past fifteen years. But Juan also captures all the attention in the room because he is a moving object. His body never rests. He is in endless, perpetual, restless motion, a fever of motion: jerking his arms, rubbing his arms, flexing his hands, dipping one shoulder and now the next, rocking his torso forwards and backwards. He is never still. He must burn an immense amount of calories every day. As the *Valley Morning Star*'s "Battle-Hardened Veteran" story reported, when Mr. Guerra first returned home

Juan Guerra
—Photo on right courtesy of Juan Guerra

from Korea he had to be restrained at night because his jerking during nightmares was so violent.

DR. ADAMS: YOU WERE RECALLED TO THE ARMY IN OCTOBER 1951. HOW DID YOU GET TO KOREA?

Mr. Guerra: We went by boat—a line of boats, seven or eight boats. We left from Japan, from Tokyo. We hit the coast of Korea.

DR. ADAMS: WHAT WAS YOUR UNIT?

Mr. Guerra: 2nd Division, 23rd Regiment.

DR. ADAMS: WHAT HAPPENED ONCE YOU LANDED?

Mr. Guerra: We started pushing the Chinamen, pushing all the Chinamans all the way to the Yellow River. [Mr. Guerra actually means the Yalu River.] It was real terrible. It was real cold. Nothing but the ice and snow.

DR. ADAMS: I KNOW FROM THE NEWSPAPER ACCOUNTS THAT YOU WON THE DISTINGUISHED SERVICE CROSS FOR LEADING A HANDFUL OF MEN TO BREAK A ROADBLOCK HELD BY OVER 100 CHINESE SOLDIERS, AND THAT YOU SUCCEEDED AND KILLED 78 OF THE ENEMY IN THE PROCESS. CAN YOU DESCRIBE TO ME EXACTLY WHAT HAPPENED?

Mr. Guerra: I started with twenty-five men. When I got to the Yellow [Yalu] River I had eighteen men. I was ordered: "Sergeant Guerra, I want you to open up that roadblock." So I lined up my eighteen men I had left and we started pushing up and up that hill. A grenade launcher was giving us hell from the top. When I got to the top I went right straight at it. I got two grenades thrown at the launcher. There was a whole bunch of Chinese. I knocked the launcher out.

I had a B.A.R. (Browning automatic rifle—an exceptionally large and powerful rifle), and started shooting at a machine-gun nest. There was a bunch of Chinese there, too. I fired with the B.A.R. and threw a grenade into that bunch.

Then we kept on pushing forward, forward. There was a pillbox about twenty-five to thirty feet from us and it was giving us hell. I don't know how many Chinese were inside that pillbox. I had a good B.A.R. man with me, Joe Acuña. I told Joe Acuña, "I want you to fire into that hole [a portal in the pillbox], and give me a chance to throw in a grenade." He was a good man, a good B.A.R.-man. He fired well. I ran like hell and threw a grenade into that pillbox. There was a bunch of Chinamans inside.

DR. ADAMS: WHAT DO YOU FEEL WHEN YOU ARE KILLING PEOPLE?

Mr. Guerra: I was real angry and real mad 'cause I was losing a lot of my men. I was pretty angry at those people. Some of my men were dead and some were wounded. I was mean. I was real mean. I wasn't scared; I was angry. It doesn't pay to be scared in time of war.

DR. ADAMS: WHAT DID YOU DO WITH THE BODIES OF THE DEAD?

Mr. Guerra: We had an American crew picking up dead American soldiers, but not picking up dead Chinese. The Chinamans we just left dead on the ground. On the way back I saw a bulldozer was digging the ground to dig a big ditch to bury the Chinamen, to dump all the dead Chinamen in that hole.

[Here Joe Ibarra interjects: "Tell him how you got your feet frostbitten."]

DR. ADAMS: YES, HOW DID YOU GET YOUR FEET FROZEN?

Mr. Guerra: We crossed a field to take the next hill. It had a lake, a reservoir, four feet deep. So I got wet. It froze me up to here. [He indicates his waist.] I told my men to keep going, so my men told me: "Sergeant, we are going to leave you some flares to call a helicopter."

The helicopter came. I shot the flares straight up in the air and they saw me and threw a cable with a basket on it to where I was. I got in the basket and the helicopter pulled me up. But there was no room inside the helicopter. The helicopter was filled up with wounded people and dead people and the baskets [stretcher pods] on the sides were filled with dead and wounded. So anyway they flew me all the way to Pusan hanging in that basket!

DR. ADAMS: IT MUST HAVE BEEN COLD IN THAT BASKET.

Mr. Guerra: You're telling me! [Laughs.] When I got to Pusan I was taken to a place with ten or twenty tents with doctors, nurses, and wounded men. They took care of me. I was there about fifteen days. I thought I would go back home then, but no. After I got well they put me in a helicopter and flew me back to the front lines.

When I got to my people those Chinamans, about 4,000 or 5,000 of them, were in front of us. We had six tanks and six 155s [large howitzers] behind us. So the Chinas hit us so hard. I can see them in my mind right now. They hit us SO HARD! I don't know how they did it, but they jumped on top of our tanks and threw grenades inside. These Chinas got right on top of the tanks, and they pushed us back again.

DR. ADAMS: DO YOU THINK THE CHINESE WERE BRAVE SOLDIERS?

Mr. Guerra: Yes. [Pause.] I don't know. I'll tell you one thing: Some of those we found dead had little bags around their necks. I am pretty sure it was dope. We opened it and it was filled with a white powder. We thought that is what was making those Chinamen so brave.

[Joe Ibarra interjects again: "Tell him how the helicopter came for you to get your medal."]

Mr. Guerra: I was on the front line when a helicopter came and landed and they called for me: "Sergeant Juan Guerra!" I was taken all the way to Tokyo, where Ridgway was waiting for me to pin the medal [Distinguished Service Cross] on me. When he put it on, I thought I was going home to my wife and kids, but no. They threw me back into the front lines again. There was nothing I could do about it. That's the army. They put me into a really big helicopter with fifteen or twenty other soldiers and flew us all back to the front lines.

DR. ADAMS: WHAT DID YOU DO, MR. GUERRA, WHEN YOU FINALLY DID GET HOME?

Mr. Guerra: We were migrant farm workers. Me and the whole family. We worked as migrant farm workers all over—from California to Michigan—all over, until I retired.

DR. ADAMS: MR. GUERRA, IS THERE ANYTHING ELSE YOU'D LIKE TO TELL THE READERS OF THIS BOOK?

Mr. Guerra: I got good things from the country and there's no other country for me. It's been so good to me.

Harold L. Adams
Interviewed by William L. Adams

I interviewed my 86-year-old father at my home on November 28, 2003. Chief Adams joined the navy in 1940 and served on a Pacific-based submarine tender throughout the course of World War II. He again saw action in the Korean War and finally retired form the navy in 1960 and later became a schoolteacher and principal in Oklahoma. For the past sixteen years he and his wife, Clella, my mother, have spent a portion of each year in Brownsville.

DR. ADAMS: DAD, WHEN THE KOREAN WAR BROKE OUT YOU WERE ALREADY A CHIEF. YOU REALIZE THE PUBLIC'S PERCEPTION OF A NAVY CHIEF IS NOT PARTICULARLY FLATTERING. WHAT THE TITLE CONJURES UP TO MOST PEOPLE IS A REAL TOUGH NUT: A HARD-DRINKING, HARD-FIGHTING, SKIRT-CHASING BRUTE. IF HOLLYWOOD CASTS A CHIEF, THEY DON'T PICK A HANDSOME, SENSITIVE-LOOKING GUY LIKE ROBERT REDFORD. THEY'LL PICK SOME COARSE,

42 Korean War

MEAN-LOOKING GUY WITH A FACE LIKE A FIST—SOMEONE LIKE ERNEST BORGNINE. WOULD YOU SAY YOU PRETTY MUCH FIT THE STEREOTYPE?

Chief Adams: [Laughs.]

DR. ADAMS: WHEN AND HOW DID YOU GO TO KOREA?

Chief Adams: I was on the destroyer *Chevalier* out of San Diego at the time. We went over with a battle group that was to join in with the fleet going into Inchon with MacArthur. Our particular battle group was made up of just four destroyers and the cruiser *Toledo*. Later the *Toledo* got the nickname of "the Galloping Ghost of the Korean Coast," and we usually operated with her. We stopped at Pearl to refuel, then on to Inchon. At Inchon we were laying down a barrage so they could land. We were shooting right over the heads of our own troops.

The *Chevalier* was classified as a DDR, "destroyer-radar." We had special radar equipment. We had the commodore of the four destroyers aboard, a full captain, Blake B. Booth. Communications was kind of bad. We were getting our communications from NPM (Radio Honolulu). I was used to working with Radio Honolulu during World War Two, and we had the best comm. gang on our ship. We knew how to pick up Honolulu on alternative frequencies, and we were getting and relaying all the messages for the ships around, including the *Helena*. The old man really liked that.

DR. ADAMS: I'VE SEEN NEWSPAPER PHOTOGRAPHS OF THE

Harold L. Adams

—Courtesy of Harold L. Adams

Harold L. Adams

CHEVALIER. SHE LOOKED VERY HEAVILY GUNNED. DID YOU USE THOSE GUNS OFTEN?

Chief Adams: We used those guns every day. We went over to the east side of Korea—the Sea of Japan side—and went up and down the coast shooting up railroads, railroad tracks, railroad cars, and trucks at night if they put their headlights on—before they learned to put them off. We shot up bridges. The bridges were the hardest to knock out, so eventually we sent small boats in from our ships and they set explosives on the bridges and blew them up. We shelled towns along the coast of North Korea. One of the most interesting things is we would get reports of haystacks moving down the highway. These were tanks moving along covered in straw. We'd fire over the mountains and hit those tanks after three or four shots. Airplanes would give us reports—they were spotting our shells for us.

Train engines would hide in tunnels, but planes could skip bombs into the tunnels. But amazingly trains would be running on those lines the next day. That's when we started to send in boats to blow up the bridges.

Once we caught a barge moving down the coast and started firing at them. (Barges are hard to hit. You know, they don't have much structure.) And they beached the barge and ran off. Our gunners couldn't hit that barge, so they shifted their fire to where the people had run off to and were trying to hide. And darned if those people didn't run back to their barge and move off. And the gunners still couldn't hit it. We really gave it to our gunners over that.

Several times the Chinese pushed our soldiers down to the beach and they had no place to go. We'd pick them up with boats and bring them out to the ships. We'd feed them sardines and crackers and take them down the coast a mile or so and put them ashore again. We'd do that two or three times. We'd keep moving them on down. They were in retreat, but trying to slow the retreat.

DR. ADAMS: THAT SOUNDS KIND OF TOUGH.

Chief Adams: Yeah, it was. They didn't even get time to warm up or anything.

DR. ADAMS: HOW DID YOU FIND THE KOREAN WINTERS?

Chief Adams: Cold. Very cold. Our ship was solidly encased in ice. It was so cold it could freeze that salt water. The destroyers with carriers would try to pick up downed pilots in the water, but they only had a minute or two to get them or the pilots would freeze to death. I stayed down in the boiler rooms a good bit because it was warmer down there.

DR. ADAMS: DID YOU HAVE ANY RECREATION AT ALL?

Chief Adams: We didn't have anything except when we went into Japan. Otherwise it was just maintaining daily life on the ship. We did have movies, but only during the summertime when it was warm enough to be out on deck where they'd set up a screen. But not many movies. Almost every day we were engaged and we wanted to sleep at night. We'd shoot up all our ammunition almost every day and had to restock from an ammo ship almost every night.

Once when we went down to Sasebo [Japan] for repairs and R&R, we got word that the Chinese were going to attack Taiwan with hundreds of junks. We went down there to repel the attack and sailed up and down the Formosa Strait, patrolling it. We never let them get anything started. We trained to repel the Chinese if they tried to board our ships from the junks. We were given .45s and knives. We were to shoot them in their heads as they came up over the side.

DR. ADAMS: WHAT WERE YOUR FEELINGS TOWARD THE NORTH KOREANS AND CHINESE? DID YOU HATE THEM?

Chief Adams: Not really. You never saw them. I suppose you don't have much feeling toward people when you don't get to see them. I expect the soldiers actually doing the fighting in combat would.

DR. ADAMS: WHAT ARE YOUR FEELINGS ABOUT MACARTHUR AND HIS FIRING? DO YOU THINK WE SHOULD HAVE FOLLOWED MACARTHUR'S ADVICE AND GONE AFTER CHINA ITSELF?

Chief Adams: I didn't like MacArthur's idea of starting a huge war with China.

USS Chevalier *refueling at Pearl Harbor, 1950.*

—Courtesy of Harold L. Adams

USS Chevalier *encased in ice in Sea of Japan, 1951.*
—Courtesy of Harold L. Adams

You know, "Chinese" is a scary word when you think of the hordes China has. MacArthur was entirely wrong. MacArthur did a good job of taking over and running Japan, but I agreed with his firing. He was *so-o-o* arrogant, even toward the president.

DR. ADAMS: WHAT WAS YOUR BEST MEMORY OF YOUR KOREAN EXPERIENCE?

Chief Adams: I thought it was kind of fun to shoot up the trains. We sailed right along the coast as close as we could, and you could see the boxcars just explode when we hit them. We could riddle those trains in no time. We never saw the people being killed or anything.

We had good gunners. Well, they got in a lot of practice.

Lorenzo Ramos, Jr.
Interviewed by Leo Villarreal

I interviewed Sgt. Lorenzo Ramos, Jr., at the Brownsville Coffee Shop on 13th Street on Friday, June 6, 2003. I met Mr. Ramos through the phone when I called the Veterans Service Office at about 1:00 P.M. I asked the person on the phone if he knew of any Korean War veterans, and he told me he had one sitting right in front of him. I asked if I could speak to him, introduced myself, and asked if I could interview him about his experience in the Korean War. So now, in the Coffee Shop, Mr. Ramos asked me if I was the person he spoke with on the phone, and I said yes. He then asked me to take a seat. After we chatted a little we began the interview.

MR. VILLARREAL: WHAT BRANCH OF THE MILITARY DID YOU SERVE IN AND WHAT WAS YOUR RANK?

Mr. Ramos: I served in the army. I was a sergeant by the time I retired in 1968. I entered the army in 1948. I began as a cook and then moved up to combat.

MR. VILLARREAL: WHERE DID YOU GO FOR BOOT CAMP?

Mr. Ramos: I went to Fort Ord, California, for boot camp, and then they sent me to Okinawa where I was stationed for fifteen months, and then I was stationed at Fort Howard in Baltimore, Maryland.

MR. VILLARREAL: WERE YOU MARRIED WHEN YOU ENLISTED IN THE ARMY?

Mr. Ramos: No, I wasn't. I did not get married until 1960.

MR. VILLARREAL: WHERE WERE YOU STATIONED WHEN YOU GOT SENT TO KOREA?

Mr. Ramos: I was still in Baltimore, Maryland, when I got my orders that I would be leaving to fight in Korea.

MR. VILLARREAL: HOW DID YOU FEEL WHEN THEY SENT YOU TO KOREA?

Mr. Ramos: Well, I had no choice. President Truman sent us over there and we had to fight. I was afraid, but I had a job to do: I had to defend my country.

MR. VILLARREAL: WHEN DID YOU GET SENT TO KOREA?

Mr. Ramos: I got sent to Korea in 1952. I was in the 8th Army Division in the Far East. We landed in Inchon and bombarded the city. We did our fighting and headed south. I was then stationed fifteen to twenty miles north of Pusan. There we did more fighting and drove the Koreans back. I was sent to Japan on a special mission, transporting nuclear machinery. We stayed in Japan for ten to thirteen days and then went back to Korea. We continued to fight and defend the line. We were hiding behind hills and I saw people die right next to me. Some I tried to save. You don't leave anyone behind. You try to save who you can. Even if they die you bring them back so that they can receive a proper burial. I fought next to British and Turkish troops. We would all form a line protecting the hill and the ammunition area. The enemy wanted to take out our supplies, and at the same time our navy ships would fire missiles into the enemy area to take out their ammunition.

One time I accidentally went into no man's land, which is in between the lines, and was captured and tortured. [Mr. Ramos has lost most of his teeth. They were knocked out of his mouth with a rifle butt.] I was able to escape within fourteen hours. On the way back to camp I was confused for a Korean by U.S. soldiers because I did not realize I had on a Korean jacket. It was cold and I guess I looked like them because I was dark and had small eyes.

While I was in Korea I was trained and became what is called a sniper hunter. I would work eighteen hours straight sometimes doing my job, clearing the enemy out of the way. It was tough fighting. It takes a lot out of a person. We would fight at night and during the day. It wasn't easy.

MR. VILLARREAL: WHAT WAS THE WEATHER LIKE IN KOREA?

Mr. Ramos: The weather was bad. The weather was 40 below. I was frostbitten.

I had to go to the hospital for a few days, but I was released and sent back to my division.

MR. VILLARREAL: WHAT WAS YOUR MOST FRIGHTENING EXPERIENCE?

Mr. Ramos: I had to fight the enemy hand to hand, and I survived. That is why I say they taught me good. I scared the enemies one time when I had the confederate flag with me, and it had the word banzai. The enemy probably thought, "That crazy Mexican!" [Mr. Ramos and I laugh.] After the war I would get flashbacks, but it has settled down. I don't get them anymore.

MR. VILLARREAL: WHAT WAS YOUR MOST MEMORABLE MOMENT?

Mr. Ramos: I received the Purple Heart, the Korean Ribbon, the Presidential Citation, and the United Nations Ribbon. [Mr. Ramos is showing me the different medals that are on his military hat and explains some of them. One of the medals is from Korea. At this time he pulls out a large envelope and shows me some of his pictures from his army service.]

MR. VILLARREAL: DID THE KOREAN WAR CHANGE YOU IN ANY WAY?

Mr. Ramos: Yes, it did. I told you already I would get flashbacks after I retired from the army. I also remember seeing children with hardly any clothing. They were really poor. I would give the children some of my extra gear so they could have something to put on. I wasn't the only one. The other soldiers did the same thing. It is tough when you see things like that, children who are poor and have nothing, and seeing friends die. [Mr. Ramos pauses for a minute or two.] Some of my friends died right in my arms, and there was nothing I could do to save them. Stuff like that stays with you. It is hard to forget. I still remember after all these years, and I am a seventy-one-year-old man. I saw some men all cut up. You really couldn't tell who they were; you had to read their tags.

The war has made me hate. For example, I don't trust the Russians even though they are not the enemy anymore. I don't like them. The British people, I like them and the Turkish also. They are good soldiers. I have also become angry with the U.S. government because I fought for them, never asked why they sent me wherever and I would do what I was told, and I did my job well. Now when I need help because my vision is bad they don't want to help me. The doctors said there was nothing wrong with me. I have a meeting at the Veterans of Foreign Wars (VFW) with someone who is helping with my situation, and the Veterans Office at the Cameron Courthouse is helping also.

MR. VILLARREAL: WHEN THE KOREAN WAR ENDED, DID YOU HAVE TO STAY IN KOREA OR DID YOU RETURN TO THE UNITED STATES?

Mr. Ramos: No, I did not have to stay in Korea. I returned to the United States when the war ended in 1953, and I was stationed in El Paso. Then they sent me to Germany in 1957 for three years, and I returned in 1960, got married, and was stationed in Austin. Went back to Germany in 1962, and then retired in 1968. I served for twenty years. I should have served ten more years and completed thirty. My pension would be more.

[Mr. Ramos and I concluded the interview though I stayed to listen to him explain his problem receiving the medical assistance that he claims he deserves for the twenty years he served in the army. Mr. Ramos is an interesting man who has been affected by the war and spends most of his time at Brownsville Coffee Shop Number One. During our interview, people would walk into the restaurant and say "hi" to him. One can see that Mr. Ramos is a regular. In fact, when I asked for his phone number he did not have one at his residence. He gave the restaurant's number. He explained to me that he is here most of the time having a cup of coffee, smoking a cigarette, listening to the music from the jukebox. After an hour of interviewing and small talk, I excused myself and thanked him for the interview.]

Jesus F. Rodriguez, Sr.
Interviewed by Jesus F. Rodriguez, Jr.

Jesus F. Rodriguez, Sr., is my father. His snow white hair and the furrows etched on his forehead display his age, and he often reminds me that the events of half a century ago are slipping from his memory except for the horror of war. He often closes his eyes and quietly thinks during the questions asked for the interview at his home in Brownsville, Texas. When I was a kid, my father would rarely talk about the war and, when he did, it was usually about someone he remembered or about having a good time at an army base away from Korea and the combat zone. I never saw his medals, and I am indebted to my mother for showing me the photos taken by my father during the Korean Conflict which had been stashed away for decades. This is his story.

MR. RODRIGUEZ: WHEN DID YOU ENTER THE ARMY?
Mr. Rodriguez: I enlisted on December 7, 1950, Pearl Harbor Day, in Littlefield, Texas. I was picking cotton there at the time and was in damn good shape. I had tried to enter during World War II when I was fourteen years old, but I got rejected because I was underweight! It's funny now, but I was really mad at the time. So when Korea came along, I volunteered.

MR. RODRIGUEZ: WHERE DID YOU TAKE TRAINING?
Mr. Rodriguez: I took basic training at Fort Sill, Oklahoma, and remained there for advanced training in artillery as a forward observer. They called them OPs then. It seemed fun at the time, and I was in good shape then. Artillery is hard work, and I could lift a 155-millimeter projectile with one arm. It helped during bar fights! [Laughs.]

MR. RODRIGUEZ: WHERE DID YOU GO NEXT?
Mr. Rodriguez: I was sent to Babenhausen, Germany, near Frankfurt. That's where I lost these. [He shows his left hand and there is a missing index finger and half a thumb.] This is what happens when you toss projectile fuses. After having screwed thousands of these things on, one is bound to have your name on it. Five of us got

hurt that day. [He closes his eyes and thinks.] Yeah, I believe it was five. Lucky the fuse hadn't been screwed onto the projectile yet. You wouldn't be here! [We both laugh.]

MR. RODRIGUEZ: WHAT HAPPENED NEXT?

Mr. Rodriguez: I was sent to Westover Field Hospital in Massachusetts and from there to William Beaumont Hospital in El Paso, Texas. I lost my eyesight on my left eye for thirty-nine days. I counted them! My fingers were amputated in Germany out in the field by a medic. I couldn't feel them and, besides, they were a mess. I was scared about being blind and prayed a lot for eyesight to return. Thank God it did! I still have pieces of steel removed occasionally at Audie Murphy Hospital in San Antonio.

MR. RODRIGUEZ: HOW WAS HOSPITAL LIFE?

Mr. Rodriguez: Terrible. I wanted out of there quickly. I couldn't stand being there. I saw many guys coming back from Korea in bad shape. One guy in the bunk next to mine was from Brady, Texas. His name was Solomon Barraza. The war lasted two hours for him. He got shot while out on patrol, and you could still see the tips of the bullets sticking out of his back. He was a good guy. I was released before Christmas and was sent to Fort Story, Virginia. I now requested a combat transfer to Korea and was given thirty days' leave. When I came back from leave, I was assigned as a truck driver to Korea. You would think they needed infantrymen, but all I wanted was to go to Korea.

MR. RODRIGUEZ: SO HOW DID YOU GET THERE?

Mr. Rodriguez: We went the long way around, through the Panama Canal. When we left Virginia, it was cold and we were wearing wool uniforms and overcoats. A few days later we were in Panama and some guys began tossing their overcoats overboard because it was hot and humid. But we arrived okay. From the Canal Zone, we traveled to San Francisco. We were there for a week.

MR. RODRIGUEZ: WHAT HAPPENED THEN?

Mr. Rodriguez: We boarded a ship that took us from San Francisco to Yokohama, Japan. I remember a marching band at the docks when we left playing the "Stars and Stripes Forever." It tugs at your heart to see America fading away in the distance while that song is being played. [Stares blankly at the window.] This is the best country in the world. Don't you forget it! You are studying history, and soon you will be teaching history, and it is your obligation to remind your students of the price we have paid for their freedom. Many good kids provided it at a price. It doesn't come cheap.

MR. RODRIGUEZ: WHAT HAPPENED WHEN YOU ARRIVED IN JAPAN?

Mr. Rodriguez: When we were traveling on the ship, everybody was seasick. I would not have made a very good sailor. The breakfast was usually powdered eggs with toast. The eggs had an oily sheen to them and smelled like diesel. I remember parts of Yokohama being burnt. We were at a troop depot for three weeks. There were soldiers, airmen, and marines there. A sergeant came over and warned the airmen about the Japanese civilians spitting on airmen. See, the air force had pounded Japan during World War II and the sergeant told them that some of these people had lost family dur-

Jesus Rodriguez, Korea, 1952.
—Courtesy of Jesus Rodriguez

ing the fire raids on Tokyo. The soldiers and marines had never attacked the Japanese homeland, but the air force did, and they were hated because of that.

MR. RODRIGUEZ: WERE YOU SURPRISED BY THAT?

Mr. Rodriguez: Not really. I wasn't air force, but I do remember the warning.

MR. RODRIGUEZ: WHEN DID YOU ARRIVE IN KOREA?

Mr. Rodriguez: I arrived in Pusan in May of 1952. All troops went through Pusan, and there we got our orders. I was assigned to the 7th Infantry Division and wondered what had happened to me being a truck driver for the army. We boarded a train that was all shot up. It was full of bullet holes and we wondered who had been in there when this happened. We arrived in Seoul a couple of days later.

MR. RODRIGUEZ: WERE YOU IN SEOUL LONG?

Mr. Rodriguez: I don't remember much, but I took some pictures there of the Capitol building and the train station. I bought a Nikon camera there and this is it. [Picks up an antique camera in a leather protective case.] Look! It still works! [Clicks it for effect.] I'm going to give it to Kiko. [His grandson.] He'll like Grandpa's camera.

MR. RODRIGUEZ: WHERE DID YOU GO NEXT?

Mr. Rodriguez: We were sent to a replacement depot where we were playing grab-ass and horseplaying with each other. This was in Inchon. The horseplaying stopped when we saw some of the raggediest people I have ever seen. They looked a hundred years old and had sunken eyes and looked gray-skinned. They looked all messed up. These were U.S. soldiers going back to the States. We were their replacements. Nobody talked and we stared at these guys and they stared back. They must have thought: "Poor guys." I'll never forget that moment.

MR. RODRIGUEZ: WERE YOU SCARED?

Mr. Rodriguez: Not yet. Just surprised at how old they looked. We grew up that day. Korea is a tough place and doesn't care about you.

MR. RODRIGUEZ: WHEN DID YOU MOVE OUT?

Mr. Rodriguez: It was shortly after that we shipped out. We got our rifles and ammo issued and we were taken by truck somewhere near the 38th Parallel to some village that doesn't ring to me. It didn't mean much back then either. From there we walked north.

MR. RODRIGUEZ: DID YOU SEE ANY FIGHTING?

Mr. Rodriguez: [Sighs.] Yes, and it was only once that we got into any shooting with the Chinese. There were no North Koreans left by this time and all were Chinese kids fighting. Once was enough. We marched to a place called Hill 155. On the way there, we passed a column of civilians going the other way. I don't know where they were going or where they were coming from but they knew something we didn't. As we kept walking, it became very quiet and lonely. Sort of like walking in the desert, you know? There wasn't a soul around anywhere except us. It's a strange feeling being away from the world.

MR. RODRIGUEZ: WHERE WAS HILL 155?

Mr. Rodriguez: In Korea! [Laughs.] The whole country all looked the same when I was there. It was nothing but rocks and ravines. All the villages and cities were all torn to bits, but we had a guy in our platoon that had been a merchant seaman before World War II and he said that Korea had been a beautiful country with millions of trees. A hillbilly from West Virginia said that he was probably mistaking some other country because this one was all messed up and there wasn't a tree in sight. Come to think about it, I don't remember seeing grass either. Or birds. They're smart; they run away from war.

MR. RODRIGUEZ: HOW LONG WERE YOU AT HILL 155?

Mr. Rodriguez: I think it was about two weeks, maybe longer. It's been a long time, and I don't remember those things anymore. I do remember seeing hills nearby or small mountains, and U.S. jets would fly over us in the day on their way to North Korea. We could sometimes see dogfights away in the distance, but we could not tell who was who.

MR. RODRIGUEZ: WAS IT BORING OUT THERE?

Mr. Rodriguez: Yeah, but the Chinese saw to it that we would not be bored long. One night, some of us were on guard and we could hear sounds in the distance. It's strange how your senses sharpen in combat. It sounded distant, but eyesight is not reliable at night. A sergeant told us to get down and be ready. He had fought in Okinawa during the Second World War, and we took his advice as the Word of God. Now I got tense. I remember a bugle blowing and lots of whistles, like the ones the referees use. I did not know what was going on, but I knew it wasn't good. We were then given the firing order and saw the sergeant begin shooting his carbine at the noise. Let me get some water. [He gets up and heads to the kitchen. I see his eyes open up a bit more when he tells about this incident. Soon he returns.] I could now see mortars falling behind us and, having been trained in artillery, I knew that they were ranging us to knock us out. Now I got scared. But they never ranged us. I think they did not know where we were at or were firing at something else. Some guys got hurt during the shooting and one guy got killed. I had the standard load of two bandoliers and a web belt with ammo. I wondered if this would be enough. We saw several enemy go by us, and the .30-caliber machine gun got them. We were told to remain in our foxholes and not jump out or risk getting shot by our own guys. I can see how it happened before because it is hard to see who is who during all the noise and confusion. The .30 machine gun crew had removed all the tracers on the bullet belts because it made it easier for the Chinese to see them. Machine gunners were usually the first to be killed by the enemy or mortar crews, and these guys didn't want to make it easy for the enemy. Some of us picked up the tracers and placed them in clips earlier, just in case. You can never have too much ammo.

MR. RODRIGUEZ: HOW LONG DID THIS FIREFIGHT LAST?

Mr. Rodriguez: It could have been thirty minutes; it could have been several hours. I don't know. [Closes his eyes and thinks for a moment.] I now believe that it was probably several hours long. Who cares? I remember the Chinese coming in waves, like a football kickoff. Many didn't have weapons, just sticks or pipes. Many of the Chinese troops were even barefoot. They were in pretty bad shape. I could now hear some tanks coming and hoped that they were ours. Someone had called the 5th RCT (Regimental Combat Team) which had "quad fifties." Two half-tracks with four .50-caliber machine guns on a mount showed up and began firing at the Chinese. These were originally made for anti-aircraft use but they worked fine against troops also. They stopped the Chinese cold. Those things make an awful lot of noise and, yes, they used tracers. They shoot lots of bullets and this stopped the waves of people coming at us. Thank God those things were on our side. I would have hated to be on the other end of those things. Only the quad fifties and napalm would stop the

Chinese prisoners stripped naked to detect booby traps, Korea, 1951.

—Courtesy of Jesus Rodriguez

human waves. The Chinese were terrified of those two things. After seeing what they could do, I would be scared, too.

MR. RODRIGUEZ: WHAT HAPPENED IN THE MORNING?

Mr. Rodriguez: We saw some dead Chinese about 100 yards in front of us, and a sergeant and two other GIs were sent to look for intel. Seeing the shape the Chinese were in, I doubt that they even had had something to eat, much less maps. There were some rifles and grenades, but most of them had sticks and pipes. We were told to be careful of booby traps on the Chinese. It smelled horrible [pauses], and I threw up. Some of these kids had been mangled badly by quad fifties. I took some photos but they got taken away from me later. Even if I would have kept them, I think I would have burned them. Those kids deserve to rest in peace. They were [picks up his hand in the air and waves] ripped apart, too much blood.

MR. RODRIGUEZ: DO YOU FEEL THE U.S. SHOULD HAVE GONE TO KOREA?

Mr. Rodriguez: Well, I volunteered, so I asked for it, right? If you got drafted, you were just doing your duty. Many people don't know that we are still at war with North Korea. There was only a ceasefire in 1953, and I was there in Panmunjon when the first prisoner exchange took place. I could see the tents where the peace talks were held and remember seeing the buses with the North Korean and Chinese POWs coming there. The buses had chicken wire on the windows and the driver had a plywood screen with a hole for the driver to see. This wasn't for the prisoners not to escape but so that the South Korean civilians would not kill the POWs. The South Koreans would throw rocks at the buses and pelt them badly. I have never seen a country where people hated each other so much as Korea. The civilians had to be kept away by ROK military policemen. These guys take no crap! They beat you over the head and are mean. But they have to be because those people understand no other form of law.

MR. RODRIGUEZ: DID YOU SEE ANY U.S. TROOPS BEING EXCHANGED?

Mr. Rodriguez: Yes, and they looked sick and weak. Poor guys. Our GIs have always been treated worse than dogs when taken prisoner. You could see their ribs and skinny arms. I was very mad at this and knew that I had to leave Korea. So much hate! [He closes his eyes and drinks water.] I waited three months to leave. The tour there was nine months but I remained there thirteen. I finally found space in the brig of a ship coming back to the States. I didn't get in trouble or anything; it's just that it was the only space available. I took it.

MR. RODRIGUEZ: WHERE DID YOU END UP AFTER KOREA?

Mr. Rodriguez: I spent the rest of my time in Puerto Rico and Panama. My truck driver orders caught up, and that is what I did afterward. I was also in Norfolk, Virginia, as an executive driver for battalion executives. I had pull, man! [My son shows up now and my father hugs him tightly.] I was discharged from Camp Chaffee, Arkansas, on May 25, 1955. I got the "Eisenhower Year" added on, so I was in the army almost five years.

MR. RODRIGUEZ: WHAT DO YOU THINK ABOUT THE WAR NOW?

Mr. Rodriguez: [My son sits next to my dad and drinks some of his water. My father puts his arm around him.] I don't think about it. It's there and I remember mostly the kids who were there. War is a disease that kills everything, so I don't let it get hold of me. Life is too short and, besides, ask me about the "1-2-3 Club" in Lawton next time, okay? [We all laugh.]

Juan Lopez
Interviewed by Santiago Salazar, Jr.

This interview with Mr. Juan Lopez was conducted on June 9, 2003. Mr. Lopez was repairing his truck and was scheduled to be in San Antonio the following day.

MR. SALAZAR: CAN YOU TELL ME A LITTLE ABOUT YOUR FAMILY AND HOW THEY FELT TOWARD THE KOREAN WAR?

Mr. Lopez: My family did not want for me to go to the military. They wanted me to go to school and get an education. Education was very important to them. They did not want me to enter the military. I come from a good family. We worked hard and had very little, but my father provided us with everything. The military was not the answer. My father and mother wanted me to go to school.

MR. SALAZAR: SO YOU GOT DRAFTED INTO THE MILITARY?

Mr. Lopez: No, I volunteered for the military. I was part of the Paratrooper Infantry Regiment, 82nd Airborne Division.

MR. SALAZAR: HOW LONG WERE YOU IN KOREA?

Mr. Lopez: I was there from 1953 to 1954. One and a half years. After that they sent me to Munich, Germany, for another three years.

MR. SALAZAR: SO YOU WERE A GI?

Mr. Lopez: Yes, and no. I was a paratrooper. I was very skilled at what I did. Not anyone can be a paratrooper. It was very dangerous work. It took guts to jump from a plane and then land on the ground. I was never scared of dying from jumping. In fact, I found it fun sometimes.

MR. SALAZAR: HOW DID YOUR FAMILY FEEL ABOUT YOU BEING A PARATROOPER?

Mr. Lopez: They did not like it. Well, my mom didn't. She was always afraid that jumping from a plane was dangerous. But my dad took some pride for what I was doing. When I came back, my sister used to tell me that he was very proud of what I was doing for my country. I think that he was proud, but my mom was always scared. She did not understand why the war had started and why we were fighting. But my dad didn't care about the war. He just wanted me to be careful and watch out for myself. "Don't trust anyone" is what he used to tell me all the time.

MR. SALAZAR: WHEN YOU VOLUNTEERED, IN WHAT CITY WERE YOU LIVING?

Mr. Lopez: I was living in Brownsville.

MR. SALAZAR: DURING THAT TIME HOW WERE BROWNSVILLE RESIDENTS REACTING TO THE WAR?

Mr. Lopez: It was not called a war at first. It was called, I think, "police something." ["A police action."] Anyhow that's what they called it at first. They didn't change the name until one or two years later. The people of Brownsville reacted good to the war. They supported the war because no one knew the bad things about the war. A lot of people thought it would be the same as the World War II. We won, and no one thought that we could lose.

MR. SALAZAR: SO WERE THE CITIZENS OF BROWNSVILLE ANTI- OR PRO-WAR?

Mr. Lopez: I don't think they were what you call anti-war. Being poor Mexicans, a lot of us used the military to get out of being poor. They used the TV very good to get you to volunteer for the military. That is why I volunteered. My friends were going to join and they pushed me to enter the military. I thought a long time, but my friends told me because I was Mexican they were going to draft me anyway. So I volunteered. Many of my friends ran away to Mexico or went back home. They did not want to fight.

MR. SALAZAR: WHY DO YOU THINK THEY FLED THE COUNTRY?

Mr. Lopez: See, what you don't understand is that people were scared, especially the poor people. We knew that we were the first to be drafted, so they left. I think some came back, but we did not remain friends.

MR. SALAZAR: CAN YOU DESCRIBE YOUR TRAINING?

Mr. Lopez: It was very hard. First you had to make sure your parachute was in good condition. We would spend several days learning how to pack the parachute. No one did it for us. If the chute did not open, then you knew you were going to, well, not make it. We had several accidents where I was training. My boss told me and the rest of the men to learn so that it would not happen to us.

MR. SALAZAR: WERE BLACKS ALLOWED TO BE PARATROOPERS?

Mr. Lopez: Yes, but not many. They did not want them to do this work. It was very dangerous for any man, but they kept the blacks in the infantry, not the paratroopers.

MR. SALAZAR: WHILE YOU WERE IN TRAINING, DO YOU FEEL THAT THE TRAINING WAS ADEQUATE FOR YOUR ASSIGNMENT?

Mr. Lopez: Yes. They taught us how to jump very well. The commanders were tough, but they knew that wrong moves kill soldiers. They were tough, but they trained us well.

MR. SALAZAR: HOW DID THE CITIZENS OF JAPAN TREAT THE AMERICAN SOLDIERS?

Mr. Lopez: Very well. The Japanese people had no bad feelings toward us. They were very nice and they helped us out a lot. They would help us unload equipment and supplies, and they always treated us with respect. They were very nice people.

MR. SALAZAR: DID YOU EVER FEEL THAT ANYTHING WAS GOING TO HAPPEN TO YOU?

Mr. Lopez: No. I knew that I was worried, but I trained very hard and I kept praying. That's what you did: you prayed every day. That's why I knew I was coming home.

MR. SALAZAR: HOW LONG DID YOU TRAIN IN JAPAN?

Mr. Lopez: Not very long. I think, if I remember, about three to five months. But they needed us real bad, so it was not very long.

MR. SALAZAR: WHAT DO YOU MEAN THEY NEEDED YOU REAL BAD?

Mr. Lopez: We were dropped behind enemy lines because we were going to start fighting a two-front war. That's what the generals wanted. They wanted us to land behind the Koreans, and when we pushed north we attacked from behind. It was crazy, because sometimes you didn't know who you were firing at, but we knew that we had to be firing at the Koreans. They gave up very quickly. They knew that the army meant business. We were trained to kill, not play around. Many of the soldiers took pride in killing. I didn't. I just wanted to make sure that I was not shooting at American soldiers because it was so hard to tell.

MR. SALAZAR: WERE YOU AND YOUR FELLOW PARATROOPERS EXCITED ABOUT THE JUMP?

Mr. Lopez: Yes and no. We trained real hard, and we knew what we were going to do. I think I must have checked my parachute several times. I was ready. Many soldiers were praying and we had a church service the night before, but we were ready.

MR. SALAZAR: HOW WAS THE MORALE OF THE SQUAD?

Mr. Lopez: Good. We were trained and we were ready. The commander told us to have our guns ready and loaded because it was going to be "hot" when we landed. That was scary. I fired my gun several times, but I don't know what I was firing at.

MR. SALAZAR: DID THEY INJECT YOU WITH VACCINES?

Mr. Lopez: Yes, there were so many. I don't know how many, but when you were standing doctors used both of your arms. Then when your arms got tired they put shots on your ass.

MR. SALAZAR: CAN YOU DESCRIBE YOUR FIRST NIGHT IN KOREA AFTER YOU PARACHUTED?

Mr. Lopez: Yes, it was very dangerous. We had to take a head count to make sure that our guys were all right. We lost several soldiers, but most got there safely. We then had to set up a perimeter so that we could advance to the south. We waited for orders to move, but the first night was scary. You heard bombs all the time and gunfire. That first night, I didn't sleep. No one did, because we knew the Koreans were coming. So we sat up and waited. The next day they told us to get ready because we were moving south. I promised myself for God to watch over me and take care of me.

MR. SALAZAR: WERE YOU CONSTANTLY HEARING BOMBS AND GUNFIRE WHERE YOU WERE?

Mr. Lopez: Yes, the bombs kept coming. We set them up because our guys were attacking from the north and waited. The Koreans had no idea we were there. When we first saw them I wanted to kill all of them, but many surrendered. They just wanted food and water. They were so tired, and a lot of them had no bullets. They were just running.

MR. SALAZAR: CAN YOU DESCRIBE THE DIFFERENCE BETWEEN SOUTH KOREAN SOLDIERS AND AMERICAN SOLDIERS?

Mr. Lopez: The South Koreans were good fighters, but they gave up too quickly. They would surrender very quickly. They did not want to fight.

MR. SALAZAR: WHY DO YOU THINK THEY GAVE UP SO QUICKLY?

Mr. Lopez: That's a good question. Think about it. It's like fighting your own race, like Mexicans. You don't kill your own people. That's why they gave up so quickly. You don't kill your own people.

MR. SALAZAR: WHAT WAS YOUR WORST EXPERIENCE IN KOREA?

Mr. Lopez: The cold. It was very cold. They gave us summer clothes but never winter clothes. They made big mistakes when it came to clothes.

MR. SALAZAR: WHAT WAS YOUR BEST EXPERIENCE IN KOREA?

Mr. Lopez: I didn't get injured. I made it back alive.

Raul J. Leal
Interviewed by Edith Lizbeth Cano

I met Mr. Raul Leal at the IHOP on Wednesday, June 4, 2003. He served in the U.S. Navy during the Korean War. Currently Mr. Leal is the commander of American Legion Post #43 in Brownsville.

MS. CANO: WHEN AND WHERE WERE YOU BORN?

Mr. Leal: I was born in Harlingen, Texas. We were originally from Brownsville, Texas, but at the time my family happened to be living in Harlingen. I'm the second oldest. I got an older sister; of the boys I'm the oldest.

MS. CANO: HOW DID YOU JOIN THE NAVY?

Mr. Leal: I volunteered. When I was in the 11th grade I dropped out of school and joined the navy. During the Korean War, I joined in [starts laughing, trying to remember] January 17, 1952, and I was in the navy for eight years. So I came out or was discharged on January 16, 1960. I put in a total of eight years. It was four years active and four years in the reserve.

MS. CANO: WHERE DID YOU RECEIVE YOUR TRAINING?

Mr. Leal: In San Diego, California.

MS. CANO: ON WHAT DATE DID YOU GET TO KOREA?

Mr. Leal: Well, I enlisted. I volunteered. I was seventeen years old and my dad had to sign for me. Then we went to basic training for about six weeks. Then, right after that, they shipped us out to Korea. After two and a half months of training, I was in Korea.

MS. CANO: WHAT WAS YOUR SPECIALTY?

Mr. Leal: I was a gunner's mate, United States Navy. I took care of all the guns onboard ship, cleaning them.

MS. CANO: DO YOU REMEMBER THE SHIP YOU WERE ON?

Mr. Leal: Oh, yes. The first one was the USS *Shovler*. I was there for about a year and I was a minesweeper. What they do is they send us close to the coast and we have some gear that strips the mines because the enemy will always put mines right below the water, right at the edge of the water, below the waves. They would drop them out on cables. The mine would float. [Mr. Leal shows me on the table how the machine worked to get the mines from the water.] When the ships would pass, they would hit the mine and blow up. So we had to go in there to clean them up. [Starts laughing.] I'm still here so I never hit any, but we were able to cut them. [Mr. Leal shows me using silverware as the ship and the mine.] The ship has some cables going down and it has some cutters like scissors. So if there is a mine it would cut it and then after you cut it, it floats up to the surface. That's when we would see them. We would blow them out of the water and get rid of them. So we would clear the water by so many yards this way and so many yards that way. That was my first tour of duty.

Then from there I went to the Air-Sea Rescue, on an LST landing ship. We had helicopters on top of that. And we would rescue all the pilots that were shot down. We would try to rescue them and go out and bring them in.

From the LST, I went to destroyers. The LST landing ship was number 799. The last tour of duty was *John Thompson*, 360. I carry that in my wallet forever with me. That was my last tour of duty.

MS. CANO: HOW WERE THE DESTROYERS ARMED?

Mr. Leal: They have two cannons in the front and two in the back. [He shows me using his hands.] Then we have the anti-aircraft guns on the side and on the back. So you could fire.

MS. CANO: WHAT WERE THE SAILORS' FEELINGS AT THE BEGINNING OF THE WAR? HOW DID EVERYBODY FEEL?

Mr. Leal: Personally, I was so young and inexperienced that the fear was not there. To me it seemed like it was some kind of game. That's the way I've always analyzed it. You know sometimes we would come under fire and you just laugh about it because, I'll be honest with you, it didn't seem real. It seemed like if I was in a movie and I was seeing cowboys shoot each other. [Starts laughing.] As I got a little older then I realized. Once I experienced it a little bit and I started seeing, you know, more people getting hurt and everything, it began to set in. I was eighteen and a half, and you grow up overnight. You grow up or you don't come back. I mean you learn to take care of yourself. So that helped me mature by the time the conflict was over. I was there when they signed the armistice in June of 1953. As a matter of fact, I was on the LST landing ship. That's when we evacuated. We evacuated the troops that were in North Korea. We went around the coast to evacuate all the troops that were in North Korea. They were all up and down the coast, up to the Yalu River. [I take out a map of Korea from class.] We were up in North Korea going up and down the Sea of Japan and picking up troops. In Wonsan harbor, we did a lot of stripping. See, what you normally do is send minesweepers in to clear the entrance to ports of the mines. We tried to clear as many mines as we could in the water. When they would plan an invasion, it would be ready. We were port patrolling a lot back and forth.

MS. CANO: WHAT WAS THAT HARBOR WHERE THE SOLDIERS INVADED?

Mr. Leal: Wonsan harbor. You see, during World War II the Japanese had laid a lot of the mines. Personally, I came seven years later, [but] there were still a lot of mines there.

MS. CANO: DESCRIBE THE AREA OF KOREA THAT YOU EXPERIENCED.

Mr. Leal: From the sea we would go into Korea once we got the area cleared. We would dock like in Pusan. When I got off the ship we would play baseball. We would play against the air force, the ones that were stationed there, in Pusan. From what I saw there was a lot of poverty. War is hell. There is no other way to say it. You keep things you'd rather not talk about, let me put it that way. In general, war brings a lot of misery to the people. Families split up and a lot of kids [are left to] fend for themselves. They do anything they can to survive ... both male and female. It is hard. I can get into more details, but I'd rather not.

MS. CANO: DID YOU EVER GET TO BE WITH THE ROK TROOPS?

Mr. Leal: Yes, we met. They were very friendly with us. I only met them when they let us go to shore. They let us mingle with them.

MS. CANO: DID YOU EVER PARTICIPATE IN ANY MAJOR BATTLES?

Mr. Leal: From the ship, nothing. We were shot at. We would fire the guns. They would give us a target. We would set it up from the ocean and fire at a certain distance. When the troops would get in a bind, they would call the ships so that we could fire. They would tell us everything that was within range.

MS. CANO: DID YOU EVER CROSS THE 38TH PARALLEL LINE?

Mr. Leal: Yes, as a matter of fact we got a certificate. [Starts laughing.] They issued a certificate because I had crossed the 38th Parallel Line. It's funny, I don't even know if I have it anymore.

MS. CANO: WHAT WAS THE HARDEST PART OF THE WAR?

Mr. Leal: The hardest part was seeing all the suffering of the people just because some other nation wanted to invade another nation. It was a very eerie part of the war in the sense that they, North Korea, would keep you and brainwash you if you were captured. That was one thing that is hardly said about the Korean War. They would get the prisoners and try to brainwash them to the point they would say that the United States and South Korea were wrong. They would get them to sign documents. They were the aggressors. After the war, South Korea became a superpower with the American technology. If North and South Korea would have been united, it would have been wonderful today.

MS. CANO: WOULD YOU TELL ME ONE INTERESTING EXPERIENCE THAT YOU HAD WHILE YOU WERE THERE IN KOREA?

Mr. Leal: When I was with the Air-Sea Rescue LST, one of the helicopters was shot at pretty bad so that we needed to rescue them. They would land on the ships and unload, but this helicopter was so badly damaged that they told them to get as close alongside the ship and drop in the water. I was standing on the deck with a boat, ready to get them out. When the helicopter hit the water, the pilots jumped out and we picked them up. Then the commander of the ship decided that they wanted the helicopter out of the water. Three days later we raised it, and as it hit the air it exploded and caught fire. The LST was right next to it. I was on top of the tower seeing this. As soon as it exploded, I jumped down the ladder and ran toward the fire with a hose. When I got there, it hit me that I was by myself. So if somebody had turned on the hose, it would have taken me all over the place. But my reactions were automatic. There was a fence there and I wrapped the hose around it and turned on the water. Now it is like a laughing matter. When the soldiers saw what I was trying to do, they came and helped me, but they had to drop the helicopter back into the water and later they got it out. The commander was very appreciative.

The Enemy

To interview enemy soldiers, to get some balance and to see the war from their perspective, I have to go to China, a nation in which I've taught in the past and have visited several times in recent years. But this visit turned out to be more of an ordeal than I had bargained for.

Northwest Airlines Flight 19 for Tokyo with onward service to Beijing lifts off from Minneapolis at 2:55 P.M. Virtually every seat on the 747 is taken—packed with Asians and a smattering of Americans: an old tourist couple, a few businessmen sprawling in business class, a knot of military types in civilian clothes but unmistakably identifiable nonetheless in their burr haircuts and their jacket patches with military logos: "101st Screaming Eagles"; "Band of Brothers." They are bound via Tokyo for American bases in Okinawa, Japan, and Korea.

Thirteen hours of confined misery are ahead of us, flying at first over Minnesota lakes, then over vast, rectangular fields of Manitoban, Saskatchewan, and Albertan grain. As we reach ever further north and west, there are increasingly desolate stretches of wasteland. Villages play out. The road grid plays out. From 37,000 feet you look down on dark smudges of water-logged scrags and just the occasional farmstead with odd-shaped fields—not rectangles—scratched out of marginal lands. Then trees start. Wilderness. Lonely logging camps, mining camps. The onboard screen tracing the flight path displays names like Yellowknife and Uranium City. It is hard not to imagine stark, lonely, horrible lives being lived down there.

As we approach the Yukon and then Alaska, the patches of snow dusting the fields, forests and mountains give way to blankets of snow.

Over Alaska, Northwest's cabin crew, composed as are most American cabin crews of graying males and middle-aged women clinging on till retirement, orders all window panels closed and douses the cabin lights. Since our westward flight paces the westward moving sun, we face an endless day and the crew is creating an artificial "night" for us. We stay buttoned up until just before landing at Tokyo. Passengers debark. Those continuing on to Beijing have a two-hour delay in transit while the 747 is refueled, restocked, and cleaned.

And then we reboard, and as we do so we enter an entirely new world. For one thing, the American crew has come off and been replaced by an all-Chinese crew. Our attendants are now petite, polite Chinese girls. But what you notice first is not their petiteness or politeness, what you notice first—what really jolts you—is that every one of them has their lower face enshrouded by a high-quality surgical mask and their hands are encased in transparent plastic gloves. You see, we are flying into a "hot zone"—Beijing in Spring 2003, the epicenter of the world's SARS outbreak—a city experiencing 100-plus new cases a day, and reeling from the impact that has. The city is nearly locked down: schools and universities closed, most factories closed, non-essential foreign embassy staff and families evacuated, movies, discos, karaoke bars, internet bars—all closed by government fiat. And this plane is ample evidence of the impact on China's tourism and international business. A World Health Organization "travel advisory" is in effect, discouraging all non-essential travel to China and, especially, Beijing. Consequently, this flight is nearly empty. Not more than one in eight seats is now occupied. Just a few heads are visible in each of the 747's three vast main cabins—and these heads are almost all swathed in surgical masks. As hands reach up here and there to adjust air vents, you notice the rubber gloves. Or, if ungloved people have to touch something, say turn off a reading lamp, you notice they do it with a quick jab of a finger knuckle. It is said the SARS virus can live up to four days on any plastic surface—say, a key of a keyboard, or, for that matter, a light switch. Remarkable virulence. Everyone fears his neighbor. We look at each other: nervous eyes flicker above our surgical masks. We speak in muffled voices. The girl who serves me my supper has to ask "beef or chicken?" three times before I comprehend her. Each passenger sits alone amidst the sea of seats, joylessly unwrapping and eating their way through the hermetically sealed dishes.

We land at Beijing International and the big Boeing taxis toward the terminal—passing over a reinforced bridge as we do so. The traffic of one of the city's main expressways passes below us—but the expressway is eerily devoid of traffic at 9:30 on a Tuesday evening. I see only one vehicle pass beneath us while we lumber over the bridge, and ominously it is an ambulance racing along with blue lights flashing. Another victim?

In the huge terminal building all the customs and immigration officials are masked. As I am motioned through the last checkpoint, the muffled official says, "Welcome to Beijing."

I pass into what is usually a teeming reception hall, expecting to find my friend and interpreter Jane (Yang Hua Jing), but the hall is completely deserted—not a soul is there. It, too, is an out-of-bounds area during the SARS epidemic, or, as I soon learn the Chinese refer to it, "The Special Time." But outside the terminal building, standing at curbside with a car and driver waiting, is sweet Jane. She's smiling. She's not masked. She's adopted a fatalistic approach. She tells me: "If I live, I live. If I die, I die. Let God choose."

Half an hour later we arrive at the government-run Friendship Hotel. The Friendship Hotel's literature boasts of its being one of the largest hotels in the world, with 1,900 rooms and containing 26 restaurants, but entering its pillared reception hall feels like entering a morgue: with scant guests, except for one small wing and one restaurant, the whole hotel is shut down. At the desk, before I can register, the masked desk clerk says "Special Time" and inserts a probe into my ear to check my temperature. I'm okay, they let me in. My heels echo in the cavernous hall as I head for the elevators.

Interpreter Yang Hua Jing

SARS campaign underway in Beijing, 2003. The billboard message reads: "The SARS will surely be conquered by our government under the leadership of the Communist Party of China."

The next day, May 14, Jane and I make a courtesy visit to the apartment of retired Professor Jin Dinghan. Jane, a former student of mine and now a reporter for the government's *International Talent Monthly,* interviewed Professor Jin on an earlier journalistic assignment and became a friend of both the professor and his wife. She was a frequent visitor in their home. Professor Jin taught at Beijing University for many years and is China's foremost expert in Hindi language and literature, and spent twenty years compiling the seminal Hindi-Chinese Dictionary, as well as translating the bulk of Mao Zedong's poems and thoughts into Hindi. He has been awarded numerous prizes and honors by both the Chinese and Indian governments. It is this man, through his connections, who has located three distinguished Korean veterans for us to interview, and so we wish to visit him and thank him. We change into slippers at the door, then sit with Professor Jin and his wife over tea and sweets in their living room. Since Dr. Jin had no direct service in the Korean War, I have only a couple of general questions on the war to ask him.

DR. ADAMS: DO YOU THINK IT WAS WISE FOR CHINA TO HAVE BECOME INVOLVED IN THE KOREAN WAR?

Professor Jin: No. It was a tragedy, a tragedy. So many persons died. We had been cheated.

DR. ADAMS: CHEATED BY WHOM?

Professor Jin: I think not only by the Soviet Union but our government. The war was begun by Kim Il Sung and the north, and not by the south. You could tell the northern troops advanced very far south—very fast—at the start of the war. So even though a young man I knew it must have been the north that started the war. But we Chinese were told the south started the war with American encouragement—and so we wanted to help the north.
DR. ADAMS: AND NOW YOU KNOW THAT IS NOT TRUE?
Professor Jin: Yeah. Yeah.
DR. ADAMS: WHAT DO YOU THINK OF NORTH KOREA TODAY?
Professor Jin: I think Kim Jong Il is a ... I agree with President Bush's idea about him. North Korea is not a behaved little brother of China.

Three days later, May 17, we met with the three veterans. There were a number

Jin Dinghan and the author.

of stipulations they made that had to be met before the meeting could take place. They would only agree to meet collectively—not individually—so as to refresh each other's memories, they claimed. Also, they insisted that the meeting take place in a quiet room—no crowds—with good air circulation due to SARS. Also they wished us to book a private sedan—no taxis—to fetch and return them from the meeting place. After some investigation with the hotel's assistant manager, we determined my own hotel room was the best alternative. He arranged for his staff to set up a table and chairs, and provide tea service in my room.

These three Chinese veterans were in no way common foot soldiers. All held positions of considerable authority during the war and in their subsequent lives. The most genteel of the group was retired philosophy professor Lin Qingshan, who is a well-known Chinese biographer and who held the post of vice-president of the Beijing Social Science Institute prior to his retirement. He is a tall man, slightly stooped by age, who has an aura of calm dignity. He is a reflective man, and he is a man who has had much to reflect upon: battle wounds from both his service in the People's Liberation Army (PLA) and in fighting the Americans in Korea. Moreover, his attainments proved a ruinous liability during The Great Proletarian Cultural Revolution (1966-1976). In 1964 he published an article in a philosophical journal containing these enigmatic lines:

One scene can be separated and
   reunited together.
One scene can have conflict and
   be harmonious.

In consequence he was accused of being an anti-Mao revisionist and branded as a member of "The Stinking Ninth Category," i.e., an "intellectual." A revolutionary tribunal sentenced him to seven years of hard labor in Henan Province. The first few years he spent as a toilet cleaner before being elevated to farm laborer.

Lin Qingshan

During the Korean War, Professor Lin served as a political commissar in charge of over 500 soldiers. He was on the battlefield five months before being wounded in the back by American artillery fire and evacuated to China for rehabilitation.

Mr. Lu Yunkui was born in Shanxi Province in 1926 and joined the PLA's famous 8th Route Army in 1939 when he was just thirteen years old. With such sterling revolutionary credentials he rose rapidly and at the time of the Korean War was serving as a political commissar in the 66th Route Army—and was supervising 4,000 soldiers. In more recent years, and until his retirement, Mr. Lu was a high official in China's Department of Food and Grain. Mr. Lu remains a feisty, exuberant, competitive man. This was evident throughout the interviews and also at the banquet I hosted afterward. Mr. Lu asked me how much my son earned. I told him and immediately he trumped me. His son works and lives in San Jose, California, and makes $150,000 a year. Mr. Lu smiled with deep satisfaction.

The final of the threesome was Mr. Hao Ru, born in Liaoning Province in 1933. He served as an officer in the artillery. Despite being seventy years old, he is fit and powerful-looking. He still has jet black hair and youthful, severely Asiatic features. Frankly, he's vicious-looking, and you can well imagine he would have been a formidable foe on the battlefield. He brought to the interview a number of his medals for me to examine and also showed me a photograph of him taken in 1948 when he was just fifteen years old and serving with the PLA against the Nationalists. He stands erect and grim in his uniform with a big automatic pistol tucked under his belt. He chuckles as he shows the photograph to me and then pantomimes whipping the pistol out and pointing it around at the rest of us in the room: "Pa-TOW! Pa-TOW!" He shoots us all and laughs.

Lu Yunkui

For the next two and a half hours, we sat around the table and these three veterans answered my questions—put to them through Jane, my interpreter—and offered up some spontaneous reminiscings.

DR. ADAMS: PROFESSOR LIN, HOW DID YOU COME TO ENTER THE PLA? WHAT MOTIVATED YOU TO JOIN?

Professor Lin: In 1945 I was a student in Jilin Province in northeastern China. China was still under the control of the Japanese, and I studied in one of the schools set up by the Japanese. As the PLA approached my city I ran away and joined the army—the 38th Route Army. I took part in many battles between 1945 and 1949. Then I was in the army in Korea until 1951 when I was wounded.

DR. ADAMS: WHERE AND HOW WERE YOU TRAINED? WHAT WERE THE CONDITIONS LIKE?

Professor Lin: We were trained for three weeks in military and politics at a camp.

Hao Ru
—Courtesy of Hao Ru

The camp was very informal. It was in a village. Because I already had a high school education, which was rare in those days, I was made responsible for political thought.

DR. ADAMS: HOW DID YOU GET TO KOREA? WHERE WERE YOU SENT? WHAT WERE THE CONDITIONS LIKE IN YOUR CAMP?

Professor Lin: [Laughs.] I walked. It only took five minutes to cross a bridge and enter Korea. I entered Korea in February or March of 1951. It was very cold. It was lucky I was born in northeast China. I could stand Korean weather.

DR. ADAMS: WHAT FIGHTING DID YOU ENGAGE IN? DESCRIBE IT.

Professor Lin: I fought in the fourth of "The Five Battles." [Chinese historians divide the Korean War into five battles commensurate with the five major offensives and counteroffensives of the two sides. The "Fourth Battle's" main action was in January-May, 1951.] Remember I was a political commissar. My main duty during battle was to write about the brave actions of soldiers and to write the history of battles. Every day I collected information on the battle and printed it up. I made hand copies and passed them out to the soldiers. I praised the brave actions of soldiers as an example for others.

[At this point, the planned orderliness of the interview session was disrupted when Mr. Hao, apparently bored with the slow-paced humdrum questions, interjected: "You Americans bombed us with germ bombs!" When I denied the truth of this, the others angrily chimed in and insisted it was true. Even Jane turned on me: "You don't want the war except in your viewpoint. You weren't there; these men were there. If you don't want to hear what they say, why did you invite them to this interview?"

So even though I know these accusations to be false—there is absolutely no evidence of the use of chemical or bacteriological agents by either side during the Korean War—I allowed Mr. Hao to continue.]

Mr. Hao: I am very surprised you don't know about Americans using germ warfare. There are many books about this. I saw many soldiers get hurt. We vaccinated our soldiers against all types of germs popular with the Americans. Every soldier carried a card saying what germs he had been vaccinated for. We also vaccinated the North Korean citizens in our area.

DR. ADAMS: PROFESSOR LIN, WHAT WAS THE WORST THING YOU EXPERIENCED DURING THE WAR?

Professor Lin: The most terrible experience of the Korean War, which was a terrible war, was seeing that people were starving and frozen. Our army was not well equipped and our soldiers did not have good shoes. Some were even barefooted. Even some soldiers starved to death. We had to amputate soldiers whose arms had frozen, sometimes all the arms and all the legs. General Peng, the senior Chinese war general in Korea, was very angry and went back to Beijing to complain during the war. This was during January 1951. But the generals back in Beijing said they were doing the best that they could. General Peng was furious. He said you generals should go to the front and see what is happening to our soldiers in -20° and -30° weather. The Chinese soldiers respect General Peng very much.

DR. ADAMS: I HAVE SEEN REPORTS THAT IN SOME BATTLES MANY CHINESE SOLDIERS DID NOT EVEN HAVE RIFLES, THAT ONLY HALF WERE CARRYING RIFLES IN SOME BATTLES.

Professor Lin: Everybody had a rifle, but often might run out of ammunition.

DR. ADAMS: MR. LU, WHAT WAS YOUR WORST EXPERIENCE IN THE WAR?

Mr. Lu: The most worst experience was when the two armies—American and Chinese—are face to face. You are trying to strike us, and we are trying to stop you. My responsibility was our soldiers were fighting on the mountain and during the daytime I stayed in the bunker, and during the nighttime I would climb the mountain and bring and carry down the dead. It is very simple to bury a soldier—just dig a hole and put them in. There were so many. Also when I climbed the mountain there were so many dead I stepped on them. Also, we dare not move during the daytime. All supply was done at night. Often in fighting of 100 men, only one or two would survive. Sometimes none. So the next night we would bring up another 100 men. This was during the Fourth Battle. In the Third Battle the Americans tried to flee. Your tanks and trucks ran over many of your own soldiers. Many Americans died of that. You Americans might not believe that.

DR. ADAMS: MR. HAO, WHAT WAS YOUR WORST EXPERIENCE IN THE WAR?

Mr. Hao: There were many. To see so many men killed during bombing and also to see my comrades starving. It is foot soldiers who mostly starved.

DR. ADAMS: HOW WERE YOU FED?

Mr. Hao: During the daytime we wouldn't eat because the planes are in the air. After 4:00 P.M. in the wintertime it got dark and we could send the food. People will bring a big basin of food up to the mountain. Rice or millet was the usual food. Or food would be wrapped in a sack.

DR. ADAMS: WHERE DID YOU SLEEP?

Mr. Hao: Dig a hole about four feet deep. Up to the chest.

Another worst experience was when one of my comrades got injured. He was bombed and got a hole in his stomach. Everything in his stomach flowed out. He still shouted out [Mr. Hao pantomimes with fist raised in the air]: "We shall still fetch death to drive the Americans out of Korea! We will keep our country safe!" Another worst experience was one night when I went out with one of my comrades. We had a light and the American planes found us and shot at us. Half my comrade's ass was blown off by the plane's shooting. And we had just set out from our camp area, so I carried him back quickly. On each soldier's head is a sign to say their blood type. My comrade's blood type was "O" and so was mine. So I supplied my blood to try to save him.

DR. ADAMS: DID YOU SAVE HIM?

Mr. Hao: Yes, he lived, but my comrade had no muscle left in his ass and he became a cripple. I was sad in my heart.

And another thing that made me sad was when I came to Korea there were no houses in North Korea—not in the country or in the cities. All of the houses were bombed into nothing by the Americans.

The American air force controlled all the air. It made it very dangerous for us Chinese to march in the daytime. We only marched at night.

There is another thing I can't forget. After the war I tried to find a wounded comrade in hospital in the northeast of China. I didn't find my comrade, but I saw many men in this hospital with no arms and no legs and some blind. There were all kinds of crippled and blinded heroes. They lost all the ability to do anything, like pouring hot water from the Thermos to the cup or even eat by themselves. But still they would try to do this by themselves. They did not want to be dependent on others. One had to pour hot water into a cup and many times spilled boiling water on his chest. Also there was one with no hands trying to clean the window in his hospital room with his stumps. Our government sent people to help take care of them, but they wanted to do everything by themselves.

Hao Ru
—Courtesy of Hao Ru

DR. ADAMS: PROFESSOR LIN, WHAT DID YOU THINK OF YOUR AMERICAN ENEMIES AS SOLDIERS, AS PEOPLE?

Professor Lin: Naturally we hated very much the American soldiers, but we never thought anything about the American people at that time.

DR. ADAMS: WHAT DID YOU THINK ABOUT THE AMERICANS, MR. HAO?

Mr. Hao: We hated the American soldiers very much, especially because of the bombing. They bombed people's homes in North Korea. Also our political officers told us to hate them. We were not so educated back then and we did not really separate the American soldiers from the American people, although our political officer told us the American people actually love peace. Our Chinese army captured some of your soldiers and we tried to educate them—teach them that they should want peace and not invade our country. One of my comrades took care of those captured soldiers: "We won't torture you; we won't harm you. We will teach you it is wrong to come to this country. You are not right to wage this war." He got feedback from these American soldiers. We learned most were hired to fight— paid a lot of money to come to

Hao Ru

fight here. [Mr. Hao, like many of the Chinese at the time, could not conceive of the high wages paid to American soldiers and concluded that they were mercenaries.]

All these captured soldiers had much better conditions than our own soldiers. Our soldiers would dance and sing for the captured American soldiers, and we fed them even better than our soldiers. We also gave them good clothes and organized them for basketball. When the captured soldiers left our center they shed tears and didn't want to leave. And some volunteered to stay in China.

Mr. Lu interjects: I know one who stayed here in Beijing. A Black American. He married a Chinese and stayed here.

Mr. Hao continues: But you Americans treated our captured soldiers very badly. Many died in your captured camps. When we exchanged captured soldiers you American soldiers had been well treated, but our soldiers were in bad shape. You tortured captured Chinese soldiers. There are many books about this.

DR. ADAMS: YOUR FRIEND, PROFESSOR JIN, TOLD ME A FEW DAYS AGO THAT HE FELT CHEATED BY HIS GOVERNMENT ABOUT THE KOREAN WAR. HE SAID THE CHINESE WERE TOLD THAT THE AMERICANS AND SOUTH KOREANS HAD INVADED THE NORTH. HE WAS SUSPICIOUS OF THIS AT THE TIME WHEN HE SAW HOW RAPIDLY THE NORTH KOREANS ADVANCED. AND NOW HE KNOWS IT WAS A COMPLETE LIE. WHAT DO ANY OF YOU THINK OF THIS?

Mr. Hao: I don't quite agree. At the beginning of the war the Americans bombed at the border of North Korea-China. Planes had intruded on the Chinese border and bombed Chinese territory. And you sent the Seventh Fleet to take control of Taiwan. And your planes flew into our territory many, many times. If it was not for those two reasons we would not take part in the war. And General MacArthur said, "We will celebrate our Christmas Day in China!" Professor Jin is not being objective. He did not know the situation then.

Professor Lin: Many of our leaders, even Lin Biao, argued we shouldn't take part in this war because the Americans are strong and we are weak. Lin Biao said we still have two million Kuomintang soldiers in the southwest of China still not destroyed and we still have problems in newly-liberated China. Many people without work. We don't have enough supplies. We are short of everything, including food.

But the Soviet Union supported very hardly that China should take part in the war and the Soviet Union would help supply the Chinese army. Mao Zedong finally decided to support the war. General Peng was brought to Beijing and went to a meeting and next day Mao Zedong talked to General Peng and convinced him. General Peng loved Mao Zedong very much.

Later we were angry that the Soviet Union demanded we pay back 35 billion yuan [about $4.5 billion] for the supplies they gave us for Korea. We paid it but knew the U.S. loaned billions in money and supplies to Russia in the war with Hitler, and Russia argued they shouldn't have to pay the money back since they paid in lives. Well, Chinese paid in lives for the common world socialist cause and Russia demanded we pay them back. Mao Zedong was a fool for doing this. He made some mistakes. If we didn't pay the Soviet Union back our economy would be much more advanced today.

Mr. Lu: The true reason ... at first it was just a domestic war and none of our business. But when North Korea started to win, you Americans got involved and pushed close to our country. We had to protect our country.

DR. ADAMS: WHO DO YOU THINK WON THE WAR?

Professor Lin: To some extent both won the war. The Americans still kept hold of South Korea, but the Chinese, who had just set up a new country, still unrecognized by many countries and weak in our economy and every aspect, but when we fought against the most powerful country in the world, America, we still got a fair outcome of the war. So we also won.

Mr. Lu: No one won. [Pause.] But taking all things into consideration, China won to some extent. We fought a United Nations Army of seventeen nations led by America and we got a balanced outcome. So we think we won.

Vietnam Overview

To understand the Vietnam War—America's longest war—and the causes of our defeat there, an appreciation of both the nature of the geographical locale and the nature of the people who dwell there is essential. Both played a significant, albeit secondary, role in America's defeat.

The land of Vietnam stretches a thousand miles from north to south in the shape of an elongated "S." At its hour-glass waist (the Demilitarized Zone, or DMZ of wartime fame) the nation is a mere thirty miles across, but at the two extremities of the "S" it flares out to 360 miles in the north, 150 miles in the south. These flared areas coincide with the nation's two great river valleys—the north's Red River Valley and Delta and the south's Mekong River and Delta—which together sustain the bulk of Vietnam's population and produce most of the nation's rice.

The land presents extraordinary difficulties for a modern military power while simultaneously abetting guerrilla forces. The terrain outside the valleys and deltas is rugged. There are mountains in the far north and northwest, while the Annam Cordillera, or "Central Highlands," stretch from just south of the Red River Valley to within 200 miles of the Mekong. These highlands shoulder to within a few miles of the sea, allowing for only a slender coastal plain. Along this narrow plain, seldom more than three miles in width, if that, snake the nation's two north-south transportation arteries: Highway 1 and the North-South Railroad, both which can easily be cut (and were) by blowing trestles and bridges and by creating rockslides in narrow passes.

The broken nature of the land precluded the use of armor in most areas. Vietnam presented few vistas of open ground where tanks could be employed en masse, fan out, and exploit their true capability. What was encountered were narrow

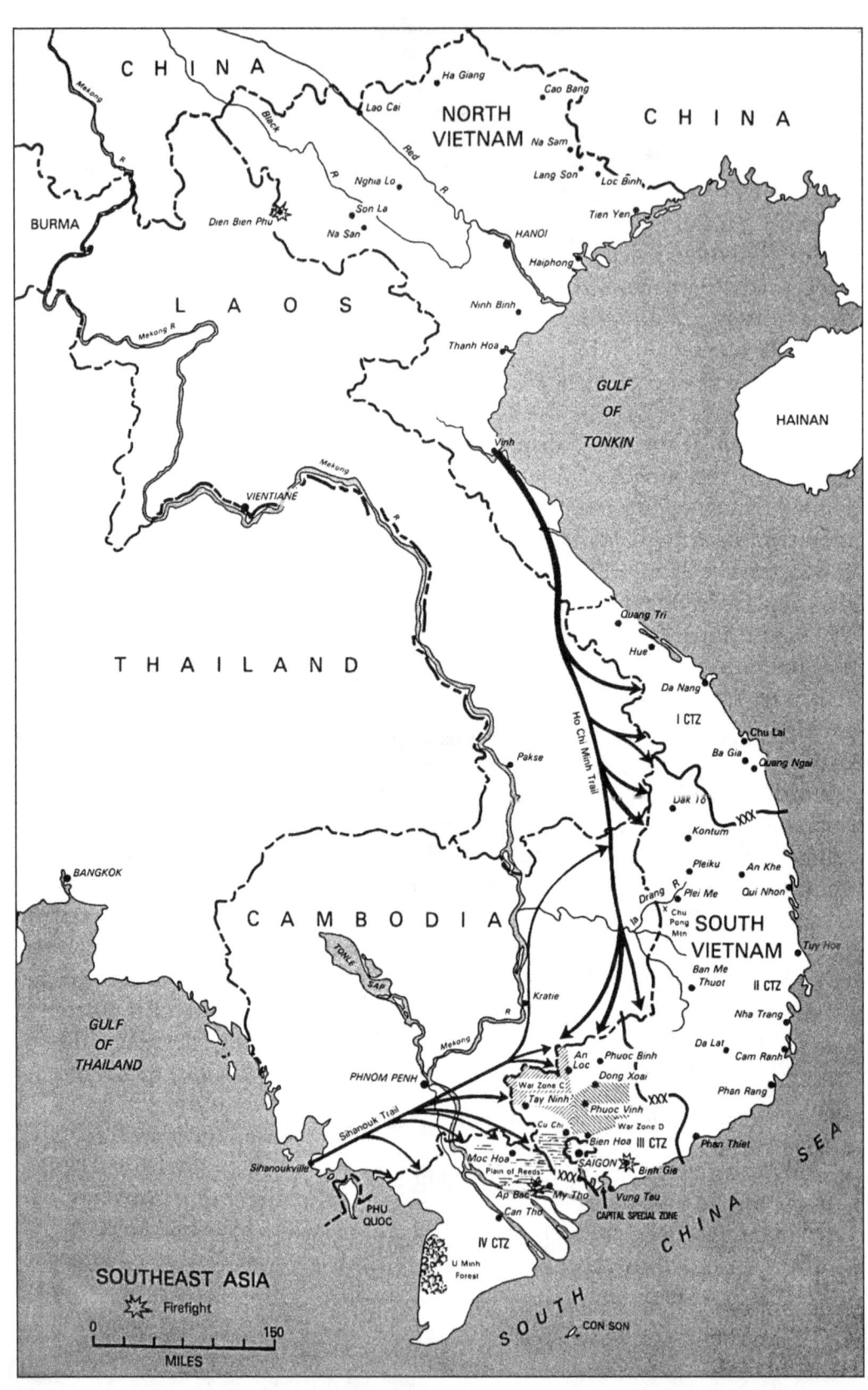

defiles, twisting, sub-standard roads, jungle tracks—terrain that forced armor to advance in column whereby a clever enemy could immobilize a whole column if he could incapacitate the lead tank.

The ruggedness of the terrain, coupled with the abysmal road network, also restricted the effectiveness of artillery. Not only was artillery difficult to move in many areas (heavy-lift helicopters were of some help), but the convoluted topography in most areas meant that the enemy was seldom far from a convenient hill or mountain and the safety of its reverse slope.

The triple-layered jungle canopy which shrouded two-thirds of the Vietnam landmass—a landmass entirely within the tropics (Saigon itself being at the approximate latitude of Cebu, Philippines, and Abuja, Nigeria)—severely curtailed the utility of air reconnaissance and air attack. Defoliants such as "agent orange" were partially successful, but by-and-large guerrillas and even mainline forces could move about the country with reasonable assurance that they would neither be located nor bombed.

Climate proved another ally of the enemy. From May to October the "wet monsoon" blew in from the warm equatorial waters to the south and east, soaking the landscape and making tank and vehicular travel even more difficult, particularly in the soggy lowland paddy areas of the Mekong and Red River Deltas. Moreover, the monsoon's accompanying clouds would overlay the area to such an extent that aerial sorties would be restricted to ten, five, or even fewer "flying days" per month. Indeed, even ground operations were difficult for friend and foe alike. The heat and nearly continuous drizzle, punctuated by occasional downpours, was so deleterious to soldiers' health that opponents usually restricted active campaigning to the cooler, less enervating months of the "dry monsoon" which runs from November to April.

The nature of the Vietnamese people also bears reckoning. The Vietnamese people are—as several foreign armies have discovered—an exceptionally nationalistic and resilient people. The Chinese know this better than most. Time and again over the past two millennia the Vietnamese have been subjected to invasions by their vast northern neighbor. Invariably, however, some local hero would rise up to lead a resistance, and China never successfully subdued the area for any length of time and had to content itself with a token tribute and a loose suzerainty over the area. [What immediately comes to mind is China's ill-fated 1979 incursion into Vietnam's northern provinces to, in Deng Xiaoping's words, "Teach Vietnam a lesson" for running off China's genocidal communist ally (Pol Pot and the Khmer Rouge) in Cambodia and installing a Vietnamese puppet regime (also communist) in its place. Within a few months of its invasion the Chinese giant was forced to declare "victory" and beat a hasty retreat. Its nose had been badly bloodied by its smaller but more battle-hardened southern neighbor.]

There is some irony here. The Vietnamese are themselves a branch of the Chinese racial family. The Viet were a migratory hunting group who inhabited southern China for thousands of years. Indeed, the Chinese ideogram for "Viet" consists of two characters: one means "run," while the other is composed of the symbols for ax and lance and means "hunt." About 2,500 years ago, an offshoot of this virile group migrated to their current location south of China. "Nam" is "south" in Chinese. In other words, "Vietnam" means "the hunting people (Viet) of the south (nam)."[23]

This people, whose very name is symbolized by the ax and lance—poor, physical, inured to hardship, unused to creature comforts, at home on their own terrain, thoroughly indoctrinated with an all-encompassing communist doctrine and the precepts of Maoist guerrilla tactics—would prove a formidable opponent.

From a westerner's perspective the Vietnam War of 1945-1975 was a war fought in three phases: the French Phase, 1946-1954; the American Phase, 1955-1972; and, finally, the Vietnamization Phase, 1973-1975. From the Vietnamese perspective, however, it was just one long, bloody saga.

Indochina had been a French colony amalgamating Vietnam, Laos, and Cambodia for nearly a century when World War II broke out in Europe in 1939. Anticipating a Nazi invasion of France, the Parisian government sought to bolster the homeland's defenses by recalling its forces garrisoning the far-flung French empire. Indochina was not exempted and thus left largely denuded of troops after the recall. This fact was not lost on Japan—aggressive, ever-alert Japan. To Japan, Indochina was ripe for the plucking.

With the unexpectedly quick collapse of France before the German juggernaut in June 1940, France became a compliant German puppet state—"Vichy" France—and willingly danced to the tune of Nazi Germany and, ipso facto, Germany's Axis allies, including Japan. A pro-Nazi Vichy governor-general was installed in Hanoi, and he acceded to Japan's occupation of Vietnam, although French bureaucrats continued to administer the country until 1945. In 1945, sensing their own inevitable defeat, the Japanese turned on their French partners in Vietnam, imprisoned them, and proclaimed a Japanese "protectorate" over Vietnam with Emperor Bao Dai as their stooge head of state. When, a few months later, atomic bombs fell on Hiroshima and Nagasaki and forced an immediate Japanese surrender, an extremely complex political situation confronted Vietnam. Allied forces suddenly poured into the country to round up the Japanese: Nationalist Chinese troops marched into northern Vietnam while simultaneously British troops landed and took control in the south. Bao Dai, shorn of his Japanese support and with no forces of his own, was impotent. Meanwhile, the newly liberated French government was racing out fresh contingents of troops and bureaucrats to try to reclaim its former colony. Into this void and chaos stepped Ho Chi Minh.

Ho Chi Minh, the final pseudonym settled upon by the revolutionary Nguyen That Thanh, had been educated in the law in Paris—where he converted to communism—and afterwards trained in Moscow as an agent of the Communist International (COMINTERN). He spent much of the 1920s and '30s shuttling back and forth between Vietnam and China. In China he worked clandestinely to rally expatriate Vietnamese youths to his cause. In 1930, on COMINTERN instructions, he founded the Indochinese Communist Party, but the French in Vietnam were relentless and fairly successful in containing this and other anti-colonial parties until the utter breakdown of order came in Vietnam in 1945. That tumultuous year saw the creation of the Vietminh guerrilla organization and Ho, appointed to lead it, incorporated its name into his own as the nomme de guerre he would bear for the rest of his life. In 1945, too, Ho began his longtime close collaboration with his old high school friend, the remarkable Vo Nguyen Giap, the military genius who would ultimately lead the "liberation" forces to complete victory over, first, the French, then the Americans.

The military machine that Ho and Giap constructed to fight their thirty-year war consisted of three distinct groups. First there were the Main Force units. These were well-trained, well-armed, highly motivated, year-round professional soldiers who would carry the brunt of the fighting whatever their title of the moment might be: Vietminh, North Vietnamese Army (NVA), or Viet Cong (VC), meaning "Vietnamese Communist." These soldiers were probably the equal of any soldiers anywhere. In 1946, at the time the First Phase fighting began, they probably numbered about 50,000.[24]

The second group was the Regional Forces. These were second-line troops attached to a given province or district. In some ways they might be equated with American National Guard units. They were part-time soldiers, modestly equipped and trained, who usually operated only within their own province. They could be activated at any given moment by the communist leadership to aid and assist Main Force units when combat operations were underway in their region or when Main Force units were engaged elsewhere. There were perhaps 30,000 Regional Force members available to Ho and Giap in 1946.[25]

The third group were the Popular Forces—guerrillas of any age or either sex recruited in villages and hamlets across the country. The individuals of this group had little or no training, had few if any arms, and were without uniforms. The majority of these people were farmers—the ubiquitous cone-hatted, pajama-clad figures of the paddy fields. Occasionally they might lay booby traps or attack an enemy outpost at night, but more usually just served as rice suppliers, porters, and the "eyes and ears" for Main Line or Regional Forces moving through their immediate vicinity. It is impossible to estimate their numbers in 1946, but it is certain their numbers swelled rapidly.[26]

After a brief attempt at compromise and reconciliation between the Vietminh and returning French colonial forces (Ho had disingenuously attempted to disguise the Vietminh's communist ideology by renaming the organization the "National Committee of Liberation for Vietnam"), fighting broke out in earnest between the two in the port of Haiphong in December 1946, once the French realized the true nature and intent of their foe.

For their part the French soon adopted a strategy of holding Hanoi, Haiphong, other key cities of the north (and during the French Phase of the war the conflict was fought almost exclusively within the northern half of the nation), and the north's demographic and agricultural core area: the Red River Delta. Indeed, in time Hanoi, Haiphong, and the triangular delta area became fortified behind a perimeter known as the "de Lattre Line," after Jean de Lattre de Tassigny, the general Paris sent out to oversee Indochina's defense. De Lattre was no fool. On the contrary, he was an experienced and highly competent commander, perhaps France's best. As such, he well appreciated the perils inherent in sitting behind a static defensive position, but, in truth, there was little more that he could do. He was hamstrung by his limited troop strength (with 115,000 in all of Indochina) and the half-hearted support offered by his government and the French taxpayers.[27]

Ho and Giap, driven out of the de Lattre defensive triangle by superior French firepower, withdrew to the Viet Bac, a remote mountainous area in Vietnam's extreme north, hard up to the Chinese border. Here they constructed a military and political redoubt, complete with an extensive complex of caves, underground food and ammunition bunkers, and a network of friendly, pro-communist towns and villages which gave them true defense-in-depth against French forces while at the same time assuring them of at least a trickle of supplies from their communist brethren fighting across the border in China. This trickle became a steady and assured stream once Mao Zedong and the communists emerged triumphant from their long civil war in 1949. Still later, following the conclusion of the 1950-1953 Korean War, the stream grew into a flood as Red China poured not only surplus Chinese arms and equipment, but also captured American arms and equipment (including trucks and tracked vehicles by the hundreds), across the border.[28]

Ho and Giap, both thoroughly versed in the precepts of Mao Zedong's theories concerning guerrilla warfare and the possibility, indeed near inevitably, of defeating a better armed adversary by controlling the countryside, isolating the cities, and exercising stealth and patience, determined to fight a protracted war of unlimited duration, confident of wearing the French down.

The French quibbled and debated for nearly a decade over whether it was more important to restore the prestige of French arms lost in World War II or to achieve a French "consumer" economy. In the end they decided on the latter and left their army in Indochina undersized and underequipped for the challenges facing it. (This was a precursor to the American argument a decade later between "guns or butter." The decision was essentially the same.)

But however that may be, it should not be forgotten that for eight long years, from 1946 to 1954, the French fought, and fought bravely. Few battles are more representative of outstanding courage (on both sides) than the culminating battle of the French Phase of the war, the Battle of Dienbienphu. In 1953-1954, Giap succeeded in drawing French forces outside the de Lattre Line by sending some of his Main Force units across the Laotian border to join their Laotian communist counterparts, the Pathet Lao, in making a convincing feint toward the Laotian capital of Vientiane. The French, now led by Gen. Henri Navarre (General de Lattre had returned to France gravely ill with cancer and heartbroken over the loss of his only son—a young French officer—in the fighting), attempted to forestall a more powerful lunge into Laos by assembling forces and equipment at the crossroads town of Dienbienphu, just five miles east of the Laotian border and athwart the Vietminh's line of communication between the Viet Bac and Laos. Navarre saw this Dienbienphu base as a "mooring point" from which he could launch attacks in any direction—to relieve Laos or to threaten the Viet Bac. His concept was basically sound except for one point: his forces were insufficient to successfully engage the vastly larger forces Giap was assembling in the area, for this was the opportunity Giap had waited upon for years. Giap had 10,800 French congregated in a small basin area in Vietnam's extreme northwest—at the absolute flight limit of French aircraft based in the Hanoi area. French aircraft would have no more than fifteen minutes to expend in air support for ground troops at Dienbienphu. Moreover, all supply for Dienbienphu would have to be by air and would be extremely tenuous.[29]

General Giap moved four Main Force divisions and two independent regiments (50,000 combat soldiers) into the hills surrounding the town. His plan was good; he elevated it to genius by successfully bringing off a stunning surprise—600 Soviet-built trucks donated by China along with 20,000 Popular Force peasants pressed into service as porters (many driving bicycles) managed to haul several dozen artillery pieces and over a hundred anti-aircraft guns to Dienbienphu. What is more, they brought in vast quantities of ammunition and rice—to feed the guns and to feed the soldiers. Giap's forces at Dienbienphu, which outnumbered the French by a ratio of 5 to 1, had now formed a ring of steel around the French.[30] As Ho Chi Minh stated to a British reporter: "Dienbienphu is a valley, and it's completely surrounded by mountains. The cream of the French expeditionary corps are down there, and we are around the mountains. And they'll never get out."[31]

The desperate fifty-five-day Battle of Dienbienphu opened on March 12, 1954, with a mighty artillery barrage from the guns surrounding the French. The French suffered 500 killed the first day. By the second day the base's airstrip was cratered and unusable. Thereafter General Navarre reinforced the besieged camp by airdrops of elite Foreign Legionnaires and parachutists, but never in sufficient numbers to halt the steadily encroaching enemy. The Vietminh took their time and came on slowly, employing the age-old siege tactics of digging forward in trenches and tunnels. As the French perimeter gradually shrank, airdrops of food, water, ammunition, medicine, supplies, and troop reinforcements became increasingly more difficult and eventually impossible. The communist anti-aircraft guns forced the resupply aircraft to make their drops from such extreme altitudes that the supplies and troops were more likely to fall outside the French lines than within.

Meanwhile, as the battle raged, newspapers across America and Europe chronicled the valiant stand of the trapped French troops.[32] More and more, westerners were coming to see the battle as not between just the Vietminh and France, but as a major Cold War confrontation between East and West, between communism and Western society.

Washington was profoundly concerned. President Eisenhower, whose dramatic threat to use atomic weapons the preceding year had coerced the communists into ending the Korean War, now called upon the Joint Chiefs of Staff to prepare options for lifting the Dienbienphu siege and rescuing the French. The JCS presented three options under the code name Operation Vulture: (1) carpet-bomb Giap's positions with 98 to 200 B-29s stationed at Clark Air Base in the Philippines; (2) use 60 B-29s and 150 carrier-based planes from two aircraft carriers in the vicinity for the same purpose; and, most startling, (3) use three small tactical nuclear bombs.[33]

In the end, however, Washington did nothing. Congressional leaders, especially Speaker of the House Lyndon Johnson, were opposed to any bombing—nuclear or otherwise—and even though Vice President Richard Nixon felt Eisenhower had the prestige to win over Congressional support, Eisenhower was not getting the Allied backing he felt necessary. Even Britain's Winston Churchill advised against the bombing.[34]

And so, on May 7, 1954, Dienbienphu fell. The French never hoisted the white flag of surrender. When they ran out of food, water, ammunition, and stamina they just sat down and waited. A desperate, last-minute plan for the garrison's remnants to break for the Laotian border was scotched when the surviving officers reported the men did not have the strength "to go 100 meters without passing out."[35] Thus, the Vietminh simply overran them. The French dead numbered 3,000 and a similar number were wounded so badly as to be permanently disabled. Communist losses were estimated to be between 6,000-8,000, with an additional 10,000 wounded. That Vietminh deaths were so high bears testimony not only to the French soldiers' skill and firepower, but also to the criminal indifference of Ho and Giap to casualties. To serve their four-division, 50,000-man army at Dienbienphu they provided only a single surgeon![36]

With the Battle of Dienbienphu concluded, French and Communist Vietnamese delegates met in Geneva in May 1954 to settle Vietnam's future. As one journalist covering the proceedings reported: "The men of Communism arrived smiling smugly and talking of peace."[37] By July the conference's work was done. Vietnam was divided at the 17th Parallel into two nations. There was to be a communist North Vietnam (Democratic Republic of Vietnam) led by Ho Chi Minh, and a South Vietnam which would remain under French tutelage until general elections were held in 1956, whereby a stabilized South Vietnam might decide its own course: independence, democracy, unification with the north, whatever. The French stuck to their word and their last troops departed South Vietnam in 1956. But elections were never held. The reason was that Ho had determined never to allow the situation in the south to stabilize. Hardly had the ink on the Geneva Agreement dried before he began dispatching Vietminh Main Force units and communist agitators to infiltrate the south. These infiltrators had been given a number of assignments: (1) they were to spark the nascent and heretofore weak communist movement in the south; (2) they were to assassinate South Vietnamese government officials, particularly those at the local government level, including village leaders, so as to prove to the rural peasantry the futility of resisting the communist cause and to intimidate them into providing rice, refuge, and succor whenever communists were in their area; (3) they were to identify promising young sympathizers to be sent north for indoctrination and training as communist cadres, who would then be reintroduced into the south to further spread the movement. (This third assignment was critical since regional biases in Vietnam were strong, and the northern Vietnamese, primarily Tonkinese, had a distinct dialect and were heartily disliked by the Annamites and Cochin-Chinese of central and southern Vietnam. Native Annamites and Cochin-Chinese would be needed to spread the communist message.) These combined forces—the Vietminh Main Force units and agitators from the north, coupled with their newly risen communist allies in the south—would be given a new title, "Viet Cong," and they would face a new enemy, the Americans.[38]

It was the "domino theory" that served as the rationale for involving the United States in Vietnam. America had already proven in the Korean War that it was willing to pay a fairly hefty price to preserve a relatively small scrap of land from communist expansion. And Korea represented the fag end of a peninsula from whence communism could spread no further—offshore was Japan, which was an increasingly prosperous democracy immune to communism's promises and bulwarked by more than a dozen American military, air, and naval bases. Vietnam was an entirely different story. If communism established a toehold there, it could surge on west, south, and east and perhaps engulf the whole of Southeast Asia. Laos, Cambodia, Thailand, Burma, Malaysia, Brunei, Indonesia, and the Philippines—nations which were mostly poor, recently independent and of questionable stability—were all seen as vulnerable. As President Eisenhower explained: "You have a row of dominoes set up, you knock over the first one, and what will happen to the last one is the certainty that it will go over very quickly. So you could have a beginning of a disintegration that would have the most profound influences."[39]

Therefore, to keep South Vietnam from falling and to buy time for the fledgling nations of Southeast Asia to stabilize themselves, the United States entered Vietnam. The American Phase, 1955-1972, had begun. Even before the French departure, America had been helping the French with military equipment, aircraft, and financial assistance—$10 million worth commencing in 1950 and growing to over $1 billion in 1954 (78% of the entire French war bill).[40] But now America would have to start sending men.

Eisenhower began the infusion of American troops with the creation of the U.S. MAAG (Military Assistance and Advisory Group) in Saigon in 1955. Its purpose was to help train and equip the ARVN (Army of the Republic of Vietnam). The number of Americans involved was not large—about 300 military advisors and trainers (including aircraft and helicopter instructor pilots)—and that number remained roughly constant for the next few years. It seemed sufficient. The ARVN was apparently holding its own against the communist forces. However, this lull was deceptive. What was occurring in Hanoi was a heated internal debate between the "North Vietnam Firsters" and the "South Vietnam Firsters." The former group were arguing that North Vietnam must give top priority to establishing a strong socialist economy in the north before mounting the takeover of the south. The opposing group insisted that the "liberation" of the south took precedence over all other goals. In the end, Ho Chi Minh sided with the "South Vietnam Firsters," and as the decade drew to a close, renewed North Vietnamese vigor in prosecuting the armed insurrection in the south became evident.[41]

In 1957 more than 400 South Vietnamese officials were assassinated, and in that same year Hanoi organized thirty-seven armed companies in the Mekong Delta to give them a strong base area in the south. In 1959 the pace increased. In May of that year communists killed their first two Americans—heretofore sacrosanct. Moreover, to speed the supply of equipment and troops to the south, North Vietnam formed the 559th Transportation Group, which would operate the logistical system known as the Ho Chi Minh Trail. This 700-mile-long trail commenced in North Vietnam then passed into Laos and wound southward through sparsely populated jungle areas into Cambodia before finally emerging in western South Vietnam at numerous penetration points. It consisted of roads, trails, jungle tracks and even rivers, whereby food, guns, and ammunition were floated along in airtight fifty-five-gallon drums.[42]

By the time John F. Kennedy assumed the presidency in January 1961, the number of American military advisors in Vietnam had inched upwards to 700, but clearly this number was insufficient and a decision had to be made. Either Kennedy could cut American losses and quit the game or he would have to dramatically up the ante. His own advisors were split over the issue, and in May 1961 he visited Paris to solicit Charles de Gaulle's advice. The French president did not mince his words. He told Kennedy: "The ideology that you invoke will not change anything. You want to assume a succession to rekindle a war that we ended. I predict to you that you will, step by step, be sucked into a bottomless military and political quagmire."[43]

But what was probably most instrumental in settling Kennedy on his eventual course—his decision to up the ante—was the Bay of Pigs fiasco which occurred in April 1961, a bare ninety days into his presidency. This ill-conceived CIA venture to retake Cuba by landing a few hundred Cuban exiles on the beaches of the Bay of Pigs in the hopes that they would spark a nationwide rebellion failed in part because Kennedy refused to provide them with U.S. military air cover. The exiles were all either captured or slaughtered on the beachhead, and Kennedy caught a fair share of the public backlash. The incident served to revive election campaign accusations that Kennedy and the Democrats were "soft" on communism. As Kennedy afterwards told the *New York Times'* James Reston: "Now we have a problem in making our power credible, and Vietnam is the place."[44] In the space of the next few months Kennedy increased the number of American advisors from 700 to 12,000, and by the time of his death in November 1963, he had increased it further, to 15,000. Escalation had begun.[45]

The tragic strategy of "escalation" was born of a fateful compromise in Washington. America's Joint Chiefs of Staff and its other top military leaders—all hard-boiled veterans of the Second World War—were the repository of the American military tradition of the "offense." Ever since the Mexican and American Civil Wars, U.S. officers were trained to seek the battle of annihilation—striking directly at the heart of an enemy in overwhelming force in the tradition of Winfield Scott, U.S. Grant, and, the master himself, Napoleon. This strategy was based on American strengths (a huge population and resource base and unrivaled production capacity) and weaknesses (including an apparent inability to tolerate or endure prolonged warfare). Not surprisingly, they advised President John Kennedy and his successor, Lyndon Johnson, to allow them to carry the war directly to the enemy: let them bomb North Vietnam's core region—Hanoi, Haiphong, and the Red River Delta—and launch a massive invasion of the north. They were confident of victory, and so advised first Kennedy, then Johnson. But these uniformed military leaders were, almost to a man, conservative Republicans, and held in disdain by the liberal Democrats who swept into power with Kennedy and now held sway at the State and Defense departments. Brilliant and Ivy League educated, the fresh-faced members of this new team were dubbed "the Whiz kids." Most of them had been too young to serve in World War II and had never heard a shot fired in anger, and yet they served as the civilian masters of the uniformed services. They took up posts at State and as the secretaries, undersecretaries, and assistant secretaries at the Departments of the Army, Navy and Air Force, and their titular leader and guiding light was Secretary of Defense Robert McNamara, a former Ford Motor Company president and a military neophyte. These men regarded the uniformed military chiefs as warmongering dinosaurs while they themselves were committed to an "interdependent world order" and the concept of "limited war." They wished, at all costs, to avoid a confrontation with either of the two communist giants: the Soviet Union and China. Moreover, they were extremely sensitive to international public opinion and fearful that America would appear a bully in the eyes of the world if it crushed its smaller, weaker North Vietnamese adversary. Consequently, they were committed to applying "gradual" pressure on North Vietnam just to the point where it would bend to America's will, withdraw its forces from South Vietnam, and leave it in peace. In other words, they sought a Korean-style settlement to the conflict. Tragically, they had made a fatal misjudgment: while these civilian officials restrained what they considered to be their overly gung-ho military, they mightily underestimated the toughness and resilience of their communist foe. North Vietnam was not as small and weak as they anticipated, and never was the U.S. military given sufficient forces and, more importantly, the freedom of action to use those forces as it saw fit, to break the enemy's will. The end result would be that America would not even have the satisfaction of settling for "half a loaf" as it had in Korea. Rather, American restraint was perceived by the North Vietnamese leadership as a lack of will to prosecute the war seriously, and they determined to wear down and outlast their half-hearted American opponent.[46]

In late afternoon of August 2, 1964, one of the key events in the American Phase of the war occurred. At that time the USS *Maddox*, a destroyer engaged in electronic surveillance twenty-eight miles off the North Vietnamese coast (and clearly in international waters), was attacked by three North Vietnamese patrol boats which fired machine guns and torpedoes. The *Maddox* returned fire and scored a direct hit on one of the boats, leaving it dead in the water, and shortly thereafter fighter aircraft from the nearby aircraft carrier USS *Ticonderoga* arrived on the scene and strafed and chased off the other two boats. President Johnson was immediately informed of the attack but initially chose to regard it as a mistake, an anomaly, on the part of the North Vietnamese, despite the fact that the Joint Chiefs of Staff were pressing for a powerful response. After all, the 1964 presidential election was only three months away, and Johnson was running as the "peace candidate" as opposed to the bellicose Republican candidate, Senator Barry Goldwater. However, just three days later, on the night of August 5, the *Maddox*, in company with the destroyer USS *Turner Joy*, returned to the same site in the Tonkin Gulf and was apparently again attacked by

North Vietnamese patrol boats. "Apparently" because, although sonarmen aboard the *Maddox* and *Joy* reported a total of twenty-one torpedo "splashes," no hits were scored and due to the poor visibility no visual sightings were made. Many American "doves" would subsequently claim this second attack never occurred and was simply trumped up by the military to pressure Johnson into taking action. (If that is so, though, then the North Vietnamese would have to be counted as co-conspirators: to this day communist Vietnam annually celebrates its "Navy Day" on August 5—the date of the second attack—when it claims "one of our torpedo squadrons chased the USS *Maddox* from our coastal waters."[47]

However it may be, the second attack did spur Johnson to action. "Peace candidate" or not, he felt he had to make some response. The response came in the form of Congress' Tonkin Gulf Resolution passed on August 7. It was the strongest response he felt he could wrest from that pusillanimous body and stated that the president should "take all necessary measures to repel any armed attack against the forces of the United States." In other words, Vietnam was such a hot potato, already becoming a divisive issue across America, that the congressmen—themselves up for reelection in three months—decided to dump the whole problem in Johnson's lap. Vietnam would be his war, "Johnson's War."[48]

But even with the authority of the Tonkin Gulf Resolution behind him, and despite the Joint Chiefs' pleas for vigorous and sustained retaliation against the north, Johnson refused to take any strong action. Initially he did not want to jeopardize his standing as the "peace candidate," and continued to promise in his campaign speeches that he would neither bomb North Vietnam nor "commit many American boys to fighting a war that I think ought to be fought by the boys of Asia."[49] Not surprisingly, Ho, Giap, and the other North Vietnamese leaders concluded America was a "paper tiger." Further prodding of the inert tiger followed. In October 1964, Viet Cong mortared the U.S. air base at Bien Hoa outside of Saigon. Four Americans were killed and five bombers destroyed. No response was made. In November two Viet Cong regiments seized control of Binh Dinh province. Again, no U.S. response was forthcoming. In December, at a time when the American elections were over and the "peace candidate's" hands were finally untied, the Viet Cong exploded a bomb in a U.S. BOQ (bachelor officers quarters) in Saigon, killing two Americans and wounding thirty-eight others. But, again, Johnson refused to respond. Accordingly, by the end of 1964, the north decided it could step up its invasion of the south without fear of any serious American interference. They began sending Main Force units into the south in divisional strength.[50]

The event that finally propelled America into action was the Viet Cong attack on the U.S. airbase in Pleiku on February 7, 1965. It served as a final straw. There was a growing consensus among the U.S. public and even the president's civilian advisors that something had to be done or South Vietnam would "fall." As Johnson told his biographer, Doris Kearns, by early 1965 he realized "that if we let communist aggression succeed in taking over South Vietnam, there would follow in this country an endless national debate—that would shatter my presidency, kill my administration, and damage our democracy."[51]

The first American combat troops introduced into Vietnam, as opposed to the advisors and instructors of earlier years, were two marine battalions which arrived in March 1965 to provide perimeter defense of Da Nang airbase, to prevent it from becoming a second Pleiku. Other units followed in reasonably quick order and nearly 200,000 troops were in country by December 1965. It is worth recalling, however, that in 1954, when the French despaired of winning the war, they had 190,000 troops in country and realized that was not nearly enough.[52] So more troops were needed and more troops were sent—gradually. By the end of 1966 troop strength approached 400,000; and by the end of 1967 it approached 500,000. Finally, in December 1968, American troop strength capped out at 540,000. Indeed, 1968 was the peak year, the key year, the deciding year, of the American Phase of the war. In addition to the 540,000 Americans in country, allied with them were the 750,000 of the ARVN, 45,000 South Koreans, and smaller, but still significant, numbers of Australian, New Zealand, Thai, and Filipino troops. Moreover, by 1968 America had concentrated fifty percent of its tactical airpower and thirty percent of its naval assets in the theater, and kept a minimum of three aircraft carriers on patrol at "Yankee Station" in the Tonkin Gulf.[53]

The strategy conducted by Gen. William Westmoreland, the commanding general in Vietnam during the key years of the American Phase, was basically defensive in nature due to the strictures placed upon him by Washington. He was not allowed to launch attacks on the Viet Cong's sanctuaries in Cambodia or Laos. He was not, as most of his own soldiers soon realized, allowed to win. What he was allowed to do was to try to attrit the soldiers North Vietnam was infiltrating into the south and see if he could reach a point where the losses he was inflicting were simply too great for North Vietnamese society and its government to bear. If he could, then logically the north would have to give up the war and terminate its goal of absorbing the south. At that time (1965-1968), North Vietnam had a population of 21 million and produced a yearly crop of 200,000 eighteen-year-old males to feed into its military. The problem was one of simple mathematics: could Westmoreland and the American troops, along with their allies, kill enemy soldiers at a rate greater than 200,000 per year? Could they kill them faster than North Vietnam could grow them? And, if so, could Westmoreland prove it? (Here was born Washington's obsession with body-counts.)

Westmoreland certainly tried. He divided South Vietnam into four military zones. I Corps Zone was in the far north and ran from the DMZ south for about 150 miles and encompassed such key cities as Da Nang, Hue, and Quang Tri. It was a marine command. II Corps Zone was immediately to the south of I Corps and ran south for another 200 miles and contained the bulk of the Central Highlands. Some of its more important cities and sites were Qui Nhon, Nha Trang, Da Lat, Pleiku, and Cam Ranh Bay. III Corps Zone was a narrow band, no more than 100 miles wide, running from the South China Sea coast inland to the Cambodian frontier. This zone contained Saigon and was very densely populated. It was the heart of the country. If this zone fell, South Vietnam would fall. IV Corps Zone was the Mekong Delta. This region was very heavily populated, too, but the American troop presence there, aside from the riverine patrols under the purview of the navy, was relatively light compared to the heavy ARVN commitment.

In each of the four zones the American commander was expected to cooperate closely with his ARVN counterpart. A division of labor was fostered by Westmoreland, which made much sense. The South Vietnamese troops would primarily be employed in holding and controlling the cities and the most densely populated rural areas in each zone. In that way the inevitable friction which would arise between American GIs and the civilian population would be kept to a minimum. The South Vietnamese troops naturally better understood the mores and customs of their own people and, anyway, would be far more adept at identifying and rooting out the Viet Cong and communist sympathizers in their midst.

This, in turn, would free up the Americans to concentrate on attriting Viet Cong and North Vietnamese Main Force units in the more sparsely populated areas in the north, in the Central Highlands, and in the western frontier areas up against the Cambodian and Laotian borders.

In each zone's command headquarters, G-2 (intelligence) would identify areas of active enemy presence. This intelligence was garnered by aerial reconnaissance, radio intercepts, electronic surveillance, seismic detectors, acoustical detectors, spies, prisoner interrogations and, most importantly, reports from loyal villagers. American "search and destroy" raids would then be launched, often using helicopters to achieve surprise and to overcome the handicap of the atrocious road network.

This method of warfare was just about as arduous as any form of warfare could be. It played to so many of the enemy's strengths: stealth, endurance, night-time ambushes, booby traps, and the ability to blend almost at will into the civilian population making identification of friend and foe difficult. And yet, despite all that, the American military was achieving success; it was attriting the enemy; it was gradually wearing him down.

Meanwhile, an air campaign was in progress. This was Operation "Rolling Thunder," which ran from March 1965 to November 1968. It had some impact on the enemy; but overall it would have to be judged a failure. The reason for the failure was that again President Johnson allowed the civilian policymakers at State and Defense to shoulder aside the Joint Chiefs and other uniformed military leaders and dictate not only the overall air campaign strategy but actually select the individual targets. When Johnson asked for options in a bombing campaign in late 1964, the Joint Chiefs lobbied for what became known as the "full court press" option, which called for "systematic attacks on the North—bombing rapidly, widely and intensely."[54] They were convinced they could bring North Vietnam to its knees within six months. This was opposed by the civilians who favored the option known as "progressive squeeze and talk," which boiled down to bomb a little, bomb a little more, and eventually the North will want to talk. Johnson backed his civilians.[55] For the first year of Rolling Thunder he forbade the bombing of any North Vietnamese factory; he forbade the bombing of any power plant; he forbade the bombing of, incredibly, any airbase; he forbade any bombing anywhere near the Chinese border; he forbade any bombing within a thirty-mile radius of the capital, Hanoi; he forbade any bombing within ten miles of the port city of Haiphong, which the Joint Chiefs considered the "kingpin" of targets and through which the North Vietnamese received the bulk of their military equipment and supplies from China and the Soviet Union. But Johnson anguished: "Suppose one of my boys misses his mark when he's flying around Haiphong? Suppose one of his bombs falls on one of those Russian ships in the harbor?"[56]

Such constraints sorely limited air power's ability to affect the war's outcome. As air historian Earl H. Tilford convincingly argued in his authoritative *Setup: What the Air Force Did in Vietnam and Why,* Washington had "setup" the Air Force for failure in Vietnam even before the planes arrived. Washington simply was not going to permit them to win.

Yet within the strictures placed upon it, American air power—comprising the aircraft not just of the air force but also of the navy and marines—dropped more bombs and expended more ordnance than it had in all of America's previous wars combined. But whereas in those previous wars the bombs were dropped to some purpose, say to destroy Nazi Germany's industrial capacity or to lay waste to Japan's cities, in Vietnam most of the bombs were sqaundered in what American pilots called "jungle bashing"—cratering up acres of rainforest when, for instance, a seismic detector indicated movement of something as large as a human beneath the forest canopy. (On one occasion bombers raced to the scene and, as they learned afterwards, obliterated a herd of elephants.) Such futile employment sapped the airmen's morale, and pilots left the service in droves to seek careers in the American airline industry.[57]

But, of course, there were many useful missions as well. American fighters, principally the air force's F-104 Thunderchiefs (Thuds) and the navy's F-4 Phantoms, both big, powerful aircraft, drove the MIGs of the North Vietnamese air force from the skies. Other planes defoliated much of the Ho Chi Minh trail with Agent Orange in order to expose its truck traffic. As many as 10,000 trucks might be in use on the trail at any given time, but in 1967 the U.S. claimed 3,291 truck kills, and in 1968 7,332 truck kills.[58] One of the most effective aircraft in this duty was the air force's AC-130 gunship, a reconfigured cargo plane fitted with large-caliber machine guns and a cannon with a truly wondrous rate of fire. Dubbed "Puff the Magic Dragon," it had an infrared system that could detect the heat of a truck engine at considerable distance and beneath the forest canopy. The firepower of the Magic Dragons could also be employed for ground support as could that of the ever-feared, even more awesome B-52 Buffs ("Big Ugly Fat Fuckers") which could be called in from Guam and Clark airbase in the Philippines. They were most useful in relieving American and South Vietnamese fire-base camps in sparsely settled areas when they became beset by encircling NVA or Viet Cong attackers. If the defenders could hold off their besiegers at a sufficient distance long enough for the Magic Dragons, Buffs or strike aircraft such as the nimble A-4 Skyhawks or Thuds and Phantoms armed with gelatinized incendiaries (napalm) to get to the scene, the enemy could often be quite literally "disappeared." But Giap's forces were well trained in the tactic of "hugging the enemy" so tightly that the aircraft could not release their ordnance for fear of hitting "friendlies." But be that as it may, there is no question that Rolling Thunder was contributing to attriting the enemy at a rapid rate throughout the three and one-half years of its duration. Secretary of Defense Robert McNamara believed that "from the end of '65 to March of '68 ... the North was suffering casualties at a tremendous rate ... at the rate of roughly a million a year during that period. Now if you accept that as anywhere close to the correct figure—and I don't want to argue whether it's a million or six hundred thousand or a million two hundred thousand—it was a tremendous loss."[59] As American commander William Westmoreland repeatedly asserted, America was winning the war; there was "light at the end of the tunnel."

As Gen. Phillip Davidson, Westmoreland's chief of intelligence, later asserted, by 1968 "guerrilla warfare by indigenous South Vietnamese communists had virtually vanished, and the original insurgency had been almost completely overcome."[60] Ho, Giap, and the other North Vietnamese were staring defeat in the face and realized it. They determined on one last-ditch effort to try to reverse the situation and win a psychological victory if not a military victory.

Their effort came in two concurrent attacks. In one, they would send four NVA divisions down the Ho Chi Minh Trail to invest the marine combat base at Khe Sahn in South Vietnam's extreme northwest and just five miles from the Laotian border. The similarities of site and circumstances were remarkably reminiscent of Dienbienphu. "The parallels are there for all to see," Walter Cronkite announced to the American people on the *CBS Evening News*.[61] A total of 40,000 Main Line communist troops would surround 6,000 marines in a remote mountainous area far from the main centers of American strength, and in which the besieged American troops, with just one small airstrip, would be dependent on aerial supply and reinforcement. The goal of the North Vietnam planners was to produce maximum American casualties and to divert American troops and attention to the area to facilitate the second attack, the main attack.[62] The main attack would be the infamous Tet Offensive.

On January 31, 1968, at the commencement of Tet, or the Lunar New Year, the holiest of Vietnamese holy days and a holy day the North Vietnamese government vowed it would never violate, 70,000 communist soldiers who had been infiltrated into South Vietnam over the preceding weeks and months staged simultaneous attacks across the length and breadth of the country. From the DMZ in the north to the Mekong Delta in the south, thirty-six of the nation's forty-four provincial capitals were struck. Most alarmingly, in Saigon and vincinity the attacks even penetrated into the U.S. embassy compound, the presidential palace, the headquarters of South Vietnam's general staff, and Tan Son Nhut airport. At Hue, the ancient imperial city in the far north, 7,500 communists seized control of the city and held it for three weeks, and, going house-to-house, shot, clubbed to death, or buried alive over 3,000 persons whose names had been compiled on a kill list—a list that included virtually all government and military officials (and their families), merchants, religious leaders and foreigners (except for the French who were spared since they were now seen as "anti-war" and "anti-American" by the North Vietnamese leadership).[63]

Yet despite the communists' initial successes in Hue and in every other city in South Vietnam subjected to attacks, the Americans and their South Vietnamese allies did not panic. They recovered, regrouped and counterattacked. (The performance of the ARVN was excellent—better than almost anyone had anticipated.[64]) Within a matter of days they regained control of every provincial capital, except Hue, where communist forces held out for three weeks before the marines, two army divisions, and ARVN troops finally cleared the city after some of the fiercest street fighting of the entire war. Militarily, Tet was a resounding defeat for North Vietnam as casualty statistics attest: 40,000-50,000 NVA and Viet Cong battle deaths as compared to 1,100 U.S. battle deaths and 2,300 South Vietnamese.[65]

The communists fared no better in their besiegement of Khe Sahn, which lasted from January 20, 1968, to March 10, 1968. There were, as Cronkite had mentioned, numerous parallels between the French predicament at Dienbienphu and the marines' predicament at Khe Sahn: the remote setting, the surrounding mountains, the single airstrip available to the entrapped and the numeric advantage of the besiegers (5:1 at Dienbienphu; almost 7:1 at Khe Sahn). But there was one big difference: the tremendous firepower the Americans could bring to bear. Marine artillery was able to hold the communist troops at bay—prevent them from employing the tactic of "hugging the enemy"—thus allowing American airpower to play its role. When the North Vietnamese tried to push trenches forward to the marines' encampment, A-4 Skyhawks were called in to "cleanse" the trenches with napalm. Whenever NVA anti-aircraft guns went into action, Thuds and Phantoms eliminated them. Then General Westmoreland ordered up Operation Niagara, a name he coined himself to "evoke an image of cascading bombs." Buffs were flown in from the Philippines to saturate the enemy's positions with tens of thousands of 500-pound bombs—the equivalent of five Hiroshima-size bombs in "the most concentrated bombing in the history of warfare." The enemy positions were leveled into a wasteland. An estimated 10,000 communist troops died at Khe Sanh, as opposed to 500 marines.[66]

By any objective measure used, the Tet attacks and accompanying Khe Sahn diversion resulted in an overwhelming American and South Vietnamese victory. The heart had been ripped out of several NVA divisions; northern Viet Cong infiltrators had exposed themselves and been killed or captured in the thousands, likewise their southern comrades; and, most auspiciously, the South Vietnamese had given a good account of themselves and their confidence and pride soared. So convinced was General Westmoreland that ultimate victory was within his grasp, that he immediately requested an additional 206,000 troops from Washington—a final escalation—to finish off the enemy's remnants in South Vietnam, and to prepare for America's departure with its goal having been met: leaving a safe, secure and independent South Vietnam behind. Even North Vietnam's military commander, General Giap, realized he was beaten and would have to negotiate a peace under almost any terms the Americans cared to dictate.[67]

But, alas, that was not to be. Within days, the unabashedly liberal American media began to portray Tet as a huge American defeat, evidence that the communists could strike anywhere and anytime they chose, and there was no end in sight to the war. Westmoreland's "light at the end of the tunnel" was ridiculed as being the beam of "a locomotive coming straight at him." Walter Cronkite, "the most trusted man in

America," opined on the *CBS Evening News* that the war was a "stalemate" and negotiations the only way out.[68] The anti-war faction staged renewed street and campus demonstrations, and more and more congressmen pressed for America's withdrawal from Vietnam. President Johnson, himself having been deeply disturbed by television images of the fighting in Khe Sahn and Hue, succumbed.[69] He decided not to send Westmoreland the additional requested troops, and then, on March 31, 1968, he announced to the American people that he would not run for reelection as president, that he was ordering a partial bombing halt of North Vietnam, and that he was appealing to North Vietnam for negotiations. Johnson had managed to snatch defeat from the jaws of victory.[70]

After Tet it was obvious to any cognizant observer that America was in full retreat, determined to cut its losses and run. Following the November 1968 presidential elections, Richard Milhouse Nixon, who had campaigned under the slogan "Peace with Honor," succeeded Lyndon Johnson, but everyone, including most assuredly the North Vietnamese leadership, understood American public opinion required American withdrawal—and soon. The strategy Nixon concocted was to become known as "Vietnamization." The Americans would depart in a gradual "de-escalation." As American units were pulled out they would pass on their military equipment (aircraft, helicopters, tanks, trucks, etc.) to a South Vietnamese counterpart unit that had been trained in the equipments' use. The hope was that with this equipment and this training the South Vietnamese military might be able to hold its own against its communist adversaries.

De-escalation proceeded fairly rapidly. From the 1968 high-water mark of 540,000 troops "in country," the numbers dropped to 475,000 by the end of 1969; 335,000 in December 1970; and just 157,000 by December 1971. At that point virtually all U.S. combat forces were out of Vietnam. Those remaining were fulfilling support roles in training, supply, communications, and intelligence.[71]

To "cover" the retreat of America's army and marine ground forces President Nixon showed himself willing to use his air assets much more vigorously than any of his predecessors. The pain America's air force and navy carriers could inflict on the North Vietnamese was also instrumental in inducing the North Vietnamese to negotiate "seriously" at the Paris Peace Talks, something they were reluctant to do knowing that with each month's troop withdrawal the American negotiating position in Paris was growing weaker and weaker.[72]

The North Vietnamese delegation received its wake-up call in April 1972. The previous year American peace activists visited Hanoi and convinced their communist hosts that anti-war sentiment in America was so strong that North Vietnam could now invade the south with impunity, without any fear of a reprisal from Nixon or the U.S.[73] Accordingly, on March 30, 1972, North Vietnam launched an all-out invasion of the south, an invasion that dwarfed anything since the Korean War. Holding only five of his divisions in reserve to protect North Vietnam, Giap sent fourteen NVA divisions and twenty-six independent regiments crashing across the Demilitarized Zone in a bid to seize the south and end the war. His force was spearheaded by 200 tanks.[74]

Nixon's response was prompt and massive. In February he had astonished the world by visiting Beijing and had quietly been assured by Mao Zedong that the Chinese had no intention of intervening in America's war with Vietnam. Consequently, on April 6, 1972, to stem the North Vietnamese invasion, Nixon, a keen football fan, ordered up the appropriately named "Operation Linebacker." American (and South Vietnamese) air power was unleashed. Not only was this airpower used to blunt, defeat, and decimate the invasion army, but also to punish the North Vietnamese homeland itself. Across North Vietnam bridges, railyards, POL (petroleum-oil-lubrication) storage sites, SAM (surface-to-air missile) sites were struck. He ordered militarily significant targets within Hanoi to be struck, and Haiphong to be not only bombed, but its harbor to be sewn with mines as well. And he warned his military commanders not to be "timid."[75] To punctuate his intention, he asked for the B-52s to be put into action. They were. A total of 210 were brought to the theater and from bases in Thailand, Guam, and the Philippines the "Buffs" pulverized both the invaders and targets inside North Vietnam. Not only did Operation Linebacker stop the invasion dead in its tracks, but "it so devastate[d] North Vietnam's military capabilities that Hanoi [was] compelled to negotiate seriously for the first time."[76]

Aside from the pummeling they were receiving from the air, there were several other factors compelling North Vietnam to seek a negotiated peace. With Haiphong harbor mined and North Vietnam's roads and bridges to the Chinese frontier chewed over by bombers, matériel resupply from either China or the Soviet Union was impossible. Moreover, America's rapprochement with China and growing détente with the Soviet Union was increasingly isolating North Vietnam diplomatically. A final factor encouraging the North Vietnamese to reach a settlement was the growing assurance, as reflected by opinion polls, that Nixon was going to defeat the anti-war "dove," George McGovern, in the November 1972 presidential election. They realized they faced several more years of having to deal with Nixon, and after "Linebacker" they truly feared him. (Henry Kissinger cunningly played to these fears in the behind-the-scenes negotiations—frequently portraying his boss as a near "madman," capable of the most extreme action when thwarted.)[77]

Between October 8 and 18, 1972, in Paris, Henry Kissinger and his North Vietnamese counterpart, Le Duc Tho, reached a tentative peace agreement. The key features of the settlement were: (1) South Vietnam was to have the government of its own choosing; (2) the U.S. would continue to support South Vietnam economically and with military equipment; (3) the U.S. would withdraw all of its remaining troops from South Vietnam; (4) the U.S. would cease all hostilities against North Vietnam; (5) North Vietnam would cease all hostilities against South Vietnam.

There was, however, one very important issue not addressed in the settlement. That was the issue of North Vietnamese already imbedded in South Vietnam and working side-by-side with their southern comrades of the Viet Cong. It was tacitly assumed North Vietnam would continue to resupply and support them. Kissinger and the Nixon administration just hoped the ARVN would be able to cope with this threat on their own.[78]

But even this flawed settlement eluded the negotiators at the eleventh hour.

President Nguyen Van Thieu of South Vietnam began insisting that the Viet Cong in the south had to "be wiped out quickly and mercilessly" before the settlement went forward.[79] By the time Kissinger and Nixon could bring Thieu to heel, Le Duc Tho was suddenly recalled to Hanoi. Clearly, the communists were resorting to foot-dragging. Nixon and Kissinger believe this was prompted by the November 11 elections wherein a liberal-Democratic majority had been returned to Congress, and the North Vietnamese leaders, savvy followers of American politics, realized that the new Congress might cut off all funding for the war, and North Vietnam might not need to make any concessions whatsoever to the Americans. According to Nixon, Kissinger was almost beside himself in his fury at the stone-walling North Vietnamese: "They're just a bunch of shits. Tawdry, filthy shits."[80]

Nixon was mad, too. He ordered Linebacker II, the so-called "Christmas Bombing" to force North Vietnam to sign the settlement. He wanted massive B-52 attacks on both Hanoi and Haiphong: power plants, railroads, docks, fuel storage areas, factories, etc. He told Adm. Thomas Moorer, chairman of the Joint Chiefs of Staff: "I don't want any more of this crap about the fact that we couldn't hit this target or that one. This is your chance to use military power to win this war, and if you don't, I'll hold you responsible."[81] The bombing started on December 18 and ended on December 30. Approximately 3,000 sorties were flown and 40,000 tons of bombs were dropped on Hanoi, Haiphong, and the heavily populated sixty-mile corridor between the two cities. By December 26, North Vietnam had expended all 1,200 of its stock of SAMS (which knocked down fifteen B-52s) and was now totally defenseless against the B-52s which flew well above the range of anti-aircraft fire. On that same date they appealed to the U.S. to halt the bombing and resume negotiations. The negotiations resumed on January 8, 1973, and on January 27, 1973, the peace settlement was formally signed. It contained the same terms as had been agreed to in October.[82]

In accordance with the terms of the peace treaty, all American troops were withdrawn within six months and the South Vietnamese were on their own, although President Nixon did make a written promise: "We will respond with full force should the settlement be violated by North Vietnam."[83]

For the three brief years of the Vietnamization Phase of the war, 1973-1975, the ARVN struggled to hold the Viet Cong at bay, but the situation steadily worsened. President Nixon became thoroughly embroiled in the Watergate scandal (he would resign in 1974), and was so politically weakened he could not forestall the House and Senate, now firmly under the control of anti-war liberals, from cutting aid to South Vietnam and curtailing shipments of the repair parts, ammunition, and fuel needed to keep the ARVN a viable fighting force.[84]

By early 1975 the astute North Vietnamese leadership realized that the climate in Washington was such that they could now violate the Paris Agreement and invade the south without fear of American reprisal. In February and March they launched a limited invasion across the DMZ and seized South Vietnam's northernmost province of Quang Tri. When, as expected, no U.S. response was forthcoming, the Politburo ordered the launching of the Ho Chi Minh Campaign on March 31, 1975. This was an all-out invasion to drive on Saigon and capture the whole of South Vietnam. Both Henry Kissinger and President Gerald Ford, conscious of America's promises to South Vietnam and anguished over the possibility that 58,000 American servicemen might have spent their lives in vain, pleaded to Congress to rally to South Vietnam's cause. The appeals fell on deaf ears. Congress would have none of it.[85]

The ARVN collapsed before the advancing North Vietnamese juggernaut. Hue fell, then Da Nang, then the whole of the Central Highlands. Hundreds of thousands of terrified civilians fled southward. On April 21 President Thieu resigned and in a bitter diatribe blamed the U.S. for not living up to its promises to provide matériel for his nation and to enforce the Paris Agreement: "An inhumane act by an inhumane ally."[86] Immediately afterwards the U.S. embassy in Saigon began an air evacuation of the remaining 6,000 Americans in South Vietnam and of 50,000 South Vietnamese who had been most closely associated with the Americans and were at high risk of being executed by the communists. The last helicopter lifted off from the U.S. embassy roof on April 29, and the following day the victorious communist army entered the city. The war was over.

The aftermath of the war? South Vietnam was rejoined to the north to form one communist Vietnam; Saigon was renamed Ho Chi Minh City; Vietnam went on to invade Cambodia and to establish a Vietnamese puppet government there in thorough compliance with Vietnam; the Soviet Union—to the chagrin of the Chinese—was acknowledged as Vietnam's closest ally and rewarded by being given the American naval and air bases at Da Nang for their own use; Vietnam emerged from the war with an even more powerful military—the world's fourth largest—and one now equipped with considerable captured American weaponry; hundreds of thousands of Vietnamese, particularly of the middle class, fled the country, ultimately to seek asylum in Thailand, Australia, Western Europe, Canada, and the United States; America pledged itself "No more Vietnams"; and 58,000 American servicemen were dead.

The Valley's Fighting Men

Luis Lucio
INTERVIEWED BY RODOLFO FLORES

I interviewed Mr. Lucio June 25, 2003, at the Veterans of Foreign Wars Hall located on Parades Line Road. Mr. Lucio was the commander of Veterans of Foreign Wars Post No. 2035 from 1998 to 2003.

MR. FLORES: I THANK YOU FOR YOUR TIME, AND IT IS MY PRIVILEGE TO HEAR YOUR STORY. WHAT WERE THE CIRCUMSTANCES WHEN YOU JOINED THE MILITARY?

Mr. Lucio: I graduated from high school and immediately volunteered for the United States Marine Corps. At the time, there was no Vietnam War; there were only advisors [training the South Vietnamese soldiers]. It was early in March of 1965 when we found out we were going to Vietnam as a whole battalion: 2nd Battalion, 7th Marine Regiment, 1st Marine Division. We made an amphibious landing in Chu Lai known as "Operation Double Eagle," and our objective was to secure enough territory in order to build an airport for U.S. aircraft. We needed to secure an area of approximately forty square miles. I remember on the way over [approaching the coast], I told an old Korean War vet that was with me on the ship it looked like we were running into some foul weather, and he turned around smiling and told me that it was not foul weather but the flash from the muzzles of the big guns. That is when I first realized that this is for real and not a training exercise that we were going into war in Vietnam and that maybe I'd make it back and maybe not; the Lord only knows what lay ahead. The following day we landed in Chu Lai on LSTs, boats that open up front and are like open boxes. We landed with tanks and M-tracks, which are amphibious tanks like you see in the movies. They were waiting for us—we received quite a bit of small-arms fire. It wasn't like in Normandy in World War II, where we sustained thousands of casualties, but we did have a lot of resistance. It took us three days to get the territory that the commanders wanted. They told us when to stop, and to dig in at that point and set up a perimeter. The Seabees would come in later to build the airstrip.

MR. FLORES: WHAT DO YOU REMEMBER ABOUT BOOT CAMP AT CAMP PENDLETON IN CALIFORNIA?

Mr. Lucio: Marine Corps boot camp trains you in discipline, to be motivated, to be loyal to each other, camaraderie. Never leaving anyone behind means a lot; respecting your non-commissioned officers as well as commissioned officers, and to salute your country and your flag. I believe the Marine Corps training is the best training in the world for survival, for war, for killing before being killed, protecting your comrade, your buddy beside you. If I had to do it all over again, I'd do it again. In fact, when there are wars like right now, I wouldn't hesitate to go, even at my age. It is very hard for me to justify 55,280 some odd soldiers, marines, airmen, navy personnel—mostly army and marines—that died out there [South Vietnam]. And we didn't liberate those people. They are not democratic; they're under communism. I don't like to say that we lost the war; I say the politicians lost the war. We didn't fight it the right way. We didn't have the right secretary of defense in McNamara. He cried like a baby all of the time before he died. [*Sic*: Robert McNamara is still alive at the time of this book's printing.] He had all those people [combat deaths] on his conscience; same with President Johnson and President Nixon, even President Kennedy.

MR. FLORES: WHAT UNPLEASANT MEMORIES CAN YOU THINK OF?

Mr. Lucio: What always stays in my mind is after three days of fighting, day and night, we were all exhausted. I was part of the detail to pick up the bodies. Not only the Americans, but the enemy also, Viet Cong mostly, not North Vietnamese, but South Vietnamese guerrillas that were fighting for Ho Chi Minh and North Vietnam; they were actually citizens of South Vietnam. We would throw the bodies in "sixbyes," big trucks, and drive them to a site close to the beach where bulldozers had dug big holes and we would throw them in there, like mass graves. We would put the Americans in body bags, their arms already stiff, smelly, and bloated, and they would be flown to Da Nang, a couple hundred miles south of Chu Lai, which is close to the DMZ which divided South and North Vietnam. After that, we had to endure the monsoon season. Day and night, we always had "fifty percent watch," which is two men to a foxhole; one would sleep, rest or write a letter that would be picked up and sent off every two or three days. We would all eat "C-rations" for the longest time, until we neared a place where helicopters could land and bring us hot food from the ships that were offshore. I was in there, Vietnam, one year, one month and seven days—I know exactly how long I was there.

MR. FLORES: WASN'T IT SUPPOSED TO BE ONE YEAR?

Mr. Lucio: No, the tour of duty normally is thirteen months for a marine. I don't know about the army or another branch. For some reason, I stayed seven days more.

War is hell, especially when at one time we had the North Vietnamese and Viet Cong on their knees. Haiphong harbor was mined and the B-52 bombers were hitting the Ho Chi Minh Trail, where they were running supplies on their back, on mules, whatever. The Russian and Chinese ships would bring in weapons, medical supplies, food, ammunition, artillery shells for big guns, grenade launchers, AK-47s, all communist made, anything you can imagine. But at one time they were not able to do that, and at that time I feel that they were ready to negotiate. But with all the people protesting in Washington, San Francisco, Kent State University and all over the nation, the harbor was de-mined and the bombing was stopped, because of the likes of Jane Fonda, who was protesting the war over there. In fact, I know of three [captured] pilots that gave her notes to give to their commander-in-chief and to the people of the United States that said that these people [North Vietnamese] were not treating us [POWs] right, under the [Rules of the] Geneva Convention. What she did has no forgiveness. She turned over those papers to the highest-ranking officer of the North Vietnamese in Hanoi and they clubbed them [pilots] to death. They killed those three air force pilots, and she's got their blood on her hands. I dislike that lady so much, and I don't like to use the word "hate," but I wouldn't see the Atlanta Braves when she married Ted Turner, the owner of the Braves. I would see her [on television] in the stands; I would flip the channel quickly because I wanted nothing to do with her. They called her "Hanoi Jane." All that protesting hurt the efforts of the American government and the American soldiers trying to liberate South Vietnam from communism.

[At this point, Mr. Lucio gets up to quiet some ladies that were arranging some tables for a party to be held at the veterans' hall later that evening. He returns, recounting more of his unpleasant memories.]

Mr. Lucio: I still have nightmares about picking up the bodies. I have some weird, weird dreams where I can see the faces of those [dead] people, and they are trying to take me with them ... in the middle of the night, you know, when I'm sleeping. I wake up in a cold sweat. War is hell. It is very hard to come out of civilian life and become a marine. You are sent to a war and you see all this death and noise around you. You get honorably discharged like I did and like millions of others that have gone to war before me and after me. You cannot just erase it and pick up where you left off. You have been robbed of your innocence. You see so much hate, so much killing, and so much blood that it is impossible to erase it from your mind.

MR. FLORES: I REMEMBER BROWNSVILLE'S FIRST CASUALTY IN THE SPRING OF '65, GORDON GULLET, A MARINE. WAS HE ANYWHERE IN YOUR AREA?

Mr. Lucio: The people that died or were wounded where I was at in those days were Roberto Rocha. Alberto Avalos was with my same outfit. In fact, I asked my commanding officer if I could accompany Alberto's body back to Brownsville because I know the family, and his neighbor, Roberto Rocha, who they had buried a week before. But I couldn't, because I was not next-of-kin and he needed me there. Driving a "105" [a vehicle half the size of a tank], he hit an anti-tank mine, so they just sent body parts back. We used them [105s] for villages and enemy machine-gun bunkers, but mostly it's an anti-tank gun. I was also with Felix Recio, who is now the federal judge here. We had a total of twenty-eight killed, and one missing in action from a small town, because Brownsville back then was about 47,000 people. They were all from the same high school. We all knew each other, just from different areas.

MR. FLORES: WHAT DID YOU THINK ABOUT THE SOUTH VIETNAMESE SOLDIERS?

Mr. Lucio: They were not disciplined at all, except for the ones trained in North Vietnam, if you know what I mean. Our allies [South Vietnam] had a lot of spies that were actually fighting for communism. Even some high-ranking officers were bought by the North Vietnamese, supplying information to them.

MR. FLORES: WERE YOUR MISSIONS TYPICAL, OR DID THEY VARY IN PURPOSE?

Mr. Lucio: At night, we were dug in with our perimeter set up, and would have incoming mortar rounds into the Seabee camp to keep us from building that airstrip. As soon as daybreak came, it was our mission to go out "search and destroy." Other times, we'd go out before nightfall and would not find anybody of fighting age in the villages. All we would find is women, children and the elderly who couldn't go out and fight a war. We'd ask them where the men were, and they would say that they are out in the rice paddies. We had radios and would contact the helicopters and there were no people in the rice fields. These people were in tunnels preparing to fire at us as soon as it would get dark. There was a lot of resistance during all the time I was there.

MR. FLORES: ON YOUR CAP YOU HAVE THE INSIGNIA OF THE PURPLE HEART. WERE YOU WOUNDED?

Mr. Lucio: I was shot in the leg and spent three weeks in the hospital ship, *Hope*. After that, I was sent back to my outfit. That ship was dismantled here at port [Brownsville] some years ago.

MR. FLORES: YESTERDAY ON THE PHONE, YOU MENTIONED WE COULD NOT MEET FOR THIS INTERVIEW BECAUSE YOU WERE AT THE VETERANS' CLINIC IN McALLEN. ARE YOU RECEIVING TREATMENT FOR WAR INJURIES?

Mr. Lucio: Yes, "PTSD," post traumatic stress disorder. Mostly, it's my nightmares that keep coming back. Gladly, it's not every night, but it's often. [Like] I'm back in the thick of things. Again, I repeat myself, it's something that I will never, ever forget; it will be with me forever. What medication and counseling they give me helps, but you will never forget.

MR. FLORES: WAS THERE A DIFFERENCE BETWEEN VIET CONG AND THE NORTH VIETNAMESE?

Mr. Lucio: The North Vietnamese had already fought the French and whupped them. The French got out of there in 1954, I believe, and they [the French] had made these people hard-core fighting people. The Viet Cong in the south were not as well organized, but they did know how to fight in the jungle, guerrilla warfare, and were good at it. They would hide in tunnels and pop out wherever they thought they could succeed. If we had a patrol of eight marines searching for the enemy out in the jungle or for whatever information we could get, and would get attacked, we'd get on the radio and more marines would be sent in by helicopter. They would disappear into the night. We would find blood, but very seldom would we find wounded or dead. I want to make it perfectly clear that we had the firepower and won almost every battle that we were in in Vietnam. I don't ever feel like we lost, especially during my term. People ask, "What happened in Vietnam?" It was not the marines, the air force, the navy, the soldiers; it was the people protesting the war. Personally, if I would have been up there running the show, I would have invaded North Vietnam. They bombed Haiphong harbor, the railroads, and they would come with pictures where schools were hit. Maybe they made one or two mistakes, but they would use it over and over showing children killed, resulting in more protests. When we came back from Vietnam, we had over 360 marines on a United Airlines 747 jumbo jet. The highest-ranking officer there was a brigadier general that was coming home also after his tour. He told something that I will never forget. He said, "If you're wearing civilian clothes, keep them on. If you're wearing a uniform and you have civilian clothes, put them on. If you don't have any civilian clothes, take off your rank and insignia, or anything else that indicates you are coming from Vietnam because we are landing at El Toro Marine Air Base." From there we were bused to another location and at that point I found out how it was back here in the United States. We were called "baby killers" and had eggs thrown at us. We wanted the bus to stop so we could get it on with those protesters that they call "hippies," "yippies," and "flower children," just plain protesters against the United States government. We were being punished for following orders to go to Vietnam. For years and years and years, everybody that I know of, and speak to, had a bitter taste in their mouths. For the longest time, we told no one that we were Vietnam veterans. But now it is starting to be okay, because we went and served our country in time of war. But before, you didn't want anybody to know that you had been there. It was terrible.

MR. FLORES: DID YOU HAVE FULL CONFIDENCE IN YOUR OFFICERS AND LEADERSHIP?

Mr. Lucio: I had the utmost respect in that marines follow orders from our commissioned and non-commissioned officers. I had all the confidence in the world in the United States government to back us up and win that war. I knew eventually, someday, we would keep South Vietnam from becoming communist, just like they did in Korea. Unfortunately, it didn't work out that way.

MR. FLORES: WHAT DO THINK ABOUT VIETNAM NOW, HOW EVERYTHING ENDED UP?

Mr. Lucio: I was hoping that not only South Vietnam but North Vietnam would end up as a democratic government. The people that survived the war, and the children that are growing up there now, will never know or have the freedom that we have here in the United States. I don't think Vietnam now is doing very well under a communist government. I think that they would have been much better off if they would not have fought the way they did. I don't think that they have a government that helps their war veterans like ours. I am very, very pleased that I have the medical and psychological attention that we, the veterans that served our country, are getting now, because it wasn't always that way.

[At this point, we turned our attention to the brightly colored decorations that the ladies had been working on during the interview. I asked Mr. Lucio what the occasion was, and he replied that there would be a karaoke party later on that evening, and that I was invited to join. I graciously accepted and returned to the hall later that night, accompanied by plenty of cold beer. So long ago, but yet so near.]

Raymond L. Simonsen
INTERVIEWED BY CARLOS PENA

We agreed to meet on Thursday, April 3, 2003. The setting was familiar to me since I had been there many times before. I will be interviewing Raymond L. Simonsen in his office at The University of Texas at Brownsville. Mr. Simonsen has been a mathematics professor at the university for fifteen years. If you pass by the hall and hear classical music that will be his office it is coming from, because he always has it on. The music was on in the background while I was conducting the interview. He was born in Portland, Oregon, "decades and decades ago." His parents were Raymond and Phyllis Simonsen. His dad, Raymond, was killed in a car accident when Raymond, Jr., was only a year old. His mom remarried and later had another son, who became his half-brother. He now has his wife, Joyce, as well as his daughter and her four children living with him. Having taken a few classes with Mr. Simonsen, I can tell you that he accepts nothing less than your best, because that was what was expected of him. He is a stern man who will not take you seriously if you do not take him seriously. He has a tendency to appear to be grumpy, but once you get to know him, you will find out he's not that way at all.

MR. PENA: WHAT BRANCH OF THE MILITARY DID YOU ENTER AND WHAT WAS YOUR LAST RANK?
Mr. Simonsen: Major, U.S. Marine Corps, Retired.
MR. PENA: WHEN DID YOU JOIN THE MARINES?
Mr. Simonsen: I joined in 1955.
MR. PENA: WHERE WERE YOU STATIONED WHEN YOU JOINED?
Mr. Simonsen: San Diego Marine Corps Recruit Depot, then to Camp Pendleton, California, then I was picked for the flight training program at Pensacola, Florida.
MR. PENA: AT THE START OF THE VIETNAM CONFLICT, WHERE WERE YOU STATIONED?
Mr. Simonsen: Well, it depends on what date you pick for the start because we had advisors there in the late fifties. The real full-blown war started in 1965, when we started putting in troops in mass quantities. I was actually stationed in Japan from 1964 to 1965, and our squadron would fly down once a month delivering supplies and stuff to the advisors. Then in March of 1965 we started bringing in troops from the 9th Marine Expeditionary Brigade.

MR. PENA: DURING THESE EXPEDITIONS DID YOU EVER ENCOUNTER INTERFERENCE FROM NORTH VIETNAM?

Mr. Simonsen: In those days they would occasionally fire at us during landing at Da Nang Air Base, but the results were minimal.

MR. PENA: DID YOU EVER HAVE ENOUGH INTERFERENCE TO DETOUR YOU FROM THE OBJECTIVE OF THE MISSION?

Mr. Simonsen: When you are flying C-130s you do not get too involved in the day-to-day combat or military fighting. We put troops where they had to be, delivered supplies, and did refueling for the jets. We dropped flares at night. We were combat support.

MR. PENA: WHAT BASE WERE YOU AT WHILE YOU WERE THERE?

Mr. Simonsen: When we were "in country" we were mainly in Da Nang, although we flew around most of South Vietnam and Thailand.

MR. PENA: WHAT WOULD YOU DO FOR SUPPORT OF THE TROOPS?

Mr. Simonsen: We were flying air combat support for everything that went on in there. We refueled the fighters. They would go out and drop their ordnance, come back, refuel and go back supporting the ground troops, or they would go up north and refuel on the way back. We would also drop million-candle-power magnesium flares at night.

MR. PENA: WAS THERE EVER AN ACCIDENT WHILE REFUELING?

Mr. Simonsen: There was one right after I got back in country in '69. Some second lieutenant in an F-4 was coming out and drove into a midair collision with a tanker. Killed everyone in the F-4 and the tanker. The tanker had two F-4s plugged in on either side, but those four guys got away. We lost another KC-130 over Tiger Island, probably by a surface-to-air missile. We also lost one in Khe Sanh while trying to deliver a big rubber bladder full of fuel to the troops at Khe Sanh during the siege. They took some fire in the bladder and it started burning while they were in the landing pattern. After landing, the pilot went outside to the back of the plane, opened the cargo door and released the trapped folks in the back of the plane. He got himself a silver star for that. Those are the only three C-130s I remember we lost.

MR. PENA: WAS THE BASE EVER ATTACKED?

Mr. Simonsen: Sometimes they would shoot rockets, but there was not a concentrated personnel attack on the base. They were unguided mortars, and 122mm rockets.

MR. PENA: YOU HAVE SAID THAT ONE OF THE SIDE EFFECTS WAS YOUR LOSS OF HEARING?

Mr. Simonsen: That was being around aviation. We were too macho to wear ear protectors, because we thought we did not need them, and we paid the price. There wasn't nearly as much emphasis on hearing loss in those days as there is now. It was like growing up when everyone on the movie screen smoked and it became the thing for everyone to do. We slowly came to realize that it is not good for you.

MR. PENA: NOW WHAT DO YOU THINK OF THE SERVICE YOU WERE DOING?

Mr. Simonsen: We did what was asked of us. Everyone was up in arms, and I am really disappointed in the American public. I mean it is okay to disagree with the administration with what they've done, but once you go in, there is no reason to look down at the troops. They are only doing their job. Maybe some of them thought we should not be there, but once you send in the troops you should support them no matter what. I love to see the support the troops in Iraq are getting now. Those guys are over there putting their life on the line and there should be no point at which we should look down at them and what they are doing.

MR. PENA: DID YOU EVER MEET SOMEONE THAT DID NOT WANT TO BE THERE?

Mr. Simonsen: No, it was a job, and in our unit it was not all that bad of a job. We had outhouses and outdoor showers, but it was not hardship compared to what the grunts were doing on the ground. It was difficult to sleep at night when the rockets were coming over and we had to jump into a hole somewhere, but I cannot remember anybody in our squadron who was violently opposed to the war. It was a lousy war, but it was the only war we had.

MR. PENA: ANY ADDITIONAL REMARKS?

Mr. Simonsen: I think we have come a long way since Vietnam. The military has turned around and they have gotten their act together. I am not too sure about the politicians, though. I wasn't completely sure why we are in Iraq but once we are there I love the support routine the guys are getting. Those guys are doing a fantastic job.

Ben Cortez
Interviewed by Erasmo Chapa

Ben Cortez is a lifelong resident of San Benito, Texas, who owns his own construction company and is currently teaching criminal justice classes at San Benito High School. Mr. Cortez was a United States Navy Seal. I arrived at his San Benito home in the evening and began the interview.

MR. CHAPA: WHEN DID YOU ENLIST IN THE U.S. NAVY SEALS?

Mr. Cortez: I enlisted in the navy first, going through basic training. I ran a mile and a half in under ten minutes and then swam a mile. That was just to get you qualified. Then I had to undergo BUDs (Basic Underwater Demolition Training). It was twenty-four weeks for that, but they cut it short because of the war. The first six weeks were the hardest; this was known as "Hell Week." You got very little sleep and had to go through several obstacle courses. Out of 120 men, eighteen of us graduated; the rest dropped.

MR. CHAPA: WHAT YEAR WERE YOUR DEPLOYED TO VIETNAM?

Mr. Cortez: I was deployed to Vietnam in 1965. I got transferred to Seal Team One in Da Nang, Vietnam. We got assigned a river boat squadron in a small river near the DMZ. We had two teams, A and B, and we were out thirty days at a time watching what kind of boats would go by and what they were carrying aboard. At nighttime we tried to see any movement, such as troops and unlikely traffic passing by. We moved from the DMZ to being alongside Cambodia and basically went up and down river, and they dropped us off until we got relieved. That was where I met Mr. Rey Lopez from Lopez Brothers in San Benito. He was on Team B and I was on Team A. At first we would pass each other often and I knew I recognized him from somewhere. You were always looking for familiar faces. It feels good to see someone from your hometown. [At this time Mr. Cortez gets up and walks to a safe box and brings back his pins and badges that he wore on his uniform.] You see back then there was a bounty on navy Seals. They were really after us. There was also a lot of Americans that would switch to the Viet Cong side. These were usually soldiers that were addicted to drugs or were bought off by the Viet Cong. There was a lot of opium grown over there, but you could find any drug you wanted. They would provide information to them. They also got information from little kids that would go shoeshine and do little odd jobs around the camp. They were called "houseboys." The Viet Cong used women and children to get information from us by spying or overhearing things.

MR. CHAPA: WHAT KIND OF ACTION DID YOU SEE?

Mr. Cortez: Well, the only action I saw was through intelligence gathering and running into small-arms fire. One time we got caught on purpose to see what the strength of the camp was and the status of the POWs. We tried to get as much information as we possibly could.

MR. CHAPA: HOW WERE YOU TREATED IN THE CAMPS WHEN YOU WERE CAPTURED?

Mr. Cortez: They would try to get information from us through standard interrogation. They would keep us in different huts, but the first few days they put us in bamboo cages in the river. They set us apart to see how strong we were mentally. If we fell asleep the rats would start nibbling on you. You tried to stay awake, especially at nighttime when the rats got real bad. As long as you moved you were okay. That's why they trained us the way they did. It was not that bad until 1969. In 1969 they had a lot of Soviet advisors, and that's when a lot of Americans were tortured. After the third day we were rescued because it was not very heavily guarded. We had a lot of air support during the rescue. They tried to set a perimeter by using napalm so that no more Vietnamese would come in to help. This is where they would come in to rescue us. Back then (1965) the enemy's weapons weren't as good; it wasn't until 1968 when they received more Russian weaponry.

MR. CHAPA: WERE YOU EVER UNCERTAIN THAT YOU WOULD NOT LEAVE ALIVE?

Mr. Cortez: [Shakes his head, meaning he was not.]

MR. CHAPA: HOW LONG WERE YOU IN THE VIETNAM WAR?

Mr. Cortez: We would go six months in and six months out. The first year I was inland and the last four years I was onboard a ship that was called a communications flagship. We would plot all of the operations going on as far as the navy went. We had aircraft and ships all plotted out.

MR. CHAPA: HOW DID YOU FEEL PERSONALLY ABOUT THE VIETNAM WAR?

Mr. Cortez: We weren't trying to win. We had opportunity to mine Haiphong harbor before the Russians could supply them with weapons and supplies. Of course we didn't see it like that back then. I kind of resent it now. It was an unpopular war, and there were a lot of protesters. I really didn't feel appreciated. We lost Juan Garza, Jr., last week [2nd Gulf War] and the community really reached out to the family. Back then I lost a friend and there wasn't any recognition or comforting like they did for this guy. There wasn't any support for the war, yet the soldiers were still willing to put their lives on the line and just come back to know that you weren't appreciated. When you're out there you think you're doing the patriotic thing, and when you come back you don't know if it was really worth it or not.

Richard Ghionzoli
Interviewed by Ruben Garcia

I met Mr. Ghionzoli through a friend from work. He struck me as a very no-nonsense kind of man. Yet the manner with which he carried himself made me feel at ease during the interview.

MR. GARCIA: WHEN DID YOU JOIN THE NAVY?
Mr. Ghionzoli: I enlisted in 1963 and served for two years.
MR. GARCIA: WHAT WAS BOOT CAMP LIKE FOR A NAVY RECRUIT? WHERE WAS IT HELD?
Mr. Ghionzoli: Basic training was held at Great Lakes, Illinois. It was the same as any other. Waking up at 5 A.M., exercise, swimming for fifteen minutes. It gets cold after a while. About every two to three weeks we would have man-overboard or abandon-ship drills.
MR. GARCIA: AFTER BASIC TRAINING, WHERE WERE YOU STATIONED?
Mr. Ghionzoli: I was stationed aboard the USS *Rangel Ranier* as a boatswain's mate-2nd class, E5. It was an East Coast ship with a crew of 300 men. The ship's purpose was carrying ammo and supplies.
MR. GARCIA: HOW DID YOU END UP IN VIETNAM?
Mr. Ghionzoli: Our ship was transferred to the Pacific fleet. We had to cross the Panama Canal. Our homeport was Olongapo in the Philippines. We were to resupply ships in the Tonkin Gulf.
MR. GARCIA: WHAT DO YOU MEAN RESUPPLY—HOW WAS THAT DONE?
Mr. Ghionzoli: We would pull up next to the destroyer, carrier, or other ship and latch on. Using winches on the bow and stern of the ship we would hoist about 3,500 pounds of ammo or supplies to the awaiting ship with cargo nets.
MR. GARCIA: HOW LONG WOULD THIS GO ON?

Mr. Ghionzoli: Depending on the size of the ship, the average time was three to four hours.

MR. GARCIA: IN THIS TIME WAS IT POSSIBLE TO BOARD THE OTHER SHIP?

Mr. Ghionzoli: No, we were traveling about 12 knots. That's about 14 miles an hour.

MR. GARCIA: WASN'T IT DANGEROUS LOADING 3,500 POUNDS OF ARMAMENT?

Mr. Ghionzoli: Yes, but they did not have the fuses in place. I was told that out of a thousand one might go off. The danger lay in falling objects. One night I was working off hatch two when a bomb slipped through the cargo net and fell two levels down. It happened so quickly; I only had time to yell a warning to the gunner's mate. Everyone's eyes grew as they saw the bomb fall. All I heard was a loud thud.

MR. GARCIA: WAS ANYONE HURT?

Mr. Ghionzoli: No, but the nature of the job is unforgiving. It leaves no room for error. This guy we called "Spider" was driving a forklift and another load slipped falling on his head. He had to be airlifted off the ship.

MR. GARCIA: DID ANYONE EVER DIE?

Mr. Ghionzoli: No, out of the 300, we all made it back home together, with the exception of "Spider" that came home early.

MR. GARCIA: WERE YOU IN ANY BATTLES?

Mr. Ghionzoli: No, our ship was only armed with two 3-inch guns. We were not prepared to defend ourselves. Luckily we usually had a larger ship nearby. Even if they were far off, they were so fast that they could reach us in minutes.

MR. GARCIA: DID YOU SEND LETTERS BACK HOME?

Mr. Ghionzoli: Why? I didn't want to worry my parents. I didn't even tell them that I was leaving for Vietnam. My captain sent out a general letter to all the families of the crew that we were off to war. That didn't make my dad too happy. Eventually I did write back in response to their letters.

MR. GARCIA: HOW ABOUT PHONE CALLS IN PORT?

Mr. Ghionzoli: I did make some phone calls, but the calls then were expensive because they used underwater cables.

MR. GARCIA: WHEN WAS YOUR TOUR OVER?

Mr. Ghionzoli: By 1966 I was en route home. And I got out of the navy in January of 1967.

MR. GARCIA: HOW WAS THE TRIP HOME?

Mr. Ghionzoli: The return home was excellent. We were in no hurry so our captain asked to go around the world. We passed through the equator and saw about twenty-five different countries.

MR. GARCIA: HOW WAS IT WHEN YOU REACHED THE U.S.?

Mr. Ghionzoli: The band played "Anchors Away." Everyone had tears in their eyes. As it turned out I happened to be the first sailor to set foot on U.S. ground. I was in charge of the gangway and had to secure the ship to the pier.

MR. GARCIA: DID ANYONE PROTEST THE WAR THEN?

Mr. Ghionzoli: The protesting was not what it would become then; no one protested our trip home.

MR. GARCIA: DO YOU THINK THE UNITED STATES OVERSTEPPED THEIR BOUNDARY BY ENTERING A CONTROVERSIAL WAR?

Mr. Ghionzoli: No way, no way. We were there to clean up after the frogs [French]. The United States would have won if we had gone beyond the DMZ.

MR. GARCIA: SO YOU BELIEVED IN THE WAR?

Mr. Ghionzoli: I believed 100 percent in the cause. There are two things in the world: discipline and chaos. Without one you get the other. If we hadn't been there, we would have had more Saddams.

MR. GARCIA: SHOULD THE U.S. POLICE THE WORLD?

Mr. Ghionzoli: Yes, the U.S. has to be the peacekeeper. If not us then someone has to. We belonged there then, just like we belong in Iraq today.

MR. GARCIA: BUT AS PEACEKEEPERS, WE HAVE PEOPLE WHO OPENLY HATE THE U.S. WHAT DO YOU THINK ABOUT THEM?

Mr. Ghionzoli: It'll go away. Truth is, more people want to help than those who don't.

James Franceschi
INTERVIEWED BY WILLIAM L. ADAMS

James Franceschi was born in San Diego in 1945, the son of a navy chief. His father, mother, and older brother had all been at Pearl Harbor when it was bombed in December 1941. It had been "understood" that Jim would in due course make the navy his career as well—and, in fact, Jim has spent the bulk of his life on and around ships.

From 1968 to 1991 he worked on sea-going tugs operating out of New York, Philadelphia, Tampa, and Lake Charles, Louisiana. Since 1991 he has served as a pilot for the Port of Brownsville. However, during the Vietnam War, Jim found himself in the army, not the navy.

I have known Jim ever since 1966, when he kindly let me serve as his piloting sidekick and ride with him aboard a big Chinese

James Franceschi
—Courtesy James Franceschi

bulk cargo vessel, the *Hai Wang Xing* ("God Neptune"), he was piloting into Brownsville. Jim is a tall, rangy, meticulous man. He is very serious and articulate. In the years since his return from Vietnam he has sought to understand that conflict and has read widely and deeply on the topic.

Over the course of a few hours, and a few beers, I interviewed Jim in my attic office the evening of November 30, 2003.

DR. ADAMS: WHY DID YOU VOLUNTEER FOR THE ARMY, JIM?

Mr. Franceschi: Had nothing else to do. It was 1963; the war was not really on yet. I had expected to make a career of it because my father had served in the navy thirty years, but I soon found I didn't like it. I didn't like the regimentation. I chose the army because the army was three years at that time and everything else was four years.

DR. ADAMS: WHAT WAS YOUR TRAINING LIKE?

Mr. Franceschi: Just basic training. I was sent to Ford Ord, California, for basic. I was in pretty good shape. I had been working on a ranch in the state of Washington the year before. The training didn't bother me. Afterwards I went to Fort Leonard Wood, Missouri, for engineering training. We were taught to build bridges, build roads, maintain roads, blow things up (demolition), road reconnaissance, lay and pick up mine fields. Made rope bridges and made bridges out of wood. Made pontoon bridges that you assemble.

There is a way you lay a mine field. People think you lay a mine field indiscriminately. You don't. There is a definite way you lay mine fields. You map your mine fields; you mark your mine fields. The division or regimental commander decides where to put the mine field, where to set up the defense. Usually it's in three lines. You lay them on a compass bearing that will then zigzag. You plant an anti-tank mine like maybe every fifteen steps. The first one would be to the left, next to the right. Left, right, left, right, all the way down the zigzag. The mine is placed just slightly below the surface with just enough dirt to cover it. A certain number would be booby trapped. A little box the size of a matchbox is underneath the mine—attached to the mine. Pull out the pin, and it is armed. If anyone picks it up, it will blow up. Around the tank mine—which will only go off under the pressure of something heavy—you spread anti-personnel mines in a semicircle in front of the tank mine a few paces from it.

DR. ADAMS: AFTER YOU HAD COMPLETED YOUR ENGINEERING TRAINING, WHERE WERE YOU SENT?

Mr. Franceschi: [Laughs.] I was assigned TDY (temporary duty) to the 802nd Military Police Company right there at Fort Leonard Wood as assistant—assistant—post dog catcher.

DR. ADAMS: DO YOU LIKE CATCHING DOGS?

Mr. Franceschi: Never caught a dog. Just traveled around in a pickup truck. Never caught anything. I did that for a couple of months. From there they sent me to the 25th Infantry Division, Schofield Barracks, Hawaii. The 65th Engineering Battalion (Combat). That was in May 1964.

DR. ADAMS: DESCRIBE HOW YOU GOT TO VIETNAM AND YOUR FEELINGS ON THE WAY OVER.

Mr. Franceschi: We flew from Hickam in Hawaii. Our equipment would follow by ship. At Hickam there were Red Cross ladies in gray uniforms and hats who gave us cookies and coffee. They gave us the old "V" sign. We just looked at them. We didn't think much about it.

We flew on a C-141 for fourteen hours. Stopped at Wake and stopped at Clark in the Philippines just for fuel. The C-141 had paratrooper seats down one side—seats made for people with parachute packs on, so you sat way back. Very uncomfortable. For fourteen hours. We engineers were on one side of the plane and artillery pieces were down the other side. Ammunition was piled way high down the center of the big C-141.

James Franceschi

Got to Pleiku just at dusk, just as it was getting dark. They threw us out of the back of the airplane. Didn't even fully drop the ramp and never fully stopped the airplane—just pushed you out, and we had our rifles and machine guns.

DR. ADAMS: DID THEY FEAR INCOMING?

Mr. Franceschi: Yeah. They wanted to get out of there! Minimum time on the ground. Trucks beside the runway. They put us right on the trucks and took us inside the perimeter for the night.

DR. ADAMS: DID YOU HAVE SANDBAG BUNKERS?

Mr. Franceschi: No. Nothing. Just laid on the ground.

DR. ADAMS: WHAT DID YOU DO IN VIETNAM?

Mr. Franceschi: I was a combat engineer. We did road reconnaissance. We built bridges and guarded them, and we built roads. We had four dump trucks and a loader in each platoon. Built airstrips; cleared trees for helicopter landing zones. This is in '65 and '66. [He shows a photograph of a scrubby-looking airstrip out in the middle of nowhere.] We built this airstrip. We built these roads. [With pride and some awe in his voice.] We built all of this!

DR. ADAMS: DID YOU EVER FEEL IN DANGER?

Mr. Franceschi: Oh yeah. Oh yeah! We were out there with the infantry. Two Corps area. We set up our base area. We were short of food. We were starving to death. Well, we weren't starving to death, but we were hungry boys. We weren't there very long and then we started operations.

Once we went to a supply base run by air force for a truckload of concertina wire. We got to this base and the supplies went for hundreds and hundreds of yards. Rows and rows ten-feet high with room for trucks to drive in between. We got to the section where the concertina wire was and were loading it when we saw in the next row were C-rations. We were starving. We started to load it, pulling it under the concertina wire to hide it, when an air force sergeant saw what we were doing and came screaming at us: "Put those C-rations back!" We were all dirty and had our rifles with us and we lowered them at him and screamed back: "We're taking it!" He held up his hands and just backed away from us.

Sometimes we would run convoys into Qui Nhon from our base camp outside Pleiku. Sometimes use every truck in the brigade and go to Qui Nhon for supplies: ammunition, C-rations, all our supplies. The wreckage of war along that road was tremendous: bridges blown, tanks on their side, everything. The wreckage of war was tremendous. The road would come down out of the mountains, very steep, to a flat area. Rice fields. A shimmering, emerald-green area. So beautiful.

DR. ADAMS: DID YOU EVER GET "REST AND RELAXATION"?

Mr. Franceschi: No. Never.

DR. ADAMS: NO BOB HOPE? NO GIRLS? NO TRAVELING TROUPES OF SINGERS AND DANCERS?

Mr. Franceschi: Nope. Nothing. No fun. Really, the war for me was grueling work all day. Pick and shovel stuff. Driving trucks. And at night if was fifty percent security—only half the people could sleep at any one time. The other half were on guard. But I guess that was better than being in the infantry.

VICTORIA Bar
13ᴬ, Nguyễn-thái-Học — PLEIKU

We have a great pleasure to invite you to come and refresh yourself.

The most comfortable one in the Town, having many charming pretty hotesses to serve you together with excellent music.

Pleiku bar advertisement.

DR. ADAMS: WHAT DO YOU THINK OF JANE FONDA?

Mr. Franceschi: What pisses me off about Jane Fonda—and will until I die—is seeing her sitting atop that North Vietnamese anti-aircraft gun laughing and clapping when that gun was being used to shoot at American planes. That really pisses me off even to remember it.

DR. ADAMS: WHAT DID YOU THINK OF THE PEACE PROTESTERS?

Mr. Franceschi: I got out in 1966, and I could look at it from the perspective of someone who wasn't going to be drafted and sent off. The whole hippie movement and the whole anti-war protest movement was just a big American fad. The largest percentage were doing it just to be cool. Only a small percentage were doing it out of conviction. And even Jerry Rubin sold out; everybody sold out. But they were right: the war should never have been fought.

DR. ADAMS: WHEN YOU HEARD ABOUT THE FALL OF SAIGON TO THE COMMUNISTS, HOW DID YOU FEEL?

Mr. Franceschi: I don't remember feeling anything. But the war itself ... all I could think of was "why?" Why did so many people have to die? Why did so many people have to fight and get so totally fucked up? For what?

DR. ADAMS: HOW DO YOU FEEL ABOUT THE WHOLE EXPERIENCE, LOOKING BACK ON IT?

Mr. Franceschi: Now I know—having read about it years later—that it was all a part of the containment policy, the domino theory. Well, look what happened.

DR. ADAMS: ARE YOU A BETTER MAN FOR HAVING SERVED IN VIETNAM?

Mr. Franceschi: Probably.

DR. ADAMS: HOW? IN WHAT WAY?

Mr. Franceschi: I don't know. I guess because I got to go to a war. [Pause.] I'm a lot more suspicious of the government.

DR. ADAMS: WHAT DO THE READERS NEED TO KNOW ABOUT THE WAR—SOMETHING YOU THINK THEY MIGHT NOT KNOW?

Mr. Franceschi: It was the junior officers that came out of that war that built the superb military we have today, not just the army, but the whole military.

Feliciano Saldivar
Interviewed by Santiago Salazar, Jr.

This interview with Mr. Feliciano Salidivar was conducted at his home on June 26, 2003. Mr. Saldivar was sitting at the dinner table with several documents from the Vietnam War.

MR. SALAZAR: CAN YOU TELL ME A LITTLE ABOUT YOUR FAMILY AND HOW THEY FELT TOWARD THE VIETNAM WAR?

Mr. Saldivar: My name is Feliciano Saldivar and I was born November 11, 1945. I was born in Brownsville and I have two sisters and three brothers. I went to school in Port Isabel and I went up to the tenth grade. I worked with my dad in the fields until 1966 when I got drafted into the armed forces. I then joined the Marine Corps in San Antonio.

MR. SALAZAR: SO YOU WERE DRAFTED INTO THE MILITARY?

Mr. Saldivar: Yeah, I was drafted. I was a 1A. I was drafted into the army in 1966.

110 Vietnam War

I joined the marines in San Antonio. So I volunteered into the Marine Corps.

MR. SALAZAR: SO DID YOU SEE YOUR DRAFT BALL ON TV?

Mr. Saldivar: I don't know how that works. All I know is that I was a 1A.

MR. SALAZAR: SO DID YOU COME FROM A MILITARY FAMILY YOURSELF?

Mr. Saldivar: Yes, my stepdad was in the army in World War II.

MR. SALAZAR: HOW DID YOUR FAMILY FEEL ABOUT YOU JOINING THE MILITARY?

Mr. Saldivar: Well, he was okay about it. He wasn't too sure about it. My stepbrothers and sisters were okay about it too. The only times they said "no" was when I wanted to reenlist. Things were going real bad at that time in 1967. They didn't feel good about me going twice up there.

Feliciano Saldivar

MR. SALAZAR: WHAT SECTION OF THE MARINES DID YOU JOIN?

Mr. Saldivar: 1st Battalion Headquarters, 1st Marine Division.

MR. SALAZAR: DURING THAT TIME, HOW WERE BROWNSVILLE RESIDENTS GETTING INFORMATION ABOUT THE VIETNAM WAR?

Mr. Saldivar: By the radio. During the time I was in school I would love to read stories about the war. I had made up my mind about joining the marines. It was all planned out. So it happened that I got drafted. It gave me an opportunity to go. I had made up my mind. I wanted to go.

MR. SALAZAR: DESCRIBE YOUR FIRST EXPERIENCE WITH THE MILITARY IN SAN ANTONIO.

Mr. Saldivar: Well, the way they do it, you go in there and they check you out. No physical, just talk to you about it, from there they put you in a hotel and the following day they sent us to Camp Pendleton in California.

MR. SALAZAR: CAN YOU DESCRIBE YOUR TRAINING?

Mr. Saldivar: I was trained to kill. Doing all kinds of exercises: mountain climbing, marching, running. They did their jobs, the drill instructors, as best as they could. What can I say? As long as you made it, they did a good job.

MR. SALAZAR: WHAT WAS THE FEELING OF BROWNSVILLE RESIDENTS REGARDING THE WAR?

Mr. Saldivar: Well, I think most people know that every ten to twenty years there should be a war for the population. So I figure the people from Brownsville, those that have been in the service, think that way. Eventually my dad thought about it that way, and his dad thought about it that way. It was tradition. Every ten to twenty years for tradition, to control the population. And I feel that people in Brownsville were for the war. I don't think there were people against the war. That was in the beginning, before I left. When I came back, that was something else. But going up there, everybody said we were doing a great job. But that was going. At the end, that was something else.

MR. SALAZAR: CAN YOU DESCRIBE YOUR EXPERIENCE OF HOW YOU GOT TO VIETNAM?

Mr. Saldivar: We got there by plane. We took off in June in a C-130. That's a military plane that's used to move equipment. We boarded the plane in El Toro, California. From there we went to Seattle. From there we took off to Hawaii. While going to Hawaii, we had engine problems. I guess I was the first one to notice that the prop was standing still. Then everyone saw it. Everyone was thinking what the hell was going to happen. So eventually, the captain told us he had to turn off the other engine and we were flying on two engines. Then they told us to get our life vests on just in case we had to make an emergency landing. You could see the water real close to the plane. Eventually we got to Hawaii and we stayed there overnight while they were fixing the plane. The next day we got on the same plane and we headed to Wake Island. We slept there and the next morning we went to Guam. Slept there overnight and took off to Okinawa. From there the same C-130 has the same engine problems on the same engine. We had to turn back. They worked on the plane, and put us on a commercial plane, a 747 airliner, that took us to Da Nang, Vietnam. We were going around in circles. They took us to some air force base, "something Bay" [Camh Ran Bay]. But the problem was that all the airfields were being bombed by mortars and rockets. We stayed in the air for more than one hour just circling bases.

MR. SALAZAR: WHILE YOU WERE IN THE AIR, WHAT FEELINGS DID YOU HAVE ABOUT A POTENTIAL BATTLE AS SOON AS YOU LANDED?

Mr. Saldivar: You know that it is dangerous. You know that when you land, you are in a war zone. Every chill goes through your head. What the hell is going to happen? They told us to get ready. When we landed, everything was okay. They had everything squared away. They had a perimeter around the airfield. The "gooks" weren't there. They were just shooting mortars and rockets. When we landed, there were no lights on the airstrip. What you could see were flashlights. We went straight to the trenches and slept there. At daylight, all you could see were tents. They started moving around and showing us where the mess hall was and where the shower tents were. They moved us around. We were there for a couple of days.

MR. SALAZAR: HOW MANY MEN WERE IN THE PLANE WITH YOU?

Mr. Saldivar: There must have been about 200. There were about fifteen percent Mexican.

MR. SALAZAR: WHEN YOU GOT YOUR ORDERS TO LEAVE BASE CAMP, HOW DID YOU FEEL?

Mr. Saldivar: I felt great that what I was doing was the right thing to do. It was all for me. I had my mind made up. I told my parents that if I don't come back, every GI had insurance for $10,000. If something happens to me take that money and buy a door because every time you walk through the door I'll be there. I was ready. I wasn't married, so I was ready.

MR. SALAZAR: HOW WAS THE MORALE OF THE TROOPS WHEN YOU GOT TO VIETNAM?

Mr. Saldivar: Well, since everyone was young—I was 20—when you're young you don't think what can happen to you. Everybody was happy. You weren't thinking about getting blown away or killed. You were out there to do a job. You had passed your training. You were doing a job and coming back. The training was okay. Now that I look at it, they should have spent more time with more drill instructors. Less people and more drill instructors on the platoon. It's kind of hard to have 200 to 300 people to really pay attention. If something goes wrong, and one of the guys wasn't paying attention, then my life was in his hands.

MR. SALAZAR: WHAT WAS THE BEST ADVICE ANYONE GAVE YOU TO SURVIVE THE WAR?

Mr. Saldivar: You better eat more tortillas and tamales. Stay together and be one, instead of being separate. Be a unit. If you want to come back, be a unit. Think together. That helps.

MR. SALAZAR: DID YOU INTERACT WITH THE VIETNAMESE PEOPLE?

Mr. Saldivar: Not really. Our training was to go out and kill, not talk to the people. There were VCs everywhere. I did not shake their hands. The problem was to do your job and come back home.

MR. SALAZAR: CAN YOU DESCRIBE YOUR MENTAL STATE THE FIRST TIME YOU ENCOUNTERED THE ENEMY?

Mr. Saldivar: We knew they were there. Some were shot or killed at night. We would never see them. We never saw them face to face. Most of the battles were done at night. Can't say I wasn't scared. There were rounds and mortar rounds, machine guns are firing at you, you think the world is coming to an end. You can't describe the feeling. Chu Lai was the first battle. At night. The people at the village were friendly, but at night those same people were shooting at us. They would pass you and wave at you, and at night they were the same people shooting at you, throwing rockets and mortar rounds. I didn't trust them. They were dressed in black. You couldn't tell if he was a regular person or a "gook." It was real hard to find out. Many Vietnamese people got killed.

MR. SALAZAR: WERE THERE ANY SPECIAL PRECAUTIONS THAT YOU HAD TO TAKE SINCE THE BATTLES WERE AT NIGHT?

Mr. Saldivar: The only precaution was that if you had to go to a village and you thought there were "gooks" there, you had to be fired upon before you could fire back. That was the only rule. Other than that, you never knew. A lot of guys were trigger-happy. The night was so dark that you could stretch your hand in front of your face and couldn't see your fingers. You waited to hear something. You couldn't see who you were firing at. You knew someone was out there.

MR. SALAZAR: CAN YOU DESCRIBE HOW THE ENEMY FOUGHT AGAINST THE AMERICANS?

Mr. Saldivar: Well, they just came in and did what they had to do and left. They stood their ground, but most of the time they fired mortar rounds and rockets. You couldn't see them. They were just firing mortar rounds and rockets.

MR. SALAZAR: WERE YOU PREPARED FOR THE ENVIRONMENTAL DIFFERENCES THERE?

Mr. Saldivar: No. It was full of grass, hot weather, and rain. It was hard to get used to it. They sent us, during basic training, to "La Pulga" and it's hot during the summer. This place is about the same as Vietnam. It's hot. For six months it's hot and then you get monsoon season. Nothing but rain for six months. We were sort of prepared for it. It affected everyone.

MR. SALAZAR: DID YOU EVER GET TO WRITE OR CALL HOME?

Mr. Saldivar: Write home, yes. Never did call home. I had an opportunity, but something went wrong and I didn't call.

MR. SALAZAR: WHAT YEAR WERE YOU IN VIETNAM?

Mr. Saldivar: From 1966 to 1967, and I served one tour. Thirteen months.

MR. SALAZAR: WHAT WAS YOUR BEST EXPERIENCE IN VIETNAM?

Mr. Saldivar: There was no good experience in Vietnam. The worst thing that happened was when I wrote a letter to my best friend and it came back that he was KIA. A good time was when I was told I was going home.

MR. SALAZAR: WHILE YOU WERE IN VIETNAM, HOW DID YOU FEEL ABOUT THE PROTESTS CONCERNING THE WAR?

Mr. Saldivar: I heard about them from the newspaper that we got. But I know why people were being drafted into the war. The VIPs didn't want their sons in the military. These kids didn't respond to orders very well. They thought just because they had college time he was to be my superior. The only news we got about the protests was from the *Stars and Stripes* newspaper. Once in a while we would get the information. My letters from my parents told me about the war. We didn't care about the protests. We thought we were doing the right thing. But the real reason why the protests started was because the VIPs didn't want their sons to go to war. It wasn't trying to help us but themselves.

MR. SALAZAR: HOW DID THE MILITARY TRY TO CONVINCE THE TROOPS THAT WE WERE DOING THE RIGHT THING?

Mr. Saldivar: Money was what they offered to troops if they reenlisted. They offered $10,000, thirty days off, and two more tours of Vietnam. My family did not want for me to go. I thought about it, but the protests were going on and I realized that I did the right thing.

MR. SALAZAR: AFTER THE WAR, DID YOU CONTINUE TO REMAIN IN CONTACT WITH YOUR FELLOW SOLDIERS?

Mr. Saldivar: No, I didn't. I was better off not having contact with anyone.

Willie F. Canant, Jr.
INTERVIEWED BY CARLOS RODRIGUEZ

I interviewed Mr. Canant inside the local federal building. He is a Brownsville native and a 1960 graduate of Brownsville High. Today he serves as a court security officer with the U.S. Marshal's Service. Mr. Canant joined the Marine Corps immediately after high school and served from June 1960 until October 1967.

MR. RODRIGUEZ: MR. CANANT, COULD YOU TELL ME YOUR EXPERIENCE WHEN YOU FIRST JOINED THE MARINES?

Mr. Canant: I was sent to Camp Pendleton, California, for marine basic training for three months. From there I was sent for a month to advanced infantry training. Afterwards I went to Okinawa for about seven months and was then shipped to the Armed Forces Staff College in Norfolk, Virginia. It was an officers' school, and we were also in charge of security at the base.

MR. RODRIGUEZ: YOU SERVED IN VIETNAM. COULD YOU TELL ME ABOUT YOUR EXPERIENCE THERE?

Mr. Canant: I was sent to Vietnam in February of 1965, and for the first four months we were on a floating battalion. Whenever help was needed we were sent in. Around June we finally landed and stayed and made a base camp at a place called Qui Nhon. We were there for several months and set up perimeters around certain areas they wanted protected. You would stay one week on the perimeter, one week on patrol, and one week resting inside the perimeter. We'd go out on reconnaissance patrols where we would locate the enemy and report on how many we saw, how many they were. Intelligence type of things to send back to the base.

MR. RODRIGUEZ: WHEN DID YOU START ATTACKING THE ENEMY?

Mr. Canant: See, we didn't start attacking the Viet Cong until August. Before this we were ordered not to shoot unless you

Willie Canant
—Courtesy Willie Canant

got shot at first. There were some advisors that advised the South Vietnamese's military on how to conduct operations. From August on it was fair game, our patrol missions were now on "search and destroy." In our first mission we got on some helicopters and it was at night; it had just gotten dark. Our company was dropped at a point. We gathered all together and proceeded to go help these people and we came under heavy mortar fire. I think about five in my company got killed and, if I remember, about twenty-something got wounded. It was my squad's responsibility to go get the wounded out of the rice paddies and bring them back. Then there was a lieutenant that was flagging in the helicopters. The wounded and dead were placed in the helicopters, and they would take off. We continued helping the units that were under attack until they weren't under attack anymore. Then there came daylight and we had captured several prisoners. We had to walk about twenty miles to a place that the helicopters could come and pick us up.

MR. RODRIGUEZ: WHAT WERE YOUR FEELINGS TOWARD THE PRISONERS?

Mr. Canant: During this time everybody was kind of angry with the POWs we had. Some started saying that we should kill them, but we never did. It was the way we were trained. Then an outfit came and took over the prisoners and then we could finally go back to the ship. For four months all we did was stay in the ship. If someone needed us, we were out there.

MR. RODRIGUEZ: SINCE YOU WERE ONE OF THE FIRST TO ARRIVE IN VIETNAM, WHAT WERE YOU EXPECTING?

Mr. Canant: This was a different kind of war; we were one of the first units deployed. We didn't know what to expect. This was guerrilla warfare where there were snipers; two or three guys would shoot several rounds and disappear into the jungle night. We didn't train for this type of warfare. We were only trained for conventional style of warfare.

When we were in Qui Nhon, it seems like every night the Viet Cong would set off booby traps and we'd shoot in their direction. By the following morning we would set off to locate bodies and we would find none. Six months later we got a report that some caves were found in Qui Nhon filled with many dead bodies. Our spirits lifted knowing that we were killing the enemy. The Viet Cong would take the bodies and take them to the caves; this is why we never found bodies.

On one occasion there was one

Willie Canant

guy that had us pinned down. We were up on a hill and he was down below. He would shoot two or three times and all of us would hit the floor. We would shoot back and he would disappear. We even sent in a helicopter to fire some rounds at him. Thinking he was dead, we proceeded, only to be shot at again. After a while it seemed comical that this one guy was keeping back 200 men until one of our guys shot and killed him.

In the first missions we were all scared and everybody was supporting everybody. After a few months of being there it seemed just like a job. You didn't think about getting shot at as much as when you first got there.

MR. RODRIGUEZ: WHEN DID YOU LEAVE THE AREA?

Mr. Canant: Around December my outfit got transferred to Okinawa and me and three other sergeants got picked to stay in Vietnam. They needed experienced men to teach the newcomers the patrol routes and everything. We showed them where the mines and booby traps were set up. We stayed until around May 1966, then I came back to the States. Once here I became a weapons instructor until I got out. I thought I would get out in June, but President Johnson had signed an order that extended everybody's stay. I finally got out in October 1967.

Compared to nowadays, you look at all the equipment and technology around. I wish we had the same technology back then.

Reynaldo Aguinaga
INTERVIEWED BY JUAN L. MARTINEZ

I had the honor of interviewing Mr. Reynaldo Aguinaga at his residence located on the east side of Brownsville. We sat comfortably at his dining table. Mr. Aguinaga and I started talking about the situation in Iraq and compared it to what the situation was in Vietnam when he served. A few minutes later, we got started on the interview of his tour in Vietnam.

MR. MARTINEZ: WHAT WERE YOU DOING BEFORE YOU WENT TO VIETNAM?

Mr. Aguinaga: I was working at the time that the Vietnam War was going on. I would hear the news about the situation in Vietnam. I recall that the situation looked to be worsening.

MR. MARTINEZ: HOW DID YOUR FAMILY REACT TO YOUR BEING DRAFTED?

Mr. Aguinaga: You could say that they were sad to hear the news that I had been drafted. They knew that I was off to war and that there was a possibility that I could be seriously wounded or killed.

MR. MARTINEZ: WHERE WERE YOU TO REPORT FOR TRAINING?

Mr. Aguinaga: I was sent to Fort Lewis, Washington, to receive my basic training. Fort Lewis is the largest army training base. After my basic training, I was stationed at Fort Ord, California. There I received individual training as a field telephone communication operator.

MR. MARTINEZ: AFTER THIS INDIVIDUAL TRAINING, WHAT HAPPENED NEXT?

Mr. Aguinaga: I was shipped out to Long Binh Army Base in Vietnam. On my way there, I could remember the sad faces and tears that were shed by my parents and family members. It's very hard to leave behind loved ones. You start to wonder whether this will be a temporary departure from their side or whether this might be your last goodbye and that there is the possibility that you might never see them again.

MR. MARTINEZ: WHEN YOU ARRIVED IN VIETNAM, WHAT WAS THE SCENE THERE?

Mr. Aguinaga: There was a lot of tension and stress. There were many soldiers who were seriously wounded. There were soldiers departing to the front lines and there were also soldiers returning in stretchers or in plastic body bags coming from the front lines. I was attached to the 101st Airborne Division. I served as a telephone communications operator in the fields of Bien Hoa, Tay Ninh, and Song Be in Vietnam. There was a lot of heavy combat during this time. There were a lot of incoming mortar firings. During the night I would stay in underground bunkers or in trenches whenever possible to avoid being hit. There were many casualties due to the heavy incoming mortars during the night. During the day you would find many dead in the fields. There were times that anywhere from 50 to 100 enemy corpses were found around the combat area.

MR. MARTINEZ: WHAT WAS DONE WITH THESE BODIES?

Mr. Aguinaga: The corpses were burned and taken to a dumping place. These corpses had to be cleared from the perimeter that we were in. The U.S. soldiers that were wounded or killed, they would be airlifted to Bien Hoa Army Base. The dead U.S. soldiers were flown back to the States, and the seriously wounded soldiers, too.

MR. MARTINEZ: COULD YOU TELL ME WHETHER YOU HAD ANY CLOSE COMMUNICATION WITH THE SOUTH VIETNAMESE SOLDIERS?

Mr. Aguinaga: I never had any involvement or close communications with South Vietnamese soldiers. They normally communicated with the officers.

MR. MARTINEZ: HOW OLD WERE YOU WHEN YOU WENT INTO THE SERVICE, AND HOW LONG WERE YOU IN THE SERVICE?

Mr. Aguinaga: I was twenty-two years old when I went into the army; I served from 1966 to 1970. I was in Vietnam for one year and then sent back to the U.S. I was sent to Fort Bliss in El Paso, Texas. I was stationed there for about sixteen months. [Then I was sent back to Vietnam.] This time around I was attached to the 1st Cavalry Division for the entire sixteen months while in Vietnam. After this second tour of duty in Vietnam, and having completed my tour and obligations to my country, I went out of the military service.

MR. MARTINEZ: WHAT CAN YOU TELL ME ABOUT MEALS AND WHETHER YOU HAD THE OPPORTUNITY TO BATHE?

Mr. Aguinaga: At campsite there were always hot meals. During field expeditions we carried canned food and "lurps" (meals mixed with water). Concerning your question in regards to bathing, you could take sometimes up to three weeks to bathe while you were away from camp. It was hard to find a place to bathe out in the combat fields.

MR. MARTINEZ: WHEN DID YOU RETURN TO THE STATES, AND HOW WAS YOUR LIFE BACK HOME?

Mr. Aguinaga: I returned back to the States in September 1970. I was happy to be back in the States and thankful to God for keeping me safe while I served in Vietnam. For about ten years, I went through bad dreams, anxiety, nervousness, and nightmares. I would recall in my dreams the combats and the heavy mortar firings while I was in Vietnam. I could see soldiers wounded or killed in my dreams. I will say that war is something that I would not wish anyone to go through.

Edward Moore
Interviewed by William Adams

This interview was conducted in my own home—in my study—on October 29, 2003. Colonel Moore is an old friend and colleague of mine at UT-Brownsville, where he now teaches courses in government and international affairs. He served in the U.S. Army from 1965 until his retirement in 1992. At retirement he held the rank of full colonel, and the latter years of his service were spent in army intelligence. The last position he held was deputy director for current intelligence at the Defense Intelligence Agency, and during Gulf War I he regularly briefed President George Bush. More recently, during Gulf War II, Colonel Moore was given a leave of absence from the university to serve as a military analyst for CNN-Turk, appearing in daily broadcasts to the Turkish people (Colonel Moore is fluent in Turkish) and offering expert commentary on the American invasion of Iraq and its diplomatic implications.

Colonel Moore served in Vietnam from October 1967 to January 1969, much of that time commanding a platoon of the 1st Infantry Division in the II Corps area, up near the Cambodian border. He earned a silver star, "two or three" bronze stars, the Air Medal (for more than twenty-five helicopter missions into and over hostile territory—including one mission into Cambodia to recover the body of the 1st Division's commanding general), two purple hearts, and the distinctive Combat Infantry Badge (a rectangular badge with a silver rifle on a sky blue background). "That was real status in Vietnam. You wore that."

DR. ADAMS: WHAT WERE YOU DOING BEFORE THE WAR?

Colonel Moore: Working at a textile mill in Martinsville, Virginia. I was in managerial training. I volunteered for the army. I wanted to leave town. I wanted to do something different. Plus I knew I would be drafted eventually. I wanted to put things in my own hands to some degree.

DR. ADAMS: HOW DID YOU ARRIVE IN VIETNAM? WHAT WAS THE FEELING?

Colonel Moore: Flew. From San Francisco on a civilian airline under contract to the military. I think it was Continental. Regular flight crew. San Francisco-Hawaii-Guam-Bien Hoa, outside Saigon. As a twenty-three-year-old—not really politically aware of what was going on in terms of the war—you didn't know what to expect. Apprehension of going somewhere new; apprehension of going into a combat zone. "Why did I do this to myself?" I don't think I felt fear—mainly apprehension. We were all quiet, reserved. No alcoholic beverages were served on the flight.

Col. Edward Moore
Courtesy of Edward Moore

Once we landed we were put in a bus with wire-mesh over the windows to stop grenades. That created a little bit of awe. We went to Long Binh to be processed. We were issued jungle fatigues, jungle boots. Then I was called to go on the back of a deuce-and-a-half and we drove to Di An. The 2nd Brigade, 1st Division was there. No one had bothered to give us a weapon yet.

DR. ADAMS: WHAT WAS A TYPICAL DAY LIKE?

Colonel Moore: If we were lucky we had one hot meal a day. Sometimes it was breakfast, sometimes it was lunch, sometimes it was supper. Start our patrols early in the morning, do whatever designated patrols we had from a base camp. We were sent to patrol near the Cambodian border to do search and destroy missions. Sometimes we would go into position for an ambush. Typical day? There was no typical day. Your day was determined by the battalion headquarters, brigade headquarters. You just had to be ready all the time. A lot of days were boring—posting highways for convoys or walking the same patrol over and over to secure U.S. base camps. A lot of rain, a lot of heat, a lot of leeches, a lot of red ants.

DR. ADAMS: DESCRIBE AN AMBUSH TO ME.

Colonel Moore: After the Tet Offensive—we fought in the streets of Saigon during the Tet Offensive—we moved east of Saigon to conduct patrols. I had a brand-new company commander—an ROTC captain.

My platoon was assigned an ambush, a squad-size ambush. We were going down into a rice paddy area to set up an ambush, expecting Viet Cong or NVA to pass. We had our backs to a water-filled dike area. Our claymore mines were out in front of

Tank

—Courtesy of Edward Moore

us. (They were the first thing we would blow in an ambush—to invoke terror.) When the bad guys came they were so close they were within the ambush! I radioed that I was about to blow the claymores ... and the company commander on the radio told me to: "Wait. Out." [Colonel Moore throws up his hands in despair recalling the stupidity of his company commander telling him to wait under those circumstances.] I went ahead and blew the ambush. Maybe fifteen enemy were in the ambush. We had mortar support. We got about nine and captured a couple. The rest got away.

DR. ADAMS: WHAT DID YOU DO WITH THE DEAD BODIES?

Colonel Moore: We left them there for their own people to reclaim.

DR. ADAMS: WHAT DID YOU DO WITH THE TWO PRISONERS, AND WHAT WERE THEY—VIET CONG OR NVA REGULARS?

Colonel Moore: Viet Cong. Black pajamas. Both had been wounded and stunned. We dragged them out to our back-up unit, who put them in tracks and hauled them off. Turned them over to battalion headquarters.

DR. ADAMS: WERE THEY YELLING, CRYING, WHAT?

Colonel Moore: I never saw a Vietnamese cry. Never. They were deathly quiet. Scared to death. They thought we were going to kill them.

DR. ADAMS: DID YOU EVER SEE PRISONERS KILLED, MISTREATED, OR CUT UP? ANY "SOUVENIR" TAKING?

Colonel Moore: I saw situations where soldiers were angry enough to do that, but

OFFICERS AND MEN IN THE 25 th U.S INFANTRY DIVISION

There will be more shelled attacks and annihilating battles which are fearer coming to you.

Our people's liberation armed forces are revolved to defeat the U.S aggressors who are causing a mourning of our native land. Our hostility towards the U.S aggressors and Thieu—Ky dictatorial traitors and determination to use ourselves blood and bone in view to winning independence and freedom will be our strength for overcoming of the enemies.

The day when the U S bellicose ringleader band still carry out the aggressive war and cover Thieu—Ky traitors, then we look you as the enemy number one of our nation.

However, the South Vietnam people have highly honoured and grately thankful the U.S people who have sympthized and supported our struggle for peace, independence, freedom and neutrality. That mean :

— The South Vietnam National Front For Liberation strictly observes its lenient policy towards the U.S presoners of war and enable and help them to return to their family if they recognize their sins against the Vietnamese people as the case of Claude Mc. Clure RA.14.703.075, black american and George Edward Smith RA.13.522.780.

— The Front kighly welcome the U.S citizen's struggles to demand Johnson administration to stop immediately the U.S aggressive war in South Vietnam.

— The Front highly praise the courage actions of your friends to opposse to your being sent to the battlefront massacreing our peasants in the liberated area. Only so doing you can look yourselves for away out.

— The Front will arrange the repatriation of anti—war US GI's crossing over to the Front's side.

ĐVĐX.01

there were almost always controls in place against this. I did once see an ear cut off a Viet Cong, but he was dead already. That was the only mutilation I ever saw.

The worst thing, the most hurtful thing to me, was when firefights started near villages and the Viet Cong used villagers as shields. Civilians ended up getting killed. It couldn't be avoided.

DR. ADAMS: DID YOU HATE YOUR ENEMY?

Colonel Moore: No. Well, I guess … No. I didn't hate them. The country was beautiful, the people exotic. The people wanted peace. The people we fought were pawns of their government just like we were. The most overriding feeling is the desire to survive. It's not about how many people you kill, but what you have to do to survive and get home. It outweighs any feeling of hatred.

DR. ADAMS: DID YOU HEAR OF ANY INSTANCES OF "FRAGGING"? [THESE WERE INSTANCES OF AMERICAN TROOPS SHOOTING OR THROWING FRAGMENTAION GRENADES AT THEIR OWN OFFICERS OR NON-COMMISSIONED OFFICERS.]

Colonel Moore: O-o-o-oh yes! Most of the fragging was in logistical units, transport units, not in the combat units. I never knew of any fragging in forward combat units.

DR. ADAMS: WHY DO YOU THINK THAT WAS?

Colonel Moore: In the rear areas the troops had much more time and freedom and resented their leadership. At rear areas they went drinking, had clubs, saw strippers, but factions between groups and races grew up. Also rear area officers were administrators and managers and not chosen for their leadership skills. We called them "REMFs"—"Rear Echelon Mother Fuckers," every word capitalized. Our men would shout it out to them from the back of trucks when we entered rear areas: "REMFs!"

When we went into a rear area our stand-down duty was to take care of their perimeter defense. We [combat units] had constant fighting, tight camaraderie, team spirit. We shared the same threats every day. We depended on each other. The others had peacetime army jobs. They had more resentment in the rear areas.

DR. ADAMS: WHEN YOU HAD MEN KILLED, WHAT WAS YOUR DUTY?

Colonel Moore: Evacuate them. No letters. That was taken care of by our company executive officer. Same with wounded. We evacuated and went on to our next operational responsibility. My job was to operate in the field.

DR. ADAMS: YOU HAVE TWO PURPLE HEARTS, ED. TELL ME HOW YOU GOT THOSE.

Colonel Moore: The first time was after Tet. One day on patrol we were out in a company-sized operation and made contact with the enemy. We brought in artillery and gunships and we were in a tree-line overlooking some rice paddies. And the enemy was along the rice paddies going into a stream bed. The gunships were making rocket runs parallel to our lines and one of the gunships fired more towards our position and shrapnel hit me in the right shoulder. I was treated at the battalion aid station.

Several months later we entered an enemy base camp area and were in a firefight that went late into the evening. We were low on ammunition and had helicopters coming in, dropping ammunition to us. And because it was dark, we had to have a way of letting the helicopters know where we were. So I had a strobe light (as company commander), and I put it in my helmet to hold it steady and turned the strobe light on. As soon as I did, the enemy started shooting rocket-propelled grenades at me and I took shrapnel in my back. It was two days before they could get us out. The medics did what they could for me until then.

DR. ADAMS: ED, I CAN'T ALWAYS GUESS THE RIGHT QUESTIONS TO BE ASKING IN THESE INTERVIEWS. WHAT STANDS OUT IN YOUR MEMORY AS SOMETHING THE READERS OF THIS BOOK MIGHT WANT TO KNOW, SHOULD KNOW? TAKE A COUPLE OF MINUTES TO THINK ABOUT IT IF YOU LIKE.

Colonel Moore: [After thinking for a bit, Colonel Moore, a large, "comfortable" man, who has up to this point been lounging rather comfortably on my study's leather sofa, sits up straight and places his hands firmly on his knees.] American soldiers are the greatest soldiers in the world. What stands out to me is how loyal soldiers are to each other in a crisis, in a firefight. I have watched people you'd never suspect of being a hero do things that demonstrated great heroism—and usually it was to protect their buddies. Most of the soldiers in my platoon were poor, disenfranchised, uneducated young men, and most of whom were minorities: Navajo Indians, African-American kids from the poorer urban areas of America, poor white kids right off the farm, one Mexican national who was told this would get him citizenship faster. And, in general, when the first shot was fired there was only one common goal: and that was to survive. These young men didn't think about color, ethnicity, or how much money they had. We had just that one common goal, and that was to survive.

DR. ADAMS: HOW DID THE WAR CHANGE YOU, FOR BETTER OR WORSE?

Colonel Moore: I think surviving that ordeal gave me a great deal of self-confidence. I think the self-confidence is derived from surviving that experience, where your life was on the line every day. The rest of your life will be relatively easy. I think whereas some of my counterparts from Vietnam, both officers and soldiers alike, got caught in a time warp and were never able to get over the experience, I moved on. I hope most of the young men I served with did the same. The American public, with all their anti-war sentiment, was telling all these young soldiers from Vietnam that they were losers. Unlike today with all the yellow ribbons and positive public opinion of the military, soldiers coming home from Vietnam were spit on and called "losers," blamed for the political failures of the entire nation. And for many of those Vietnam veterans that caused them to get caught in this time warp. Many started using drugs; many couldn't hold down a job. Vietnam veterans did their jobs the same as soldiers today, but the politics then were different and the public disowned them.

DR. ADAMS: ANYTHING ELSE, ED? ANYTHING AT ALL?

Colonel Moore: [He thinks for a few moments and then scatterguns this information at me.] We lived in holes, holes in the ground.

We depended on helicopters. If we were in the field for more than twenty-five days a helicopter would come out and drop us clean uniforms and pick up our dirty ones and take them away.

I was supported by every kind of fire while in Vietnam. I was supported by naval gunfire—even sixteen-inch shells coming from the *Missouri*. It was like Volkswagens coming in over your head. On a humid night the sound was like "swooooosh!" I was supported by napalm, by B-52s, and that was before smart bombs and the bombs were so inaccurate they wanted us at least ten kilometers away when the B-52s came in. Very dumb bombs!

My OCS class sticks together. We have raised money to create memorials in their hometowns for all of our classmates who were killed in Vietnam.

The 1st Infantry Division didn't allow drinking in the field. It had pride. It had people who wanted to be in it. It had a great history: the Battle of the Bulge in World War II; the Second Battle of the Marne in World War I.

My battalion commander in the 1st Division was Richard Cavazos of Kingsville, who later became a four-star general and has General Cavazos Drive named for him in Kingsville. Two of my medics were from the Valley. One was from San Benito; one from Rio Grande City. The one from San Benito is now in charge of special education in the San Benito School District. His daughter Melissa was one of my students here at UTB. We went to her wedding when she was married. Those two medics introduced me to Mexican food in Vietnam: tamales out of a can.

Luis Martinez
Interviewed by Edith Lizbeth Cano

I had known Mr. Martinez for a while since he worked at the county courthouse. I met with him on June 24, 2003, at the bowling alley in Brownsville. I got the impression that he didn't want to talk too much about the Vietnam War.

MS. CANO: WHERE WERE YOU BORN?
Mr. Martinez: I was born here in Brownsville on October 31, 1947.
MS. CANO: DID YOU VOLUNTEER TO GO INTO THE ARMY?
Mr. Martinez: I graduated in 1967, from Brownsville High School. At that time the Vietnam War had started and people were being drafted. As a Valley resident, I decided to enlist in the service rather than to go to college because we didn't have the money to pay for the college tuition. I thought that it was better to join the service and get an education through the service, so I volunteered.

MS. CANO: HOW DID YOUR PARENTS REACT WITH YOU GOING TO VIETNAM?
Mr. Martinez: Well, back then it was pretty regular that family members lost their sons or daughters to the service. At the time I believe it was only one child could go to Vietnam if two or more were enlisted to the service. I believe that was it, but I was the oldest of the family and I was the one that was sent.

MS. CANO: WHEN DID THEY SEND YOU TO VIETNAM?

Mr. Martinez: July 9, 1967.

MS. CANO: HOW DID YOU GET TO VIETNAM?

Mr. Martinez: After the completion of basic training at Fort Hood, they sent me home for a thirty-day leave. I was here in Brownsville for thirty days. Then I was flown to Seattle, Washington. From there we flew to Cam Ranh Bay, Republic of Vietnam. That was like a depot for all arriving troops in Vietnam at that time. When we got there we had incoming fire and it was a hostile environment. Afterwards, we flew to Pleiku. I was in the north central highlands, thirty miles from Cambodia.

MS. CANO: HOW WAS THE MORALE OF THE TROOPS THROUGHOUT THE VIETNAM WAR?

Mr. Martinez: Well, Vietnam was not a very popular war. It was not a supportive war. We were sent there. We had to look out for our own lives so we did the best we could, but the morale was not very high because we knew we didn't have the support of the people. I mean back in the States they were burning the flag, and you saw that right after the My Lai incident they started calling the United States soldiers "baby killers." We felt we didn't have the support of the people and that is not a morale builder. Morale was low.

MS. CANO: HOW DID YOU REACT TO THE PEACE MOVEMENT THAT WAS GOING ON IN THE UNITED STATES?

Mr. Martinez: Well, we didn't know what we didn't hear. When we were out in the jungle—and I'm talking about doing everything over there—we didn't know about the peace movement. We knew it was going on because we had read it. When we got newsletters, they sent us newspaper clippings and we knew what was going on, but we didn't hear of them on an everyday basis. We were out fighting, out in the bush. We had no radios, no TV. We had no means of communication except among our squad leaders and company commanders that were giving us orders. We knew that it was not a happy environment in the States.

MS. CANO: WHAT WOULD YOU SAY WAS YOUR FIRST REACTION TO VIETNAM?

Mr. Martinez: As an eighteen-year-old kid, that hasn't seen anything, didn't know what killing was, I didn't know what a dismembered body looked like. I was scared. I cried for a whole week because I was scared. But you get used to it. I was a young boy who hadn't been anywhere before.

MS. CANO: WERE YOU IN ANY MAJOR BATTLES?

Mr. Martinez: All battles were major because you fight to save your own life. That's a major thing, a major battle. You talk about "major battles," every day we had to fight.

MS. CANO: WHAT WAS YOUR SPECIALTY?

Mr. Martinez: Infantry. I was with Three-Five Cav., First Cavalry Division, Third Battalion.

MS. CANO: BOB HOPE WENT TO VIETNAM TO LIFT THE MORALE OF THE TROOPS. DID YOU EVER SEE HIM?

Ms. Martinez: No, I was a fighting man. I was not a "take-it-easy soldier." Bob Hope went to where there was peace.

MS. CANO: COULD YOU TELL ME AN INTERESTING ASPECT OF VIETNAM?

Mr. Martinez: Beautiful country. It was a shame that it was messed up with bombs.

MS. CANO: COULD YOU TELL ME ONE OF YOUR WORST EXPERIENCES IN THE VIETNAM WAR?

Mr. Martinez: Killing of my friends, dead, every day.

MS. CANO: DID YOU EVER COME IN CONTACT WITH AGENT ORANGE?

Mr. Martinez: I don't know. Possibly. I know that over the years I developed a heart condition. I have what they call "Jungle Rot PC" because I was in water all the time. My toenails are long and easy to take off. They are not like yours that are shiny. I was in water in the rice paddy. We hardly ever kept our clothing dry. It was always wet. Our feet were always wet.

MS. CANO: WHAT WAS YOUR OBJECTIVE IN THE NORTH CENTRAL HIGHLANDS?

Mr. Martinez: Killing the North Vietnamese. The objective was to kill.

MS. CANO: HOW LONG WERE YOU IN THE VIETNAM WAR?

Mr. Martinez: One year. We were replaced by fresh meat.

MS. CANO: WHEN YOU CAME HOME, HOW DID THE PEOPLE TREAT YOU?

Mr. Martinez: It was very ugly. We were not looked at as today's Desert Storm and Operation Freedom troops. They had parades for them. During the Vietnam War, people looked at us with the uniform and called us "scum." We were not honored at the American Legion Post, and the Veterans of Foreign Wars Hall did not honor us as veterans because supposedly it was the "Cold War," not a real major war like World War I and World War II. It was a "conflict." To this day I don't feel that we get the recognition that we deserve. I mean we did what the government asked us to do. We didn't want to be there. Like the boys that went before us to Korea and Japan, they were paraded, celebrated and called "heroes." We were called "baby killers." That is not something you can be proud of. You look at his perspective: if you killed a child, it was because that child was armed with grenades. The enemy has no age limit. A child, a woman, an elderly person can kill. So you have to protect yourself and your buddies, the American soldiers. Any time in a hostile environment, you have to look after your welfare. You cannot let your guard down. Anybody is a potential killer. Even your own soldiers. What happened here in Iraq, a soldier that dropped the grenade into the commanding camp? People go crazy. It is very hard. You are always on guard. I think they took that My Lai incident out of perspective and they labeled every American soldier a "baby killer" because of that incident.

MS. CANO: HOW MANY PEOPLE MADE IT OUT OF YOUR PLATOON?

Mr. Martinez: My company was 200 and something. I know I lost abut forty or fifty of my fellow soldiers. They were killed.

MS. CANO: HOW DID YOU FEEL WHEN VIETNAM BECAME A COMMUNIST COUNTRY?

Mr. Martinez: Well, the time that I was there and the time that I left, I always thought that we were fighting for something where we had no business. People didn't really believe in themselves. They just gave up. The North Vietnamese just overran the South Vietnamese right after we left. So the lives we lost and the blood we shed was to no avail. They gave up so easily.

MS. CANO: DID YOU MEET ANY OF THE SOUTH VIETNAMESE TROOPS?

Mr. Martinez: I lived with them. We lived with them.

MS. CANO: DID YOU TAKE ANY TYPE OF IMMUNIZATIONS BEFORE YOU LEFT FOR VIETNAM?

Mr. Martinez: Oh, yes. We took every type of immunization there is: yellow fever, small pox, tetanus. I mean we just walked the hallway and they let us have it in both arms with air guns. When we came back we spent one week in quarantine in San Francisco. We were placed in an air base for a whole week. They never told us why. They said that everybody that comes back to the States has to be quarantined.

MS. CANO: HOW WAS IT DIFFERENT WHEN YOU CAME BACK?

Mr. Martinez: Brownsville had an expressway. It didn't have one when I left. We had some major road changes. And the town had grown a little more. It was not the Brownsville that I knew. I smoked and drank when I came back. I didn't smoke or drink when I went into the service. Basically, I knew how to be on my own. When I left to the service I was freshly out of high school. It had only been fifteen days that I had graduated and went to the service. From there I learned how to cook, sew, dress my uniform, and do laundry. It was different.

MS. CANO: DO YOU REMEMBER YOUR COMMANDER?

Mr. Martinez: My unit commander was Colonel Greene. He was killed.

MS. CANO: DID YOU BRING ANYTHING FROM VIETNAM?

Mr. Martinez: Bad memories. Real bad memories. That is all I brought back. I didn't want to bring anything back.

[Mr. Martinez today works at the Pro Shop at the Galaxy Bowling Alley. He still feels very strongly about Vietnam. He doesn't believe that there is any respect for the American flag. He also believes that veterans are not being honored for their sacrifice, especially here in the Valley. Mr. Martinez feels that veterans need the help. There are homeless and sick veterans in the Valley that he feels the government should provide for. After all, they went to Vietnam with no questions asked.]

Richard Wilson
Interviewed by Justin Lawrence

Richard Wilson, a native of Memphis, Tennessee, came to the Rio Grande Valley in 1953. During the Vietnam War he served with the U.S. Army Security Agency from 1967 to 1970.

MR. LAWRENCE: WHAT DID YOU DO IN THE ARMY SECURITY AGENCY IN VIETNAM?

Mr. Wilson: I ended up being a courier—top secret and secret courier. Intelligence. You know, what's going on, troop movements.

MR. LAWRENCE: HOW DID THEY GATHER INTELLIGENCE?

Mr. Wilson: Late '67 and early '68, the U.S. Army Intelligence Agency captured a code book of North Vietnam, without them knowing it, so for the next eighteen months we broke all their codes. We knew everything they were doing.

MR. LAWRENCE: WASN'T THAT THE YEAR OF THE TET OFFENSIVE?

Mr. Wilson: The Tet Offensive started in January of '68.

MR. LAWRENCE: SO YOU SAW IT COMING?

Mr. Wilson: Yes...well...yes and no. We knew there was something going on, but I don't think we had any idea of how big it was going to be. You realize, the Tet Offensive was over in thirty-five to forty days.

MR. LAWRENCE: SO YOU WERE A COURIER. DID YOU LIKE HIKE THROUGH THE JUNGLE AS A COURIER?

Mr. Wilson: Every courier is assigned an area and I had four cities, four landing zones near cities. I would go to those four, pick up what they had, and transfer it to wherever it had to go.

MR. LAWRENCE: DID YOU SEE ANY ACTION?

Mr. Wilson: Well, yeah, the landing zones were always attacked; the bases were always attacked.

MR. LAWRENCE: WHAT WOULD THE LANDING ZONE LOOK LIKE? WOULD IT LOOK LIKE A FORT OR LIKE A CLEARING IN THE JUNGLE?

Mr. Wilson: No, it would look like a hill with the point chopped off. They were the highest peaks in the area next to the city. My cities were Hue, Khe Sahn...it's been a long time. There are four areas in Vietnam, they call them "Corps." The first one at the top is called "I Corps," where the DMZ is, and that's where I was. I was stationed just a mile or two from the DMZ.

MR. LAWRENCE: THEN YOU PROBABLY SAW THE MOST ACTION THERE, RIGHT?

Mr. Wilson: No, it depends. It depends. I think the most action was probably on the border between Cambodia and Laos.

Again, when you saw action, it was not like the war you saw last month. [Referring to the 2nd Iraq War.] We went in and established bases. The smaller bases were called "landing zones" and the 101st Airborne had a landing zone. The 1st Cavalry had a landing zone. The 3rd Marines were in Phu Bai until they were transferred up to the DMZ area, which was some pretty heavy stuff.

During the time I was there, you know strategy shifted from what they call big heavy pushes, where you would go in and just destroy an area, to search and destroy missions, where, with specific intelligence, you snuck out at night and stayed out and you would search a village and destroy whatever you could and then another village and another village. Remember, we're not fighting a uniformed enemy.

MR. LAWRENCE: SO YOU HAD ACCESS TO CLASSIFIED DOCUMENTS?

Mr. Wilson: We had documents on anybody who was senior sergeant and above.

We had their photograph, where they went to school, what they studied, and the books they read. Everything. From the sergeants and up.

MR. LAWRENCE: DO YOU REMEMBER ANYTHING INTERESTING ABOUT HO CHI MINH?

Mr. Wilson: Ho Chi Minh once said—we recorded him one time in his regular radio address to the people—that he was going to eat breakfast in our mess hall, because all Vietnamese looked alike to the Americans, and they would never know that he was in there.

MR. LAWRENCE: HOW WAS THE MORALE THROUGHOUT THE WAR?

Mr. Wilson: Well, it was fairly high, I think, up until the My Lai massacre, and then I think it went way down.

MR. LAWRENCE: THAT WAS WIDELY PUBLICIZED?

Mr. Wilson: You know we had so many events; we took off at night so war protesters couldn't see us take off. We landed at night so that we couldn't see how bad the protests were. Most everybody took off from Oakland and came back, and there just were hundreds of thousands of protesters. The war protesters had great influence on the morale of the soldiers. When I was over there, Robert Kennedy was shot, and so was Martin Luther King. When Dr. King was shot, almost every place in Vietnam was shut down. All the black soldiers were severely warned that they were not to cause trouble.

MR. LAWRENCE: WHEN YOU CAME HOME, WHAT WERE THE PROTESTS LIKE?

Mr. Wilson: They would threaten us and call us "baby killers." There were tens of thousands of them. I landed about one or two o'clock in the morning. They taxied us up to this barn. We changed our clothes into civilian clothes and we flew home in civilian clothes.

MR. LAWRENCE: WHEN YOU SEE PROTESTERS OF THE WAR THAT JUST HAPPENED IN IRAQ, DOES IT AROUSE ANY FEELINGS OF RESENTMENT?

Mr. Wilson: No, you know, I think war protests are good. I think it keeps the leaders honest. Military people are tough people. Their job is to kill. If you ask any marine what his job is, he'll tell you that. So, I think they encourage wars.

MR. LAWRENCE: WERE YOU DRAFTED?

Mr. Wilson: Actually, I was drafted,

Richard Wilson

130 Vietnam War

but then I joined. When you're drafted, you have no choices. When you join, then you have some choices.

MR. LAWRENCE: SO YOU WANTED TO GO INTO THE ARMY?

Mr. Wilson: No, I wanted to go somewhere where I wouldn't go to Vietnam. They promised me I wouldn't go there. They lied. But for me, it was all very interesting. My job was pretty good; I got to fly a lot in helicopters. I got overseas pay, housing pay, flight pay, on top of regular pay, which I sent to my parents.

MR. LAWRENCE: DID YOU HAVE ANY INTELLIGENCE ON RUSSIAN OFFICIALS?

Mr. Wilson: We killed a lot of Russians. You know how in Afghanistan, during the eighties, Russia invaded, and America funded the rebels? Well, in Vietnam it was the reverse. We invaded, actually coming to the assistance at the invitation of the South Vietnamese, but they took it as an invasion. The enemy that we fought, primarily, was Chinese. All of the weapons that we faced, all of those SAMs that shot down the pilots, were either Russian or Chinese made. We killed many Russians. We killed tens of thousands of Chinese. Almost all of the officers were Chinese. Probably taken out of Vietnam at, say, seventeen and trained in China, and taken back to Vietnam. All the weapons were Chinese. The rice that we found was wrapped in Chinese letters.

They had a base on the northern border of Vietnam and they had a base of about 250,000 soldiers, mostly probably supply. Huge aircraft. And we always just wanted to bomb that place, but we just couldn't. But it supplied. It was a trail. Have you heard of "Arc Lights"?

MR. LAWRENCE: ARE THEY THOSE LIGHTS THAT YOU ...

Mr. Wilson: No an Arc Light is a B-52 strike. You have intelligence, for example, this is in the old days when technology was young, for example, when a transmitter would transmit, we would have an antenna in South Vietnam; we would have one in Thailand, one in Okinawa, one in the Philippines; we would have maybe ten or fifteen antennae, and when a transmitter would go off, it would go off at a certain frequency, and we would shoot a beam from those antennae right to there, and we could get within a hundred yards of where that transmitter was. And you could tell an awful lot.

Remember the *Pueblo*, the ship captured by the North Koreans? We would have a ship that would record that information onto a plot on a map, and when we would see a number of transmitters go off, we knew there were some large troop movements. And they would talk to each other, and we knew there was a convoy, or a unit. We would call out of Bangkok, Thailand, which was flight time from the time the buzzer went off, and it would take maybe twenty minutes for that aircraft to get there. It would take five to ten minutes of flight time. They would locate the target; fly over at 35 to 40 thousand feet. We had ground intelligence units that would call in and say what we had hit. Since we were in the I Corps, quite a bit of our intelligence was coordinating Arc Lights.

The other things we would be able to control were motion sensors. We had probably 20,000 motion sensors. A motion sensor could sense probably anything big, like a man walking by, and it would transmit a frequency. Let's say if it were 50 hertz it would be a man; if it were 500 hertz it would be a vehicle; if it were 1,000 hertz it would be a big vehicle. One of the things that made the newspaper at the time, that I got to see, was that we had these enormous readings. We sent some planes to take out the site, and we went to investigate. It was about twenty-five elephants.

Jose Gonzalez
Interviewed by Edward J. Garcia

I interviewed Jose Gonzalez in his Brownsville home on April 16, 2003. Jose Gonzalez is a native of the Brownsville area and is currently working as an administrator for the local school district. After his years of service he returned to school and obtained his masters in education at Texas Southmost College.

MR. GARCIA: HOW DID YOU GET INTO THE MILITARY?

Mr. Gonzalez: I served, well, actually I was drafted in 1966. I got a letter from "Uncle Sam." In December of 1966 I went to talk to a recruiter and at that point in time I decided to volunteer for the United States Army.

MR. GARCIA: WHERE DID YOU RECEIVE YOUR TRAINING?

Mr. Gonzalez: I attended the communications school, but before that I received my basic training in Fort Polk, Louisiana, for eight weeks. From there I went to Fort Gordon, Georgia, and that's where I received my training for communications specialist.

MR. GARCIA: HOW LONG WERE YOU IN TRAINING?

Mr. Gonzalez: I was in training in Fort Gordon for sixteen weeks.

MR. GARCIA: FROM THERE THEY SENT YOU OFF?

Mr. Gonzalez: I joined the army on the 31st of January, 1967, and on July 31, 1967, I was sent overseas to Saigon.

MR. GARCIA: WHAT WERE SOME OF YOUR DUTIES IN SAIGON?

Mr. Gonzalez: Well, I didn't really start doing what I was trained for when I first got there. All I did was fill up sandbags, detail, and put on guard duty. Until five months after I got there I finally worked as a teletype operator. I did that until August of 1969.

MR. GARCIA: WHOSE COMMAND WERE YOU UNDER WHEN YOU WERE STATIONED AT SAIGON?

Mr. Gonzalez: I don't recall. I wasn't in Saigon very long. I was there for about five days before I went to Long Binh. Long Binh was this place twenty to twenty-five miles north from Saigon. That's where I stayed for eleven months and performed my duty as a teletype operator.

MR. GARCIA: WHAT'S A TELETYPE OPERATOR?

Mr. Gonzalez: A teletype operator is someone that works this machine that's like a typewriter. This machine would send messages through wavelengths. I think they're called microwaves. I don't know. [Laughs.] Basically my job was to establish communications between one base and another.

MR. GARCIA: WHAT WERE YOU DOING BEFORE THE WAR?

Mr. Gonzalez: I was a bum! [Laughs.] Before I was drafted I did attend college. I took a few hours. I went to school for about a year and a half. After that I went ahead and decided to go and join the military. I was not going to school full time; I was going part time. So that had an effect on my status. I graduated from high school at the age of nineteen, and at the age of twenty I joined the military.

MR. GARCIA: WHILE YOU WERE IN THE SERVICE DID YOU FEEL ANY TYPE OF DISCRIMINATION BECAUSE OF YOUR RACE?

Mr. Gonzalez: No.

MR. GARCIA: DID YOU TALK TO ANY SOUTH VIETNAMESE, AND, IF SO, WHAT WAS THEIR OPINION OF THE WAR?

Mr. Gonzalez: Well, the people that you would talk to are pro-American of course, and you don't know if they're being truthful or not. But most of the people in the local area did need help because it was a country that was in war and had been in war for many years ... even before the Americans got there. So the locals were really looking forward for somebody to liberate them from what their country had been going through for so many years. I think they were sincerely grateful.

MR. GARCIA: WHAT DID YOU DO FOR ENTERTAINMENT WHEN YOU WERE STATIONED IN LONG BINH?

Mr. Gonzalez: For entertainment we played chess. Basically we just hung around until we were assigned an assignment. I don't remember the date, but Bob Hope came by with some entertainer to entertain us.

MR. GARCIA: WHAT MEMORIES ARE YOU LEFT WITH AFTER PARTICIPATING IN THE WAR?

Mr. Gonzalez: Well, you kind of learn to appreciate what you have here. You know we have a lot to be thankful for. So I guess I experienced how other people live and compared to that country I think we have a lot more privileges and freedom here than other nations.

MR. GARCIA: DID YOU LOSE ANYONE CLOSE TO YOU?

Mr. Gonzalez: Yeah ... my cousin died. He was a POW. They never found his body so ... [his voice crumbles] they declared him dead. Some close friends of mine also died in the war and they entered the military the same time I did.

MR. GARCIA: HOW DID IT FEEL COMING BACK HOME?

Mr. Gonzalez: It felt great! Even though I did not engage in any firefights or anything, we did experience a lot of "incoming." So I got a taste of what it was like being shot at also being around explosions and things of that sort. So for me coming back home was really great because it was so peaceful comparing it to over there. You know you wake up every morning and expect the unexpected. It's not an easy life when you live in a place like that and you feel more for the people that live there because they're kind of stuck there. If you were lucky, you were there for a year and out.

MR. GARCIA: HOW DID YOUR FAMILY FEEL WHEN YOU LEFT?

Mr. Gonzalez: It was a sad moment. I'm sure my family didn't know what was going to happen, especially when you hear in the news that people are dying. Even people in my unit were dying. It wasn't a frontline attack; it was more of guerrilla-type warfare.

MR. GARCIA: WHAT WAS YOUR OPINION OF THE WAR AT THAT TIME? DO YOU STILL FEEL THE SAME WAY NOW?

Mr. Gonzalez: For one thing you serve your country whether you think your government is right or wrong. You feel that you're doing it for the well-being of your country. When you're over there you see how these people are living and you feel you're doing your part to liberate them. I think this war was more of a political war. I don't know; I have mixed feelings about the Vietnam War. I feel that nothing was accomplished. I mean, had we not gone, nobody would have been killed. I think things would have turned out to be the same, which they did anyway. So I think it was a lost cause!

Juan Torres
Interviewed by David Rodriguez

Juan Torres sits outside as I pull up to his residence. As I walk up to greet him, I see that he is an easygoing man who wears a constant smile. He is a veteran of the Vietnam War, having served one year beginning April 13, 1967. Mr. Torres was in infantry until leaving Vietnam with a rank of E-5. We move inside to the kitchen area where the noise of the busy street can only bother us slightly. As we move, I notice that he is a man of short stature.

MR. RODRIGUEZ: DID YOU ENLIST OR WERE YOU DRAFTED?
Mr. Torres: I was drafted.
MR. RODRIGUEZ: WHAT WERE YOU DOING BEFORE YOU WERE DRAFTED?
Mr. Torres: I had just finished high school. I was nineteen.
MR. RODRIGUEZ: AFTER YOU WERE DRAFTED, WHERE WERE YOU SENT?
Mr. Torres: I was sent to Fort Polk, Louisiana. I was there for three months. Three months' basic training, and one more month advanced, you know, infantry training. Then I was going to be sent to North Carolina for parachute, but they were running out of people, so they sent us like that. It was actually only three months, four months. Then they sent you back home for a month. Then you went for your tour. So the day you get there, from the day you get there, a year from there. Not one day more, not one day less, unless you got wounded or get shot that bad. Then they send you back home. But actually just one year from the day you got there and the day you come back.
MR. RODRIGUEZ: AFTER YOUR TRAINING AND HOME LEAVE, WHERE WERE YOU SENT?
Mr. Torres: I was sent to Vietnam, well Saigon, then An Loc, where I was sta-

tioned. I worked out of that base. Actually it was just a base out in the woods. It was just a base, and I worked out of there, for a whole year there. But I was in different things. The first three months I was in infantry, and then my company got wiped out. Out of 150 there were only 32 of us left. So they decided they'd split us up. So they told me, "You wanna go in the 'tracks'?" [Half track armored vehicles.] You know like the tanks. So I said, "Well, why not? Beats walking." So I lasted there four months. Then after a while I didn't like it too much, because as soon as you were stopped by the enemy, we were the first ones to go in. It was all right because you knew you had metal, but you could still hear the "*pip, pip, pip*." [Mr. Torres uses an audible sound to explain bullets hitting the vehicle he was in.] So then I went to basic command they had there for scout teams. So I said, "Well, I'm gonna go apply for that." So I went in there, and the guy told me look at my size. You know how guys are. And I said, "Uh, I want to see if I can get into the scout team. How does this work out?" He said you only go out three days a week, which would be Monday, Wednesday, and Friday. You only go out in a group of six, and then all night. They go and leave you around 5:30 or 6:00 at one checkpoint. Then you walk about eight or ten clicks, which is in miles, and they'll pick you up in the morning. All you do is scout. And that's what we did all night. So I did that for three more months.

MR. RODRIGUEZ: YOU WERE SAYING BEFORE THAT WHEN YOU FIRST GOT THERE THAT YOUR SQUAD WAS WIPED OUT. WAS THAT IN FIGHTING?

Mr. Torres: Oh, yeah. It was going up a hill. Yeah, up on my perimeter.

MR. RODRIGUEZ: DID YOU FIRE ON ANY PEOPLE?

Mr. Torres: Oh yeah! [I can see a thought come over his face, and his smile temporarily leaves.] It's like my sergeant told me, "Everything you see here, you're gonna see it. So when you see it, don't get scared, 'cause you already saw it." I mean, the guy who trained me had been there two years in Vietnam. "Like I told you, I'm gonna show you everything I can, and so when you see it, don't panic, don't hesitate, just do it, and we'll talk about it later." There's no law out there. It was dog eat dog. Women or whatever, anything that's out there in the woods didn't belong out there. That's very simple. It gets to a point when you have to shoot them, too. I don't like it. It's a different issue of war for me, because over there you couldn't see them. It was all jungle. It was bad. All green, green, green.

MR. RODRIGUEZ: WERE YOU EVER SHOT?

Mr. Torres: Yeah, I got shot three times. Shot once in the shoulder. [He points to his left shoulder just above the collarbone.] One right here. [He now points to the far right side of his stomach.] And one on the back with a shrapnel. [He reaches around to touch his back.]

MR. RODRIGUEZ: WHAT'S IT LIKE TO BE SHOT?

Mr. Torres: It hurts. [The words leave his mouth with a laugh.] Well, the good thing is, it didn't hit the bone. [This is in reference to his shoulder.] See the bone here. It just went through. Burned the hell out of me. That really helped. That's why I got sent back. If it would have broken my bone they probably would have sent me home. The second time was just a flesh wound. It came in through here and out through here. [He gestures toward the entry and exit of the wound.] The guy just came out of nowhere. Good thing I turned. If I wouldn't have turned I would have gotten it good. So I just turned, and boom! He got me right here. I fell down and the other guys got me. I got sent back that time too. Every time it was two weeks in Japan. Which was nice. I would go back, and they would say, "Nope, send him back." So I went back. It was real bad because there was not enough infantry at the time. When I first got there.... "Huh!" you all go as the plane comes in. Every plane was like 300, 400 soldiers going that way. So I was there for five days in this depot where they disciplined the soldiers. So then I told the guy, "Hey, how come every company gots their different amounts? You know twenty, eighteen, five, fifteen." He said, "No, those are the replacements for the ones who got killed last night." So if the amount was twenty-five, then twenty-five got killed last night, and we're replacing those guys. That's the way it was. The more days you're there, you get the hang of it, you know. *Asi* [like that] you come right now and by five o'clock you would be in a plastic bag there. So actually, you didn't have time to really think. You rely on the guy you're with, but you could you know *asi como estamos* [as we are]. Only the platoon that you're with, two, three months and you start getting those bonds with them. So everybody knew their jobs. And didn't matter the size, as long as you did. You know I was short compared to them. I gonna show you a picture of that. They're all about 6'1, and I'm the shortest one. But like I said, when I went out there, those guys there were on their second tour, so it really helped me out. Because I would have been in bad shape if I had gone to a green company. They helped me out. As long as I did my part and that was it. If a guy said stay and watch our backs, okay I did my part.

MR. RODRIGUEZ: SO YOU BASICALLY FED OFF THEIR KNOWLEDGE?

Mr. Torres: Until I learned more and more.

MR. RODRIGUEZ: YOU SAID AFTER TWO OR THREE MONTHS YOU WOULD ESTABLISH A BOND WITH A COUPLE OF GUYS THERE. DID YOU EVER LOSE ANY FRIENDS?

Mr. Torres: Oh, yeah. We lost a whole bunch. And the people who complain about this war [Second Iraq War] that they lost 140 or whatever, we used to lose 200 a night. I mean in the whole day. So why are they crying? In a war you're gonna lose people. I mean that's the way it is. [Mr. Torres lets out a sigh, and seems upset at thoughts in his head.]

MR. RODRIGUEZ: WITHIN YOUR SQUAD, WHAT RESPONSIBILITIES DID YOU CARRY?

Mr. Torres: After my third month, I had my own "track." We went to the meetings and we just followed what they put up on the map in the morning for our sector, and what we had to do and just sweep. Well actually the big tanks would just sweep the area. There were like twenty of us, so they could hear us. If you were miles away they could hear if you were coming. Sometimes there would be like forty "tracks." Ten maybe go one way, then we would set up an ambush. Sweep so when they would come out we would catch them over here. Everything was like a hunt, a rabbit hunt. That's all it was. You would go out there, they knew where you were at all the time.

Cause they were in their country. Americans were clumsy, *hablando* [talking]. Sometimes when I had the company I would go all the way to the back. Good thing I was flexible. I go back and forth. But once you got on that mountain they learned their lesson. But see I was a rookie, just two or three months each guy. Then you get these lieutenants that knew it all. Say you know the books and everything, but it's on-the-job training out there. Yeah, when I was about eight months or nine months I had my own squad. I would say, "Just hang on. No disrespect, just hang on. You know where you go I'll follow you." Then you say, "I was just telling you to wait." Ah, two weeks later they popped him, *pobre vato* [poor guy]. They wouldn't take your advice. I mean I was just advising you not ordering you. Just hang on, I ain't in no rush to get up there. Haven't you seen that movie "Hamburger Hill"? Sometimes we had those hills like that and you have to go up, and, hey, why rush? I didn't have to be the first one on top. At first I didn't care if I got shot. Hey, I go home. But yeah, when I got to about two or three months, then I started worrying about getting out of there.

MR. RODRIGUEZ: WHAT DOES IT FEEL LIKE TO TAKE THE LIFE OF ANOTHER PERSON?

Mr. Torres: The first time you feel sick, you feel like throwing up. But once you get over the first one, it's just "yeah." Because you already saw it from the training. You just have to. You don't wanna do it, but it got to the point where it was you or him. The guys make fun of you. Yeah, just get over. You just got here. You still have a lot more to go. The guys that were there, like I said, had been there for a while. So they would make fun of you as you were throwing up. But, after you get the first one … After my fourth day the sergeant said, "Can you shoot?" And I said, "Yeah." So when we go on patrol you're always the third guy. So when we go to the villages, you go out about twenty yards and set yourself. We're gonna go and flush them out. If anything comes out running, you get him. If you miss him, you need to go look for him. So you couldn't miss him. So one or two guys, they would go to the village, and you start seeing them running in black fatigues, running like hell. So you had to catch them in the fields. Back then I had a "14." It was a lot heavier than an M-16; for what we used it for it was good, like snipers. At 350 yards it was a sure thing; after that it was kind of hard. The sergeant got mad. Too many came out, you can't get them all. You missed him, you can go look for him. And no prisoners, because we would have to stay up all night guarding them. At first—real dummies—we would get them and they would come for them in a helicopter and the South Vietnamese would take them back to Saigon and throw them out of the helicopter. So what was the point of working our butts off two or three hours to get one then throw them out? It was just a big chaos.

Epitacio Lopez
Interviewed by Carlos Garza

On a sunny day, typical of a Brownsville, Texas, April afternoon, I was lucky to secure an interview with Epitacio Lopez, a four-year veteran of the United States

Army, 1966-1969. His first year he was stationed in Germany and the remainder in Vietnam. The interview was conducted in the third-floor boardroom of the South Building at the University of Texas at Brownsville. The boardroom made for an ideal setting, because of its beautiful view of the Fort Brown Resaca and the vast military history of the area.

MR. GARZA: DID YOU ENLIST, OR WERE YOU DRAFTED INTO SERVICE?

Mr. Lopez: I enlisted in 1966, but I was disappointed because I was sent to Germany; I wanted to go to Vietnam. I asked for a transfer and received one in 1967.

MR. GARZA: HOW OLD WERE YOU?

Mr. Lopez: I was nineteen years old.

MR. GARZA: WHERE DID YOU LAND IN VIETNAM?

Mr. Lopez: I received a thirty-day leave, which I took in Brownsville. I flew out of Brownsville on what I believe was a Braniff Airlines 707, which took me to Oakland and, after several stops along the way, we landed at Cam Ranh Bay, Vietnam.

MR. GARZA: CAN YOU TELL ME ABOUT AN INCIDENT OR BATTLE THAT YOU WERE A PART OF?

Mr. Lopez: During the Tet Offensive was the worst part of my stay in Vietnam. Everyone in South Vietnam got involved; there was a constant attack on our camp, and I could actually see the enemy.

MR. GARZA: WHAT DID YOU THINK OF THE VIETNAMESE?

Mr. Lopez: The Army of South Vietnam was not eager to fight; when I was there I could sense that. They let us do the fighting for them.

MR. GARZA: DID YOU AT THE TIME OF THE WAR THINK IT WAS A WORTHWHILE CAUSE, AND HAS TIME CHANGED YOUR MIND ON THE ISSUE?

Mr. Lopez: I did think the war was worthwhile. As far as time changing my mind on the issue, I don't think it has. We left diplomacy to the diplomats; we took care of our business and felt a sense of duty.

MR. GARZA: WHAT WAS YOUR VIEW OF ANTI-WAR PROTESTERS?

Mr. Lopez: I think everybody is entitled to their opinion, but it hurt to see the protesters burning their draft cards, and especially the burning of the American flag.

MR. GARZA: WERE YOU INJURED, OR DID YOU INFLICT ANY INJURIES ON THE ENEMY?

Mr. Lopez: I wasn't injured. And I don't know about me injuring the enemy. I don't know. I don't know.

MR. GARZA: WERE YOU DISCRIMINATED AGAINST BY FELLOW SOLDIERS OR BY THE CITIZENS OF BROWNSVILLE?

Mr. Lopez: By soldiers, no. It was totally different. We might joke about it [discrimination], but on the battlefield we were buddies. We had to lean on each other. If I experienced any discrimination it was in Brownsville.

MR. GARZA: DID YOU HAVE A SWEETHEART WHEN YOU LEFT BROWNSVILLE?

Epitacio Lopez
—Photo on right courtesy of Epitacio Lopez

Mr. Lopez: No, but I had a few female friends. [Smiles from both of us.]

MR. GARZA: DURING THE EVENINGS IN VIETNAM, WHEN AND IF YOU GOT SOME QUALITY TIME BY YOURSELF, WHAT DID YOU THINK OF?

Mr. Lopez: I would always think about my family. [Not one moment of hesitation.]

MR. GARZA: DID YOUR EXPERIENCE IN VIETNAM LEAVE ANY LASTING SCARS?

Mr. Lopez: It's something I'll never forget. It will be there forever. I especially remember about my war experience right now, because of the media coverage of the war in Iraq. It's very different now. I can see the battles and envision myself back then.

MR. GARZA: HAVE YOU EVER FELT LIKE A FORGOTTEN SOLDIER, I.E., THE FACT THAT MANY AMERICANS WOULD RATHER JUST FORGET THE WAR EVER HAPPENED?

Mr. Lopez: I have deep regrets that up to today we have not been welcomed home. We didn't lose the war; we did our duty. We lost 58,000 men. Even in our own city we are not allowed to use Elizabeth [Elizabeth Street is the traditional parade route in Brownsville] for our parade. We use Southmost. [Southmost is one of the poorest areas in Brownsville.]

MR. GARZA: DO YOU THINK THAT THE GOVERNMENT HAS PROVIDED YOU AND OTHER VETERANS WITH THE POST-COMBAT MEDICAL AND PSYCHOLOGICAL SERVICES THAT YOU DESERVE?

Mr. Lopez: They have, but I encounter discrimination and they try to treat us like we're asking for *limosna*. [*Limosna* is Spanish for "handouts" for beggars.]

Jose Ibarra
Interviewed by William L. Adams

This interview took place in my Brownsville study the night of December 2, 2003. Mr. Ibarra is a large, powerful, plain-spoken man who wears a cowboy hat and cowboy boots. He was born in the small farming community of El Ranchito, Texas, in 1939. He attended Los Fresnos High School up until his junior year, when he dropped out to make a twenty-year career of the army (1958-1978). He rose to the level of sergeant first class. He spent 1968 to 1969 in Vietnam. After the war he attended St. Edward's University and received a degree in criminal justice. Today he works as a civil process server in Harlingen.

DR. ADAMS: WHAT DID YOU FEEL AS YOU APPROACHED VIETNAM IN THE AIRPLANE?

Mr. Ibarra: What I remember was I started thinking—we all started thinking. We had no idea what would happen. We expected the worse. You always have a sense of apprehension, a fear of the unknown.

DR. ADAMS: WHAT DID YOU DO IN VIETNAM?

Mr. Ibarra: I was a platoon sergeant with "A" Company, 188th Ordnance Battalion. My job was to make sure ammunition kept flowing to the units in the field. I was stationed at Camp Hollaway, Pleiku. We were assigned to an ammunition supply point way out in the boonies, about fifteen to twenty miles from Pleiku. The supply point was not inside Camp Hollaway for fear of an explosion.

DR. ADAMS: PHYSICALLY, WHAT DID THIS SUPPLY POINT LOOK LIKE? HOW WAS THE AMMUNITION KEPT?

Mr. Ibarra: It's kept in different categories: projectiles, different calibers, your grenades, small-arms ammunition, your fuses, 200-pound bombs, 500-pound bombs for the aircraft, Agent Orange, napalm.

The ammunition dump covered about five square miles—that's how big it was. Earthen berms separated the different categories with required distances in between. Not covered. For security we had regular infantry patrolling in foot patrols and watching from towers. And we also had artillery up on a hill in case of a ground attack.

DR. ADAMS: DID YOU GET ANY GROUND ATTACKS?

Mr. Ibarra: No, but mortar attacks and RPGs, rifle-propelled grenades. But we were lucky they never hit our ammo dump. Either the rounds fell short or they missed.

Around Christmas I got sent to Kontum to set up another ammunition supply point for special forces up near Dak To and Ben Hat near the Cambodian border.

DR. ADAMS: HOW DID THE AMMUNITION GET TO THE TROOPS? DID YOU DELIVER IT BY HELICOPTERS, OR WHAT?

Mr. Ibarra: The ammunition normally went out in trucks, semis. Or course, if you had an emergency, helicopters were used.

DR. ADAMS: WERE YOU INVOLVED IN ANY FIREFIGHTS?

Mr. Ibarra: The only action we would see other than mortar attacks on the ammunition dump was back at headquarters at Camp Hollaway when the enemy made probes. These were usally at night, two or three o'clock in the morning. Mortar attacks and perimeter probes.

DR. ADAMS: DID YOU SEE ANY VIET CONG OR NVA?

Mr. Ibarra: Dead ones. I saw lots of dead ones in the morning after they made their night probes. Mostly they were not in black pajamas but mostly in light blue. Viet Congs usually, not regular North Vietnamese Army. Mostly young—sixteen to nineteen, I'd say. No one gray amongst the corpses.

DR. ADAMS: WHAT WOULD YOU DO WITH THEIR CORPSES?

Mr. Ibarra: They would be taken away and given a proper burial. They were disposed of properly.

DR. ADAMS: DID YOU EVER FIND YOURSELF IN GREAT DANGER?

Mr. Ibarra: You had to be careful every day and every night. I went with convoys and you had to be careful of ambush, especially on convoys from Pleiku to Qui Nhon on the coast.

Once when I was riding in the backseat of an open Jeep I heard a "slap" right next to me. A bullet hit the seat between me and the other guy. It missed me just by inches. I knew right then I was going to make it back home. That was the bullet that had my name on it, and it just "went away" from me. Never saw where it came from—probably a sniper aiming at the driver to stop the convoy.

DR. ADAMS: DID YOU GET ANY R&R, ANY REST AND RECREATION?

Mr. Ibarra: I took three days and went to Saigon and two days to go to Vung Tan, an R&R place near Cam Ranh Bay, but I never felt at ease. I felt that the Viet Cong were taking R&R in Saigon too and were right beside us.

The mail service was good except around Christmas time. My wife made me a fruitcake with rum in it and the rum had fermented. When I opened the lid it nearly knocked me on my butt. We got a cheap drunk out of that one.

Jose Ibarra
—Courtesy of Jose Ibarra

DR. ADAMS: WHAT DID YOU THINK OF THE

WAR PROTESTERS?

Mr. Ibarra: I sure wasn't very happy when I heard what was going on back in the States. I was a sergeant and it was hard to keep the morale up of the troops. Being called "baby killers" sure didn't help. I have no respect for those people who protested back then.

DR. ADAMS: ARE YOU A BIG FAN OF JANE FONDA?

Mr. Ibarra: [Laughs.] I don't even want to hear about that woman. I can't understand why people like her who sympathized with the enemy still enjoy the liberties and freedom of this country.

DR. ADAMS: HOW DID YOU FEEL WHEN YOU GOT BACK TO THE STATES?

Mr. Ibarra: I was lucky when I came back that after I took thirty days' furlough at home, saw my family, I was still in the military and went back to it for another ten years. This helped my adjustment—still being in the military.

I feel bad for the nineteen-or twenty-year-old soldiers who were plucked out of the rice fields and then went straight home to civilian life. They needed some time to adjust. They should have kept them in the military for another six months or so to let them make the transition gradually. You know, it took some adjustment when you came out of that war.

First, they weren't loved by their country. The only support you got was from your own family. You begin to wonder if you did the right thing. You needed time to adjust from the war environment to this environment.

How did the war change me? I became more patriotic and I really got to appreciate the freedoms we had in this country. At nights back then I'd look up at the stars and I thought, at least my family back home is doing okay. I had a wife and a six-year-old daughter at that time.

Manuel Torres
INTERVIEWED BY RODOLFO R. FLORES

I interviewed Manuel Torres June 27, 2003, at Duffey Plaza, where we both work for the University of Texas at Brownsville. Manny and I go back many years to elementary school at St. Joseph Academy, when it was located in downtown Brownsville. Both of us began in the first grade with

Jose Ibarra

Catholic nuns as teachers. We actually played marbles and scampered about the playground, just a few blocks from where we spoke. It seems like a lifetime ago.

MR. FLORES: I THANK YOU FOR YOUR TIME, AND IT IS MY PRIVILEGE TO HEAR YOUR STORY. WHAT WERE THE CIRCUMSTANCES WHEN YOU JOINED THE MILITARY?

Mr. Torres: I had taken one college course after graduating from high school, when I moved to Corpus Christi. I decided to move back and, after a few weeks, received my draft orders because I had left school and lost my student deferment. I actually did not want to join the army. Nothing against it, but I had no wishes to join it. On a humorous level, I couldn't join the navy because I couldn't swim and I still can't swim. So I sought enrollment in the air force, but the air force at the time had a six-month waiting list. Actually, the only guy that was there [to take applicants] was a recruiter, and I still remember his name, Staff Sergeant McDonald, from the Marine Corps. My family has all been marines, but actually I did not want to be a marine. My father was a marine in World War II, my brothers were marines during Korea, but I ended up joining the marines. I left for boot camp, MCRD [Marine Corps Recruiting Depot] in San Diego. The rumbling against the war could already be heard in the United States, even in '66 and '67. The morning that I left, I remember quite clearly, there were six other men, boys, with me that left from Brownsville. There were, I believe, another four or five from the Valley. I know that one, de la Rosa from Mercedes, was a slender young man, very short. The irony was that he became our machine gunner. We left for San Antonio, spent the night there, and the following morning we were put on a plane to San Diego. We spent thirteen weeks in boot camp, quite an ordeal. Even till today, you have to experience it to believe it.

MR. FLORES: WHAT DO YOU REMEMBER MOST ABOUT IT?

Mr. Torres: What I remember most of all is that a lot of the men, or boys, that I was there with was their inability to accept the regimentation. I was blessed because I came from a very strict, disciplined

Manual Torres

family. My father, good Lord. And all the years that I played football gave me a very disciplined environment. To me, the Marine Corps was another level of discipline, quite out of the ordinary, but just the same. There was constant moving. You never walked; you ran everywhere you went. As we evolved in our studies there in boot camp, ultimately, we went to the rifle range in Camp Pendleton. We went back to San Diego and everyone received their orders the day we graduated. I remember that from my platoon everyone went overseas to Vietnam, except for one individual.

MR. FLORES: DID YOU RECEIVE ADVANCED INFANTRY TRAINING?

Mr. Torres: Yes, it was known as "AIT." In advanced infantry training we were exposed to all different types of weapons and survival training. We were actually put in a Viet Cong village, held captive, and expected to escape. The thing with me is that I wear glasses, and it was the first thing that they took off. I had to rely on a friend of mine; but we were able to escape. My friend and I and another two guys were the last to be recovered the next morning. We had successfully escaped. During that period of training, I happened to be with Capt. Charles Robb, President Lyndon B. Johnson's son-in-law [married to Lucy Baines Johnson], who was getting ready to go overseas. Of course, the difference is that we ran in, and a helicopter brought him; a little bit of a fringe benefit, if nothing else. I came home on leave for twenty days, and then went back to school, and in late February of '68, I went overseas.

MR. FLORES: HOW DID YOU GET OVERSEAS?

Mr. Torres: They bused us from Camp Pendleton to an air force base in San Bernardino, had breakfast, and then boarded an aircraft to Anchorage, Alaska, and then from there we went to Okinawa. We spent a few days there for more training, shots, orientation, the whole nine yards. From there we were flown to Da Nang, where I was assigned to the 3rd Marine Division, and that area of operation was up in the "I Corps" which is from the DMZ [Demilitarized Zone] to south of Da Nang. I awaited for a unit to pick me up and that was the 2nd Battalion, 12th Marines, 3rd Marine Division that was being regrouped because they had lost quite a considerable amount of men up in Khe Sanh, and other little sorties up in Kon Tien, up north in the DMZ, but east to the Gulf [of Tonkin]. So I joined them, an artillery unit. That unit had been involved with the lifting of the siege at Khe Sanh.

MR. FLORES: HOW DID YOU ACCUSTOM YOURSELF TO THE HOSTILITES SINCE YOU HAD JUST ARRIVED IN VIETNAM AND WERE INEXPERIENCED?

Mr. Torres: I remember the humorous things more than anything. Standing outside one of the hooches, I could see at a distance what I thought was puffs of dirt going up, and could hear a distinct *"thoomp, thoomp"* when one of the guys comes at me, in sort of a flying arm tackle, pushing me into a hole. What was actually occurring were incoming [mortar] rounds. To this day, the sound of rolling thunder reminds me of that. It has a very distinct sound to it. Our rear area compound was at Dong Ha, and another humorous thing is, and I never could understand, even today, why it is, the marines are always outside of a town or of a village, while the army and air force were always within a populated area. From there we went out to the LZs [landing zones] where we kept our guns and along the way is when we came under sniper fire and the danger of mines on the road.

MR. FLORES: DID YOUR MISSIONS VARY?

Mr. Torres: They differed. An artillery unit, by and large, would carry a contingent of marines to guard its perimeter. Often the case, if there were a lot of enemy activity in the area where we were at, we would come under attack by snipers, mortars or their own artillery. They would make an attempt to overrun the hill where we were at, and there were two or three incidents where they tried to overrun our perimeter, our location. Luckily, they never succeeded, but it got kind of hairy, to say the least. [Laughs.]

MR. FLORES: DID YOU HEAR OF ANY CASUALTIES FROM BROWNSVILLE?

Mr. Torres: No, while I was there, the only guy I met was Ignacio Campos. In fact, he lived in my old neighborhood and is back now in Brownsville working for the post office. My neighborhood was in the area of 19th or 20th and Jackson. A personal friend of mine that got killed early on was Anthony "Tony" Perez that I've known since we were in grade school at Cummings [Junior High]. He was a real quiet individual, friendly, and loving to everybody. After graduation, he joined the marines, and shortly after he was in the country, two or three weeks, he got killed. The other was Steven Mullin, a good friend.

MR. FLORES: WHAT UNPLEASANT MEMORIES DO YOU HAVE?

Mr. Torres: I don't remember seeing stars. I just saw black sky, total darkness. You could put your hand in front of you and not see it. The other, again, is humorous, but maybe not at the time. We were being flown into our LZ in a "56," a turbo type of aircraft. It circled and when it came down the rear opened up and we were expected to jump. One of the things that I suffer from is depth perception, and, standing at the door, I couldn't hear what the guy behind me was saying, but he finally pushed me out.

MR. FLORES: DID YOU GET IN ANY CLOSE CALLS?

Mr. Torres: Early in my tour, we took a lot of fire when we were being transported in the air. Travel was by helicopter. You'd hear those "thumps" and you don't realize that it is a round passing right next to you.

MR. FLORES: DID YOU HAVE A LOT OF INTERACTION WITH THE SOUTH VIETNAMESE SOLDIERS?

Mr. Torres: No, we were strictly on our own.

MR. FLORES: I HAVE SEEN YOUR PICKUP AND YOU HAVE A VIETNAM VET LICENSE PLATE. IS IT A DISABLED PLATE? WERE YOU INJURED?

Mr. Torres: No, just a Vietnam Vet plate that identifies that I went.

MR. FLORES: ARE YOU ON ANY MEDICATION DUE TO THE WAR?

Mr. Torres: No, no. I did when I came back in the '70s with a little problem. But I was blessed that I had a good counselor that got me out of my situation, caused by the experience that we went through; the fact that when I came back, we were not accepted at all. When I came back to El Toro Air Base there in California, we were told to get home quickly. If we were harassed, we were told to keep walking and not make an issue. The country called me and I went. Here on the border, we wouldn't have gone to Canada, but I could have gone with my aunt in Querétaro [Mexico], spent the duration of the war, and I would still be there, you know. But I chose to go, it was my duty and the duty of every young man and woman to serve in the armed forces if called upon. Often, we don't have a choice, we go.

MR. FLORES: DID THEY EVER CALL YOU "GROUND POUNDER" OR "GRUNT"?

Mr. Torres: We were just "grunts," "cannon cockers."

MR. FLORES: I HEARD FROM A KOREAN VET THAT MEDICS WERE CALLED "PECKER CHECKERS." DID YOU ALL USE THAT TERM?

Mr. Torres: [Laughs] *Chingao*, no. We just called them "doc."

MR. FLORES: WERE YOU AWARE OF COMING ACROSS AREAS THAT WERE SPRAYED WITH AGENT ORANGE?

Mr. Torres: We were sprayed, and it is a current concern. I'm supposedly okay. All my five children have come out okay. They're saying that the probability decreases as the generations progress. I have six grandchildren, and they seem to be okay. So, hopefully, I wasn't affected; we were sprayed quite a lot.

MR. FLORES: WERE YOU AWARE OF ANY DIFFERENCE BETWEEN THE VIET CONG AND THE NORTH VIETNAMESE REGULARS (NVAs)?

Mr. Torres: The only people we saw were NVA. At no time do I recall hearing them being referred to as Viet Cong. They were hard-core soldiers that had come from the North to fight us.

MR. FLORES: DID YOU HAVE FULL CONFIDENCE IN YOUR OFFICERS AND THEIR LEADERSHIP?

Mr. Torres: Oh yes, I did.

MR. FLORES: WAS THERE A MORALE PROBLEM?

Mr. Torres: No, even though there was scuttlebutt from other outfits that they didn't like their officers. There were rumors of them getting shot or shot at. But in our outfit we didn't have that. Starting from the lowest rank of our NCO all the way up to our captain, they were all good leaders. Our captain was from Midland.

MR. FLORES: WHEN DID YOU BECOME AWARE OF THE ANTI-WAR MOVEMENT AND PROTESTS?

Mr. Torres: Well, my sister would send me copies of the *Brownsville Herald* that I would read or new guys coming into the outfit would tell us about what was going on back in "the world," as we would refer to it. The thing with us is that we were kept busy. There were very few times for us to actually sit and think about, you know, things. If we weren't up in the LZ, we were back in the rear breaking a gun down or going to get provisions.

MR. FLORES: WHAT DO YOU THINK ABOUT VIETNAM NOW THAT IT'S COMMUNIST, IN RELATION TO YOUR SACRIFICE FOR HAVING SERVED THERE?

Mr. Torres: The only thing that I can say is that, what is probably said in many, many circles, is our lack of commitment. I think that at one time, with the amount of men there, we could literally have stood side by side from the Delta to the DMZ. The amount of firepower, and you actually have to witness this firepower, that we had at the time, with B-52s flying across and you are standing on a hill or on a side of a mountain, you see a valley or mountain range pummeled. I've never been through an earthquake, but I've been there when the 52s dropped their loads, and the ground just shook. I'm thinking, "Those poor guys under there." Or you see a gunship we called "Puff the Magic Dragon." It is a C-130 equipped with miniguns shooting tracer bullets, and it appears like one solid red line as it sweeps the width of a football field. It breaks and kills. It's horrific. Poor guys. But it was the lack of will to let these guys loose and kick some tail. In my opinion, it was lack of resolve to do that which is now evident in what's going on in the Middle East: to begin, to do, to end.

MR. FLORES: HOW WAS YOU TRIP COMING BACK HOME?

Mr. Torres: I wasn't treated in a negative way because I kind of kept to myself. I did what the guys over at El Toro said, hurry in, hurry out, and go home. I went from LA, where we encountered a lot of heckling, to Dallas, where I stayed in a hotel and bought a bottle of booze. The next morning I flew to Brownsville. No, we had to fly out at night, and landed in Brownsville in the evening. On a positive note, the taxi-cab driver asked where I was coming from and I told him from Vietnam. When we stopped in front of my house and I asked him how much I owed him, the driver replied, "You don't owe me anything." [Mr. Torres' voice breaking.]

MR. FLORES: WAS EVERYONE HAPPY TO SEE YOU?

Mr. Torres: Oh, yeah, they were happy to see me and everybody wanted to know about ... Shortly thereafter, I had my problems. It was more of an adjustment. I couldn't adjust. I just stayed home until I came out of this shell.

Raul Saavedra
Interviewed by Edith Lizbeth Cano

I had the chance of interviewing Mr. Saavedra this past weekend [June 28, 2003]. He was very detailed in recounting his experiences in Vietnam.

MS. CANO: HOW DID YOU BECOME AWARE OF THE VIETNAM WAR?

Mr. Saavedra: I found out through the news and the TV.

MS. CANO: DID YOU VOLUNTEER, OR WERE YOU DRAFTED TO THE ARMY?

Mr. Saavedra: Are you crazy! I would never have volunteered. I was drafted. I went to college one year and got out. I made some money on the side. I was then drafted on November 15, 1967. I was supposed to report to San Antonio.

MS. CANO: WHERE DID YOU RECEIVE MOST OF YOUR TRAINING?

Mr. Saavedra: Basic training was in Fort Polk, Louisiana. I think it was the biggest training center. It was divided into north Fort Polk and south Fort Polk. I was there for about eight weeks. Then I got two weeks off. After that I went to advanced training.

MS. CANO: WHAT WAS YOUR SPECIALTY?

Mr. Saavedra: In basic training you don't get a specialty until the basic training is over. Then they assigned you to where they need you. Most of my friends were going to infantry. I was just one of the lucky ones that got to go to armor, which was in Fort Knox, Kentucky. I was there for another two months, eight weeks. It is called advanced training because they specialized you in weapons and how to drive an APC (armored personnel carrier). They have a .50-caliber machine gun. It is usually manned by the platoon leader or the commander. Then you have two machine guns like M-16 machine guns, one on each side, left and right, and those are manned by the crew. Those are machine guns, which have the bullet size of 7.62 millimeter. The .50-caliber, that's the heavy weapon. That thing is very huge. Those bullets were huge.

MS. CANO: WHEN DID THEY TELL YOU THAT YOU WERE GOING TO VIETNAM?

Mr. Saavedra: One week before training ended, we got our orders. Each of us had a piece of paper stating where you were going to be. More than ninety percent were going to Vietnam. The lucky ones were going to Germany. So I was not lucky.

MS. CANO: WHAT WAS YOUR ROUTE TO VIETNAM?

Mr. Saavedra: When we finished our advanced training, I came home. We had two weeks' leave. From there I traveled to Fort Lewis, Washington. That was like a staging area, where we would fly to Vietnam. The flight went from Washington and arrived in Hawaii. It stopped there for a couple of hours. Then we went to the Philippine Islands. There we stayed two hours. The next stop was Cam Ranh Bay.

MS. CANO: WHAT WAS YOUR FIRST REACTION TO VIETNAM?

Mr. Saavedra: Well, I remember, and even took a picture, I was sitting by the window of the plane. It was a huge plane, one of those commercial planes. As it was coming down we could see the coastline of Vietnam. As soon as we got closer and closer, we saw a dull gray area. We could see Cam Ranh Bay. It was dull, no vegetation, forest or jungle around the area. As a matter of fact, it was one of the main bases where troops would arrive from the United States. The first thing we saw was those F-4 fighter jets that were stationed there. Camouflaged real nice, good-looking. They were camouflaged green and brown. They were parked right there, and my first impression was "Wow!" I can't believe I'm here. I was not excited, but scared. We were there for two days. Every day they would assemble everybody in a big field. I'm talking about thousands of people. They had a guy climb onto the tower, and he would say some [of the soldiers' names and where they were going]. These names are going to Saigon or Da Nang. All these names are going to Chu Lai. I wanted to go to Saigon, but Chu Lai was up north. Vietnam was divided into four areas or corps. First Corps, Second Corps, and Saigon was in the Third Corps. We got there and they took us to a school where they would teach us about booby traps and do a refresher course. It only lasted for one week. After that, I got assigned to a certain outfit, which was south of Chu Lai in Duc Pho. That was where the 11th Infantry Brigade was located. At Chu Lai it happened to be the division headquarters of the Americal Division. I was to go to the 11th Infantry Brigade.

MS. CANO: WERE YOU IN ANY MAJOR BATTLES?

Mr. Saavedra: We did have one that was not a major, major. We went up north close to Da Nang, and we had to go to a place called "Pinkville." It was supposed to be an area where there was enemy movement. So we had to go in there and search the village. Most of the battles were in the daytime for us. Since we cannot move at night, we moved during the daytime because of the APCs being that they were so vulnerable to the RPGs (rocket-propelled grenades). It was so easy for just anybody to throw one of those things at us. That was a main weapon for the enemy.

MS. CANO: WHAT WERE SOME OF THE DUTIES THAT YOU HAD TO PERFORM?

Mr. Saavedra: Most of the security was performed by the infantry soldier. We were infantry, but we were with the cavalry. There were three jobs that we had to do. We were the second platoon. There was a first platoon and a second platoon. Those three were the "E" troops. We were supposed to be stationed at Duc Pho. Not all three would be stationed at Duc Pho. We would alternate. We would be stationed at Duc Pho, and we would provide security against the people trying to come through the wire trying to sabotage, or just trying to overrun us. The other job was to secure bridges and the highway: Highway 1. Highway 1 actually ran parallel down the coast. They would run north and south. Usually the highway would run through bridges. We had to secure those bridges at night. Then what we had to do was go on search and destroy missions, either with the infantry or by ourselves. We would go to a place where we suspected the enemy would be. We even searched the villages. So there were three jobs that we had to do and we would alternate.

MS. CANO: HOW DID THE VILLAGERS REACT TO THE SEARCHES?

Mr. Saavedra: They didn't say anything. They would just move out of the way.

MS. CANO: HOW LONG WERE YOU IN VIETNAM?

Mr. Saavedra: Ten months.

MS. CANO: WERE YOU INJURED?

Mr. Saavedra: I was wounded in action. We were supposed to be in the base camp at Duc Pho. One of our jobs was to secure the bridges. We got the orders to go down and secure the bridge. We were there during the daytime. We set up our security. It was a bridge that on one side we had a friendly village and on that same side a South Vietnamese base was there. On the other side of the bridge was pure jungle. So our main concern was the jungle. You wouldn't think nothing would come from the other side because of the Vietnamese army there. I remember that I was securing something on the APC's tracks [Mr. Saavedra shows me how he got hit], and then I saw sparks flying. You do see stars. When that happened, the first thing I remember were the sparks. Then all of a sudden I remember picking myself up. As soon as I picked myself up, my eyes went blank. Then I started to get scared and tried to clean them. Then when I could see, my shirt was all wet, but everything was blood. That was so scary. The first thing I did was check myself. When something like that happens, you don't feel anything. My face felt like when a firecracker blows up in your hand. I had that pain in my face.

MS. CANO: WHERE WERE YOU WOUNDED?

Mr. Saavedra: I was wounded right there [points to his nose]. I had surgery twice. Like I said, I was checking myself. I put one of my fingers in my nose. It was kind of torn up just like a piece of paper. I had lacerations in the head. That's why most of the blood was running into my eyes. That's why I couldn't even see when I cleaned my eyes.

We had guards. As soon as it would get dark we would have our security ready. Most of the guards were looking at the jungle. We never expected that. There was a village. There was a little church—I don't know what religion. It was two stories. Somebody had gone up there and [fired] a rocket at us. Not just one, about three or four. See, we weren't the only APC available to provide security. There was another one on the other side of the bridge. As soon as they hit us, they next hit him [the other APC]. At that time my instinct was, "Why the hell are they shooting at you from the South Vietnamese base side?" I didn't think twice, I went around the APC and placed myself down on the other side of the APC, toward the jungle. As soon as I hid, I was crouching and I heard a noise. I looked back toward the end [of the APC] and there was another explosion. In other words, if I had been there I would have been killed—if I wouldn't have moved and thrown myself behind the APC. Then, as soon as that happened, I tried to get inside the tank, but it was burning. We had all kinds of explosives inside. We had grenades, ammunition galore. I remember seeing my machine gun burning. It kind of traumatized me. Some guys came in and used the fire extinguisher... When I was crouching on the other side I was afraid that they would come in and shoot us. It would have been easy with the confusion. Myself and the other guy on the other side got wounded. There were about three of us.

[Later on that day, Mr. Saavedra was picked up by a helicopter and flown into Duc Pho. He couldn't get up. So he was picked up on a stretcher and the medical service started injecting him with shots, while cutting off his clothing. On the right-hand side of Mr. Saavedra's body are scars caused by the APC explosion. Afterwards he was taken to the hospital near the air base in Chu Lai. There he had x-rays taken and he saw himself covered in blood. He has never forgotten that moment. He just asked God that if he were to die, let it not be in Vietnam. Later he had surgery and awoke days later in the ICU. He was in the hospital for two months. Afterwards, on the day he was to leave Chu Lai, the North Vietnamese were attacking the air base. Mr. Saavedra, along with everyone in the hospital, had to place a mattress on top of himself. He was worried that the runway would be damaged and he wouldn't be able to fly to Japan, but he was able to leave at five in the morning. He was in Japan for three days, and on the fourth he returned to America.]

Garrett Tyra
Interviewed by Joel Rodriguez, Jr.

I interviewed Garrett Tyra at the Elks Lodge in San Benito. Mr. Tyra is in his late fifties and is currently retired.

MR. RODRIGUEZ: WHERE WERE YOU BORN, AND WHAT WERE YOU DOING BEFORE THE SERVICE?

Mr. Tyra: I lived in El Paso, Texas. I attended college in Alpine, Texas. Man, those were weird times! I had the time of my life, and if I was not married I would tell you. [Mr. Tyra winks at me and starts to laugh.] My tuition was $300 a semester. However, that was some time ago. I bet the cost of tuition has gone up.

MR. RODRIGUEZ: HOW DID YOU GET INTO THE ARMED FORCES?

Mr. Tyra: When I was younger, I did some rodeoing and thought, hey, I would like to join the armed forces. However, the navy recruiter would not enlist me so I ended up being recruited by the Marine Corps.

MR. RODRIGUEZ: WERE YOU DRAFTED?

Mr. Tyra: No, I was not drafted. When we went to war I decided that I wanted to serve and do my part. The thought of me getting killed never occurred to me. I was young, and I guess you can say that I was stupid, and when you're younger you feel indestructible.

MR. RODRIGUEZ: WHERE DID YOU TRAIN?

Mr. Tyra: I trained in San Diego, California. They sent me to Camp Pendleton, where I trained in basic training for twelve weeks. Later, I trained for eight weeks in infantry training.

MR. RODRIGUEZ: WHAT WAS THE NAME OF THE PLATOON AND HOW LONG WERE YOU IN VIETNAM?

Mr. Tyra: I served in the 5th Infantry, 3rd Division. I spent three years in the hot jungle of Vietnam. Let me tell you that it was no picnic; it was hell on earth. [At this point Mr. Garrett gets quiet and his eyes get misty, so I immediately jump to the next question.]

MR. RODRIGUEZ: WHERE IN VIETNAM DID YOU GO?

Mr. Tyra: They sent me to Da Nang, and that's where I stayed mostly.

MR. RODRIGUEZ: WHAT WAS YOUR JOB?

Mr. Tyra: I was a radio operator, and from there I climbed the ladder. When I left the service, I was a lieutenant. I received this commission after Khe Sanh, in which [of my group] 178 soldiers went in and only sixteen returned.

MR. RODRIGUEZ: DID YOUR PLATOON EVER GET ATTACKED?

Mr. Tyra: Hell, yes! I did get in several firefights. Those damn sons of bitches were everywhere. I would go take a piss and they would be somewhere in the bushes. I was involved in several battles, but they were mostly "hit and run" when I was with reconnaissance.

MR. RODRIGUEZ: WAS THERE ANY ILLEGAL DRUG USE IN THE ARMED FORCES?

Mr. Tyra: There was illegal drug use among the soldiers. I guess that some soldiers could not take the pressure and, to tell you the truth, I don't fucking blame them. Those that do have never been in fear of their life that could come to you in a hundred ways.

MR. RODRIGUEZ: WHAT DID YOU THINK ABOUT THE WAR PROTESTERS?

Mr. Tyra: They were fucking idiots. How could they protest a war in which American soldiers were dying? These people had no idea of what was going on in Vietnam. One of the phrases that to this day gets to me is when they would call us "baby killers." These fuckers don't know, but I never hurt a child; I was a soldier, not a monster. It was ironic that we were also fighting for these idiots' rights also. The only reason that they had a chance to protest the war was because they were living in a free country. I would have liked to see these protesters go to another country and see how long they lasted.

MR. RODRIGUEZ: WERE YOU EVER WOUNDED?

Mr. Tyra: I was wounded three times. The first time we saw the Viet Cong down below a ridge, so we decided to take them out. However, what we did not realize was that they were walking "point" of a platoon, so when we attacked them all hell broke loose. We were pinned down under heavy enemy fire, and as we tried to evacuate I was shot in the leg. The second time that I got wounded was in Khe Sanh. I did not get into my hole fast enough. The third time was along a river. We were jumped by a lot of those sons of bitches.

MR. RODRIGUEZ: DID SOLDIERS TRUST THEIR OFFICERS?

Mr. Tyra: They were treated well. However, the officers did not even wear insignia. [Mr. Tyra laughs.] If you saluted an officer, they would knock you on your ass. Although it was common knowledge that the radioman with the antenna sticking out from his ass was always next to some kind of officer or staff sergeant, so the dirty bastards tried to take them out first.

MR. RODRIGUEZ: AFTER THE WAR, DID YOU KEEP IN TOUCH WITH OTHER SOLDIERS IN YOUR PLATOON?

Mr. Tyra: After the service I did keep in touch with some of my friends. Although you know how it is—you start to lead your life and you start to drift apart. Besides, sometimes seeing my old army buddies would conjure up old, painful memories.

MR. RODRIGUEZ: DO YOU THINK THE WAR WAS WORTH FIGHTING?

Mr. Tyra: At the time I did believe that the war was worth fighting for. If they would have let us fight a complete war we would have been in and out. I guess what it all comes down to is that I would do it all over again if I had to. I love this country and what it stands for.

MR. RODRIGUEZ: WHAT DID YOU THINK OF JANE FONDA DURING THE VIETNAM WAR?

Mr. Tyra: Back then, if I had any way of getting to that bitch I would. I would have liked to splatter her ass in a million pieces. That is just the way I feel. [Mr. Tyra starts to laugh.] The whole platoon felt like that. We all thought that it should have been treason. Although it all goes back to what we were fighting for: freedom.

MR. RODRIGUEZ: WAS THEIR ANY INSUBORDINATION TOWARD OFFICERS, AND, IF SO, HOW WAS IT HANDLED?

Mr. Tyra: Once in a while you had a soldier who was insubordinate toward their commanding officer. The one who took care of it was usually the sergeant. He would take you out and beat the shit out of you. Then, after that, if you did not learn your lesson, the whole platoon would threaten to kill you in the jungle. Out in the jungle you learned very quickly that there was only one color and that was green so eventually you learned to get along with people from different backgrounds.

MR. RODRIGUEZ: WHAT DID YOUR FAMILY THINK ABOUT YOU ENLISTING IN THE SERVICE?

Mr. Tyra: My family was not too thrilled about me enlisting, especially my mother. After I enlisted she told me that if she had known that I wanted to enlist, she would have tied me to the bed. I guess that I do not blame her for not wanting me to enlist since I had two brothers already in the service. They were also in the Marine Corps.

Joe Serrano

Interviewed by Alejandra Sainz

On a Thursday night, I had the pleasure of having a cup of coffee at the Serrano home a few blocks away from the busy traffic of Boca Chica Boulevard. Mr. Serrano is watching the news as his wife shows me into the living room.

MS. SAINZ: MR. SERRANO, WHERE WERE YOU BORN, AND WHAT WERE YOU DOING WHEN THE WAR BROKE OUT?

Mr. Serrano: I was born in Mexico and came to the United States with my parents as a child, and I grew up here in Brownsville. I was here in the U.S. when the war broke out and was attending college.

MS. SAINZ: DID YOU VOLUNTEER, OR WERE YOU DRAFTED?

Mr. Serrano: I enlisted in March 1968. I was twenty-two and I was single. I was not married but married my girlfriend when I returned.

MS. SAINZ: HOW DID YOUR FAMILY REACT WHEN YOU ENLISTED?

Mr. Serrano: Well, I didn't have a choice because they would call you up anyways, so I decided to enlist because it was better. So before they called me I went in and enlisted because you could choose your field of study. My family knew I was going to do my duty like everyone else.

MS. SAINZ: WHAT BRANCH OF THE MILITARY WERE YOU IN?

Mr. Serrano: The U.S. Army.

MS. SAINZ: WHERE WERE YOU SENT FOR BASIC TRAINING?

Mr. Serrano: My basic training was in Louisiana, but I went for aircraft mechanic school in Fort Rucker, Alabama. I was then stationed in Savanna, Georgia, at the army airfield there to work on aircraft before being sent overseas. I graduated as a mechanic for helicopters.

MS. SAINZ: WHERE WERE YOU STATIONED IN VIETNAM?

Mr. Serrano: I was stationed fifty miles north of Saigon.

MS. SAINZ: WHAT DID YOU DO WHEN YOU WERE IN VIETNAM?

Mr. Serrano: Since I chose to go to aircraft school, my job started at 7:00 P.M. and went through the night since we had to fix the choppers by morning so that the pilots could do their missions. I was assigned twenty-six helicopters to maintain with a crew that were assigned to me. Anytime the choppers came in in the afternoon, they had to be ready by morning. With the 145th Aviation Battalion we dropped off supplies, did med evacuations and some combat.

MS. SAINZ: DID YOU ENCOUNTER ANY DANGER FROM THE VIETNAMESE?

Mr. Serrano: There was no safe place in Vietnam. We were sitting ducks at night. We had missiles, mortars, and even snipers shooting at us. Since we always did our work at night all we had to do was try to stay safe. But there was no safe place. We were in the jungle and it was hard not to be shot at. They used the darkness. One time a pilot and I had to get parts and pieces we did not have at our station for the helicopters, so we had to go in the dark to another place to look for parts. Since we didn't have a supply station we relied on each other's help to fix the choppers.

MS. SAINZ: WERE THERE ANY OTHER TIMES YOU WERE IN DANGER?

Mr. Serrano: One time we were being fired on and a rocket or something exploded three feet away from me. Luckily I was in a bunker and the sandbags protected me. I was hugging the ground. That was very dangerous. Another time a pilot and I were flying without any protection. I didn't take my M-16 to work and neither did the pilot. All of a sudden we saw a flash of light right in front of us, but it was a flare. It was startling. It really scared us. Being shot at at night, after a while you get accustomed to it.

MS. SAINZ: HOW LONG WERE YOU OVERSEAS?

Mr. Serrano: One year. After I had done my job, they asked me to stay another three months. So I volunteered to stay. So I was there one year and three months.

MS. SAINZ: DID YOU EVER FACE ANY DISCRIMINATION BECAUSE YOU WERE A MEXICAN-AMERICAN?

Mr. Serrano: Yeah, I did. As Mexican-American or Hispanic, white people weren't used to living with us so there were sometimes that I did. Some white boys didn't like us, but most of them were really nice.

MS. SAINZ: DID YOU BUILD ANY LASTING FRIENDSHIPS WITH YOUR CREW?

Mr. Serrano: I did make a lot of friends, but not many were from the Valley. So I didn't have any pen pals. It was really wild over there because it was so dangerous, and as a young person you don't feel the danger. As we get older we see the danger and could have been killed on some occasions.

MS. SAINZ: WHAT WERE YOUR THOUGHTS ON THE VIETNAM WAR?

Mr. Serrano: Back then lots of people were for it and against it. I was just doing my duty and did the job I had to do. We had to protect our country and just like what happened with the World Trade Center, it's kind of the same. Somebody had to take care of the security, people locally or abroad. Our country is great because some gave up their time and some their life to fight for the right of freedom of our country. Those were and are my thoughts. One of my favorite quotes was from one of my favorite presidents, John Fitzgerald Kennedy: "Ask not what your country can do for you, but what you can do for your country."

MS SAINZ: WHAT DID YOU FEEL WHEN YOU WERE ON THE WAY BACK HOME?

Mr. Serrano: I was just in shock. I couldn't believe I had made it back. I couldn't sleep since our trip took twenty hours, then we had to be bused over towns where we would fly home from. When I got home I took a real shower, ate good food, unlike the C-rations, and slept like twelve hours that day. But I was glad to be back home.

Roberto Garcia
Interviewed by David Cantu

We are here with Mr. Garcia, at his sister's house in Brownsville, Texas. Mr. Garcia has a daily routine of checking up on his father, who resides with his sister. He stands around 5'11, and is in good physical condition. Mr. Garcia is a veteran of the Vietnam War, in which he participated from 1968 to 1969. Since the war he has been working for the Brownsville Independent School District and now heads one of its maintenance departments. Mr. Garcia is a very humble and modest person, and I would like to thank him and his family for sharing his memories.

MR. CANTU: WHAT WERE YOU DOING WHEN YOU FIRST HEARD ABOUT THE WAR IN VIETNAM?

Mr. Garcia: I had graduated out of high school in 1965 and started college at Texas Southmost College. I was taking business courses when I was drafted. At that time the draft was very active. It had a date to report. Do you want me to give you the whole scenario? Okay, the draft here was in San Benito and that's where we reported. It was August 1967. After reporting in San Benito we were shipped to San Antonio, to Fort Sam Houston, and went through the physical. After passing the physical they sent us to Fort Polk, Louisiana, for basic training. Came out of that and specialized in artillery, in the fire direction center, where you compute all the data for the gun to fire (artillery piece: 105mm howitzer), such as angle, trajectory, and all of that. So, anyway, I qualified for the artillery fire direction center, where I was trained in Fort Sill, Oklahoma, and that became my MOS (military occupation specialty).

MR. CANTU: DO YOU RECALL YOUR FIRST DAYS IN SERVICE?

Mr. Garcia: When I went in? The first thing I remember was the haircut. Bald headed as can be. I can still remember the barber asking me how I wanted my haircut. [Mr. Garcia, with a big smile, describes his experience.] I said just a trim around the edges, and the first thing the son of a bitch did was go down the center, *asi* ["like this," in English, as he demonstrates the hair clippers going from front to back], and then from ear to ear. The barber then asked, "Do you like that?"

MR. CANTU: OBVIOUSLY YOU GOT ORDERS FOR VIETNAM. TO WHAT UNIT WERE YOU ASSIGNED?

Mr. Garcia: Most people from Fort Sill were getting orders for either Germany or Vietnam. I got my orders to Vietnam; I was able to go home on thirty-day leave, then I reported to Fort Lewis, Washington. We left there to Vietnam and arrived in one of the main areas, which was Cam Ranh Bay. One of the high points when we were getting there, you know how we celebrate Christmas here, they, too, had a similar holiday, they call it in military terms as the Tet Offensive. I remember arriving at Cam Ranh Bay at night. You would see out through the window of the plane and see it going off like the Fourth of July. *Uno de inocente* [As innocent as one was], we thought they were celebrating, but we arrived and found out it was mortars landing everywhere. Anyway, we went through the in-processing and I was in the 5th Battalion of the 27th Field Artillery, Charlie Battery. It was a battery of 105s, which consisted of six guns. We supported infantry—you know infantry and artillery are like brothers—so they provided the security and we provided them fire to clear the way. And one side depends on the other.

MR. CANTU: WHERE EXACTLY DID YOU GO?

Mr. Garcia: We served near Phan Rang and in a beautiful city where there was a lot of French culture, Da Lat. From there we supported the 101st Airborne Division. We were in direct support, and you know that it involved a lot of flying around. They were always moving. You know the Chinook helicopter? The one with two rotors? We would attach the gun to it while we were inside and we just kept moving. [Mr. Garcia has a serious look on his face as he describes the scene.] The 105mm only reached, max range, about seven miles, so we had to move a lot, a lot of air assault missions.

MR. CANTU: YOU JUST MENTIONED CASUALTIES, AND THERE WERE MANY DURING VIETNAM. DID YOU LOSE ANY CLOSE FRIENDS?

Mr. Garcia: In our battery we lost a guy, but it was not due to any incoming fire. I think this guy overdosed on pills.

MR. CANTU: IS THERE A MOST MEMORABLE EXPERIENCE THAT YOU CAN TELL ME ABOUT?

Mr. Garcia: Yes, you know a battery has six guns, but because of the demand in support of the infantry we had to split the battery and the crew. This is toward the end of my tour, like the ninth or tenth month, we split with three guns. We made our perimeter with wire guards. On this particular night we encountered enemy, pretty much in the perimeter where we were. In artillery, when you have a situation like that, the guns have a set elevation pointed up for angle, but we had to lower it for a direct shot because they had breached perimeter. We checked the following morning to see if there were any kills and obviously we didn't locate anything. It was funny because those people were bastards, they would hide everything. If there were any of them dead they would take them with them. They were bastards. But we held our ground.

MR. CANTU: IT IS OBVIOUS YOU RETURNED HOME IN ONE PIECE. WAS THERE SOMETHING SPECIAL YOU DID FOR "GOOD LUCK"?

Mr. Garcia: No, I just carried a crucifix and remained focused.

James A. Scanlan
Interviewed by Billy G. Karavasilis

On April 13, 2003, I had the pleasure of interviewing James A. Scanlan. Mr. Scanlan is a native Brownsvillite. I met Mr. Scanlan when my family moved to Brownsville in 1990. He has been our neighbor ever since. I interviewed Mr. Scanlan at his home in Rio Del Sol, a Brownsville subdivision, where he has lived for the last twenty years.

Mr. Scanlan was born August 1, 1949. During his junior year in high school he enlisted in the navy to avoid being drafted. Mr. Scanlan is now a foreman for the Brownsville Independent School District.

James Scanlan (left) on riverine patrol with friend who died in Vietnam.

—Courtesy of James Scanlan

MR. KARAVASILIS: WERE YOU DRAFTED, OR DID YOU ENLIST?

Mr. Scanlan: I enlisted because I wanted to be in the navy.

MR. KARAVASILIS: WHY?

Mr. Scanlan: Because I love boats and the open seas.

MR. KARAVASILIS: HOW DID YOU FEEL ABOUT THE WAR BEFORE YOU ENLISTED?

Mr. Scanlan: I [long pause] really didn't give any thought to it.

MR. KARAVASILIS: WHAT WERE YOUR DUTIES WHILE YOU WERE IN VIETNAM?

Mr. Scanlan: I was what you call a river rat. My job was to ride down the rivers and look out for enemies. I was the machine gunner. When we came upon an enemy patrol or camp, I opened fire and just kept blasting and blasting.

MR. KARAVASILIS: HOW DID YOU FEEL HAVING TO SHOOT PEOPLE?

Mr. Scanlan: At the time I was just scared and I wanted to get it over with and get back home. You know, it was either me or them, and they sure didn't mind shooting at us.

MR. KARAVASILIS: HOW DID YOU FEEL THE FIRST TIME YOU WERE IN COMBAT?

Mr. Scanlan: Scared to death.

MR. KARAVASILIS: HOW DID THE NORTH VIETNAMESE FIGHT? IT WAS SAID THEY USED GUERRILLA TACTICS.

Mr. Scanlan: Very, very guerrilla. They used a lot of ambush and surprise tactics, and they were very effective with it.

MR. KARAVASILIS: HOW WAS THE MORALE OF THE SAILORS?

Mr. Scanlan: Sometimes good, sometimes not so good.

MR. KARAVASILIS: HOW DID THE SAILORS RELAX AND UNWIND?

Mr. Scanlan: Well, we had some periods to relax. Most of the time we drank. Oh, there was a whole lotta beer. Best thing is we didn't have to pay for it. Once in a while we would have some barbecues and sit around drinking and talking about back home, or we'd play cards. We tried to do all we could to take our minds off the war, but we all knew we still had a war to fight.

MR. KARAVASILIS: THROUGHOUT ITS HISTORY THE U.S. HAD USUALLY FOUGHT FULL-SCALE WARS, BUT IN THIS CONFLICT THEY USED A THEORY OF LIMITED WAR, SO THAT THE AMOUNT OF FORCE USED IN ANY SITUATION WOULD BE LIMITED TO THE AMOUNT NEEDED TO ACHIEVE THE POLITICAL AIM. HOW DID YOU FEEL ABOUT THIS?

Mr. Scanlan: We needed a little bit more.

MR. KARAVASILIS: HOW DID THE SOUTH VIETNAMESE AID YOU?

Mr. Scanlan: Well, when they weren't running, they helped us.

MR. KARAVASILIS: WERE THEY GOOD FIGHTERS?

Mr. Scanlan: I had a couple that were good, but I heard that most of the time they weren't up to expectations.

MR. KARAVASILIS: WAS THE U.S. SURPRISED BY THE TET OFFENSIVE LAUNCHED BY THE NORTH VIETNAMESE IN 1968?

Mr. Scanlan: They caught some of them, especially in the fire camps, off guard.

MR. KARAVASILIS: HOW DID THE U.S. RESPOND TO THIS?

Mr. Scanlan: Well, they had an all-out bombing run; they launched the B-52s out of Guam and bombed the hell out of them.

MR. KARAVASILIS: DID YOU FEEL THAT THE NORTH VIETNAMESE WERE BEATEN AFTER THIS BATTLE?

Mr. Scanlan: Oh, heck no! They were tough and determined fighters. I don't think they ever would have given up.

MR. KARAVASILIS: MANY IN THE U.S. WERE OPPOSED TO THE WAR. HOW DID THIS MAKE YOU AND OTHER SOLDIERS FEEL?

Mr. Scanlan: Bad. I wish we had more support. We were fighting an unpopular war.

MR. KARAVASILIS: DO YOU THINK THIS GAVE THE NORTH VIETNAMESE THE WILL TO CONTINUE FIGHTING?

Mr. Scanlan: Oh, yeah. They knew that our country wouldn't support the war the longer it took.

MR. KARAVASILIS: HOW DID IT MAKE YOU FEEL ONCE THE U.S. WITHDREW ITS FORCES AND SOUTH VIETNAM FELL?

Mr. Scanlan: Well, it was inevitable. We knew it was coming. They [the U.S. leadership] wouldn't go after the major cities and ports and stuff. So we knew it was going to go down. I guess it felt like, you know, we came back feeling like a whipped dog with its tail between its legs.

MR. KARAVASILIS: DO YOU HAVE ANY REGRETS ABOUT GOING TO VIETNAM?

Mr. Scanlan: Nope.

MR. KARAVASILIS: DO YOU HAVE ANYTHING ELSE YOU WOULD LIKE TO TELL ME ABOUT VIETNAM?

Mr. Scanlan: Not really. It was an awful time and we lost a lot of good men over there, and I'll never forget that. I'm just glad you didn't make me talk about body counts, because it was awful and I don't think I can talk about it, not even today, probably never.

Catarino Murillo
Interviewed by Santiago Salazar, Jr.

This interview with Catarino Murillo was conducted at his home on June 27, 2003. Mr. Murillo had been watching TV and keeping up with the latest information on the war with Iraq. Mr. Murillo seemed very eager and anxious to conduct this interview.

MR. SALAZAR: CAN YOU TELL ME A LITTLE ABOUT YOUR LIFE BEFORE THE VIETNAM WAR?

Mr. Murillo: I came from a large family—eighteen total. My father was married twice. Half-brothers and half-sisters. I was the second one drafted into the service. The rest of my family consisted of several cousins entering the military. I was born on May 1, 1948. We didn't really know what the military was about.

MR. SALAZAR: SO YOU GOT DRAFTED INTO THE MILITARY?

Mr. Murillo: I volunteered because I wanted to get into the marines. I found out I was drafted. The marines wanted me to be enlisted for three years, but I only wanted to be in the military for two years. So I told them that I was going into the

Catarino Murillo

army because they were offering two years. Then they came up with this program that made the enlistment for two years, so I joined the marines. I was by myself. I went in as a volunteer. I knew that I was drafted. I just beat them to the punch.

MR. SALAZAR: SO DID YOU SEE YOUR DRAFT BALL ON TV?

Mr. Murillo: No, nothing like that. We went to San Antonio and they gave us a physical. After the physical, they would notify us if we got in. It was real easy to get in.

MR. SALAZAR: SO DID YOU COME FROM A MILITARY FAMILY YOURSELF?

Mr. Murillo: No one was in the military in my family. I was the first to join.

MR. SALAZAR: HOW DID YOUR FAMILY FEEL ABOUT YOU JOINING THE MILITARY?

Mr. Murillo: My mom didn't like it at all. My dad told me it was up to me. I was close to twenty years old. My mom was afraid. The way I looked at it was that if I didn't volunteer I was still going to be drafted. If you don't go you had to go to Mexico. There was no way for me to get out. I was the only one who got drafted. I had two other brothers, but they never got drafted.

MR. SALAZAR: WHAT SECTION OF THE MARINES DID YOU JOIN?

Mr. Murillo: 3rd Marine Division. I think they are stationed in Hawaii, but I am not sure.

MR. SALAZAR: WAS THAT INFANTRY?

Mr. Murillo: Yes. I was a "grunt." You walked all the time. That's the reason they call you a "grunt." I went to San Antonio to become a "grunt."

MR. SALAZAR: HOW DID YOU GET TO SAN ANTONIO WHEN THEY NOTIFIED YOU THAT IT WAS TIME FOR YOU TO SERVE?

Mr. Murillo: Once you got your letter you got a bus in Harlingen and they took you to San Antonio. From there you got another physical and they would divide you into groups. From there they told you what division of the military you were going to.

MR. SALAZAR: DESCRIBE YOUR FIRST EXPERIENCE WITH THE MILITARY.

Mr. Murillo: I wanted the blue uniform. I didn't know how bad it was going to be. I figured it would be a little easier for me since I volunteered. I was by myself. I got to know another friend from Brownsville. He and I became friends. We went to training together. In basic training, toward the end, I got injured from a rifle exercise. So I was always two weeks behind everyone else. I lost my strength in my arm, so that's why I was two weeks behind.

MR. SALAZAR: HOW LONG WERE YOU IN CALIFORNIA AND BASIC TRAINING?

Mr. Murillo: Twelve weeks. They cut it down. It used to be longer, but they cut it down.

MR. SALAZAR: CAN YOU DESCRIBE YOUR TRAINING?

Mr. Murillo: That was terrible. Early in the morning they started you running. After the run they would feed you breakfast. From there they would make you run. After that they would take you to classes. The classes were about everything. They trained you how to take care of yourself. You became very self-reliant: how to dress and take care of your weapon. There were about seventy-five men in the division. All of us were from Texas. We competed in everything from rifle and marching to physical exercise. We were better than everyone else. We were trained to give first aid and treat the physical demands. I used to work in the fields, and I knew how to take care of the wounded. They put us in the woods and trained us there. They had some nice wooded areas in San Diego. It was very organized. We had to look for traps and mines. I was good at finding that stuff.

MR. SALAZAR: WHAT WAS THE BEST ADVICE YOUR DRILL INSTRUCTOR GAVE YOU TO SURVIVE THE VIETNAM WAR?

Mr. Murillo: The first thing they tell you is that only a small percentage will come back. Most injuries were gunshots. They knew how you were going to get hurt. You make yourself think that it won't happen to you. I hated my drill instructors. If I ever saw one over there I was going to chew his ass out. They treat you very rough. Not everybody gets treated that way. The best and worst ones get the worst of it. So you stayed in the middle of the group. Stay in the middle and you were going to be okay.

MR. SALAZAR: CAN YOU DESCRIBE HOW YOU GOT TO VIETNAM?

Mr. Murillo: I really didn't want to go. They flew us from El Toro, California, to Hawaii. We stopped there and refueled. It was a commercial plane. The plane was full of soldiers. From there we flew to Japan and then to Da Nang, Vietnam.

MR. SALAZAR: WHAT WAS THE MORALE OF THE SOLDIERS IN THE AIRPLANE?

Mr. Murillo: Everyone was singing and dancing in the plane. The ladies gave us water and soda. They were nice to us. We were in a C-130. When we got there, in Vietnam, things changed.

MR. SALAZAR: WHEN YOU LANDED WAS THERE A PERIMETER SET UP FOR SAFE LANDINGS?

Mr. Murillo: Incoming the night before, there were bombs all over the airfield. When we landed it was in the afternoon. We went straight to the bunkers, and we ran like hell because we had "incoming." We were scared. We didn't know where to go. We had our weapons but we didn't have any ammo. We stayed in the bunkers for about two hours. Later in the day, we got ammo. Da Nang was supposed to be a secure area, but they were still being attacked by mortars every once in a while.

MR. SALAZAR: WHEN YOU GOT YOUR ORDERS TO LEAVE BASE CAMP, HOW DID YOU FEEL?

Mr. Murillo: Just show me the way. Everyone wants to shoot. You had to check in and out. From there we went to a specific division and went to work.

MR. SALAZAR: WHAT WAS THE BEST ADVICE VETERAN TROOPS GAVE YOU WHEN YOU WERE IN VIETNAM?

Mr. Murillo: "Keep your eyes sharp. Everyone is the enemy." Of course, in Da Nang, you couldn't tell the difference. In the day the civilians were nice to you, but at night they became VC. Those people fought at night. They had special mortars and fired at you. Most of the fights were at night. During the day they knew that they would lose. They didn't have helicopters or planes to help them. After I got close to the DMZ, anything that moved was the enemy. There were no civilians in this area. So if it moved it was the enemy.

MR. SALAZAR: WHAT YEAR WERE YOU IN VIETNAM?

Mr. Murillo: I was there in the end of 1968. I was there for about eleven months.

MR. SALAZAR: HOW DID YOU INTERACT WITH THE VIETNAMESE PEOPLE?

Mr. Murillo: They didn't say much. They spoke a different language. They avoided us and talked to the officers. They used the translator. They didn't speak English.

MR. SALAZAR: CAN YOU DESCRIBE YOUR MENTAL STATE THE FIRST TIME YOU ENCOUNTERED THE ENEMY?

Mr. Murillo: It was not a battle. It was a sniper. Everyone got off the vehicle and did what they were trained to do. Once I got into my group it was a long while before we actually had a battle. I didn't think. You just react and do your job. If you think, you were dead.

MR. SALAZAR: WERE THERE ANY SPECIAL PRECAUTIONS THAT YOU HAD TO TAKE SINCE THE BATTLES WERE AT NIGHT?

Mr. Murillo: You really don't think about it. What helped me was that I knew what noise people make and what noise animals make. You would close your eyes and listen for the noise that was being made. What happened was that at night the enemy tried to get close to you. "Claymores" are set up so that they shoot small pellets and cover about fifteen to twenty yards. If your enemy is out there they are going to get hurt. You don't use your rifle because they are going to shoot at your rifle. We used grenades and flares to fire at the enemy. If the flares go up then you use grenades so you don't use your rifle.

MR. SALAZAR: DID YOUR PLATOON FOLLOW THE "RULES OF ENGAGEMENT"?

Mr. Murillo: No. The areas that I was at, you knew the enemy was out there.

MR. SALAZAR: WHAT WAS YOUR HIGHEST RANK WHILE YOU WERE IN VIETNAM?

Mr. Murillo: I came back as lance corporal. The officers didn't like me. I was a bad boy. Sometimes doing things by the book got you killed. The officers wanted to follow the book and I knew better. That's why I came back without a scratch. I knew where the enemy was and where he was hiding. I didn't get along too good with the officers. They kept me at "point" all the time. I only used my machete and I didn't follow trails. I made my own trails. That's what the officers didn't like. The point man was the first man they killed. I can remember at least four times that when I changed from being point they would shoot and kill the next guy. They kept following the trails. They didn't kill him just to injure him. All they wanted was to damage the helicopter. There were rumors that they paid the VC by "dogtags" and the amount of damage they did to the helicopter. They paid them American money for this information. Those were the rumors going around.

MR. SALAZAR: WAS THE ENEMY A FIERCE FIGHTER?

Mr. Murillo: Yes. The VC were good during the day and bad boys at night. We mostly fought the regular soldiers. One time we killed thirty-two of them in the morning and about forty in the afternoon. They came in early one morning and we surprised them. The "listening posts" were out there and we were cover for some tanks going through. I then saw the enemy and we surprised them.

MR. SALAZAR: HOW DOES IT FEEL KNOWING THAT YOU MAY HAVE TAKEN SOMEONE'S LIFE?

Mr. Murillo: You don't think about it. You just react. You don't shoot at anyone. Everyone shoots at the same time and you don't know if you hit them or not. Now, if someone from your group gets killed, then that's a different story. You know that person for a good while. We were just talking this morning. That's when your morale gets down. Somehow the VC knew when the morale was low and that's when they would fire at you.

MR. SALAZAR: WHEN YOU WERE "POINT," DID YOU FEEL RESPONSIBLE FOR YOUR GUYS?

Mr. Murillo: Yes. There is no two ways about it. I was lucky enough to know the terrain and have like a sixth sense about it. Something just didn't look right. We had an operation called "Hamburger Hill." It involved everyone. There was a big hill near Laos and we needed this hill. The enemy had the hill and they had some big cannons. We had to walk into it. I had a lot of fun during that operation. The hill was real steep and they had bunkers. The planes couldn't help us because of the hill. I was able to stand on top of that hill for about three days. The back of the hill was straight down. We had to use ropes to get down. That operation cost a lot of lives. Green berets, special forces, army, and the navy was firing at the hill. We needed the hill for observations. We needed to know what the enemy was doing.

MR. SALAZAR: WERE YOU EXPOSED TO AGENT ORANGE?

Mr. Murillo: I think we were. The places that I was there were some big trees. You couldn't see daylight from the floor. They wanted the trees to lose all their leaves. They had spotter planes and bumblebee helicopters. There were always two jets in the air. They would use flares and then the jets would drop bombs on the trail. The spotter planes and the bumblebee helicopters would do a good job. Elephant grass was also another enemy. We didn't see this type of grass in America. It was always raining and hot. You would sleep and it was raining and you would wake up and it was raining.

MR. SALAZAR: DID YOU EVER CALL HOME?

Mr. Murillo: No, but I did send tapes home. One time I was talking and in the background you could hear the Cobra helicopter firing and my mom was really worried. After that I started to write instead of using tapes.

MR. SALAZAR: HOW DID YOU FEEL ABOUT THE PROTESTS OCCURRING IN THE UNITED STATES?

Mr. Murillo: I didn't really care about the protests. Nothing was happening. That's why the people were protesting. It was a small nation. Most of us called it a political war instead of a real war. The politicians were controlling the war, not the soldiers. I got mad when I found out that some guys got special privileges just because of their families. I found out later that by joining the National Guard you would avoid going to Vietnam. If I had known that, I would have joined the National Guard.

MR. SALAZAR: WHAT ADVICE WOULD YOU GIVE TO SOLDIERS WHO ARE GOING TO WAR?

Mr. Murillo: Know your terrain. Like the soldiers in Iraq. You have to know the terrain. They got lost because they weren't paying attention. Instead we call them heroes. But in reality it was their fault. You have to know your terrain. They trained them but you can tell that they weren't paying attention. How can you get lost from your platoon? That's why you have to know your terrain.

Jose G. Leal, Jr.
Interviewed by Arturo Juarez

It was a Sunday night, April 13, 2003, when I interviewed my father-in-law, Jose Guadalupe Leal, Jr. He has been a resident of Brownsville, Texas, his entire life. A recent hailstorm had hit Brownsville, breaking his skylights and damaging the living room area. The whole week had been very hectic for Mr. Leal. He was kind enough to take time at the end of the day to do the interview. He seemed tired but relaxed. We decided to do the interview in his kitchen. Mr. Leal served himself a glass of water and we began the interview.

MR. JUAREZ: WHERE WERE YOU WHEN THE WAR STARTED?

Mr. Leal: I was in high school. I don't remember the war starting, but on June 14, 1967, I enlisted. This is the same day as Ashley's birthday. [Ashley is his granddaughter.] I went into the army, to Fort Polk in Louisiana. After basic training, my advanced training was as a mechanic. From there another advanced training was as a truck mechanic, like tanks. I went to Fort Sill in Oklahoma for that one.

MR. JUAREZ: WHERE DID THEY SEND YOU AFTER YOUR TRAINING?

Mr. Leal: From there I volunteered for airborne school. I went to Fort Benning in Georgia. I was there for about a month.

MR. JUAREZ: WHAT MADE YOU VOLUNTEER?

Mr. Leal: Really, a challenge for myself. You had to be fit to put up with the training.

MR. JUAREZ: WHAT DO YOU REMEMBER MOST ABOUT THE TRAINING?

Mr. Leal: Running. You do a lot of running, and then you do your regular airborne training, where they teach you to jump off platforms.

MR. JUAREZ: HOW MANY JUMPS DID YOU MAKE THERE?

Mr. Leal: To qualify—five. Then I got my wings.

MR. JUAREZ: WHAT DOES IT FEEL LIKE JUMPING OUT OF A PERFECTLY GOOD AIRPLANE?

Mr. Leal: Great! [Sarcastic smile.]

MR. JUAREZ: HOW WAS IT JUMPING OUT THE FIRST TIME?

Mr. Leal: I can't remember, but I must have been real scared.

MR. JUAREZ: WHERE DID YOU GO AFTER GETTING YOUR WINGS?

Mr. Leal: I finished airborne training then came home on leave for about ten days. Then I reported to New Jersey/New York area and left for Germany from there.

MR. JUAREZ: DO YOU REMEMBER WHERE IN GERMANY YOU WERE STATIONED?

Mr. Leal: In Mainz, right on the Rhine River. Wiesbaden was the air force base. I reported to the 8th Infantry Airborne Division. By this time the war was real heavy. This is about the same time the Tet Offensive happened.

MR. JUAREZ: HOW WAS IT IN GERMANY?

Mr. Leal: [Laughs.] Good, lots of wine, lots of beer! It was different, snow and hills and stuff. In Germany I jumped like ten times, once at night. Then we went to war games in Greece.

MR. JUAREZ: HOW LONG DID YOU STAY IN GERMANY?

Mr. Leal: Approximately seven to eight months. I was there when they assassinated Martin Luther King. [Mr. Leal closes his eyes and shakes his head.] When it happened, it got real ugly in Germany. There was fighting when people went out at night, mostly at the white people. They didn't fool around with the Hispanics; they knew better. You had to be careful when you went out at night.

MR. JUAREZ: THEN FROM GERMANY WHERE DID YOU GO?

Mr. Leal: I got disillusioned about the things that were happening in Germany, about the fights, everything. I just wanted to get out of there, so I volunteered to go to Vietnam. That was the only way, or the quickest way, to get out of Germany. Once I volunteered they cut my papers to go. So I came home toward the end of November for about a week or two to visit. Then to Washington to Fort Lewis. Then I left to Vietnam.

MR. JUAREZ: YOU KNEW THAT IT WAS PRETTY BAD OVER THERE AND YOU STILL WENT?

Mr. Leal: Yes, because of all the crap that was going on there in Germany. I couldn't see myself there. I wanted to go somewhere I would make a difference.

MR. JUAREZ: HOW DID YOUR RELATIVES FEEL ABOUT YOU GOING TO VIETNAM?

Mr. Leal: [Shrugs his shoulders.] Scared, I guess, but it was something that I had to do. I was a member of the armed forces, just wish for the best, and then I was gone.

MR. JUAREZ: WHAT WERE YOUR FIRST IMPRESSIONS WHEN YOU LANDED IN VIETNAM?

Mr. Leal: I arrived in Cam Ranh Bay. It was super hot, and it was December! It was just the ... I don't know, you're going through the processing center. It's just go, go, go. Fill this out, and fill that out. You're on the move, but you have to stay there till they cut your orders where you'll go.

MR. JUAREZ: WHEN YOU GOT YOUR ORDERS, WHERE DID YOU GO?

Mr. Leal: Lai Khe. It was in the "Iron Triangle." I was assigned to a M.U.S.T. unit, 2nd Surgical Hospital in the 44th Medical Brigade.

MR. JUAREZ: WHY WAS IT CALLED THE IRON TRIANGLE?

Mr. Leal: I'm not sure. [Laughs.] It had to do with being a stronghold. I never asked. Probably because of the fighting, incoming rounds all the time. They were continuous. That area, the main forces were the Big Red One and the 1st Cavalry, a helicopter unit.

MR. JUAREZ: WHAT WAS YOUR RANK?

Mr. Leal: By that time I was a motor sergeant. I was in charge of all the vehicles. I got a bronze star for this. They didn't want me to leave. They offered me staff sergeant. From being a mechanic to staff sergeant in two and a half years, that's something else. I probably would have, but I felt that I had been there fourteen months. That was enough. It was a hard decision to make.

MR. JUAREZ: WHEN YOU ARRIVED IN VIETNAM, WHAT DID YOU THINK THE WAR WAS ABOUT?

Mr. Leal: [Looking up, thinking.] It was about democracy, saving people from the communists. When you're nineteen, twenty years old, it's really about being patriotic.

MR. JUAREZ: DID YOU KNOW ABOUT NORTH VIETNAM INVADING SOUTH VIETNAM?

Mr. Leal: Not really.

MR. JUAREZ: DO YOU THINK YOUR FELLOW SOLDIERS KNEW?

Mr. Leal: I think, for the most part, not really. It's like this war. [Second Iraq War.] You're young and you do what's expected of you.

MR. JUAREZ: WERE YOU APPREHENSIVE TO MAKE FRIENDS?

Mr. Leal: No, because as you go you meet people for a second, a minute, days or months. So you never knew who you'd be around.

MR. JUAREZ: WHILE YOU WERE THERE, DID YOU LOSE ANY FRIENDS?

Mr. Leal: I did, but not friends from the same unit.

MR. JUAREZ: WHAT DID YOU DO TO PASS THE TIME?

Mr. Leal: At night we would hear music. They had a tent like a club. We'd drink beer and listen to music, and get ready to run like hell if you heard "incoming." For the most part you don't pay attention to time. I had four trailers. Each trailer had a huge generator—an a/c unit. I had to make sure they were fueled, get the lights ready, make sure everything is working and prepared to move out. When you're done you have to tear it down and do it all over again, like in the carnival. You don't have time to think about anything.

MR. JUAREZ: DO YOU THINK THAT YOU SUFFERED ANY ILL EFFECTS FROM ANY CHEMICALS THAT WERE USED IN VIETNAM, LIKE AGENT ORANGE?

Mr. Leal: I don't know, it was all over the place. We were in a plantation setting, where they did use it. It's been very hard to prove. Every day they accept new ailments that were caused by chemicals. The list keeps growing. According to the armed forces, Agent Orange didn't affect anybody, but now, thirty years later, they have a list of ailments that are or have been linked to the herbicides.

MR. JUAREZ: WHAT IS ONE OF YOUR MOST MEMORABLE EVENTS IN VIETNAM?

Mr. Leal: I got sent out. Our unit had been moved from the Central Highlands to Lai Khe. We had been where the Americal Division was located. They sent me out to look for two 2½-ton trucks. All I had was a .45 and an ammo belt. I traveled through Vietnam for two days to look for these two trucks that were missing. I hopped from airport to airport. While I was traveling I ran into a friend of mine from Germany. We had shared a room when I was there. His name was Gary Whitman.

MR. JUAREZ: DID YOU FIND THE TRUCKS?

Mr. Leal: I found the rails. They had cannibalized the trucks to keep the other ones running. We wrote them off. The trucks were left behind, so when I got back there was nothing left. It's funny because while you're scared to be doing this, it was an adventure. So you just do it.

MR. JUAREZ: BEING IN VIETNAM DURING THE WAR, WHAT DOES THAT DO TO YOU MENTALLY?

Jose Leal

Mr. Leal: You know, it's funny because it depends on your position, where you are. I want to say that I was able to adjust because I had it better than other guys. You had some that went crazy.

MR. JUAREZ: HOW WAS IT WHEN YOU RETURNED HOME FROM VIETNAM?

Mr. Leal: I tried not to let it bother me, but at that time when everyone came back the public was against the war. It's not like now. Back then they didn't look at you the same way. There were no parades or anything. It was bad. When I got into the States, it was at 2:30 in the morning, so I didn't have to deal with the protesters.

MR. JUAREZ: IT HAS BEEN SAID THAT THE ANTI-WAR MOVEMENT UNDERMINED WHAT THE U.S. WAS TRYING TO ACCOMPLISH IN VIETNAM. WHAT ARE YOUR THOUGHTS ON THIS?

Mr. Leal: It added fuel to the fire with the Vietnamese. This made them think that what we were doing was wrong. As a soldier you do your duty. It's easy for people that are Stateside to talk, they're not getting hurt. They enjoy the liberties of freedom and free speech at someone else's expense. How would they act if their country fell and they had to live under someone else's rule? Would they have acted the same way?

MR. JUAREZ: DO YOU THINK THAT VIETNAM WAS A VALUABLE LESSON?

Mr. Leal: It was a valuable lesson, in different ways. I think that Washington had us fight a war with one arm tied behind our backs. We were ineffective, not like today's army. There was more that we could have done.

MR. JUAREZ: LIKE WHAT?

Mr. Leal: There were more helicopters and infantry. We could have used a different type of offense. We could have used different kinds of bombs or any other means available.

MR. JUAREZ: HOW DID THE MILITARY CHANGE YOUR LIFE?

Mr. Leal: It made me a better person. It disciplined me. During my youth I was... who knows where I might have ended up. I attribute my successes in part to having been in the armed forces.

Doss Kornegay, Jr.
INTERVIEWED BY JORGE PENA

On Sunday, April 13, 2003, I had the distinct honor of interviewing Doss Kornegay, Jr., at his home in Harlingen, Texas. I arrived at his home at around 1:00 P.M. as we had agreed. Mr. Kornegay greeted me outside and then led me to a small room in his home where the interview took place. Mr. Kornegay keeps all of his important achievements on display here in this room. As I walked in, I noticed many pictures and medals, and Mr. Kornegay proudly told me the story for each. As I sat down on a small sofa, Mr. Kornegay sat in a rocking chair and we began the interview.

Doss Kornegay

—Courtesy of Doss Kornegay

MR. PENA: DID YOU ENLIST OR WERE YOU DRAFTED?
Mr. Kornegay: I was drafted as soon as I graduated from college May 29, 1968.
MR. PENA: HOW OLD WERE YOU AT THE TIME?
Mr. Kornegay: I was twenty-one.
MR. PENA: AFTER BASIC TRAINING, WHERE DID YOU GO?
Mr. Kornegay: I went to Fort Polk for regular troop training. There they shaved my face, and cut my hair. I learned how to clean my rifle and take it apart, as well as survival skills and some navigational skills.
MR. PENA: WHERE DID YOU GO AFTER THAT?
Mr. Kornegay: I went to Fort Benning, Georgia, for officer's training. That's where I got my small infantry command.
MR. PENA: WHAT WAS YOUR JOB DURING THE WAR?
Mr. Kornegay: I was a lieutenant of the 196th Light Infantry Brigade. I was also a reconnaissance platoon lieutenant in command of about twenty-five to thirty men, which included a sergeant and platoon leaders.
MR. PENA: WHEN YOU LANDED IN VIETNAM, HOW WERE YOU RECEIVED BY THE POPULATION?

Mr. Kornegay: I was well received. I developed a respect for those people, although many veterans didn't and still don't hold these views.

MR. PENA: WERE YOU EVER WOUNDED IN COMBAT?

Mr. Kornegay: I was wounded in November 1969, and then again on August 8, 1970. The Vietnamese that shot me was perched up in a tree in camouflage. As I was coming down a hill, I was shot in the buttocks, and rather quickly the guys isolated him and shot him before he could inflict any more damage to anyone else.

MR. PENA: WHAT WAS YOUR WORST MEMORY IN PARTICIPATING IN THE WAR?

Doss Kornegay

Mr. Kornegay: One was Mike Conklin's death. [He says this and quickly points at a photograph of Sergeant Conklin, who was his platoon sergeant.] The day he died I was taking a patrol out for reconnaissance. Mike told me he felt like going instead, that I should stay and rest. So I briefed him on it. As he left with the patrol, something didn't feel right. As I looked upon them leaving I could see the ambush coming from where I was standing. So Mike was shot. He told me as he lay there to make sure I gave his wife a ring that he had bought her. I immediately called the medic to try and stop the bleeding, but he just couldn't. Had I gone with him maybe he wouldn't have died. [Stops for a moment and eyes get watery.]

You know, Mike's widow wrote to tell us she was going to pray for us to return home safe. One thing that made the guys and myself just break down was when she told us that Mike's baby would have to be raised now by one parent. This brought all of us down to tears.

MR. PENA: DO YOU HAVE ANY SOUVENIRS FROM THE WAR?

Mr. Kornegay: Actually I have a Type 56 Chinese Communist Carbine SKS. [Leaves the room for a moment and returns with the carbine.]

MR. PENA: HOW DID YOU ACQUIRE IT?

Mr. Kornegay: Well, I killed a guy with an M-16. We were two patrols, and we just surprised each other. We opened fire on each other, and we ended up killing seven of them and they got none of us. As we moved in closer to assess the damage, I saw the SKS lying on the ground, so I picked it up and brought it home.

MR. PENA: WHAT WAS THE MORALE OF THE TROOPS YOU WERE WITH?

Mr. Kornegay: Morale was pretty high. Sometimes someone would get killed, but my guys knew how to handle stress.

MR. PENA: IN YOUR OPINION, WAS IT RIGHT FOR THE ANTI-WAR PROTESTERS TO BE ASKING FOR A STOP TO THE UNITED STATES INVOLVEMENT IN THE WAR?

Mr. Kornegay: The people protesting had a right to do that. They live in a country where they have a right to express themselves. You know, I'll tell you that when I got back, I became one of them for a while in the '70s. [Laughs.] I don't think that what they did is unpatriotic. In fact, they are one of the reasons why we got out of the war.

MR. PENA: HOW DID THE WAR AFFECT YOUR LIFE?

Mr. Kornegay: [Takes a big breath and begins to speak.] The war affected me in both good and bad ways. However, the bad ways overwhelm the good. My son, for example, died of cancer. [Stops for a minute and clears his throat.] Now that cancer is the leading cancer in veterans exposed to Agent Orange. There's a good chance my exposure brought my son's illness and death. On the other hand, because of my involvement in the war, I became a man by my standards. I also developed maturity.

Roberto Miguel Rodriguez
Interviewed by Sandra Vargas

This interview was conducted at Roberto Miguel Rodriguez's parents' home. My family, the Vargas', and the Rodriguez family have known each other for the past forty-five years and have been neighbors for just as long. The interview takes place in his father's living room.

MS. VARGAS: DID YOU SIGN UP FOR THE SERVICE, OR WERE YOU DRAFTED FOR THE VIETNAM WAR?

Mr. Rodriguez: On August 16, 1962, I enlisted in the U.S. Army. By enlisting in the armed forces, it would mean a better life and way of life for me with opportunities to learn a trade. I always knew and felt that it was my duty to serve my country and represent my family in a good way, and I also needed a sense of direction and I knew that the military would somehow help me with that. Coming from a family of nine brothers and three sisters, I only attended school until the ninth grade. I attended Central Junior High School. Times were hard, and coming from a poor and large family it made sense.

MS. VARGAS: DID ANYBODY ELSE THAT YOU KNEW SIGN UP AS WELL, AND WHAT WAS YOUR RANK IN THE ARMY?

Mr. Rodriguez: My oldest brother had enlisted in the U.S. Air Force and I promised myself that same day I would do the same. My rank was staff sergeant.

MS. VARGAS: WHERE DID YOU GO FOR YOUR BASIC TRAINING?

Mr. Rodriguez: I did my basic training at Fort Polk, Louisiana, and I stayed there for my advanced infantry training.

MS. VARGAS: DID YOU EVER ENCOUNTER ANY KIND OF PREJUDICES ALONG THE WAY?

Mr. Rodriguez: During the periods of my training, we never were separated because of races. I had never had any problems with that, until I got orders to ship to Germany. On the way to Fort Dix, New Jersey, the bus made a stop in Jackson, Mississippi, and at the bus station there were two doors, one said "For Whites" and the other "For Blacks." So, needless to say, I stayed on the bus and did not get to eat or drink anything until later that day. That was my first encounter with the separation of the races.

MS. VARGAS: ONCE YOU FINISHED YOUR TRAINING AND REACHED YOUR DESTINATION WHAT DID YOU EXPECT TO FIND?

Mr. Rodriguez: When I arrived in Germany, I didn't expect anything but to be exposed to another culture and more military training. During my stay in Germany there was more training and long stays out in the fields. There was not much time to get to know and see Germany, but that was all right because I was getting to be a better soldier and a better person.

MS. VARGAS: ARE THERE ANY SPECIAL ENCOUNTERS YOU MIGHT HAVE HAD WITH THE ENEMY WHILE IN VIETNAM?

Mr. Rodriguez: While in combat, my unit did a lot of "seek and destroy" missions. We had to go into the jungles and wetlands [rice paddies] of Vietnam.

MS. VARGAS: HISTORY HAS SAID VIETNAM VETS WERE NOT SEEN AS HEROES, NOR WERE THEY RECEIVED WITH OPEN ARMS UPON THEIR RETURN. WHEN YOU RETURNED, WHAT WERE YOUR REACTIONS SEEING ALL THESE PROTESTS ALL OVER THE UNITED STATES?

Mr. Rodriguez: On my first return from Vietnam in 1968-69, I did notice these protests. Upon my return from Vietnam and arriving in California, we were welcomed with protests and called names. However, I was thinking more on getting home and to my family that I didn't pay much attention to the protests and the name calling. I believe everybody has a right to speak up and express their own feelings, so I took the protests as that and nothing more. On the return after my second tour (1970-71), I did not see as many protests.

MS. VARGAS: DID YOU FEEL THE WAR WAS FOR A JUST CAUSE?

Mr. Rodriguez: The war of Vietnam might have had one reason or another, but my reason for going was because my country called and I answered. Sometimes to keep the peace and freedoms wars are fought and someone has to do the fighting.

MS. VARGAS: DO YOU HAVE ANY REGRETS ABOUT ANYTHING YOU MIGHT HAVE BEEN ORDERED TO DO WHILE IN COMBAT?

Mr. Rodriguez: As a soldier you do what needs to be done, and as a leader you take orders and give orders and get the mission done. Wars are not nice and lives will be lost, but that is the price some pay for freedom, as we all know.

MS. VARGAS: ANY REGRETS?

Mr. Rodriguez: I have no regrets serving my country or anything that I went through in the military. If the call ever came for me to serve my country again, I would do so without question. Being in the military and serving one's country is an honor you remember with lots of pride. There is no other feeling like it, and it is a privilege to be able to serve today especially if the person is willing and volunteers of their own free will. One never knows what will happen while serving, but one thing is certain: the memory will live with you as long as you live.

MS. VARGAS: LOOKING BACK AND KNOWING WHAT YOU KNOW NOW, WOULD YOU ENCOURAGE OR DISCOURAGE OTHERS TO JOIN THE ARMED FORCES, AND, IF SO, WHAT WOULD YOU TELL THEM?

Mr. Rodriguez: I would always encourage young people to join the armed services for the experience, travel, training, and the chance to serve their country. I know that if I had not joined the army, I would have never gotten to travel the United States as well as other places around the world. I might not have gotten the experiences that made me the wiser and better person I am today.

MS. VARGAS: DO YOU HAVE ANYONE SPECIAL IN THE ARMED SERVICES AT THE PRESENT TIME?

Mr. Rodriguez: Now I have a son who is in the U.S. Army and doing real well. He is out there doing what the army says to do, "BE ALL YOU CAN BE."

Alonso "Tiny" Barrientes, Jr.
Interviewed by Erika Longoria

The reason I remembered Tiny, when I was considering a veteran to interview, was because of the tailgate of his truck. I had seen it several times. It has a customized picture of the Vietnam memorial statue of the three soldiers walking together. Tiny's face had been drawn into the memorial and "Vietnam Vet" was written beside the artwork. Yellow ribbons and flags adorn his home in Brownsville. Purple Heart license plates hang from the car parked in his driveway.

He sits me down and brings out an array of tri-fold project boards covered with old photos of him while serving in Vietnam, newspaper clippings from the time, and an AK-47 similar to the one he carried around with him more than thirty years ago in the jungles of Vietnam. These days Tiny organizes Memorial Day events and makes presentations at local schools. This was by no means his first interview.

MS. LONGORIA: WHAT YEARS DID YOU SERVE IN VIETNAM?
Mr. Barrientes: From 1969 to 1970.
MS. LONGORIA: HOW OLD WERE YOU?
Mr. Barrientes: Not old enough to drink; not old enough to vote. I was nineteen. I was drafted.
MS. LONGORIA: WHAT WAS YOUR RANK, POSITION?

Mr. Barrientes: United States Marine Corps. I was a G-4. I was an O-3-11. What was that? I was infantry. You were a number.

MS. LONGORIA: WHAT WERE SOME OF YOUR RESPONSIBILITIES?

Mr. Barrientes: I was out there to protect a hill and I took care of a perimeter, and on that hill we took care of telecommunications, where helicopters land, and if there was any activity at night we would go in the day and check it out. Of course our perimeter was surrounded by wire. Concertina, barbed wire, you know. Concertina wire, that's what we called it. I was to guard a hill, Hill 327, just outside of Da Nang. During the day we would go on patrols.

MS. LONGORIA: HOW DID YOU FIND OUT YOU WERE GOING TO VIETNAM?

Mr. Barrientes: You didn't find out, you knew. Well, everyone that graduated either you went to college or you went to the service. You got in trouble with the law, the judge says, "You want to join the service, or you want to go to jail?" That doesn't happen anymore. It's against the law to do that. I graduated. Then I got a scholarship, and I couldn't hack it. So I got drafted. I was nineteen, 103 pounds.

MS. LONGORIA: DID YOU HAVE ANY EXPECTATIONS? WERE YOU SCARED, NERVOUS, OR EXCITED?

Mr. Barrientes: Oh, yes. You know, when you're over there, everybody carries a cross and everybody prays. You come back home, nobody prays. You know, we shouldn't do that. You forget. You shouldn't. You should always be grateful to God. At the beginning it's like the first day of school when you're a kid, you know, wondering what's next. Then after a couple of months you catch the ropes. My first two months I was caught sleeping on post and I had "office hours," which means I could get court-martialed, but since I came out with honors at boot camp, things like that, they gave me a break. So what they had me doing as punishment was putting wires around a hill and burning shit cans. You know, potty cans. You pour out the can and put distillate oil on and burn it. That was my punishment for two weeks. The guy that caught me was a "pothead" and later I caught him because I became a security guard at the entrance of the hill, like the check man at the entrance of the hill. I was in charge of anyone that came in. I would check to see if any bad people were coming in, and I caught him. He had marijuana stashed in his rifle, and I turned him in. I was taking care of the hill. I became an MP for two months. I caught him with drugs and he was sent to the ... he was busted ... and sent to the jail, and he threatened to kill me. But he was sent away. From then on, after I got caught, hey, I got to take care of myself. So you go out at night and you drink "moon juice" to stay awake. Speed, we called it "moon juice." You sip on that stuff and you jaw-jack all night long. You remember when you were a kid the things that you did and you talked all night. So you stayed awake.

MS. LONGORIA: WHAT WAS YOUR FIRST IMPRESSION OF VIETNAM?

Mr. Barrientes: I was scared. I was scared shitless. You know, "You're goin' this way. you're goin' that way." And you've got your bag and then your rifle and then you're like, "Where am I goin'?" And they've got you in a "4-by." A "4-by" is one of those big trucks you know, and there you go, you know. Once you're settled in it's nothing like when you're getting married and you know where you're goin'. This was like, you don't know where you're going.

I never imagined what it [Vietnam] was. I knew it was a jungle out there. You would see hills and then you're up in a hill. It was all jungle. It was tropical. I always carried a 35 millimeter. It was one of those things that I had over there. I always took snapshots. I lost a lot of them. But they trained you how to survive over there and we knew we were going to a jungle. I got to see a lot of people not coming back. After I got wounded, I was sent back to this place close to the airport. Those big trailers, you've seen those big trailers that we have going to the port? But without the box, just the bed, boxes, piles of GIs. You would see them every day. You know how many died in Vietnam? You know how many died per week? One-hundred-and-fifty, for seven years. And that's a true story. Fifty-eight thousand soldiers. That was the average: 150 soldiers a week for seven years. And that was not a war; it was a "conflict."

MS. LONGORIA: WHERE WERE YOU FIRST SENT?

Mr. Barrientes: I was sent to Da Nang. Da Nang City. I basically could stay there. I traveled a lot. After I became a security officer, I was traveling with a guy who had tactics information and I flew with him on those helicopters they use now. I flew with him for about two months. We would fly to China Beach. I was like his guard. Can you imagine me, a small kid, carrying a weapon? I had a .45. Those were some of my assignments. Then after I got wounded, they had me doing artwork. They found out that I could do art. Art has always helped me throughout my life. On the hill when the helicopters would land you would have this plywood all over so the dust wouldn't blow to the tents and I did a big logo. So they had me doing tactics, how we were going to shoot or how the airplanes were going to hit enemies. I was drawing tactics. Now they do that through the computer. I did that for my last few months there. Me, 103 pounds, right there [points to a picture of himself], an MP, come on. I looked like a little Vietnamese. I was a gook. That word was used a lot: "Gook." Considering us, that we were there, we were the gooks. If you crossed to Mexico, you were a gook. We called the Viet Congs gooks.

MS. LONGORIA: WHAT DOES "GOOK" MEAN?

Mr. Barrientes: I don't know. I guess a foreigner. Gook. They used to call them the gooks. "I shot three gooks," or "The gooks are coming from the north." The Viet Congs, the gooks.

MS. LONGORIA: HOW DID YOU GET THERE? HOW WAS THE TRIP?

Mr. Barrientes: From here we went on a humongous plane; none of this type that had three rows. This was a big, humongous airplane. Then they shoot down this screen where you see like a drive-in theater and you watch a movie. A big plane. It landed in Hawaii. From Hawaii it went to Okinawa. From Okinawa it went to Vietnam. And at Okinawa the plane was so heavy, I actually remember, the plane was so heavy with troops and had so much fuel left over that it had to throw some of the liquid out, jet fuel, because it was too heavy to land. And that's what it did. It just went around and dropped some of the jet fuel so we can land in Okinawa. I didn't know that until they told us later. How was the trip? I couldn't go to sleep. None of us could go to sleep.

MS. LONGORIA: DID YOU SEE ANY ACTION?
Mr. Barrientes: I was one of those fortunate guys that was not constantly in the bush. That's what they called it, the bush. I was taking care of a hill. There were people that were constantly in combat. They lived in combat; they lived in the jungle, the infantry. I was a fortunate infantry that was based on a hill, went on patrols, saw action and came back to the hill. The other guys on the ground, the only way to get back to your ground was to get shot.

MS. LONGORIA: WHEN WERE YOU WOUNDED?
Mr. Barrientes: On a patrol. Ask me where? In the ass. See, and people laugh, and that's cool. People always want to know, "Hey, where did you get shot at?" They think I'm kidding you know. I was patrolling on the bottom of the Hill 327 and there was movement that night and I had to go out on patrol. As a matter of fact we were out on patrol with the 5th Marines. We were scattered and had to go into the Vietnamese houses and ask for any enemies. When we got ambushed we were in a wave like this [makes V-shape with hands]. Our patrol man was up front and we got fire up front, so everybody goes down and the sergeant was saying, "Move forward, move forward." I was like, "Shit, I'm not going to move forward." They kept shooting so I got shot in the back.

MS. LONGORIA: IS THERE ANY PARTICULAR DAY OR EVENT YOU REMEMBER THE MOST?

Alonso Barrientes

—Courtesy of Alonso Barrientes

Mr. Barrientes: Yeah, I was in the hospital. A lot of soldiers from different branches come in with broken legs and that's when I picked up a cigarette for the first time, to relax. At like one o'clock or five o'clock in the afternoon that's when the helicopters used to come in and I used to carry around my camera. That's when they would bring in their wounded soldiers. They would say, "No pictures beyond this point," and I would sneak in there just like I was sneaking out of the bush and "click." But all those pictures that I had, when we came back we went through this process center and they would look at all your photos, books, and take all the nasty pictures away.

MS. LONGORIA: WHAT PEOPLE, THINGS, OR PLACES DO YOU REMEMBER MOST FROM THE TIME YOU SERVED?

Mr. Barrientes: The guy that caught me asleep, that's the one I remember the most. I was sitting in a bunker, you've got sand bags in front of you and you're looking down the hill, and I was asleep. The sergeant got me from here [grabs throat in choke position] and was choking me, and he told me that's what would've happened if the enemy would have come in here and because of you we would have lost more people. That's the guy that burned me. That's the guy I burned later. But it's true; anybody that sleeps on post in a combat area is automatically court-martialed, dishonorable discharge. But I was a brand new kid on the block, you know, "Here, here's your weapon, Jack." You are a guard—how can you stay awake at night? That's the most gross part of my time there, but the most memorable. The one that I liked the most, I think, was having Christmas parties for the orphanages, for the kids that didn't have dads or moms.

Ralph J. White, Jr.
Interviewed by Miriam V. Briones

I interviewed Mr. White on April 16, 2003, at his office at the Gloor Lumber Company. Mr. White is originally from Louisiana but moved to Brownsville as a child. He was drafted in 1969 at the age of twenty through the "lottery" draft.

MS. BRIONES: WHAT WERE YOU DOING BEFORE YOU GOT DRAFTED?

Mr. White: I was an avionics technician. I worked on navigational equipment on airplanes; we had a contract with the navy.

MS. BRIONES: WERE YOU IN THE ARMY?

Mr. White: Correct, army infantry.

MS. BRIONES: HOW DID YOUR FAMILY FEEL ABOUT YOU BEING DRAFTED?

Mr. White: Ah, my father wanted me to join the navy. He said it'd be safer, but I didn't want to give them more time. I'd go through the system like everyone else.

MS. BRIONES: ONCE YOU WERE DRAFTED, WHERE DID THEY SEND YOU?

Mr. White: My father took me to the corner of Stenger and Sam Houston in San Benito (Texas), where all the Cameron County boys go. They put you on a bus there; you were taken to San Antonio. Then they put you on an airplane, send you to Tacoma, Washington, which is near Fort Lewis, and I'm on basic training there for eight weeks. I got one day off, a Sunday, then that Monday I started my advanced infantry training. That was another eight weeks. Then they gave me a five-day "delay enroute." Not a leave, it was a "delay enroute" and they gave me 50 cents to go by bus, from where my training was, to the partition point right there on the same base. So I borrowed money from the Red Cross so I could come home. [Laughs.] They didn't give me leave; they just gave me "delay enroute" and 50 cents for the ride.

MS. BRIONES: SO YOU HAD TO BORROW MONEY?

Mr. White: I had to borrow money to come home.

MS. BRIONES: THEY LOANED YOU THE MONEY RIGHT AWAY?

Mr. White: Oh, yeah, and I paid them back.

MS. BRIONES: HOW MUCH DID THEY LEND YOU?

Mr. White: $500, that's how much it cost.

MS. BRIONES: HOW DID YOU FEEL ABOUT THE WAR?

Mr. White: I didn't have an opinion. I just figured I was just gonna take care of myself so I could come home. I didn't have no political views. I guess at our age, being from down here, we figured whatever our government says we do, we do. You know.

MS. BRIONES: WHERE WERE YOU FIRST SENT?

Mr. White: Cam Ranh Bay. That's in South Vietnam.

MS. BRIONES: WERE YOU IN ANY SPECIAL TRAINING?

Mr. White: Well, it's really kind of funny. When I was there, they had everybody lined up. They hadn't really decided what to do with you yet, other than they know you're in the infantry. Well, when I was there they asked, "Are there any hand-radio operators here?" And I said "I am." And they said, "What's your call sign?" And I said, "Well, I'm a novice and I haven't got my final license." "Put your hand down." That was 'cause they had what they called a MARS station, meaning, GIs could go to these hand-radio operators in Vietnam and talk to their parents for free, if you're in a rural area. So, I didn't get it.

MS. BRIONES: WERE YOU IN ANY BIG BATTLES?

Mr. White: Well, let's not get there yet. Then from there they sent me to my battalion headquarters. They decided I was going to be a member of the 1st Infantry, 11th Brigade, Americal Division, and they sent me to Chu Lai. There you go to two more weeks of more training and you go to sapper school and you learn the tricks that the enemy has. Well, actually, Chu Lai was the actual division headquarters. After that, after the two weeks, they sent me to Duc Pho and that was our battalion headquarters. There they gave me my gear, my rucksack, my basic stuff that I needed: my gas mask, my weapons, ammunition, grenades, and smoke bombs. Then they put me on a chopper and they said, "You're going out to Field 411." I said, "What is that?" "It's a hill; it's a firebase." So I said, "Oh, okay." So they sent me there, and you could see it off at a distance. They didn't drop me off there; they dropped me on a little dike on a rice paddy, so I could walk in, so I'd fall on the mud and get muddy. I'm the new guy! There's another way of saying it. They call it the "FNG," the new guy, the "freaking new guy" you know. That's what I was. So, they all saw the chopper come in and they're all looking to see the new guy. They want to see him fall. Your pack weighs like 80 pounds and it's high. It takes you a little bit to adjust to. And I fell, of course, and I had a good laugh.

Then we started going on patrols around this firebase. We had a certain area that we covered and then, past that, a certain area where we had a marine group that covered another area, and we were in the mountains a lot. It was what they called a "free-fire zone." We'd go looking for trouble. We'd set up ambushes at night. We'd look for booby traps. It rained a lot. Got to camp for free. [Laughs.] It rained so bad sometimes that if you're on the side of the hill, you'd be in an air mattress, the air mattress would float out of the tent and you'd wake up and get wet. [Laughs.] It rained a lot and when it wasn't raining, it was hot. Real hot!

MS. BRIONES: WAS IT HUMID AS WELL?

Mr. White: Yeah, real humid. Probably at about two, three o'clock in the afternoon nothing would move. You'd set up these little blankets that they gave you as little tents to get into the shade. It was so hot, even the locals wouldn't go out. You just kinda have a little peep time there, for an hour or two. So hot for everybody.

MS. BRIONES: WHAT DID YOU DO FROM THERE?

Mr. White: We did patrols and about every three weeks we'd go back to the firebase. Spend three or four days on the firebase and have hot meals. Then they'd send us back out on patrol again. It was company patrol: that was four platoons and the "palace guard." The "palace guard" is the commanding officer's group. We were in a big company. We didn't travel; we were close to each other. There'd be five groups in an area. We'd cover a grid that would be one kilometer by one kilometer. We all had a map of that; we all knew where we were. It's pretty close, you know; it's not that big, but it was a jungle and I think that I did that for about a month, and they'll send you to FNG. You get to do "point." You're the front guy!

Ralph White

You have the machete and you're cutting through the brush. You're the guy that's either gonna get shot or bit by a snake or something like that. The FNG, he's the point man, and they rotate you. There's a couple of them, you don't do it all the time. It's very hard to do. So then our radio operator got wounded, and since I knew radios and stuff, and I knew that the radio guy could call breaks 'cause he'd carry more weight than anybody, so I said, "I'll do it." So I was radio operator for two months and we had combat, we had different things happen, people got hurt, people got killed, we killed people. It's not a good thing, you know, and we did it and then ... I got hit.

MS. BRIONES: YOU GOT WOUNDED?

Mr. White: Mm, I stepped on a land mine.

MS. BRIONES: WHERE DID YOU GET HURT?

Mr. White: I was lucky enough. Well, lucky and unlucky. It was a homemade thing made in a macro can, like a sardine can, but an oval one and they'd fill it up with nails and glass and anything to make you get infected. They didn't want to kill you, they wanted to wound you, so when the helicopter came to get you, they could get the helicopter, too. But anyway, about eight guys walked over the thing. We were in elephant grass up to our chest. Eight guys walked over. We're three to five meters apart because there were a lot of booby traps, lots. Golly, as soon as I stepped right on top of it, they hit it. Knocked me out. I flew straight up into the air. They got my feet, my legs, and my groin area; they got this hand [pointing to his right hand], my right hand and arm. We had a firefight then. And I could hear the commanding officers and captain on the radio: "Who authorized blowing up that booby trap?" Because we blew them up when we found them. "Who authorized it?" But he didn't get any answer back. We could receive, but it blew a hole in the back of the radio, but it didn't kill me, 'cause it got the radio. We couldn't transmit, so they realized something was wrong, so they called for a medivac. The medivac came in; he couldn't land.

MS. BRIONES: HOW COME HE COULDN'T LAND?

Mr. White: Too much fire! So then they had this guy; he was a "cargo ship" or a "dust off" guy. He was coming back empty and he said, you could hear him, he says, "I'll go in. If you hear me, pop smoke." So we popped smoke. He went in and he didn't have a stretcher or anything. They just put me on the floor, in there, and it was co-oo-old because it blew my clothes off, too. He had to get up real high so he wouldn't get shot at, and I think the rest of all that I remember, I was just cold all the time.

[Mr. White then recounted months of being transferred around different hospitals.] And the last place I was was the fort hospital at Fort Sam Houston, and then I had about six months left and they asked me what I wanted to do. I said, "I want out!" They said, "No, we want to keep you in because you still have some problems. We don't just want to turn you over to the VA right away." So they said, "Where do you want to go?" I said, "I want to go somewhere where there is no KP, no guard duty." I was just being facetious. They said, "We got a place like that." Mineral Wells, Texas, called Fort Walters. It's a helicopter school. They had civilian cooks, civilian guards, everything. So I just sat and worked at a print shop for six months and then they let me out and that was it.

MS. BRIONES: WHAT DID YOU GUYS DO FOR FUN IN YOUR SPARE TIME?

Mr. White: Well, we listened to cassettes and drank beer.

MS. BRIONES: DID YOU EVER ENCOUNTER ANY TUNNELS?

Mr. White: Yeah, the whole time, sure.

MS. BRIONES: DID YOU EVER GO INTO THEM?

Mr. White: No, the little guys would go in there, some of the smaller fellows. We never really cared to. We'd have to crawl in. They never really looked used, most of them that we saw. So we figured they were abandoned, and we'd just throw grenades in them and blow 'em up. We'd put CS gas in them. CS gas, it's not lethal, but you want to get out real quick. But we never found any people in them.

MS. BRIONES: WHAT DO YOU CONSIDER YOUR MOST INTERESTING EXPERIENCE?

Mr. White: I guess every now and then, we'd ah ... the companies would get together out in the brush. Then one platoon would stay with all our gear, and choppers would pick us up with our grenades and our guns and a lot of ammo and stuff, and we'd go on "eagle flights." Just looking for trouble. We would have these [small helicopters] in front. They would be flying trying to draw fire at night. Trying to draw fire! These guys are something else. And we would be behind in the "hueys" looking for these tracers because the Vietnamese like to shoot those tracers. They love watching that, you know, shooting out, like you saw in the Iraqi thing. And we would see where they would come from and then we'd shoot into them and they'd drop us off. We'd go after them. Sure, that was neat. But I enjoyed the helicopter part of it and the landing and all that, and of course seeing these big craters that some of those bombs would make. You see them on TV and they don't look that big; when you see them though, golly!

MS. BRIONES: HOW BIG WERE THEY?

Mr. White: They were like thirty to forty feet deep. The big ones, like those big tubes, like 500-pounders and when you'd fly over Vietnam it looked like it had acne. Bombs everywhere, everywhere, everywhere.

MS. BRIONES: DID YOU RECEIVE ANY RECOGNITION?

Mr. White: I got a Purple Heart.

MS. BRIONES: HOW WAS LIFE OUT THERE?

Mr. White: Well, you didn't get a lot of sleep.

MS. BRIONES: HOW MUCH DID YOU SLEEP?

Mr. White: Well, you have guard duty every night. So you're lucky if you get five or six hours, and you'd take a little nap in the afternoon when it was real hot and also there was another time we were there and a typhoon came in. A typhoon, it's like a hurricane, and all our helicopters were grounded. So when it started we were just about out of food. I think we didn't have any food for about three or four days and then the typhoon was over, and we saw a helicopter coming and we thought it was food. It was the mail, but that's all right though. We got mail. Then a few hours later we got food.

MS. BRIONES: WHAT DID YOU EAT FOR THE FOUR DAYS?

Mr. White: We were "fragging" rivers and stuff. We'd throw a grenade into the river and we'd have a guy downstream and he catches the fish that float up. Some of these little teeny streams, some of these guys there were Montagnard guys. They'd show us how to build little dams with sticks and stuff, and leave them alone and come back two to three hours later and you'd find these little fish. They were about three to four inches long. Build a little fire and just cook them whole; peel them and eat them. Just throw them on the fire! Cooked them with scales and all, and just peel them like you're peeling the skin off a whole kernel corn and eat that. It wasn't enough, but it calmed the hunger.

MS. BRIONES: WHAT YEAR WERE YOU SENT OUT?

Mr. White: I went out in '69. I don't remember exactly what date. I was in twenty months; I got a four-month "early out" for Christmas. At that time, you're already back in the country and they decided I was in good enough health and they gave me four months off. Instead of twenty-four months it was only twenty months.

MS. BRIONES: YOU WERE HOME IN 1970?

Mr. White: Right. For Christmas.

Leonardo Villarreal
Interviewed by Leo Villarreal

I interviewed Leonardo Villarreal, my dad, at his house. This was a great opportunity to find out what my dad went through in Vietnam. Although he was not in combat, it must be frightening to be sent to a nation that is at war. I had never really spoken to my father about his experience during Vietnam. When I was younger I would ask him, but he would keep his answers short and say, "I was only a mechanic. I was not in combat." The short and quick answers only raised my curiosity. How does someone go to a nation during a time of war and not have any experiences? In addition, the war was political, and Americans were protesting against the war. Thus, I had my suspicions and was determined to probe for answers.

MR. VILLARREAL: DAD, I KNOW YOU WERE IN THE AIR FORCE. WHAT WAS YOUR RANK WHEN YOU ENTERED AND WHEN YOU WERE DISCHARGED?

Mr. Villarreal: Yes, I was in the air force. I believe my rank was "airman." We did not go by "private" like in the army. Let me make sure. [My dad goes to his room for his discharge papers.] Let's see, I was an airman when I entered and a buck sergeant when I was released.

MR. VILLARREAL: I UNDERSTAND THAT YOU ENLISTED IN THE AIR FORCE, BUT THE ARMY DRAFTED YOU. CAN YOU EXPLAIN WHAT HAPPENED?

Mr. Villarreal: Well, I joined in February 1969, through the delayed enlistment program. I received a letter from the army in April, two months after I already joined the air force. I took the draft letter to the air force recruiter and he said, "Don't worry about it. You're ours." [We both laugh.] So I ended up leaving in March 1969 to San Antonio.

MR. VILLARREAL: IS THAT WHERE YOU WENT TO BASIC TRAINING?

Mr. Villarreal: Yes, I was sent to Lackland Air Force Base for basic training. I was there for about six weeks. Then from there I was sent to Rantoul Air Force Base in Illinois. They sent me for training on jet engines for six weeks. Then I was stationed for one year at Holloman Air Force Base in New Mexico. During my time at Holloman, I was sent to Germany for an exercise which lasted one month. I then returned to Holloman until I was sent to Vietnam.

MR. VILLARREAL: WHEN DID YOU GET SENT TO VIETNAM?

Mr. Villarreal: I was sent to Vietnam in 1971. I was stationed in Da Nang the whole time I was in Vietnam.

MR. VILLARREAL: WHAT WAS YOUR REACTION WHEN THEY SENT YOU TO VIETNAM?

Mr. Villarreal: I had no choice. It was not the duty station that I wanted. I wanted to go to Europe, but with the war going on I knew I would be going to Vietnam.

MR. VILLARREAL: CAN YOU DESCRIBE THE ATMOSPHERE OF VIETNAM WHEN YOU ARRIVED?

Mr. Villarreal: Let me see, the base was located right outside the city of Da Nang. It was a busy airbase. There were troops all over, and you could hear the noise of the jets taking off all the time. There were army troops, Korean troops, South Vietnamese troops, and there were business people there, too. You could hear the gunshots and the rockets firing throughout the day and night. In fact, my first night in Da Nang a cargo plane was hit, while it was on the ground, by a rocket. The explosion was loud. I jumped off my bed. I told myself: "Welcome to Vietnam." You would hear shooting around the base, outgoing artillery, the tracers, and the B-52s. Tracers were bullets that were lighted so that you could see where you were shooting. The army soldiers would adjust if needed to hit the target. They had combat troops around the base protecting it. There were army outposts around the base. They

Leonardo Villarreal

had marine troops, South Korean troops, and South Vietnamese troops all protecting the base.

I would go to Da Nang with friends. We would go and eat at restaurants. It was a busy city. There were businesspeople all around, but you would see army personnel walking around patrolling the city. Then they put the city off limits to air force personnel because it got too dangerous. That is what they told us. I guess there were too many Viet Cong soldiers in the area. They did not tell us much, so that was the end of that.

Also, when I was in Vietnam we did not use "green." That is what they called U.S. money. We used MPC, which is like play money. I don't know how this worked, but we all had a "mamasan," which is a Vietnamese lady who would clean the barracks. My mamasan would ask me to ask my mother to send 20 dollars hidden in an envelope. She would tell me, "You give me 20 dollar 'green,' I give you 30 or 40 dollar MPC." They would do that and make a lot of money. These ladies would also do our clothes, but we had to pay them. They also would smuggle stuff off the base. They had some GIs that would buy stuff for them and they would smuggle it off the base and sell it outside. Each barracks had their own "mamasan."

There was also a lot of racial tension between the blacks and the whites, especially outside the base when we were allowed to go out. There were a lot of Hispanics there, but most of the fighting was between the whites and the blacks. Remember, this was back in the early '70s. Times were different.

MR. VILLARREAL: WHAT WAS YOUR ROLE IN VIETNAM?

Mr. Villarreal: I worked in the shop, the main shop, and we would all work on the planes. I worked on the engines only. Other people worked on the flight line. These people worked on the actual planes. They would tell me if I needed to replace or repair parts. I only dealt with the jet engines, which is what I was trained for. The flight crew would take the engine off the plane; take it to the shop where I would work on it.

MR. VILLARREAL: DID YOU KNOW ANY PILOTS?

Mr. Villarreal: No, I did not know them personally. I would only salute them. They were officers.

MR. VILLARREAL: WHAT WAS THE WORST EXPERIENCE YOU WENT THROUGH IN VIETNAM?

Mr. Villarreal: The worst experience was a barracks getting a direct hit. What was scary was that it was right next to mine and these barracks were only made of wood. I was working the night shift and I had gone to eat breakfast. I came back and I was lying on my bed reading a magazine when the warning siren had gone off. Not even a second later we heard the big explosion: "boom BOOM." I even heard the rocket coming in before it hit. There was another barracks that was hit further down. The barracks that was right next to mine was like twenty to thirty feet apart. When I ran outside to see what happened, the barracks was V-shaped. It was a two-story barracks and you can see where the rocket hit right in the middle. People were trapped at the ends of the barracks, and you can hear guys screaming because they were being burned alive. Some guys survived, but they were badly injured. The other barracks that was hit was half a block down from mine, but only the edge was hit. It was chaos. There was a helicopter flying over, people running and screaming, trying to help the people get out. There were people lying on the ground. It was bad. One guy I remember we tried to help was trapped by his legs. He was burning from the heat. He wasn't in flames. We could not get him out because of the debris, so he threw himself out. But those barracks had some aluminum on top. So when he threw himself out, the aluminum tore him up. And we saw all his insides. I don't know what happened to him, but we did stay with him until the medics came. We did not want to move him because, well, we were afraid. The fire spread and my barracks caught on fire, but no major damage. There was smoke inside but that was all.

After that incident, whenever the warning sirens went off, I would freeze and look up even if I was in a building. One time the warning sirens went off and we heard [a rocket] fly right over us, "zoom," and it hit somewhere down the flight line. That was my worst experience in Vietnam. These men were not best friends, but I knew them by face because our barracks were next to each other.

MR. VILLARREAL: HOW LONG WERE YOU IN VIETNAM, AND WHEN DID YOU LEAVE?

Mr. Villarreal: I was there for about a year and I left Vietnam in February 1972. Let me tell you, I was happy to get my ass out of there.

Joe Castillo
Interviewed by Leo Villarreal

Joe Castillo is my uncle, and until this interview I knew nothing of his Vietnam experience, other than the fact that he was there. My father, who was in Vietnam as well, told me that my Uncle Joe's experience in Vietnam would be interesting because he had been in the marines. I called my uncle, and he agreed to do the interview. He said he needed a break from all the housework he was doing. After I rescued my uncle from the housework, we headed to Whataburger for some coffee, breakfast, and the interview.

MR. VILLARREAL: UNCLE JOE, I KNOW YOU WERE IN THE MARINES. CAN YOU TELL ME YOUR SITUATION BEFORE YOU SIGNED UP?

Mr. Castillo: I graduated from high school and I needed a job. I looked around and I could not find one. It was hard to find a job back then. There were a lot of graduates that stayed in Brownsville and they were all looking for jobs, too. I went to a job interview; it opened my eyes. The job was for an aircraft painter. The guy was asking me questions like what I knew about painting aircraft and I answered what he wanted to hear. I told him that if I were given a chance I would learn. He told me that he did not want to hire me because I was eligible for the draft. He said it would be expensive for the company to train me, and I could be gone next month. After that interview I thought maybe that was the reason it was hard for me to find a job. So then I went downtown to see the army recruiter. I spoke with him and he guaranteed me a job with computers. That is what I wanted to do, work with computers. He had the contract all written up for me, ready to sign. But I did not sign it. I went to the other recruiters to see what they had to offer. I went to the navy recruiter, but I did not like the uniform. Then I went to the marines. This guy was thin, tall, and he looked sharp with his uniform. The army guy was fat. Anyway, I told the marine recruiter that I wanted to work with computers, and he told me he could not guarantee me anything. I told him the army recruiter was able to. He told me, "Well, go sign up with the army." I went home, but I did not sign anything. The next day the marine recruiter and army recruiter came to my house. The marine recruiter comes in and tells me there is an opening for logistics. He has me do a typing test for one minute, but it felt more like five minutes. I had the whole page filled out and he says, "Good job." I signed on with the marines, and thirty days later I was on a bus to San Antonio for my physical.

MR. VILLARREAL: WHAT YEAR WAS THAT?

Mr. Castillo: The year was April 1971, and I served up to May 1975.

MR. VILLARREAL: WHERE DID YOU GO FOR BOOT CAMP, AND WHAT WAS IT LIKE?

Mr. Castillo: I went to the Marine Corps Recruit Depot in San Diego, California. When I first arrived, we loaded up on a green bus. This instructor gets on the bus and begins yelling. He says, "From now on your ass is ours!" I was like, "Who the hell does this guy think he is?" Anyway, we get to the marine depot and we are standing on a yellow line. We don't know what is going on. We are standing there and they have us go into this building for our haircuts. They tell me, "How do you want your hair cut?" I told them, "Just a little bit off the sides, sir, please." They said, "all right," and zoom. I was like, "Ahhh shit." In the Marine Corps they shave everything off. I mean everything! I wanted to cry when I saw myself in the mirror. Then after that you go to "processing," where you take off all your clothes, and they give you a box. You put all your civilian clothes in the box. You seal up the box, put your home address on it, and they send it home. You stay naked. You have a towel wrapped around you and that's it. Then you go to the next station, where everybody takes a

Joe Castillo
—Courtesy of Joe Castillo

shower. Then you go and get your clothes. They give you a shirt, pants, socks, underwear, and tennis shoes. They give you two of each. Well, then you get dressed and the tennis shoes don't fit you. You go, "Sir?" And he answers, "I don't want to hear your problems." Then I said, "But these shoes don't fit." He replied, "I said I don't care." So there you are, asking people and you trade off with other people's shoes. This was like two o'clock in the morning when we are doing all this stuff. So we start going into the barracks to go to sleep. I was one of the last ones, so I took one of the top beds near the entrance. About 4:30 in the morning someone comes in, two hours later, and turns on the light. I was like, "What idiot turned on the light?" Since I was on top I had this bright bulb right in my face. The instructor comes in and says, "Everybody up!" He has one of the tops of the trashcans, the aluminum ones, banging it with a stick: "Bam! Bam! Bam!" I put the pillow over my face. I did not want to hear anything. He comes over and says, "Didn't you hear me?" He grabs the mattress and flips it over, and I'm on the mattress. He flips me over all the way to the floor. This was my first day there. [We laugh.] That was the last time I slept near the entrance.

You get into the swing of things after the first few days. Boot camp was nothing more than physically making sure that you are capable of carrying out the task, and mentally, too. They gave us history training, weapons training. We had to break down our weapons, clean them, and put them back together. We did survival skills where we had to choke our partners and I did not pass out. I saw black, but I did not pass out. Then they asked whose partner did not pass out, and my partner raised his hand. Then they wanted us to do it again, and I faked it. Man, I did not pass out, but I faked it. I saw how the other people passed out, so I copied them. After graduation I came home. Then I reported back and I went through more training, advanced training, where we did night training, weapons, night survival. We did that war paint where we camouflaged our face, and we did training with booby traps. These traps were loud, man. They were explosives, and you can feel the ground shake. So we graduated from there, and then that is when we went to Okinawa.

MR. VILLARREAL: IS THIS WHEN YOU GOT SENT TO VIETNAM?

Mr. Castillo: Yeah! I got my order and all it said was "Far East," and I did not know what that was. I was sent on August 9, 1971, on my birthday. That was my birthday present. I got to Okinawa and that is where they ask me if I wanted to "float" or "rock." I asked, "What the hell is that?" They told me "rock" was you stay in Okinawa and "float" was you go on a ship. I got mess duty my first week on the ship. We were on a rotation. Well, the first three days I was sick as a dog. I was serving chow and there I was throwing up. They would tell me, "You big badass marine, you can handle it." I was up until two in the morning cleaning the kitchen spotless. Then I had to wake up at four in the morning to prepare breakfast at six. I did that for the first two days and after that I said, "The heck with this!" I went into another area and I bunked there so they would not find me. I did not get up until ten that day. Man, everyone was pissed off with me. Everyone was looking for me. I told them I was so tired I went to the wrong place and slept. They bought it the first day, but then I did it again the second day and they did not buy it the second day. I was in trouble. I did not care what they did to me. I was so tired, but I was getting better. I began to eat again so I was feeling better. It just so happened that that day I was not supposed to be on mess duty anymore, but nobody bothered to take me off. The petty officer in charge wanted me to work another week. So I messed with him another week or so. And at the end of the following week this guy was so ticked off with me he wanted my butt. I went to go complain to my gunnery sergeant. I said, "Look, you guys told me I was only supposed to be on mess duty for a week, and I've been there for two weeks." He said, "Yeah! You're supposed to be there one week." So he told me he was going to look into it. We went to the captain and I explained what had happened. He got mad. He said, "What! How come no one has told me about this, gunny? I don't want no one taking advantage and abusing my men, gunny." I told him that they wanted to write me up because I did not report to mess duty that day. He said for me to stay up there with him, and if anyone had a problem with that they would have to answer to him. The captain and me became best buds after that. I would take his laundry and I snuck mine in there, too. I had mine washed and pressed. I did not have to do it myself like everyone else.

It just so happened that he was in charge of the S-4, the whole unit. The S-4 was logistics, supplies, and ammo-techs. So the captain got more comfortable with me. He started giving me different assignments. And that is when I began to branch out into different areas, for example, the ammo-tech where we trained the companies, because we had companies like the Golf Company, Fox Company. We had four to six companies. I forget now. It's been awhile. Anyway this Golf Company went out to the field, and they had this new lieutenant right out of West Point. Real gung ho. Well, he orders 1,000 rounds of ammo. So I told him, "Sir, don't you think that's a lot of rounds?" He tells me, "Who are you to tell me what I need? I am telling you what I want, and you get me what I need." I said, "Yes, sir." So I went to tell the captain and he was like, "What?" So the captain tells me give him what he wants. So I go to the ammo dump and I got a truck and a trailer to pick me up. We get to the ammo dump and the people are looking at me like, "Damn, man, what the hell are you going to do with all this ammo?" So I signed the requisition, and said, "Just load up the trucks, man." One of the rules was whatever you checked out, you couldn't bring it back to the ammo dump. We took it out to the field where the lieutenant was. They had eight grenade launchers, but five of them broke down. So the lieutenant calls me back and asks me if I could pick up the ammo and take it back. I told him, "No, sir. None of it can be returned back. You have to exhaust it all." They had to stay there another week until all the rounds were used.

MR. VILLARREAL: WHAT WAS YOUR ROLE IN VIETNAM?

Mr. Castillo: We used to go out and set camps. We call it the recon advance party team. We would fly out to camps that were going to be occupied and make sure there were no booby traps. We made sure that the water was hooked up and working and stuff like that. So we had like four helicopters that would fly out, and then we would start making assessments and reports. Then we would take another team out there to secure the perimeter. And then once the perimeter was secure, we would bring other guys to set up showers and latrines. We did this in Thailand and Vietnam, but sometimes in Vietnam the stuff did not flow. So we had to get fifty-five-gallon drums, cut them in half, and shove them under the hole. I felt sorry for the shit birds that had to take them out and go dump it somewhere else. That was nasty stuff.

I would also do search and rescue. I was not a pilot. Those guys were crazy. It's like you see on television. They got the rock-n-roll music going and they are going fast. They must have been high on something, because they were calm and cool, and to have people firing at you had to make you nervous. We went to this camp; we had a squadron of helicopters taking troops. And we were flying low, close to the treetops, and they are shooting at you. So you really can't see who is shooting at you. You just see like a little spark from the gun. If you have a good eye you can see it, or at night you can see it better. You just hear when it hits the helicopter, but we were okay. We got in and out of there.

MR. VILLARREAL: WHERE WERE YOU STATIONED IN VIETNAM?

Mr. Castillo: Our first camp was in Thailand. We had a camp out there, but my main stay was on ships. The ships were docking about five miles from the shoreline of Vietnam. The ships would provide gun support at night. They would fire like crazy: "Boom! Boom! Boom!" We would provide helicopter support; basically our mission was search and rescue. Mainly downed pilots, but we had other missions we would do. The weirdest mission I went on was a submarine watch. We would go around looking for periscopes around our perimeter of ships. And we spotted some Russian submarines very close by. At night they have a little red light, and I spotted the red light. As a matter of fact, I took a picture, but all you see is a red light. But they were there. They were close by. A week later we lost our first helicopter; it just disappeared from the sky. We believe the Russian sub blew it out of the sky. Then we continued on the mission and the second one goes down, and guess what? On the third one I was scheduled to go but something happened. I could not make it, and that one goes down. After the third one, we did not go on submarine watch. It got dangerous so they canceled it. We went out on a Saturday where the chopper was on location. We saw the chopper's helmets floating in the water and the tail of the chopper. And some of our helicopters were equipped to spray Agent Orange, and that was floating. We stayed around to look for bodies, but there were so many sharks in that ocean I couldn't believe it.

MR. VILLARREAL: WHAT WERE THE NAMES OF THE SHIPS?

Mr. Castillo: The first ship was the USS *Tripoli* and the second ship was the USS *New Orleans*.

MR. VILLARREAL: WHAT WAS YOUR WORST EXPERIENCE IN VIETNAM?

Mr. Castillo: I guess the worst was when we brought back the body bags. We would go pick up the bodies at the LZs, which were landing zones. We would ask them to pop up a flare and we would tell them what color to pop up. To make sure they were the right people, because the Vietnamese had flares, too. Right before we landed, we told them which color to use, and if it was not the right color we were not landing. We would pick up the wounded and the dead, sometimes without the body bag. We would bring them back to the ship, and on the ship we had a huge icebox where we kept the dead bodies. One time I had to do guard duty and it gave me the chills. The carpenters would do the coffins for the bodies, and every coffin had the American flag over it. They would take all the coffins to the Philippines and from there I think they took them to Norton Air Force Base in the United States. That was the saddest part, seeing all those coffins.

I was not one of those guys that were always in there. I was an "in-and-out guy," which I don't know which is worse because you don't know when your number was up. In fact, I thought our number was up once because we had a mission, and it was an easy one. We had to go to one of the bases in Thailand for some supplies; we needed milk and other supplies for the ship. On the way out they started shooting at us. You can see the bullets coming in through the skin of the helicopter. From the inside you see the lines and those lines were filled with hydraulic oil. Well, the lines busted and there was hydraulic oil in the inside of the helicopter. We were already past land and we were out at sea and we started to pick up air. The chopper was going up, up, up and all of a sudden that sucker just dropped. We lost it. I thought we were going into the water. Keep in mind I had my belt on. I had a .45 and the ammo. I had my canteen, my rifle and the ammo for that, and my boots. I was going down, so I began to take off everything so I could float. Well, what happened was we hit an air pocket and the pilots were able to stabilize the helicopter. But I thought that was it for me. It scared the shit out of me. And all this was for milk. But let me tell you, sometimes we ran low and when we saw the supply ship come in, it was like Christmas for us.

Let me tell you the best part was when we had liberty. Sometimes the ship would go into the ports like Australia, Okinawa, Japan, Philippines, and there were some others. We would get like a twenty-four-hour pass. As long as you told them where you were, it was okay.

MR. VILLARREAL: WHAT WAS YOUR ROLE IN THE HELICOPTER?

Mr. Castillo: It depends. We took rotations. Sometimes I was the gunner and sometimes a watcher. When I was using the machine gun I was hanging on a sling. And I would just shoot. You couldn't see what you were shooting at, you just shot. One time our chopper did go down. We were out there almost a week until they finally came to get us. The problem was we did not have any supplies and we had no food. When we got back to the ship, there was not much food in the ship either. So I had a friend and we had those convex boxes where you keep your weapon. I asked him to give us a box that had C-rations. It had crackers and food and cigarettes. So they gave us the whole box and we partied out. We ate and ate and ate until we exploded. I slept for two days, and they left us alone. Luckily nothing happened to us out there within those five days. We just had to stay away and lay low, in case the VC came to investigate. Yet, stay close enough to where somebody can find it and we pop a flare. We were search and rescue yet no one was coming to rescue us. The problem was we were not pilots. Those pilots go down and they scramble to get them right away. They probably thought: "They're marines. They can survive a week." But luckily they came and we got out of there.

MR. VILLARREAL: HOW LONG WERE YOU IN VIETNAM?

Mr. Castillo: Let's see: I did thirteen months. We left November in 1972. When you come back you have to come back in uniform. We came back through American Airlines and when we got back I saw all these protesters in the airport lobby. They had all these signs saying: "Baby Killers." They were yelling at us, and spitting at us. We did not know what was going on. We did not see the news like they did here. That was the first time I felt I needed to be careful who I told I was in the military. The last thing I wanted to do was to get beat up or killed by one of these protesters. So if you did not need to know I wasn't going to say anything. Anyway, when I got back I was stationed at Camp Pendleton. I was there until I was discharged in May 1975.

Ricardo Ortiz
Interviewed by Rolando R. Barron

I interviewed Mr. Ortiz at J. T. Canales Elementary School, where he is presently employed as a counselor. He makes his home in Brownsville, Texas, with his wife Martina and daughter Marisa. He shared with me how he arrived in Brownsville. Born of Spanish parents in Santander, Spain, on June 10, 1947, he moved with his family to Matamoros, Tamaulipas. They lived there till he was about fifteen and then moved to Brownsville. He became a United States citizen in 1968. He attended Saint Joseph Academy and graduated in 1965. He attended college at the University of Dallas, and received his bachelor of arts degree in history. After graduating, he decided to join the military.

MR. BARRON: HOW OLD WERE YOU WHEN YOU DECIDED TO JOIN THE NAVY?
Mr. Ortiz: I was twenty-one years of age and had recently graduated from college.
MR. BARRON: WHAT WERE THE FACTORS IN YOUR DECIDING TO JOIN THE ARMED FORCES?
Mr. Ortiz: After graduating my status as 1S (student status) changed to 1A (eligible to be drafted). So, it was either get drafted or join. I decided to join.
MR. BARRON: WHAT BRANCH OF THE MILITARY DID YOU CHOOSE?
Mr. Ortiz: I decided on joining the United States Navy.
MR. BARRON: WHY THIS BRANCH? WAS IT YOUR FIRST CHOICE?
Mr. Ortiz: I joined because I wanted to travel and see different parts of the world. Yes, this was my first choice; my second would have been the United States Air Force.
MR. BARRON: AFTER ENLISTING, WHERE DID YOU GO FOR BASIC TRAINING?
Mr. Ortiz: After enlisting, I reported on September 1, 1969, to RTC (Recruit Training Center) in Orlando, Florida. Training lasted from September of 1969 to November 1969. When I completed basic training, I reported to the Naval Technical

Center in Jacksonville, Florida. There, I received training in aviation ordnance, which lasted twenty weeks, until April of 1970.

MR. BARRON: DID ANY OF YOUR FRIENDS GO WITH YOU?

Mr. Ortiz: No, but I did meet a friend at the Naval Tech Center in Jacksonville, Florida. He was Everett Lande, also from Brownsville. I also met some friends I made during basic training.

MR. BARRON: AFTER YOUR TECHNICAL SCHOOL TRAINING, WHERE WAS YOUR NEXT DUTY ASSIGNMENT?

Mr. Ortiz: I received orders to VT-24 at Naval Air Station Chase Field in Beeville, Texas. There we received training on loading munitions on fighter aircraft. This consisted of loading 2.7" rockets and the 20mm guns.

MR. BARRON: HOW DID YOU FIND OUT ABOUT YOUR ORDERS, AND WHERE WERE YOU ASSIGNED: TO A SHIP OR LAND BASE?

Mr. Ortiz: In December 1971 I received orders to Naval Air Station at Cubi Point, Subic Bay, in the Philippines. I was assigned to a land base with the ordnance armory responsible for magazines, transshipments of ammunition to and from the base, with final destination to Vietnam. We also made mine dropping exercises. Then I was temporarily assigned to the USS *Midway* and reported to Yankee Station off the coast of Vietnam in the Gulf of Tonkin. While on this assignment my primary duties were on the flight deck, loading ordnance on aircraft (A-7 Corsairs, A-6 Intruders, F-4 Phantoms).

MR. BARRON: WHAT WAS LIFE LIKE ON YOUR SHIP?

Mr. Ortiz: Depending on the flight schedule, we worked from twelve to fourteen hours a day loading weapons on airplanes. After we went off-duty we watched a little closed circuit television and went to sleep. Our quarters were located in the forward part of the ship near the catapults, and there was always a lot of noise. At first it was hard to get any sleep, but after a while we got used to it. When we got off work we were so tired that the noise did not bother us. Life aboard the ship was very routine: work, eat, and sleep. Work on the flight deck was very stressful. It was very noisy and dangerous. You had to be alert at all times and make sure that you did not violate any safety regulations. There was a safety of-

Ricardo Ortiz

ficer on the island above the flight deck ready to yell at you through the loudspeaker or write you up if you were goofing off.

MR. BARRON: WHAT WAS YOUR INVOLVEMENT IN THE WAR, DIRECT OR INDIRECT?

Mr. Ortiz: I was indirectly involved in the war by arming aircraft so that they could drop ordnance in the war zone. We were out at sea so we did not see any direct action. They did call general quarters once because they had spotted some MIGs close by. Aircraft would eventually return to the ship damaged by enemy fire.

When stationed at Naval Air Station Cubi Point, I was indirectly involved with the war by transshipping ordnance to various destinations in Vietnam through Cubi Point and NavMag in Subic Bay.

MR. BARRON: WERE YOU STILL IN THE MILITARY WHEN THE WAR ENDED? WHAT WERE YOUR FEELINGS WHEN YOU HEARD THE WAR WAS OVER?

Mr. Ortiz: I was out of the military when the war ended. I felt sad realizing that many young men had died and we did not attain our goals. I was also angry because politics had made that war drag on for so long, and that both the government and the country lost sight of our objectives and refused to give the military the backing it needed to win.

Leonel Casanova
Interviewed by Leo Casanova, Jr.

Mr. Casanova is my father and he is a veteran of the Vietnam War. He was born in Port Isabel on July 2, 1952. He was one of six brothers born to Carlos and Marcela Casanova. He always had a fondness of water, growing up in a port city. His father was a shrimp-fisherman and he became one, too, at an early age. His love of the ocean led him to make his decision to join the navy. He joined the navy for several reasons, but his main one was to avoid the draft. He decided that since he was going to get drafted anyway he might as well join something he liked. He joined on December 20, 1970, at the age of eighteen. He signed up for four years. He received an education after his release from the navy and is now a middle school counselor in Los Fresnos, Texas. He said the navy was a great experience and taught him discipline.

MR. CASANOVA: WHERE WERE YOU SENT FOR TRAINING CAMP?

Mr. Casanova: I was sent to Orlando, Florida, for thirteen weeks of training.

MR. CASANOVA: WAS TRAINING CAMP DIFFICULT TO ADJUST TO, AND WAS IT EASY TO MAKE FRIENDS?

Mr. Casanova: Training camp was difficult at first due to getting used to the routines and the discipline. Making friends was easy for me since I always had a lot of friends. Some friends of mine were Juan Jaimez of Cotula, Texas, and several African-American sailors.

MR. CASANOVA: WAS THERE ANY DISCRIMINATION AMONG THE SAILORS?

Mr. Casanova: There was really no discrimination because everyone there was from the same background. No one was really better than anyone else. Everyone basically got along.

MR. CASANOVA: WHERE WERE YOU SENT AFTER TRAINING CAMP?

Mr. Casanova: After basic training I was sent home, but then I went to Storekeeper "A" School in San Diego. The school was twelve weeks long.

MR. CASANOVA: WHAT WERE THE NAMES OF THE SHIPS YOU WERE ON?

Mr. Casanova: The first ship I was assigned to was the USS *Alamo*. This ship was an LSD, an amphibious landing ship. The second ship was the USS *Point Defiance*, this ship was the sister ship of the *Alamo*. They were used to transport marines and equipment. My ship was part of a larger battle group consisting of many ships comprised around an aircraft carrier.

MR. CASANOVA: WHERE WAS YOUR FIRST VOYAGE?

Mr. Casanova: My first trip was a public relations trip to Acapulco, Mexico. It was a trip to show off the navy to the rest of the world. However, my first combat trip overseas was in 1972 when we went to Vietnam. The marines on board would get seasick.

MR. CASANOVA: DID YOU GET TO GO ON A LOT OF MISSIONS, AND HOW LONG WERE THESE MISSIONS?

Mr. Casanova: Well, we went on what we called stations. We must have gone on at least ten of them. We would be on station for fifty-four days at a time. We would be deployed for six to eight months at a time.

MR. CASANOVA: WHAT EXACTLY IS A "STATION"?

Mr. Casanova: A "station" is a mission that our ship was sent on. We would go and patrol the Gulf of Tonkin, Tiger Island, and Tiger Beach. Since we had marines we would wait for the orders to land them at any given time. However, we were never ordered to land marines. The battle group during these stations would

Leonel Casanova

fire constantly at targets on the beach. We would have "darkened ship" when on alert. All lights were turned off at night.

MR. CASANOVA: DID YOU EVER GET SCARED ON THESE MISSIONS?

Mr. Casanova: There was two times when I really feared for my life. The first time was when we were on station, patrolling, when shots were being fired at us from the beach. The shots never hit us, and an air strike was called to bomb the beach. F-4 Phantoms were used in the attack. We could see the beach from our ship and hear the rumbling. The other time was when we were on station and I was playing cards down in the barracks. Over the loudspeaker we were told that this wasn't a drill and to man your battle stations. No one moved at first until the second announcement came on and then everyone ran to their stations. I was a first loader on a 3-inch-50 cannon. However, nothing happened and the alarm was called off.

MR. CASANOVA: WHAT WERE YOUR SHIP'S MAIN WEAPONS?

Mr. Casanova: My ship was a marine transporter and was armed with small guns. Our ship had six 3-inch-50 cannons. I was the first loader on one of these guns. We were always part of a battle group, so we were well protected.

MR. CASANOVA: WHERE WOULD YOUR SHIPS DOCK WHEN NOT ON STATION?

Mr. Casanova: We would dock at Hong Kong, Okinawa, Yokuska, Japan, and Subic Bay in the Philippines. Once docked, we would party. I had a lot of fun when we would dock.

MR. CASANOVA: WHAT WERE THE MOST EXCITING THINGS THAT HAPPENED WHEN YOU WERE IN VIETNAM?

Mr. Casanova: When we would be off station, the ships would be lined up on both sides of us. They would be firing constantly to the beach. At night there was constant bombing and light shows. They would fire on Tiger Beach in Vietnam.

MR. CASANOVA: WAS THE NAVY A GOOD EXPERIENCE?

Mr. Casanova: It was a wonderful experience for me because it helped me become a better person and it gave me a chance to see the world. I would have not done what I did in the navy anywhere else. Also it allowed me to receive an education after I left the navy. It was the best opportunity for me at the time.

Ricardo Zapata
Interviewed by Juan Velez

I interviewed Ricardo Zapata, my cousin, at his home in Brownsville, Texas.

MR. VELEZ: DID YOU ENLIST, OR WERE YOU DRAFTED INTO THE ARMED FORCES? WHAT WAS YOUR AGE?

Mr. Zapata: I volunteered to go into the armed forces, specifically the air force, but I weighed 195 pounds. That was over the weight limitation. I went back later weighing 160 pounds, which was the maximum weight allowed, and I was allowed in the air force. The year I enlisted was 1970 and I had just graduated from high school and was eighteen years old. I wanted to serve my country and at the same time see more of the world, experience new things and not to be told stories to. I wanted to see for myself and I'm glad I did. I served for four active years until 1974 and then for two more years in the reserve. The highest rank I achieved was E-4.

MR. VELEZ: WHERE DID YOU DO BASIC TRAINING, AND HOW LONG WERE YOU THERE?

Mr. Zapata: I was sent to Lackland Air Force Base in San Antonio, Texas, in July of 1970. It was very hot during this time. I spent six weeks in basic training and received training as a vehicle mechanic.

MR. VELEZ: WAS BASIC TRAINING VERY HARD FOR YOU, OR DID YOU COMPLETE IT EASILY?

Mr. Zapata: No, it was not very hard for me. In fact, when I was in high school playing football, the training was harder and more difficult. When it got too hot to be outside during basic, they would take us inside a classroom for instruction and keep us out of the sun.

MR. VELEZ: WHERE ELSE WERE YOU STATIONED DURING YOUR TIME IN THE MILITARY?

Mr. Zapata: From Lackland Air Force Base I was sent to MacDill Air Force Base in Tampa, Florida. I was there until 1973. While at this base, I worked in the transportation area as a maintenance mechanic servicing both diesel and gasoline vehicles such as troop carriers and other vehicles that supported the base. You learned a variety of different mechanical skills dealing with so many different types of vehicles. My mechanic job was 8 to 5 and it left a lot of free time that was spent going to the movies. The only exciting time was when I participated in war games in either North or South Carolina. I don't remember which state it was in, but it was in 1972. While I was at this base, I hurt my knee and had to have an operation to fix it.

MR. VELEZ: DID YOU DO ANY OVERSEAS DUTY AND IN WHAT COUNTRIES?

Mr. Zapata: Yes, I did do some overseas duty. I was sent to Thailand, to a base called Nakhon Phanom that was on the Laos/Thailand border. I spent three months there and was later transferred to another base closer to the Cambodian border called Udorn. Both of these bases were Royal Thai Air Force Bases. There was a rumor about Udorn that it could be overrun in a matter of ten minutes. Cambodia, as you know, was communist with the Khmer Rouge in power. You know, actually you could see a lot of downed aircraft at these bases 'cause the shot up planes would crash land as close to the airfield as possible. They flew missions from Thailand into Vietnam and some of the planes got real shot up. I spent the rest of the year at this base. When I first arrived at Nakhon Phanom, we were watching a movie outside and I saw some flashes on the horizon and I mistook them for lightning and thunder. I commented to the guy next to me that we were going to have a storm, but he said that it wasn't a storm, that they were bombing up north. That's the closest I got to any action, which I'm glad. I guess I was inexperienced, not really comprehending that I was in a war zone. Sometimes I was volunteered as security police guarding aircraft on the flight line, walking perimeter and spending nights on top of a tower looking out over the base. Nothing. You couldn't see anything.

When I was at NKP, that's what we called Nakhom Phanom, you had to take a bus to the town and it took thirty minutes to get there. At Udorn, you stepped outside the fence and there was the city. I lived off base at Udorn and in my free time I went to the movie theaters that showed mainly kung fu movies. Living off base I had to learn to get along with the native population and speak their language. You have to in order to survive. A lot of the GIs lived off base because you had more freedom to do what you wanted. With the air force, once you finish your shift, you're basically a civilian again and you enjoy your freedom. You're not on twenty-four hours a day unless you happen to be on call or on standby.

MR. VELEZ: DID YOU HAVE ANY INTERACTION WITH THE NATIVE POPULATION? WHAT WAS THE CULTURE LIKE?

Mr. Zapata: Well, yes. When I went to Thailand I learned some of the language, enough to get by anyway. You know, you go to town and you talk to people, but you had to be careful who you associated with or talked to because it was a very dangerous place. There was one incident that I remember: a sergeant went into the wrong section of town and he was found dead later. But the culture, the people themselves, were all right. I went to a mountainous area with a taxi driver who was a neighbor where I lived. There was a Buddhist temple near the village, but since I did not know the customs, I did not want to make a mistake and I stayed out of the temple. A Buddhist temple priest came out to talk to me and I was surprised he knew English. He talked for a while and then invited me inside the temple where I saw a lot of people around an image of Buddha. I never took any pictures, but the pictures are in my mind. They're mine and mine alone. You know I was surprised to see that the people's features were almost Latino-type features. They looked a lot like some of the people here [in Brownsville]. You remember Felipe, right? Well a guy I saw there looked exactly like him, and it could have been his twin. The people were short and brown-skinned, similar to us. You saw a lot of different nationalities there, too. The Indians and the Chinese were the merchants with their jewelry shops. Anyway, the way that people lived there, if you go to the poorer sections of Matamoros, you could probably say you are looking at a scene from Thailand. Open-air markets were another thing that reminded me of Matamoros and the eating at shops much as in Matamoros with the little eating places every few feet.

MR. VELEZ: DID YOUR SERVICE IN THE MILITARY PREPARE YOU FOR YOUR FUTURE CIVILIAN LIFE?

Mr. Zapata: The military service, in my opinion, helped me to mature. When I came back after the service, I noticed there was a big difference between myself and the people I went to school with. I really didn't have anything in common with them anymore, something had changed. I didn't know if it was because I was more mature or they had not matured at all. The military helped me become disciplined, and I learned to make wise decisions for myself and those around me. The military service also helped me educate myself through the GI Bill and also helped me buy my house.

MR. VELEZ: IN YOUR OPINION, SHOULD EVERYONE EXPERIENCE MILITARY LIFE?

Mr. Zapata: I think that everyone should experience at least two years in the military. You learn discipline, how to take care of yourself, how to interact with other people, and see new places.

Roberto Pina, Sr.
Interviewed by Alfonso Gonzalez

I chose to interview my uncle, Roberto Pina, Sr., USMC retired, because he was my inspiration for also serving in the Marine Corps.

MR. GONZALEZ: AT WHAT AGE DID YOU FIRST ENLIST IN THE MILITARY? OR WAS THERE A DRAFT SYSTEM?

Mr. Pina: I enlisted into the U.S. Marines during 1952 at the ripe old age of seventeen, and the Selective Service was drafting all males from ages eighteen and up. All of the armed forces had authority to draft for their respective service. The U.S. Marines were not drafting during 1952 because there were enough volunteers enlisting. The draft at the time was necessary because of the Korean War, which started during June 1950.

MR. GONZALEZ: WHERE DID YOU GO FOR TRAINING?

Mr. Pina: I received my training at the Marine Corps Recruit Depot, in San Diego, California, commonly known as boot camp, and then it was twelve weeks long. I remember enlisting in Brownsville, Texas, and going on to San Antonio to be sworn in. I spent one night in San Antonio and, the following day, they herded us into a train bound for San Diego, California, for boot camp.

MR. GONZALEZ: LIKE MOST SERVICEMEN THE FIRST NIGHT OF BOOT CAMP, DID YOU ASK YOURSELF, "WHAT DID I GET INTO?"

Mr. Pina: My first night in boot camp was a nightmare and I kept asking myself what I had gotten into. To be perfectly honest, I was pretty scared, but I did not lose control of my faculties.

MR. GONZALEZ: WAS JOINING THE MILITARY YOUR FIRST EXPERIENCE AWAY FROM HOME AND ON YOUR OWN?

Mr. Pina: The sudden shock was being away from home for the first time and getting homesick. First off, I came from a poor family environment and I did not have much to want or desire because there was none. But when I got to boot camp, all of a sudden life back home was priceless and the canvas cot that I slept in was a bed fit for a king. Before long I made friends with other recruits and I found that they also came from poor homes. So in a sense we found a home when we joined the Marine Corps. After the twelve weeks of boot camp, we were given ten days of furlough and I got on a bus and headed for home. At home, I was received with much love and a warm welcome. I was very proud of being a marine, and I went to the high school to show off my uniform. My ten days were up quickly. I did not even get a chance to date a couple of girls that thought that I was hot stuff in my uniform. I got back to

Camp Pendleton, California, to continue with my advanced infantry training for three more weeks, after which I was given a Military Occupational Specialty (MOS) of 0311, basic infantryman or commonly known as a "ground pounder" or "grunt."

MR. GONZLAEZ: TELL ME ABOUT YOUR FIRST DUTY OVERSEAS. WHAT WAS THE TRIP LIKE? WHAT WAS THE MOOD OF YOURSELF AND YOUR COMRADES?

Mr. Pina: My first real duty station was at the U.S. Naval Air Station, Sangley Point, in the Philippine Islands, across the bay from Manila. The duty consisted of security guard and patrols at the naval base. Our morale was high because we got to go to the beach and watch the Filipino girls wash their clothes on a rock. Some of them were good looking, but there was no comparison to our good old American gals.

MR. GONZALEZ: WHEN YOU ARRIVED OVERSEAS, WERE YOU INVOLVED IN COMBAT IN KOREA? WHAT WAS YOUR DUTY?

Mr. Pina: I was there from June '53 to August '54 and then on to Korea with the 5th Marines, where I was a mortar man, a small portable artillery cannon.

MR. GONZALEZ: WHAT WAS THE TERRAIN LIKE? THE CLIMATE? THE NATIVES?

Mr. Pina: The terrain was nothing but hills and valleys and the climate was hot, hot, and hotter during the summer and cold, cold and colder during the winter. We had a hard time digging foxholes because the ground was frozen. The Korean War was over and I returned to Camp Pendleton, California, during April '55 as a corporal (E-3). During '56 I was discharged from the Corps and I tried civilian life until '63, when I elected to reenlist and I was assigned to Camp Pendleton, California, again.

MR. GONZALEZ: TELL ME ABOUT YOUR VIETNAM EXPERIENCES: NEAR HITS, MISSES, DANGER, ETC.

Mr. Pina: During November '64, I went overseas by ship and after twenty-two days we landed in Okinawa. During April '65, my battalion was selected to go to Vietnam and we landed, in Da Nang, South Vietnam. The war started to pick up momentum when we landed, and for the next eight months we ran combat missions to our rear and to our front because this was one war that did not have front battle areas. During the whole duration of the war there were two kinds of people, the politicians and the media, that had no business in the war efforts. In my opinion, even though the powers that be will never admit it, we lost the war because Washington was dictating the moves instead of the commander in the combat zone. It is also my opinion that the Vietnamese were not good allies. They could have cared less which way the war went as long as they got foreign aid.

This point was well proven by them when the North Vietnamese made the final push of the war during April '75, and very few South Vietnamese units stood up to fight. They abandoned their positions and weapons and headed for the U.S. bases. When Saigon, the capital of the South, fell to the North Vietnamese, the evacuation of thousands upon thousands of South Vietnamese refugees ended up at Camp Pendleton, California, Fort Chaffee, Arkansas, and Fort Indian Point, Pennsylvania, refugee-processing centers. I was one of the counterintelligence specialists assigned to Camp Pendleton, California, to look for any North Vietnamese sympathizers. At any one time there were 22,000 refugees at our camp and by November '75, the last refugees were sponsored out.

MR. GONZALEZ: WHY WERE YOU WILLING TO DO A SECOND TOUR IN VIETNAM?

Mr. Pina: My second Vietnam tour was from November '68 to November '69, as a counterintelligence agent and Vietnamese linguist after attending one year of Vietnamese language school, and four months as a counterintelligence trainee.

MR. GONZALEZ: AFTER VIETNAM, WHERE WAS YOUR NEXT ASSIGNMENT?

Mr. Pina: During the spring of '73 I was a part of a team detailed to conduct intelligence debriefings of the U.S. Prisoners of War that were released by Hanoi. The purpose of the debriefings was to gain information from the former POWs about MIAs unaccounted for and we were successful in finding out the fate of them. In most cases, they were killed trying to escape or died in captivity. After the Vietnam War was over, the Cold War between major powers picked up momentum. The United States had a sound technology lead in a number of areas, i.e., weapons systems, space exploration, missile technology, to name a few. Just like the U.S. was continuously gathering data about what Russia and China were developing in the way of technology in the areas mentioned above, some members of our own technology labs and national defense information centers were involved in espionage activities for a meager monetary gain. The names of Christopher John Boyce, Andrew Daulton Lee ("The Falcon and the Snowman"), and John Walker, U.S. Navy, come to mind, just to name a few of the many involved in espionage activities against the U.S. As a counterintelligence agent, I found myself lecturing members of the units throughout the U.S. Marine Corps bases on the proper safeguarding of national defense information.

MR. GONZALEZ: TELL ME ABOUT YOUR MOST MEMORABLE EXPERIENCE (GOOD, BAD, OR BOTH) OF YOUR TIME IN THE MARINE CORPS.

Mr. Pina: The most memorable military assignments that I had were assisting the Secret Service in VIP protection for President Nixon when he was at the West Coast White House in San Clemente, California, and when he played golf at the Camp Pendleton golf course.

The Enemy

On December 12, 2003, I leave on my Vietnamese trip, the trip I had tried to make the previous May but which I had to abort when I became stranded in SARS-infected China. Vietnam canceled all flights incoming from China while simultaneously most carriers cut flights to and from China until the World Health Organization's "travel advisory" was lifted. I could neither proceed to Vietnam nor return to the States for three weeks. I was unable to obtain my interviews with NVA or Viet Cong veterans.

So now I try again. My flights are booked Brownsville–Houston–Dallas–Hong Kong–Hanoi, a grueling twenty-eight-hour flight, an endurance test which I commence on a Friday afternoon. Having crossed the International Dateline, it is 9:00 Sunday morning when I board the Vietnamese Airlines flight for the short, two-hour leg, into Hanoi. We cross the Gulf of Tonkin and cross Vietnam's land frontier directly above the port city of Haiphong. From there on in to Hanoi we are flying over the north's Red River Valley, the agricultural and demographic core of the north. Although the scene is not the emerald green of the height of the rice growing season, neither is it dull brown. Corn, vegetables, and other crops are still being produced in some fields to add a splash of green here and there amongst the stubble of the rice paddies. Villages are numberless, as frequent and ubiquitous as the central plain of China. Finally we bank and land at Hanoi's Noibai Airport, twenty-five miles from the city center.

My first impressions of Vietnam are these: it is undeniably a beautiful land. The farmlands are wonderfully well tended and the farm houses are neat. This is a much cleaner land, too, than much of the rest of Asia. Another impression: it is less poor than I expected. I was expecting a bicycle society such as prevails in most of China,

The Enemy 201

but this society has achieved the motor scooter age—that's the way 90% of the people seen to get around in Hanoi. Other impressions: the people are so fit, so physically beautiful as a people, and so friendly. If there is lingering resentment of the Americans as a result of the war, then it is very well hidden. Everyone goes out of their way to make you feel welcome. In the taxi riding in from the airport into the city, the driver and his friend, who is riding shotgun, Nguyen Van Loi, "Nam," a young man I was to see a lot of in the next eight days, asked my nationality. When I replied "American" they both gave me an enthusiastic thumbs-up sign and Nam turned around to shake my hand, saying the war's long over and we are friends now.

They take me to the Minh Thu Hotel located in Hanoi's Old Quarter. This proved to be a fortunate choice, not only because of its perfect setting but also because of the friendly staff headed by Manager Nguyen Viet Bac. Bac proved himself a true friend, and his knowledge of the city and English were such that I hired him as my guide and interpreter throughout my eight-day stay in Vietnam. Through him and his eager-to-help staff the four North Vietnamese "enemy" soldiers I interviewed were located—including Gen. Nguyen Duc Huy.

Bac also spent three days escorting me around Hanoi to view the more significant sites in Hanoi associated with the war years: Hoa Lo Prison (or the infamous "Hanoi Hilton," as it was dubbed by the American pilots imprisoned there); the Vietnam Military History Museum; the "Flower Village" in Central Hanoi, where a B-52 crashed during the 1972 "Christmas Bombing" and miraculously landed harmlessly in a pond (and where it still rests as a ready-made tourist attraction); and the Ho Chi Minh Mausoleum. It is at these official sites commemorating the war that it becomes clear the Vietnamese government's attitude to the war is much less forgiving than the general populace's. The official view is unremittingly hostile; for instance, they still refer to the war as "The Fight Against the U.S. War of Destruction in North Vietnam (1965-1973)." Especially maddening is the blatant bias maintained in the exhibits at Hoa Lo Prison. That prison is horrid: a wretched hell of tiny cells and wooden foot stocks. Today half the prison is devoted to the French period, when communist nationalists were incarcerated there—and the exhibits catalog

Interpreter Nguyen Viet Bac

this cruelty. However, the current communist curators seem to see no irony in devoting the other half of the prison (and its exhibits) to chronicling their kind treatment of American captives! It is absolutely ludicrous. Here are some captions I noticed in the section of the prison devoted to the incarceration of American pilots which were so egregiously disingenuous that I copied them down verbatim—including diction and spelling errors:

- One photograph of a pilot being examined by a purported doctor. *"American pilots were medically checked in regular and carefully treated white being in fured or sick."*
- One photograph of a pilot holding a guitar. *"American pilots were played the guitar sang a song of one's hometown in prison."*
- Three tiny black balls in a display case. *"American pilots played when they were in Hoa Loa Prison."*
- One pair of cheap, white tennis shoes in a display case. *"Canvas shoes distributed by Vietnamese Government to American pilots in Hoa Lo Prison."*

I suppose, as they say, the victor gets to write the history books, and certainly the communist government of Vietnam will ensure their exclusive version of the Vietnam War will prevail in their nation for some time to come.

Nguyen Duc Huy
Interviewed by William L. Adams

General Huy was born in Hung-Yen province in 1931. In 1948, at age seventeen, he joined the Viet Minh and went on to serve with distinction in Vietnam's communist army—through its various name changes—for the next fifty years. He retired in 1998. During his long service, General Huy participated in some of his nation's most important military engagements, from Dienbienphu to Khe Sanh (where he commanded the NVA's vaunted 351st Division) to the final General Offensive that concluded the war in 1975. General Huy is a man of considerable fame in Vietnam and not unused to interviews. With the aid of my interpreter, Nguyen Viet Bac, I interviewed the general in his lovely, five-story home in an exclusive residential area of Hanoi. As we sat sipping tea in his ever so tasteful living room, decorated with fine oriental artwork and framed photographs of him standing, sitting or conferring with such legendary figures as General Giap, Ho Chi Minh and Fidel Castro, he graciously answered my questions.

DR. ADAMS: GENERAL, WHEN YOU FIRST JOINED THE ARMY IN 1948, WHAT WERE YOU DOING? WERE YOU FIGHTING THE FRENCH?
General Huy: Yes, fighting with the French people. I was only seventeen then, so I was just a common soldier. You know, just in a trench shooting a rifle at the French, and them in a trench shooting rifles back at us.
DR. ADAMS: DID YOU FIGHT AT DIENBIENPHU?

General Huy: Yes, and by then I was an officer.

DR. ADAMS: AFTER 1954 AND THE GENEVA NEGOTIATIONS, WHICH DIVIDED VIETNAM INTO NORTH AND SOUTH, WHAT DID YOU DO?

General Huy: I still was in the army and now I was going to the South. At that time I was commanding 2,000 soldiers, uniformed soldiers. There was no big fighting, only small fighting until 1968. During that time, from 1954 to 1960, I also studied more—I took various military courses. Then there was really big fighting from 1968 on. I was at Khe Sanh.

DR. ADAMS: AT KHE SANH YOU WERE UP AGAINST AMERICAN MARINES. HOW WERE THOSE MARINES? DID YOU REGARD THEM AS GOOD SOLDIERS?

General Huy: Yes. My division was fighting mainly with the 3rd Marine Division, and they were very good, experienced soldiers. You know that 3rd Marine Division has a very long history of fighting. They were very good, very well trained. And that division was very large; it had about 20,000 men in that division, and they had much more firepower than us. Much more.

DR. ADAMS: MOST AMERICAN HISTORY BOOKS THAT HAVE DEALT WITH KHE SANH ESTIMATE YOUR COMMUNIST FORCES AS HAVING BEEN ABOUT 50,000. IS THAT YOUR RECOLLECTION?

Gen. Nguyen Duc Huy in his Hanoi home. The framed photograph in the background shows him being congratulated by Fidel Castro.

General Huy: No, that figure is wrong. We had nearly 100,000 at Khe Sanh when your air force arrived with more than 1,000 aircraft and also helicopters bringing in more men.

DR. ADAMS: I KNOW AT KHE SANH THE U.S. BROUGHT IN THE B-52 BOMBERS AND ALSO USED NAPALM EXTENSIVELY. WERE ANY OF THESE DROPS MADE ON YOUR PERSONAL DIVISION?

General Huy: Yes. Those bombs killed many of my men, over 1,000 men in my own division. My division was the 351st Division, one of the strongest and most famous divisions in the North Vietnamese Army. We had on average about 12,000 soldiers, sometimes more, sometimes less. For instance after those bombings we had 1,000 less. It took some time to build it up again. Both our sides lost quite a lot at Khe Sanh.

DR. ADAMS: YOU KNOW, IT HAS LONG BEEN SPECULATED IN AMERICA THAT THE COMMUNIST SIEGE AT KHE SANH WAS JUST INTENDED AS A DIVERSION—TO CAUSE THE AMERICANS TO DRAW MORE AMERICAN FORCES NORTHWARD AND THUS WEAKEN THEMSELVES IN THE SOUTH AND THEREBY GIVE YOUR OWN COMMUNIST FORCES A BETTER CHANCE IN THE SOUTH WHEN YOU LAUNCHED THE TET OFFENSIVE. IS THAT SPECULATION CORRECT?

General Huy: I refuse to answer that question. Many people have asked me that question before, and to this day I refuse to answer.

DR. ADAMS: WELL, THEN, YOU'LL PROBABLY REFUSE TO ANSWER MY NEXT QUESTION, TOO, BUT I'M GOING TO GO AHEAD AND ASK IT. IT HAS ALWAYS BEEN A QUESTION WHETHER OR NOT GENERAL GIAP WAS ACTUALLY PRESENT AT KHE SANH AND DIRECTING THE FIGHTING. SOME SPECULATE THAT HE WAS THERE FOR PART OF THE BATTLE BUT ONCE THE HEAVY BOMBING STARTED WAS PRESSURED IN TO LEAVING FOR FEAR HE, TOO, WOULD BECOME A CASUALTY. IS THAT TRUE?

General Huy: Yes, that is true. All of what you have said is true. He was there, but he left not only because we feared for his safety but also because he had urgent duties elsewhere. You know he was directing the fighting everywhere.

DR. ADAMS: A LOT OF MILITARY HISTORIANS ARE BEGINNING TO CONSIDER GENERAL GIAP A MILITARY GENIUS, PERHAPS NOT QUITE A GENIUS ON THE LEVEL OF NAPOLEON, BUT STILL A GENIUS. WOULD YOU AGREE WITH THAT ASSESSMENT?

General Huy: Yes. He was very clever, the cleverest of generals. And he was very experienced, having fought from the time he was young until he was old.

DR. ADAMS: YOU KNOW AFTER THE WAR ENDED GENERAL GIAP TOLD A GROUP OF WESTERN REPORTERS THAT COMMUNIST LOSSES IN THE TET OFFENSIVE WERE SO DEVASTATING THAT IF THE AMERICANS HAD KEPT UP THAT LEVEL OF MILITARY PRESSURE MUCH LONGER NORTH VIETNAM WOULD HAVE BEEN FORCED TO NEGOTIATE A PEACE ON AMERICAN TERMS. DO YOU AGREE?

General Huy: If the American army had fought some more, continued, I don't know. Maybe. I can't predict what would have happened.

DR. ADAMS: WHAT DID YOU DO WITH YOUR DEAD SOLDIERS?

General Huy: The dead soldiers I would remove to the back of the division. Other men would then bury them. Letters would be sent to the soldiers' families notifying them. Our injured would go to a hospital, but not a hospital in a city. Sometimes our hospitals were in among the trees, but usually they were in caves.

DR. ADAMS: AND WHAT DID YOU DO WITH DEAD AMERICANS?

General Huy: Usually American planes would circle a battlefield and keep us back until they could send in helicopters and recover the dead bodies themselves. But whenever we did find American bodies, we did bury them. We didn't remove their dogtags. We knew what those were for so we buried them with the bodies, and we buried the bodies in places where they would be easily found. We buried the bodies in shallow graves, and we grouped the graves together like steps. We knew eventually American or South Vietnamese forces would come along and find those bodies, get the tags, and notify those soldiers' families.

DR. ADAMS: THAT WAS CONSIDERATE.

General Huy: Let me tell you something else. Six years ago your Gen. Raymond Davis, a four-star general, brought a military delegation here to Vietnam to meet with a military delegation of ours. I was on that delegation. We did all we could to help them locate more American bodies.

Another thing. While General Davis was here he asked me my opinion on why America lost the war when they had so many more weapons and much better weapons than we had.

DR. ADAMS: THAT WAS GOING TO BE ONE OF MY QUESTIONS. SO HOW DID YOU ANSWER HIM?

General Huy: I gave him three reasons. First, and most important, I told him that the North Vietnamese soldiers were fighting from their hearts for our freedom. Second, we knew the place of the fighting. You understand what I mean? We knew the mountains; we knew the rivers; we knew so well the place of the fighting. And, third, we watched very closely the Americans. [Here General Huy does a little pantomime pretending he is crouching through the trees and jungle, spying on the Americans with binoculars which he pans left and right.] We tried to guess everything the Americans would do in advance. We attacked them very carefully. When we could we would attack them from the rear. We also had our tunnels to approach them undetected.

One thing General Davis told me when he was here was that for thirty years he had been wondering how North Vietnamese tanks could so suddenly appear on a battlefield and catch the Americans by surprise. He said it seemed like magic, that they came out of nowhere. He asked me how we managed to do that: I told him that is a secret we still keep in case we ever have to use it again. Would you like me to tell you now?

DR. ADAMS: YES.

General Huy: No! I still refuse to answer. [Laughs.] But I will tell you this. We had more than one way of doing that. There was more than one trick to doing that.

Gen. Nguyen Duc Huy and the author.

[This, of course, leaves one to speculate on what those tricks might have been: an especially effective camouflage system? Burying prepositioned tanks? An ingenious system of disassembling and reassembling the tanks? Heretofore undisclosed use of Soviet heavy-lift helicopters? The possibilities would seem to be quite limited.]

DR. ADAMS: TELL ME, DID YOU HAVE A HATRED FOR THE AMERICANS AT THE TIME OF THE WAR? AND WHAT ABOUT NOW?

General Huy. During the war, of course! Our deaths were very, very big. Of course I hated them. But about six years ago, when I met with the American military delegation, I decided we could become friends. We talked together so that we could forget the past and look to the future.

DR. ADAMS: I WONDER IF YOU EVER HEARD OF A PLAN AN AMERICAN "THINK TANK" PROPOSED FOR THE WINNING OF THE WAR. THIS WAS A PLAN PROPOSED BY HERMAN KAHN OF THE HUDSON INSTITUTE. THE PLAN WAS THIS: TO BUILD UP AMERICA'S TROOP STRENGTH IN VIETNAM TO A TOTAL OF ONE MILLION MEN. AT THAT POINT THOSE ONE MILLION MEN COULD ACTUALLY LINK HANDS AND STRETCH THE ENTIRE LENGTH OF SOUTH VIETNAM'S LAND BORDERS—FROM THE D.M.Z. TO LAOS, TO CAMBODIA—THE ENTIRE LENGTH OF THE LAND BORDERS. THEY WOULD SIMPLY PREVENT ANY MORE NVA OR VIET CONG FROM ENTERING THE COUNTRY. THEY WERE ALSO TO BE ASSISTED BY TENS OF THOUSANDS OF SPECIALLY TRAINED DOGS THAT WOULD LISTEN FOR ANY TUNNELING ACTIVITY BENEATH THE BORDERS. WHILE THE AMERICANS AND DOGS HELD THE BORDERS SECURE, THE SOUTH VIETNAMESE ARMY WOULD BE USED TO TRACK DOWN AND KILL OR CAPTURE ANY VIET CONG OR COMMUNIST SYMPATHIZERS WITHIN SOUTH VIETNAM.

WHAT DO YOU THINK? DOES THAT PLAN SOUND CRAZY TO YOU, OR DO YOU THINK IT MIGHT HAVE WORKED?

General Huy: I think that's quite funny. The South Vietnamese Army could never have tracked down all of our Viet Cong and communist sympathizers within the country. There were just too many of them. Men, women, the farmers—there were so many of them that were on our side. They could never have been stopped.

DR. ADAMS: MY FINAL QUESTION IS DO YOU HAVE ANYTHING YOU WOULD LIKE TO TELL THE READERS OF THIS BOOK?

General Huy: One thing: the war is over and I look to the future. But the poisons Americans dropped on the land continue to harm many of our people—not just this generation, but the next and the next, with diseases and birth defects. You should tell this to the American government. They should be doing something to help us with this problem.

I hope relations between America and Vietnam improve rapidly. It would be good for the economies and the lives of both of our peoples.

Nguyen Van Khien
Interviewed by William L. Adams

On December 19, 2003, I traveled south of Hanoi to Ha Nam Province with interpreter Nguyen Viet Bac, his employee, Nguyen Duc Hanh, and a hired driver. There in the village of Thanh Ha we interviewed Nguyen Van Khien in his humble home. We sat on low stools sipping tea in the living room of the three-room dwelling. His granddaughter played in the corner on a plastic mat laid on the bare concrete floor. Dogs, cats, and chickens scurried about and occasionally poked their noses through the open door. His shy wife looked on.

Mr. Khien showed me a framed certificate on the wall and a wallet card, both of which identify him as being a "First Class War Invalid"—a veteran who has suffered the most grievous wounds. There is no doubt of that. His left leg has been removed immediately below the buttock, and his right leg—as he rolled up his pants' leg to show me—has most of the flesh

Nguyen Van Khien

missing—pared right down to the bone in portions of both the shin and thigh. He has a bright, cheerful, peasant's demeanor, and is eager to please.

DR. ADAMS: WHEN AND WHY DID YOU JOIN THE NORTH VIETNAMESE ARMY?

Mr. Khien: I joined the army when I was seventeen years old. I served from 1974 to 1979, but much of that time I was in hospitals. Why did I join? Because I loved my country and I wanted to fight for its freedom.

DR. ADAMS: WHAT HAPPENED ONCE YOU VOLUNTEERED?

Mr. Khien: We were trained in the north for six months and then sent to the south. We went south on the Ho Chi Minh Trail. It was a very hard journey. We had to sleep under the trees in the forest. We had very little to eat. When we reached rivers we swam across them. We were bombed a lot. We were on the Trail three months. My unit was R-856. We moved in stages and traveled only at night. I was in a group of 400. There were many groups of 400 before us and following us, but we were spread out. If the groups were larger than that, they were easier to be spotted and bombed by airplanes. So we stayed spread out.

DR. ADAMS: YOU ENTERED SOUTH VIETNAM IN THE FINAL STAGES OF THE WAR, AND MOST OF THE AMERICANS HAD ALREADY LEFT. WHAT WAS THE MOST IMPORTANT ACTION YOU PARTICIPATED IN?

Mr. Khien: The liberation of Saigon. We got into Saigon. We were fighting and got into the city. A lot of my friends were killed inside Ho Chi Minh City. [Here he uses Saigon's postwar name.] This was in 1975.

DR. ADAMS: WHAT WAS THE FIGHTING LIKE IN SAIGON?

Mr. Khien: We were fighting house-to-house in Saigon's streets. We were fighting everywhere: in the houses and out of windows, in the trees, in the streets, laying under cars.

DR. ADAMS: DID YOU KILL ANY PEOPLE THAT YOU KNOW OF?

Mr. Khien: I had a large Russian rifle, an AK-47. I hit several people. I don't know whether I killed or injured them or what, but I did hit them.

DR. ADAMS: WHAT WAS YOUR THINKING, YOUR EMOTION LIKE, DURING THE FIGHTING?

Mr. Khien: I think nothing. [Here he pauses, no doubt recalling his indoctrination lectures.] I think just about the nation and serving it. [Another pause.] But really in combat I think nothing. Only fighting.

DR. ADAMS: WHEN AND HOW DID YOU GET YOUR INJURY?

Mr. Khien: In 1976. The war was over and I was going back home, back to North Vietnam. It was near the Cambodian border. I stepped on a mine. It was in the forest near the border.

DR. ADAMS: WHAT DID IT FEEL LIKE? OR WERE YOU EVEN CONSCIOUS?

Mr. Khien: When I stepped on it I heard a big noise and I felt my leg get very cold, and then I went unconscious. The leg halfway down was missing immediately.

It was blown clear off. My comrades took me to a little army hospital in the forest, in a little kampong. I lost much blood and they cut off more of my leg—above the knee. My other leg was also in bad shape.

DR. ADAMS: HOW LONG DID YOU STAY THERE?

Mr. Khien: One day, then they transferred me to a big hospital in Hue City, where they removed more of my leg.

DR. ADAMS: HOW DID YOU FEEL—WHAT WERE YOUR EMOTIONS, LOSING YOUR LEG?

Mr. Khien: [Very animated.] I felt very, very sad and I cried. I didn't want to think about anything. I told the army doctor to do anything he wanted with me—cut anything they wanted off of me—I didn't care. But they worked hard to save my other leg.

DR. ADAMS: DID YOU EVER THINK ABOUT KILLING YOURSELF?

Mr. Khien: I had a very bad feeling of both the spirit and the body for a very long time, but I didn't want to kill myself. Today I'm still happy to be alive. Life is still good.

DR. ADAMS: HAS YOUR GOVERNMENT TAKEN GOOD CARE OF YOU?

Mr. Khien: Yes, very good. I get some money every month, enough for living. Later I got married and now I raise some chickens and pigs.

DR. ADAMS: WHO DO YOU BLAME FOR YOUR INJURIES?

Mr. Khien: The Americans.

DR. ADAMS: ARE YOU STILL ANGRY? I'M SITTING HERE IN YOUR HOME ...

Mr. Khien: I forgive now, and it was in the past. I try to forget. Now I blame no one. And I'm okay.

Dang Thi Phuong
Interviewed by William L. Adams

Dang Thi Phuong is the wife of the previous interviewee, Nguyen Van Khien, and I also interviewed her on December 19, 2003, in Thanh Ha village. Phuong, a shy woman, was a little reluctant to be interviewed. She smiled demurely and was cheerful, but spent much of the interview hiding her face behind her hands. As a woman of the "old school" she was hesitant to speak before the males present and especially me, a foreigner. Bac, my interpreter, informed me that I was the first foreigner she has ever seen, let alone met and spoken with.

One other thing: Phuong may be shy and demure, but there was no mistaking the fact that she is physically very tough. Although in her fifties, she is fit, and has the deep tan of a Vietnamese farm woman.

DR. ADAMS: PHUONG, WHEN DID YOU SERVE IN THE ARMY?

Phuong: From 1970 to 1979.

DR. ADAMS: DID YOU WEAR A UNIFORM?

Phuong: Yes. A North Vietnamese Army uniform.

DR. ADAMS: WHAT DID YOU DO?

Phuong: At first I worked in the rear of the army, cooking rice for the army. Then I worked on the Ho Chi Minh Trail. There were many young girls like me who worked on the Ho Chi Minh Trail. We were cutting down trees and widening the trail for trucks. This was near Laos.

DR. ADAMS: DID YOU EVER GET BOMBED?

Phuong: No. Never.

DR. ADAMS: WHAT WAS YOUR LIFE LIKE WHILE YOU WORKED ON THE TRAIL? WHERE DID YOU SLEEP?

Phuong: We slept under trees; we slept in caves; we slept in the mountains. We had a blanket, but it was never enough to keep me warm.

DR. ADAMS: I DON'T WANT TO EMBARRASS YOU, BUT, TELL ME, DID YOU GIRLS GET BOTHERED BY THE MALE SOLDIERS?

Phuong: No. We had very strict army rules about that, so I was very safe in the group.

DR. ADAMS: WHERE DID YOU MEET YOUR HUSBAND?

Phuong: We met at the hospital in Hue. By then I had become an army nurse, and because he was a first-level injury my husband was assigned a personal nurse to be with him twenty-four hours a day—that was me. That was in 1978, and after two years we got married.

DR. ADAMS: WHAT QUALITIES DID YOUR HUSBAND HAVE THAT CAUSED YOU TO WANT TO MARRY HIM?

Dang Thi Phuong

Phuong: It was a very special love. [At this point Phuong speaks to my interpreter directly, and Bac informs me that Phuong would like to end the interview soon.]

DR. ADAMS: IS THERE ANYTHING ELSE YOU'D LIKE TO SAY, PHUONG?

Phuong: Only that we love each other and have sympathy for each other.

[As we prepare to depart, Bac suggests to me that since this is such a very poor household, I might like to make them a small money gift beyond the sack of fruit we brought them. To avoid humbling the man and his wife, he advises me to hand the money (the Vietnamese equivalent of twenty dollars) directly to their four-year-old granddaughter and indicate this is for her.]

Nguyen Duc Hanh
Interviewed by William L. Adams

I met Mr. Hanh the first day I checked into the Minh Thu Hotel in Hanoi. He was another of Manager Nguyen Viet Bac's male employees, three or four of whom are always present in the hotel lobby, hovering around the reception desk, or sitting sipping tea in the ornately carved chairs that line the lobby's walls. They have a variety of functions: chauffeuring the hotel's guests, opening and closing doors, shifting luggage around, providing services for guests and, in general, keeping a close eye on things. They are not uniformed or wearing labels, so it is difficult to know exactly who does what. Nguyen Duc Hanh served as one of these denizens of the lobby. He was older than the others. He wore a suit and had a great deal of personal dignity. Among other functions, he served as the hotel's electrician. He walked with a limp.

When Mr. Hanh learned of my purpose of coming to Hanoi, it was he who suggested I might wish to interview Nguyen Van Khien and wife Dang Thi Phuong, well-known veterans of his own village of Thanh Ha. When we visited that village on December 19, Mr. Hanh accompanied us, arranged the introductions, and also provided us with a splendid meal in his village home after the interviews—his wife and daughter lopped off one of their chicken's heads to provide the main course.

Back at the hotel the following day, December 20, 2003, I interviewed Mr. Hanh himself in the hotel's lobby.

DR. ADAMS: MR. HANH, I UNDERSTAND THAT BEFORE YOU JOINED THE VIET CONG YOU HAD EXPERIENCED BOMBING BY THE AMERICANS WHILE YOU WERE IN NORTH VIETNAM. TELL ME ABOUT THAT.

Mr. Hanh: Yes, when the bombs came to Hanoi in 1972, I was staying in the village. [Thanh Ha village, 55 kilometers south of Hanoi.] We had a bombing there. That was a B-52. [The previous day, while we were dining at his Thanh Ha home, Hanh had taken me outside to show me the site of the crater—which is now a pond.] In our village no one was killed, but some were injured. However, in the village next to us, Do Xa, they had over 100 deaths.

DR. ADAMS: WHY WOULD THEY WANT TO BOMB THIS VILLAGE?

Mr. Hanh: There was a military training base near our village. They were probably trying to hit that. Also, Highway 1 passes beside the village and there is a bridge. They might have been trying to cut that highway.

DR. ADAMS: DID ANY AMERICAN PILOTS GET SHOT DOWN OVER YOUR VILLAGE?

Mr. Hanh: Yes, one pilot with a parachute landed near our village, but local army forces captured the pilot. That was at the time of the Christmas bombing of Hanoi. That pilot was sent to Hoa Lo Prison, the "Hanoi Hilton."

DR. ADAMS: I UNDERSTAND YOU SERVED IN THE VIET CONG. WHAT WAS YOUR SPECIFIC JOB?

Mr. Hanh: I was a tunnel digger. I was issued a shovel. [Here he draws a picture of a distinctive, acutely-pointed spade.] Along with many other soldiers I was assigned to dig tunnels and underground chambers for soldiers to eat, cook, and sleep in.

DR. ADAMS: GIVE ME THE SPECIFICS FOR HOW THEY WERE DUG. HOW DEEP UNDERGROUND WERE THEY?

Mr. Hanh: Usually they were at least three meters [ten feet] down; at least three meters down to the roof of the tunnel. This was enough to protect us from all but direct hits by bombs.

We only came out of the tunnels at nighttime. To move about we used small flashlights provided by the army. They produced only a small light so the enemy wouldn't see us. Also, if we were approaching the enemy we never even used flashlights. We would tear up strips of material and tie these strips around our wrists. Then we tied each other together with other longer strips. Then we could advance together in a line in the dark and not get lost.

DR. ADAMS: HOW WERE YOU FED?

Mr. Hanh: One lady soldier would go to the rear to prepare the food. We used dried cakes of rice mixed with milk. These came from China. You ate the cakes and then drank water and the rice swelled up in your stomach. It made you feel full.

DR. ADAMS: HOW MUCH WERE YOU PAID? [MR. HANH DOESN'T SEEM TO UNDERSTAND THIS QUESTION, AND INTERPRETER BAC HAS TO REPEAT IT AND EXPLAIN IT IN DIFFERENT WAYS.]

Mr. Hanh: We were only given enough to buy stamps for letters. We got cigarettes, food, medicine, and fruit free from the government.

DR. ADAMS: HOW DID YOU GET YOUR HEAD WOUNDS AND YOUR LEG

Nguyen Duc Hanh

INJURY? [THE PREVIOUS DAY HANH HAD INVITED ME TO FEEL THE TOP OF HIS HEAD. BENEATH HIS ABUNDANT HAIR, ON EITHER SIDE OF THE SKULL'S CROWN, WERE TWO DEEP DEPRESSIONS THE SIZE OF GOLF BALLS.]

Mr. Hanh: I was in a tunnel when artillery shells started to hit. Those at the mouth of the tunnel were killed immediately. The smell of those weapons was powerful! Then an artillery shell hit above the tunnel where I was. Two pieces of shrapnel hit my head and one piece hit my leg. The shrapnel penetrated and collapsed the tunnel roof.

DR. ADAMS: DID YOU FEEL IT WHEN YOU GOT HIT?

Mr. Hanh: I felt nothing. I was unconscious. When I woke up, I was in the next tunnel. They had taken me there for first aid. I was there one day. After, I was transferred to a cave hospital. Then I was taken to a big hospital for an operation to remove the metals. The metal was inside me for two days. Another shrapnel broke this leg. I still limp whenever the weather changes. I still take pain tablets.

DR. ADAMS: IS THERE ANYTHING ELSE YOU'D LIKE TO SAY?

Mr. Hanh: At first, when the fighting started, I didn't think very much about it, but when I saw civilians being killed I began to hate the enemy—whether they were Americans, South Vietnamese, or whoever.

Whenever I think back about the war now, I think of how terrible war is, how terrible that so many people were killed for whatever reason.

Reflections

    I joined the navy in February 1967 and was discharged six years later in consequence of the drastic force reductions ordered by Congress in the aftermath of the Vietnam debacle.

    As with almost everyone who had served in the military, the experience forged so many aspects of my conscious and unconscious personality that I am still striving to appreciate the full impact it has had deep into my middle age. Just last week, having concluded a lecture and while packing up my briefcase and preparing to vacate the podium in favor of a colleague and his incoming class, a young man who had just plonked himself down in one of the desks asked me: "You were in the military, weren't you?" I said, "Yes, how can you tell?" He responded, "Oh, you just can." The student gave no hint of whether he considered this a good or bad thing. He was just expressing a fact. The young man was no genius of perspicacity. I do bear the outward signs of service. Having never really thought about it, I still wear the near-burr haircut the barber at Officer Candidate School in Newport, Rhode Island, afflicted on me nearly forty years ago. I've continued to loop a tie around my neck every morning of my working life, and I still unthinkingly inspect myself for a proper "gigline"—shirt buttons, belt buckle, pants zipper in careful vertical alignment—whenever I leave the house. Why do I do that? I don't even know myself. Maybe it gives me an illusion of purposefulness in what often seems a purposeless world. And, of course, the service had more substantive effects on my personality. There are my political and social biases. My limited tolerance of liberals, extremists of any stamp, or of persons who stray too far from what I consider the "norm" for human behavior. I disdain eccentrics and quirky, shrill, excitable personalities and persons who consider themselves "special cases." Conversely, I admire calm, steady, focused, and competent personalities. Blandness I don't mind at all.

There is no doubt about it, the military knocks "the corners" off you. And the process is not without some pain. I found my eighteen weeks of navy OCS something of a trial. The ferocity—the intentional ferocity—of the experience is something few forget.

As the reporting officer candidates are dropped off by parents, wives, girlfriends, what have you, in the OCS parking lot, the system loses no time in giving you a taste of the ferocity. OCS upperclassmen who patrol the parking lot with M-1s approach the arriving cars and wrench open the door next to the seated novice candidate and bark: "Get out of the car!" Almost invariably the novice responds with something like, "Just give me a minute to say goodbye." The novice has committed his first mistake. What he gets next is: "Mister, I gave a direct order which you have refused. You are in the navy and your nation is at war. Listen to my next words very, very carefully. I am going to repeat the order one more time. If you again refuse the order I am going to shoot you. I am not going to shoot to wound you. I am going to shoot to kill you." [At this point the upperclassman takes one step back and levels the M-1 at the appalled novice's chest.] "GET OUT!" Welcome to OCS. And it just gets better and better.

The first month, "Hell Month," pushed us to our limits—and a few beyond. Three in our class committed suicide. One man shot himself through the head when given a loaded .45 pistol to stand night guard duty; two others hung themselves. Suicide seemed a bit extreme. Why not just drop out? Well, they didn't make it easy. If you couldn't hack the officers' training—if you either flunked out or requested to drop out—they just busted you down to seaman recruit (the lowest rate in the navy) and assigned you to clean garbage cans for a month in front of the officer candidates' mess hall. The ignominy of your failure would be rubbed in your face every mealtime of every day as your former classmates marched to and from the hall. An indubious message for all, you see. The word went around, too, that after

William L. Adams

the month's humiliation of publicly cleaning garbage cans that the navy killed you. Oh, nothing so dramatic as executing you, but the next best thing: they would ship you off to Vietnam and assign you as a ground spotter for naval gunnery. A helicopter would drop you off on some hilltop in enemy-infested territory and you'd radio in grid coordinates for shell impacts until you were killed or captured. Did the navy actually do that? In hindsight I'm almost 100 percent sure they did not, but the rumor seemed entirely credible to us naïve candidates at the time and effectively scotched any notions we might have entertained concerning "dropping out."

And so we determined to put up with our lot during Hell Month, like being allowed eighty seconds for our meals—marching to the mess hall, pushing our trays down the cafeteria line as food was ladled out, assembling at our section's assigned table, and standing at attention with our trays—that is, holding our trays with our arms crooked at the elbows in the precisely prescribed 90-degree angle. Sitting on command. Eating for exactly eighty seconds. And let me tell you, for young men who, in addition to many hours of classroom study, had at least four hours of heavy physical exertion every day (running, swimming, calisthenics, marching and rifle drill), getting enough calories into your body in eighty-second bursts three times per day (four minutes total eating time per twenty-four hours) was some feat. We ate only the foods on our tray that we could swallow whole: eggs, mashed potatoes, peas, corn kernels, jello. We would glomb this down and then wash it through our gullets with a pint of milk, two pints of milk if we could manage it, before the dreaded: "Stand!" The breads, meats, salads on our trays were never touched. They were just dumped in the garbage cans on our way out. Once the chief cook, or whoever it was that decided our menu, scheduled us for spaghetti and meatballs. Obviously he had a sense of humor, albeit a cruel one. What a pitiful spectacle we were. A real gut-splitter for the cooks and servers watching us.

Hell Month mornings were no fun for us novice candidates either. Unlike the second-, third-, and fourth-month candidates—the "upperclassmen"—who could luxuriate in their bunks until 5:30 reveille, we were awakened by the blast of a police whistle at 4:30 A.M. If it had snowed during the night we were hustled outside to clear the OCS area's sidewalks and roadways and parade ground before the others awoke. If there had not been a snowfall, we were hustled off to the dormitory's bathrooms for "head detail." We had to make sure the toilets, urinals, and showers were absolutely spotless—clean enough for our section's chief to "happily dine on the bathroom floor," as he put it. For cleaning utensils we had hand-brushes, rags, and rubber gloves. We were allowed no mops or handled-brushes—nothing with a handle. This was so we could be "close to our work." Everything had to be made nice and tidy: "ship-shape." Pubic hairs had to be retrieved from every urinal, toilet, and shower drain by hand. Remember, as officer candidates we were all college graduates, and all of us had reasonably high intelligence. (In those days the military tested all prospective officers for IQ, and 116 was the minimal allowable score during the Vietnam era.) And yet here we were at 4:30 in the morning with our heads stuck in urinals, using our fingers to tweeze out "pubees," as we called them. It was demeaning. Of course the navy had a ready rationale: it was important for us prospective officers to appreciate the feelings of sailors we would one day be assigning such tasks. True enough, I suppose, but still it was demeaning. On the other hand, the class before us that winter had it even worse. When they had finished harvesting the "pubees" they had been made to sit bare-bottomed on the toilet seats. They were forbidden to use the toilets; their function was to warm the toilet seats for the ease and comfort of the upperclassmen who would stroll down after 5:30 reveille.

Hell Month. Hellacious days, one activity right after another the whole day long. No rest. And if we were looking for sympathy, as one chief told us, we would find it in the dictionary between "shit" and "syphilis." Looking back, the whole ordeal did have its comic side, but we couldn't see that at the time. All we were doing was trying to keep up with the relentless pace, marching from class to class: seamanship, tactics, steam-propulsion, naval history, piloting, celestial navigation. And in between times, marching, rifle drilling, calisthenics, and swimming.

Here's our first swimming class. Two burly chiefs stand either side of the pool, the depth of which is over everyone's head. The sixteen members of our section stand poolside. We're ordered in. Everyone jumps in and clings to the side. "Swim!" We swim to the other side. The chief on that side orders us back to the other side. Back and forth, lap after lap—twenty laps, thirty laps—until no one's counting the laps, just enduring. I am thinking what I suspect every other man is thinking: "Please God, let someone break before I do." On and on we go until finally, Sweet Jesus, someone did break. A cheerful, chatty sort of a fellow in our section—a law school grad, if I remember correctly—was clinging to the ledge, whining that he couldn't go on, he'd drown. The chief screamed at him, "Swim!" and tromped on his fingers to make him let go of the ledge. The man tried to make it across, made maybe three or four flailing strokes, swallowed water, and then turned back. He was frantically clinging to the ledge. Crying now. Blubbering, actually. He was broken good and proper. Finished.

You know, the strange thing is, I don't think any of us felt sorry for that man. We were ashamed of him. We averted our eyes from him. You see, he was a weak link, and we were already beginning to internalize the navy's values. We had no use for that man.

As we progressed from first-month neophytes to second-, third-, and finally, fourth-month upperclassmen, the ferocity slackened at least a degree or two and, having toughened up a bit also, we began to find life almost bearable; our mealtimes were extended to a leisurely ten minutes. Meats and other solid foods could be contemplated. We were granted liberty from 1200 hours Saturday to 1700 hours Sunday. We could go into Newport—or even to New York or Boston. That is, we were granted liberty if we didn't accumulate five or more "gigs" per week. Gigs were meted out for slovenly, unseamanlike conduct or demeanor: marching out of step; marching with your armful of classroom books in incorrect order (the correct order was with the largest book next to your body, smaller books working outward in diminishing size); having a loose thread (an "Irish pennant") on any article of your clothing or, for that matter, on your terrycloth washcloth or towel (one gig per thread); being caught with your elbows on your desk or with your feet not firmly planted in a seamanlike manner on the floor (deck) during the excruciating 7:30 to

11:30 nightly study sessions. I once got caught face down in my book, asleep. That was a ten-gigger. Two weekends of liberty lost—to be spent marching up and down on the grinder with my fellow malefactors. There was one other time I got slapped with a ten-gigger—actually two five-giggers, but on the same day. Every so often the powers that be would single out someone to lean on a little extra bit hard, to see how they responded. This day I guess it was my turn. On the march to the mess hall for breakfast, an officer standing beside the roadway ordered our section to halt. The officer called me over to him and asked me why I was smiling. I wasn't smiling; my face was set in its usual robotic mode, but, of course, I knew enough not to argue with an officer. I replied, "I don't know, sir." Then he lit into me: "Don't you realize our nation is at war? Don't you realize navymen are fighting and dying in Vietnam? Five gigs, and wipe that smile off your face." "Yes, sir!" That was the march into breakfast. When we marched over for lunch that same officer was standing there again in the same place. Again he halted our column and called me out. "Why are you frowning, mister? You're in the navy. Aren't you proud of being in the navy? Five gigs, and let's see a smile on your face." I said, "Yes, sir!" and jollied up right away. That was two more lost weekends for me.

The instruction during the final two months of OCS became more interesting. We spent some time at the rifle range, some at the pistol range. We manned mock-up models of ship bridges and learned to drive ships—first the mock-up, but later we'd spend one day a week out on Narragansett Bay driving an eighty-foot patrol craft. We had three days of fire-fighter training. They'd bus us to an area of the base where big cylindrical vats of various fuel oils and chemicals would be set alight and we'd practice smothering them with foam with the big, powerful fire hoses that took six men to control. We'd each take turns as nozzle-man. We'd practice putting out electrical fires, smoke fires, and so forth. For our final test the fire-fighter trainers had a good-sized chunk of a scrapped destroyer mounted on the pier as a training device. By flipping switches they could cause any number and any type of fires to erupt in the device. Our section got suited up in fully enclosing asbestos suits that had little viewing windows in the hood section. We wore a self-contained breathing apparatus. Then the trainers flipped some switches and had all kinds of fires breaking out in the training unit. Then we were ordered in. We clambered through hatches and up and down ladders trailing our hoses or carrying extinguishers. No sooner would we be making headway on one fire and they'd flip some switches and start two more. Then while we were battling away, they flipped a switch that caused a gas main to blow out and sent a twenty-foot flare jetting out at us. We were feeling heat! Then they started some massive smoke fire and we couldn't see our hands in front of our little viewing windows. We all came spilling back out of the hatches. The trainers told us that we were failures. Absolutely pathetic. They said that we were the sorriest sons of bitches they'd ever seen.

We had damage control training at another area of the base. The damage control trainers also had a section of an old destroyer as a training tool. Come to think of it, it was probably just another section of the same destroyer the fire-fighters were using. However, this section was actually in the bay's water and just tied up to the pier. By flipping various switches the trainers could simulate catastrophes (shell penetrations, torpedo hits, mine explosions) and flood the section so that it would sink. They could then flip other switches to pump it dry and re-surface it. It was the same sort of deal as we had had over at fire-fighting. At first the trainers taught us how to plug shell holes with bunk mattresses and/or various sized beams—2x2s, 4x4s, 8x8s. They taught us how to wedge, jack, or sledgehammer sprung plates back into position. Once we had the basics in hand they gave us our test. They would simulate various hits, and this time actual water would flood in for realism's sake. It was April, and the trainers warned us that we would find the bay water cold—"colder than a witch's titty" is how the chief put it. We got ready. We each had a jack, a sledge, a mattress or beam. We waited. Then they threw a switch. A hole the size of a basketball opened in the bulkhead and a torrent of water poured in. We sprang into action and pounded an 8x8 block into the hole and wedged smaller blocks into the remaining gaps. We almost had this under control, although we were up to our knees in frigid water by this time—the chief hadn't lied, it *was* colder than a witch's titty—when they flipped another switch to simulate a mine blowing up under us and the deck plate beneath us gave way. We frantically wrestled timber beams into place and tried to erect them vertically between the buckled deck plate and a steel girder overhead. But we were struggling. The water was up to our waists by this time and rising rapidly. Then a trainer yelled: "Torpedo! Torpedo!" and flipped another switch that caused a door hatch to burst open, and water just gushed in. We threw down our tools, scrambled up the ladders, and jumped onto the pier just as our ship went down. We stood in our sodden uniforms and squishy shoes shivering on the pier. The trainers shook their heads in despair and told us we were failures. They said we were useless bastards. The chief said that it had damn near broken his heart to watch us and that we were as useless as tits on a warthog.

In due time we graduated. Shortly before we did, our orders arrived. They came one night just before our shower time and taps. We were joyful. It seemed that it almost didn't matter where we assigned; we were just happy to see our names on official U.S. Navy Bureau of Personnel stationery with a concrete destination. Early on in our days at OCS it had been made clear to us that, as prospective officers, we were all expected to volunteer for Vietnam. It was the "right thing" for us to do, and that although only one-third of the navy's assets and personnel were in the Vietnam theater, this would facilitate the navy calling us to Vietnam if needed, but, of course, we might very well be sent elsewhere. I believe virtually everyone in my section did the "right thing." Yet, when the orders arrived, it was not just to Vietnam our section's members were sent, but to ships and bases all over the globe. We were in roaring good spirits. Hooting around, pumping each other's hands, and congratulating each other. "What did you get?" ... "USS such-and-such!" "Terrific! Sounds great!" ... "What about you?" We set off for the showers, popping each other with our shower towels. When we came out, one of the company chiefs was waiting in our dorm area to take some of the wind out of our sails. The words were about like this:

"Hey, chief, I've got orders to the destroyer *Semmes*. Do you know her?"

"Yeah. She sits high in the water. A 'rough rider.' A barf-bucket. You'll be puking your guts out."

"Chief! I got the cruiser *Toledo*. Can you tell me anything about her?"

"Sure, the chief bosun's mate on her is a pal of mine. Said they just got a new captain, a real hard-ass. You'll be bustin' your butt night and day."

"How about the *Gearing*, chief?"

"World War Two bucket. Completely rusted out. Only thing holding her together now is baling wire and prayers. She'll be a widow-maker. Sorry, son." But the chief didn't look sorry. He had a smile of firm satisfaction.

My orders were for the aircraft carrier USS *Forrestal*. I could hardly believe it. I had been aboard the *Forrestal* back in 1957—the year she made her maiden voyage. I was just a kid then, living with my family in Naples, Italy. My dad, a chief (what else) was stationed there, and the *Forrestal* paid a "good will" visit. My fifth-grade class was given a tour of her. We were all mightily impressed. We were all navy brats, of course, since our school was a navy dependents' school, and we all knew something about ships. And we all knew what the brand-new *Forrestal* was: at 78,000 tons she was the biggest and mightiest warship the world had ever seen—the world's first supercarrier. It was a thrilling, never-to-be-forgotten day for us kids. We clambered all over her in the wake of our cheerful, fun-loving sailor guides. We had lunch aboard—went through the "chowline" and, naturally, the sailor cooks dolloped us out extra big scoops of ice cream and handed us fistfuls of cookies. My fifth-grader's mind was made up: one day I would serve on that great ship. And now, in a thousand-ship navy,

USS Forrestal *departing Norfolk, 1968.*

—Courtesy U.S. Navy

I had drawn that ship. There in my hand were my orders: I was directed to take an eight-week communications officer's course there in Newport, then take a thirty-day home leave, and then fly out to join *Forrestal* on patrol at "Yankee Station" in the Gulf of Tonkin. I was delighted!

Unfortunately, events didn't play out quite like that. I completed the eight-week course, all right, and was just commencing my thirty-days' leave at my parents' home in Edmond, Oklahoma, when one evening while watching TV the program was interrupted for a news flash: the viewers were informed that at that moment a naval disaster was in progress in the Gulf of Tonkin. The carrier *Forrestal* was ablaze, heavy loss of life was feared, and there was doubt that the ship could survive. For the rest of the evening and much of the next day, the *Forrestal* was the news. The same story and the same images were carried by all three networks.

What had happened was that while preparing for an air strike on North Vietnam, one of the scores of aircraft in motion on the flight deck had grazed another one, tearing open a wingtip fuel tank. The spilled fuel immediately ignited and spread over much of the aft- and mid-sections of the flight deck. This burning fuel then began to "cook off" the bombs, slung beneath the wings and fuselages of the strike aircraft. The bombs, as they exploded, blasted down through the flight deck into the eight levels of decks below the flight deck—the living and working quarters of 4,700 crewmen. The captain kept speed on and drove the ship bow on into the wind to drive the flames backward and to keep them from spreading to the forward part of the ship. Meanwhile, other American warships on duty at Yankee Station raced to assist—bringing themselves in right alongside so that their powerful water pumps could spray *Forrestal* down. Still, it took many hours to bring the inferno under control, and the images captured by cameramen aboard the assisting ships and hovering helicopters are unforgettable and moving: swarms of men shoving burning aircraft to the deck edge and pushing them over the side; heroic sailors staggering under the weight of 50-, 80- and even 100-pound smoldering bombs that they would cradle in their arms and lug to the deck edge and drop into the sea (some of these men had to have their burnt arms amputated afterwards); fire teams by the dozen in frantic activity; and rising above it all a dense, black, burgeoning column of smoke towering upward for thousands of feet and which journalists reported was clearly visible from fifty miles away.

When I finally met up with the *Forrestal* it was several weeks later at Norfolk Naval Shipyard in Virginia. After the fire, *Forrestal* put in briefly at Subic Bay, Philippines, to unload her 138 dead and scores of men who had already received amputations or required amputations and to have the shipyard there make some necessary patch-up repairs for the ship's long voyage back to the States, where the real restoration would take place. She returned via the Pacific and, being too large to use the Panama Canal, rounded the "Horn" of South America, thence steamed northward up through the Atlantic to Norfolk.

The *Forrestal* I now saw in Norfolk Naval Shipyard was not the pristine vessel that enthralled me so when first I beheld her riding at anchor on a sunny day in the glimmering waters of Naples Bay. Oh, the ship still looked big—stunning actually—when you saw her balanced on giant blocks inside her mammoth dry-dock. For once you could see the ship "in full," and not just the part of her that rode above the waterline. But she did look beaten: smudged with soot; gaping craters in her flight deck; raw, twisted metal everywhere; and the barrels of her five-inch gun turrets melted and drooping like flaccid elephant trunks. Aboard it was worse, especially in the below-decks compartments where the majority of the deaths occurred. These were mainly sleeping compartments for off-duty crewmen, and the men had been incinerated in their bunks when the blasts came through. Despite the bulkheads having been scrubbed with lye, the aroma of burnt bacon persisted.

A few days after I moved aboard *Forrestal*, which would be my home for the next three years—half of my abbreviated six-year career in the navy—a curious incident occurred. I had gone "ashore" (yes, that terminology still pertained even though we were laying in our dry dock) on some errand to one of the shipyard offices, and on my return I came upon a group of well-dressed civilians gathered on the lip of our dry dock and staring gravely down at *Forrestal*. The focal point of this group was clearly an elderly man with a walking stick. He was a vision in white: white suit, white shirt, flowing white hair, and white goatee. And a black string tie. I asked one of the "suits" in attendance if the man were Colonel Sanders. He said it was. And shortly afterwards the group crossed the gangplank to our quarterdeck, where our captain was waiting to receive them. A couple of hours later the group left and it was announced on the public address system that Colonel Sanders had been aboard with his people to establish an education fund. He had pledged to pay for the educations of all the children of both our deceased crewmembers and of our crewmembers who had lost limbs, for as far as the children could go: high school, college, post-graduate studies, medical school, however far. I fondly eat Kentucky Fried Chicken to this day.

I enjoyed my time in the navy, especially my sea years on *Forrestal*. Much of what I craved was within my grasp—the sea, ships, travel, most particularly exotic travel. It's tough to beat a day when you've come off pleasantly exhausted from a night watch and go up on deck to greet the rising sun. You stand on the bow, braced against the wind as your colossal floating island plows through some remote sea at a steady 30 knots. And, necessarily, along your journey's way there will be ports of call where strangers might be met—preferably girl strangers. And, make no mistake, that hope is harbored at the back of almost every sailor's mind.

And I valued my time in the navy for more serious reasons as well. I found my co-workers on the whole exhibited more competence, more integrity, and less flimflam than the members of any other organization I have served. These qualities were epitomized in the two successive captains I served on *Forrestal*. The first was Capt. Robert B. Baldwin. He was an Annapolis man who came up during World War II and had an unbroken succession of important assignments. He was all business and all navy—crisp, strict, meticulous. Just the sort of man you'd expect the navy to entrust with an enormous ship, an enormous crew and enormous powers. (The *Forrestal*, like all supercarriers, was "nuclear capable.") At sea Baldwin sat in his tall, leather, swivel bridge chair at least sixteen hours out of every twenty-four. An armed marine bodyguard was always at his side. He seldom spoke. He just sat in his swivel chair, watching things with his gimlet eyes. He watched the changing bridge teams that drove the ship in four-hour shifts. On the few occasions that he spoke, it was usually to the officer-of-the-deck, and always to some purpose. "You're turning the ship too fast, damn it! You'll throw a plane off the flight deck!" Captain Balwin was eventually promoted to rear admiral and transferred to the Pentagon and an office charged with "strategic target selection" responsibilities. Yes, an office with a function just as ominous as it sounds.

My second captain was James W. Nance. He had had just as lustrous a career as Baldwin, and I think the crew liked him better. He had a certain air of sadness about him, and he seemed more human and humane. For instance, within just a couple of days of his having flown onto the ship and assumed command, he made a maiden speech to the crew over the announcement system—a "Now hear this, now hear this, this is the captain speaking" speech—in which he ordered some immediate changes to be made. He had noticed the big patches half the crew wore on the backs of their blue work jackets. The emblem on these patches was a big circle with cross-hairs and a cone-hatted "gook" in the sights. The logo read: "Tonkin Gulf Hunt Club." The captain ordered these patches to be removed within twenty-four hours under penalty of formal charges. He lectured us to the effect that no human's life was to be regarded lightly—not ours, not our enemy's. He explained that if we were called upon to kill our enemy we would do so, but not in a spirit of hatred and not in a spirit of levity. Furthermore, he went on to express his disappointment that when inspecting various divisions' living quarters he had found so many dirty magazines and pin-ups of naked women. "What would your mothers think? What would your sisters think?" He ordered all such magazines and pictures to be burned in the ship's incinerator within twenty-four hours.

The patches and pictures disappeared and, you know, I never heard any crewmember express any resentment at all. They respected the decency of the man, and I think they appreciated the boundaries he was placing on their behavior. After all, the bulk of the crewmembers were very young men, still in their teens or early twenties, and they did need some sort of a father figure.

The *Forrestal* never did return to Vietnam waters. After our lengthy interlude at Norfolk Naval Shipyard, we reverted to being an East Coast ship, and our cruises were to the Caribbean, the North Atlantic, and the Mediterranean. But excepting "the Med," which was a true plum, much of this was pretty dull steaming, especially the North Atlantic. Our cruises there lacked any pressing purpose other than to simply keep moving. Ever since Pearl Harbor the navy has striven to keep its assets dispersed and underway in order to prevent them becoming sitting ducks like they were at "Battleship Row" on December 7, 1941. So frequently our ship's assignment was as elementary as steaming in a giant circle in some remote reach of the North Atlantic. We performed this task as surreptitiously as possible so "darkened ship" was always in force at night, and we traveled at reduced speed to conserve fuel and to reduce our engine, propeller, and wake noise as a precaution against any Soviet submarines that might be prowling in the area.

One memory that catches in my mind during one such stretch of dull duty was when we were gliding quietly along the coast of Greenland in transit to our circling position. At our paltry 12 or 15 knots, for days we were creeping along that huge island's coastline—seemingly endless cliffs of ice, gleaming by day and gleaming by night, too, in the starlight. There was very little to do other than our regular rotation of watches, day after day, night after night. Well, one night in Main Comm, the ship's communication center, where I worked, one of the bored sailors on the midwatch, Wickham was his name, a big, third-class petty officer with hair and skin almost as fair as an albino's, hooked up banks of teletypewriters in tandem and printed periods—just dots—for hours onto spools of paper. He then cut the spools into long strips and taped these strips to the communication center's walls. He had planned things carefully: he had printed out exactly one million dots. When we, the members of the morning watch, came on, he said, "Look! Look at that! That's one million. That's what a million looks like." It was pretty amazing, all right. We all just stared and stared. We walked up to the strips to get a closer look. I've got no doubts we were all thinking pretty much the same thing: "That's how insignificant we are. We're just like one of those dots." And, actually, we're even more insignificant than that. There are billions of people on the planet. We're about as close to nothing as it gets. I can't speak for the others, but I didn't find this epiphany depressing. On the contrary, I found it rather comforting. Perhaps I'm deficient in ambition.

The crusty old chiefs relieved their boredom by tormenting the "fresh meat" that arrived on the ship weekly. A batch of rookies straight from training camps would be flown out on the mail plane to replace a batch of crewmen whose enlistments were up and who were being flown back on the same plane. Inevitably, there would be one rube among the new recruits who "stood out," some bumpkin from Iowa or Kansas or places like that, some simple-hearted, dull-witted farm kid hoping to do his family proud. Having spotted such a yokel, the chiefs will almost rub their hands in relish. As like as not they'll start him off with the "ship's list" scam. Now the "ship's list" is the degree the ship is canting to either port or starboard as measured by a spirit level mounted in the bridge. But, of course, the hick isn't going to know that, and no doubt envisions some important document or roster. Before he even has time to stow his gear, a chief will approach him with: "Hey, you, Swenson! The captain needs the ship's list immediately! I think Chief Watts down in the boiler room has it. Get down there quick as you can and bring it back to me. Don't just stand there! Hustle, buster!" The poor guy will blunder lost and panic-stricken until he finds Chief Watts six decks down, who'll twig immediately to the words "ship's list," and send the oaf all the way forward to Chief Anderson in the fo'c'sle, who now has the list. "And for God's sake, hurry! This is important!" For the next few hours the chiefs will have the poor devil tearing all over the ship, from top to bottom, stem to stern. Great fun. And the real kicker comes when it finally dawns on the dull-witted dupe just how dull-witted he has been.

Another favorite of the chiefs was the "mail buoy" caper. In this one the dolt would be assigned to sit on the ship's bow to keep a sharp lookout for the mail buoy. He would be given binoculars to assist him in this task. The chief will have given the innocent to understand that little postal ships hang the navy's mail on buoys spotted here and there around the oceans and passing navy ships snag the mail pouches off the buoys as they pass. The chief will also have driven home the importance of the assignment: failure to spot the buoy will result in the entire crew's disappointment. Oh, and the captain's also expecting a letter from his wife. The message is clear: miss the buoy and you'll have your ass in a sling.

I remember being on the bridge once when Captain Nance, the sad, kindly captain, arrived and took his place in the swivel chair. Almost immediately he spotted a lonely figure perched way forward on the bow, tracking slowly left and slowly right with the binoculars.

"What's that man doing?"

"Mail buoy watch, sir," replied the officer-of-the-deck.

"How long's he been at it?"

"Several hours, sir."

"Send someone down to get that boy. I won't have this on my ship."

Of course, not even the cold, gray North Atlantic was always boring. Our cruises there were periodically enlivened by "Bears." These were the big, workhorse bombers of the Soviet air force (the equivalent of America's B-52s but for being prop-driven) that would make frequent runs from bases in Russia's Kola Peninsula down to Cuba. They would leave their Kola airfields, skirt Norway's North Cape, then come barreling down the North Atlantic through the Iceland-Faeroes Gap. We engaged in a sort of cat-and-mouse game with them. If they had by one means or another (submarine, satellite, radio intercept) detected our carrier's whereabouts, the Bear would attempt to overfly us in a mock bombing run. Many miles out the Bear would drop to low, low altitude and approach our ship, just skimming above the wave tops in an attempt to stay under our radar. If they managed to escape our detection, the first warning we'd have of them would be a sighting by our lookouts atop our island superstructure. By then it was too late for us to do much of anything; our ship's inertia was such that we could not even effect a course change before the plane was upon us. It would come boring in, rise slightly from the wave tops, open its bomb-bay doors, and then buzz the length of our flight deck, delivering an unmistakable message: "Gotcha!"

In such instances our captain would be justifiably furious, and his wrath could take several forms: he could punish us by holding us at "general quarters" (battle stations) for twenty-four hours—no rest, no meals, and no movement since every hatch and water-tight door on the ship was clamped and sealed; he could drill us till we dropped; or, what we most regretted, he could cancel all liberty during our next scheduled port call. Not surprisingly, therefore, the crew took enormous interest in preventing the Bears from buzzing us. And we were usually successful. When things went as they were supposed to, our radar men would detect the Bears a couple of hundred miles out, giving us plenty of time to launch several of our fighters to harass and harry the bomber out of our vicinity. In these cases the tables were turned and our fighters would make mock strafing and rocketing runs on the Bear. As you see, this was a cat-and-mouse game, but a cat-and-mouse game with very high stakes. There was significant danger of a mistake or misjudgment having terrible repercussions, even turning the Cold War suddenly hot.

Never was the Cold War permitted to stray far from out thoughts. Whenever, and

I stress whenever—anytime, every time, no exception—our carrier was within range of Soviet territory, even within the absolute extremity of our range, we prepared to strike. The "range" was calculated as the distance our longest-range, fully fueled, nuclear-configured aircraft could fly, not on a round-way trip, but on a one-way trip in which the plane and pilot would necessarily be forfeited. That being the case, whenever the ship's navigator could confirm we had broached that range line on our chart, we prepared. Two nuclear bombs cradled on jack-up hoists would arrive on an elevator coming from our nuclear weapons magazine in the bowels of the ship. The bombs were sleek, surgically clean, gleaming white cylinders blunted on both ends. They each had several small glass viewing portholes to see into the device's interior mechanisms and coding system. While marine guards with rifles at the "port arms" position kept crewmen well back, a gang of technicians attached the bombs to the bellies of two planes. The planes were then elevatored up to the flight deck and mounted on the port and starboard bow catapults. A pilot would mount each of these aircraft, which were usually single-seaters. The pilots would sit in their cockpits, flight-suited, helmeted, and oxygen-masked. If war suddenly broke out, they would be launched. If not, after four hours they would be replaced by two fresh, ready pilots. That routine went on without let-up, day-after-day, week-after-week, month-after-month, for however long we were within range. The thinking was that under virtually any circumstances (barring a direct nuclear hit on *Forrestal*) we would manage to get at least those two aircraft up. *Forrestal*'s size and survivability were such that it would take a number of conventional missile strikes or torpedo hits to incapacitate or sink her, and almost certainly those two planes could be launched. The conventional wisdom of the time, the late sixties, held that for every two planes that entered Soviet airspace, one would make it through to target, particularly if the pilot came in low, skimming the forests, hugging the steppes. *Forrestal* might be gone, but she would avenge herself with, perhaps, a city. This was MAD (Mutual Assured Destruction) writ small: a city for a carrier.

To maximize our survivability chances, we usually had escorts attending us. Once we even had the mighty battleship *New Jersey* assigned to protect us. (Keep in mind that a carrier's "CAP," combat air patrol, is always its own best protection, but in spells of exceptionally bad weather when the planes can't be launched and "its cap's off," a carrier is virtually defenseless.) Usually, too, we had one or two HUKS (hunter-killer submarines) as invisible outriders several miles out in front of us or on our flanks to scour for enemy submarines. And always we had at least one or two destroyers assigned to us both for their anti-aircraft and anti-submarine capabilities and for rescue duties. Every couple of weeks some dink would fall over the side or, more usually, in a moment of inattention be blown over the side by a jet's exhaust blast. Unless they got sucked into the ship's propellers, they would usually survive, albeit often with a broken bone or two—it was a seventy-foot drop from the flight deck. And the destroyers also picked up pilots who had to eject because of a botched take-off or landing. If the pilots were successfully rescued, the ribbing they got once they were safe and sound back in the *Forrestal*'s wardroom was almost enough to make them wish they hadn't been. And if the pilots didn't make it—and on one par-

USS Forrestal *refueling from USS* Marias *in the North Atlantic, 1968.*
—Courtesy U.S. Navy

ticular ten-month Med cruise five didn't—the navigator carefully noted the location on his chart and within a few weeks, at our first opportunity really, we'd fly the wife, parents, kids, what have you, out to *Forrestal* and return to the exact spot. Then in a sad little ceremony, while the ship circled the location, the crew would be piped to silent attention and the widow or whomever would toss a wreath over the side. It would float there until it disappeared in our wake.

Besides having our own escorting vessels, when we were in the Med we would often have a Soviet frigate or destroyer in attendance, too. These ships were units of the U.S.S.R.'s Black Sea Fleet that would come down into the Med via the Dardanelles from their bases at Odessa and Sevastopol. They were quite brazen. They would shoulder their way through our screening ships and get right up beside us and then train their guns and missile pods at us. They'd shadow us everywhere, weeks at a time, and were at times so close we could have pitched a baseball at them. When our guys were off duty they would sometimes lounge on the catwalks that lined the flight deck and look at the Russians. They'd give the Russian sailors the Bronx cheer and shoot them the finger. The Russians would shoot it right back and shout their own brand of obscenities. Once I was alone on the catwalk at dusk studying the Russian ship—mainly marveling at the slovenliness of the vessel—when a lone Russian sailor emerged from a hatchway onto the deck. He must have been a steward of some kind, because he was carrying a tray of dishes and dinner things along to the bridge. He spotted me looking down at him from high above on the catwalk. We had eye contact. I gave him a small wave. He looked forward and aft to make sure no one on his ship was watching, and then he gave me a small, civil wave back. Then he walked off with his tray.

So, as I say, the Russians and the Cold War were never far from our minds. They were very close indeed for one of my cabin mates. I lived in an eight-berth cabin for junior officers forward in the ship and two levels down from the flight deck. The compartment had eight gray bunks with pull-up cradle rails to keep us from falling out during rough weather, eight gray desks with built-in safes for storing our valuables, eight gray wardrobes for our uniforms and "civies," and two sinks. A steward cleaned the cabin daily, made our bunks, and hauled off our dirty clothes for cleaning and pressing. Usually no more than four or five people lived in the cabin at any given time, so we had spare bunk space, and one of the cabin's bunks was given over to housing the impressive sound system—huge speakers—that one of our cabin mates owned. If no one were sleeping (a rare occurrence since we all had different shifts and duties), we would crank up the music and liven things up. But, anyway, one of the cabin's occupants was a pilot who kept pretty much to himself and had exceedingly light duties. While we ship's officers had our watches to stand and divisions to supervise, this guy lolled around in his bunk most of the day. He'd read books, listen to music, saunter down to the wardroom for meals. We couldn't figure out what his function was. He said he was a pilot, but we never saw him flying a plane. Well, finally, we found out what he was. One night he couldn't sleep and was up virtually the whole night vomiting in the sink. He'd bend over the sink and wretch awhile, lie back down, then get up again and wretch some more. He looked spent and shaky. An hour or two before dawn he opened his wardrobe and put on his flight suit. From his safe he retrieved a pistol, a dagger, a packet of plastic encased South African gold Krugerrands, and a 10- or 12-page cloth pamphlet made of unburnable asbestos fibers. Each page of the pamphlet was printed in a different language—Turkish, Russian, Farsi, Chinese, Urdu, Hindi, et cetera—and each page translated as the same thing: that he was an American pilot and if the reader would hide him and help him he would be rewarded with gold and other gifts by the American government. Our cabin mate flew a spy plane.

We had three RA-5s (reconnaissance aircraft) aboard called "Vigilantes." These were beautiful, viciously graceful-looking aircraft that had a ceiling in excess of 100,000 feet and were believed to be beyond the range of any ground-launched anti-aircraft missile in the Soviet arsenal. Late model MIGs, themselves high-fliers, might be able to reach a Vigilante with an air-launched missile, but the Vigilante could attain a Mach-3 speed and would be very hard to catch. The wings of these aircraft had a leading edge of honed titanium so sharp that they were fitted with rubber guard strips whenever the planes were aboard ship to prevent the plane handlers from cutting themselves. The Vigilantes were unarmed but carried an array of high-definition motion and still cameras in their underbellies. Whenever our ship was in the northern or eastern reaches of the Med, say up in the Adriatic or Aegean Seas, the Vigilantes could penetrate up and into the Soviet heartland and then arc over to exit via Turkey or (then) allies Iran or Pakistan. But, to make a long story short, after that we no longer ribbed our cabin mate about either his leisurely life-style or his preflight bouts of vomiting.

I, too, never forgot what our ship's primary mission was: to serve as an active component of our nation's defense policy, Mutually Assured Destruction. I was one of the six CWOs (communication watch officers) aboard ship. Among our other tasks one of us always had to be on duty in Main Comm. We supervised the shift that was manning the radio links, teletypewriters, and coding machines. We decided the routing of the hundreds of daily messages that fed into the ship from the Pentagon, the Navy's Bureau of Personnel, Atlantic Fleet headquarters in Norfolk, various NATO commands we were either attached to or cooperating with, our escorting vessels, and the bucket-brigade chain of oilers and supply ships that rendezvoused with us to fuel and feed us. But one other duty each of us six CWOs had was to keep a sequence of numbers forever etched in our brains. These were the numbers which turned the tumblers of a dual combination safe housed in *Forrestal*'s SIOP (Strategic Integrated Operation Plan) center. This safe contained the authentication codes which authorized the use of the racks of nuclear weapons in the ship's nuclear magazine. The CWO had the combination for one of the safe's dials, the IWO (intelligence watch officer) had the combination for the other. Both were required to open the safe, and both had independent means of verifying the authenticity of a sealed instrument inside. The safe contained both a sealed exercise authentication instrument (so the system could be periodically tested) and then, of course, the sealed "real" instrument, which hopefully would never be opened.

Every month or so at understandably random times of the night or day a system test would be initiated by the National Emergency Command Center located deep, deep in the ground beneath the Pentagon. Our first sign on *Forrestal* that a test was in the works was that suddenly and seemingly inexplicably our banks and banks of chattering teletypewriters and on-line coding machines would abruptly go dead. Complete silence. Then, in a few seconds, they would revive, but now would be dinging their bells. *Ding-ding-ding-ding.* Then the machines would start printing again and again: "Standby for Flash SIOP message." That would repeat for maybe ten seconds, in which time I lifted my direct phone to the officer-of-the-deck and ordered this message to be announced on the public address system: "Captain and SIOP team to SIOP center immediately." Meanwhile the message would come in. Very brief—a few printed letters of a code. These I'd rip off the teletypewriter spool and begin my well-practiced run. The SIOP center was amidships, about 150 yards distance and with foot-high watertight hatch combs ("knee-knockers," we appropriately called them) about every ten yards. I'd be hurdling through these as fast as I could. From different parts of the ship the captain and half a dozen other members of the SIOP team would be hurtling along, too. Crewmen who had also heard the announcement and knew at least something of its importance would press themselves to the passageway bulkheads to clear a path for the running officers and alert those ahead with, "Gangway! Gangway!" (It was something of a shock to crewmembers to see their captain running—unable to imagine him moving in any manner other than his deliberate authoritarian tread.) As we all tumbled breathless into the SIOP center (its sealed and coded combination door already stood open for us), we went to the safe. The IWO would have already dialed in his combination, and now I would dial in mine with trembling fingers—trembling because of my 150-yard sprint and because of the "moment" of the occasion. With the coded message in my hand and the instrument inside the safe, I could then vouch to the captain on the authenticity of the message to use our nuclear weapons. The IWO would do the same. The captain would then order me to send a confirmation message to the NECC, stating that the authorization process was successfully completed. This I would do. Now a measure of the speed with which this whole process was conducted—from origination of the message at NECC to NECC's receipt of the confirmation—was the outside allowable time limit: ten minutes. We always made it. And when you think this same scenario was being played out simultaneously throughout the SIOP system, at any U.S. commands with nuclear inventories—bomber bases, ballistic missile submarines, ICBM missile silos—it was pretty impressive. I know it impressed me.

Once the captain asked us to stay on in the center after the authentication test was complete. He wanted us all to be clear about the steps that would next be taken if ever the "real" authentication code came. He nodded to the SIOP officer, who went and fetched a big map from another safe. Pausing a moment for effect, he then unfolded this map onto a big work table. As we looked, there was silence. I think all of us were mentally taking a breath. Before us was the SIOP—the Strategic Integrated Operations Plan. The words now had true meaning. This was a plan for an overwhelming nuclear attack. The map was of Eurasia, and the whole communist bloc was spread out before us with the targets marked—hundreds of them. One person said, it wasn't really a question, more of a sad statement: "And China, too." To which the SIOP boss replied in, if not these exact words, very nearly these exact words: "Gentlemen, we're only going to do this once. We're going to take care of all our business. We're not going to do Russia now and then worry about China twenty or thirty years down the road. We're going to do this just once." This was MAD writ large.

Our own ship's color-coded little clump of targets in southwestern Russia seemed almost insignificant on this huge map and in the vast scale of things—insignificant until you looked closer, until you saw the actual names of the sites and cities. These were places and people that would be struck harder and suffer more than Hiroshima or Nagasaki—our bombs were far more powerful. My God.

After three years on *Forrestal*, I had three years of shore duty—six months as a CWO at SACLANT (Supreme Allied Commander-Atlantic) headquarters, in Norfolk, then two and a half years as officer-in-charge of the message center at COMIBERLANT (Commander Iberian-Atlantic Area) headquarters outside Lisbon, Portugal. It was now the end of 1972, and the American Phase of the Vietnam debacle was drawing to its inglorious close. A liberal Congress was gutting the defense budget, reducing a proud 1,000-ship navy to fewer than 400, and would trim personnel just as savagely. My "detailer," the officer at the Navy Bureau of Personnel whose responsibility it was to track the careers and advise officers whose last names ran from A to G in the alphabet, visited my command in Lisbon and spelled out the hard facts to me. I was due for promotion to lieutenant-commander, but he made it clear that for me to secure that promotion I had to agree to spend six of the next nine years of my career at sea. Having married just three years prior to this a Scottish girl I had met in Marseilles on my last cruise on *Forrestal*, and now having an infant son and daughter, this was not an undertaking I was willing to make. I returned to the States with my family and spent a month at Brooklyn Naval Shipyard Hospital having some medical problems taken care of and then left the navy.

It has been almost forty years, two generations, since I first reported for duty aboard *Forrestal*, and I have never looked back on those years with anything else but pride. Like almost all of my brother veterans, I am proud that I served in my country's armed forces. I feel we all participated in a great historical venture. Between the years of 1945 and 1990, the United States was locked into a Cold War to at first contain and then to defeat the Soviet Empire and communism. And we won. Surely that is a good thing: good for the U.S., good for the peoples once subjected to communism, and good for the world.

I hope that the Korean and Vietnam veterans can appreciate that those ugly Asian agonies they participated in were but part of a grander scheme and were not nearly as futile as they might appear on the surface. Korean veterans might feel frustrated that they had to settle for half a victory, and Vietnam veterans might feel they came home with even less, but I believe history has proven otherwise. The veterans of Korea and Vietnam, with their blood and sacrifices, "bought time." They held back the surging tide of communism long enough for the nascent developing nations of East and Southeast Asia to establish viable governments and economies. North Korea was not recovered and spared from the tyranny and poverty that are the twin hallmarks of communism wherever it takes hold, and neither was South Vietnam nor the two dominoes that fell with it, Laos and Cambodia. But how gratifying it is that those were the only East and Southeast Asian nations that did fall. The far more significant fact is that South Korea, Taiwan, Japan, Thailand, Malaysia, Singapore, Indonesia, Brunei, and the Philippines did not fall. Those nations, today homes to 600 million people, have stabilized and, in most cases, grown prosperous. If America had stood by and done nothing in the face of encroaching communism, almost certainly that would not have been the case.

Endnotes

1. At the close of the war in 1945 the Soviet Union claimed war losses of 16 million. Actual losses were 27 million—a fact not revealed until 1986 and the inception of President Mikhail Gorbachev's *glasnost* ("openness") campaign. Previous Soviet leaders downplayed Soviet war losses lest it expose the severity of the Soviet Union's postwar manpower shortage and thus embolden Russia's enemies.

2. For a discussion of the role Korea's exclusion from the U.S.'s "defense perimeter" had in fomenting a communist attack see Center of Military History, *American Military History* (Washington, D.C.: U.S. Army Center of Military History, 1989), pp. 544-45, and Chen Jian, *China's Road to the Korean War* (New York: Columbia University Press, 1994), pp. 119-120.

3. Center of Military History, *American Military History*, p. 545.

4. *Ibid.*, p. 546, and Robert Jackson, *Air War Over Korea* (New York: Charles Scribner's Sons, 1973), pp. 13-14.

5. Center of Military History, *American Military History*, p. 550.

6. Ever since this disastrous rout, "Task Force Smith" has served in the U.S. Army as a byword for the consequences of military unpreparedness. For a description of the force's engagement and retreat see: Russell A. Gugeler, *Combat Actions in Korea* (Washington, D.C.: U.S. Army Center of Military History, 1987), pp. 3-18.

7. Courtney Whitney, *MacArthur: His Rendezvous with History* (Westport, Connecticut: Greenwood Press, Publishers, 1977), p. 344.

8. For a detailed account of General Walker's masterful defense of the Pusan Perimeter see William Glenn Robertson's *Counterattack on the Naktong 1950* (Fort Leavenworth, Kansas: Combat Studies Institute, 1985). This study comes complete with twenty-two fold-out operational maps.

9. A thorough evaluation of Inchon's suitability as an invasion site can be found in the chapter "Inchon: The Great Debate" of General Courtney Whitney's *MacArthur*, pp. 342-353.

10. Center of Military History, *American Military History*, p. 555.

11. *Ibid.*, p. 556.

12. *Ibid.*, p. 559.

13. *Ibid.*

14. Billy C. Mossman, *United States Army in the Korean War: Ebb and Flow November 1950-July 1951* (Washington, D.C.: U.S. Army Center of Military History, 1990), p. 84.

15. The promptness of General Ridgway's dispatch from Washington was due to the army's routine contingency planning. A battlefield commander's death is always anticipated. Months before, General MacArthur had requested and Army Chief of Staff General J. Lawton Collins had approved General Ridgway as General Walker's replacement in event of the latter's death or incapacitation. Mossman, *Ebb and Flow*, p. 177.

16. *Ibid.*, p. 247.

17. *Ibid.*, p. 231.
18. *Ibid.*, pp. 230-234.
19. Center of Military History, *American Military History*, p. 563.
20. *Ibid.*, p. 564.
21. *Ibid.*, p. 567.
22. *Ibid.*, p. 569.
23. Scott Rutherford, ed., *Vietnam* (London: Insight Guides, 2001), p. 35.
24. Phillip B. Davidson, *Vietnam at War* (New York: Oxford University Press, 1988), pp. 40-41.
25. *Ibid.*, pp. 41-42.
26. *Ibid.*
27. *Ibid.*, p. 42.
28. *Ibid.*, pp. 177-178.
29. *Ibid.*, pp. 224-225.
30. *Ibid.*, pp. 225-226. Davidson estimated the Vietminh fired a minimum of 93,000 artillery rounds during the battle. Also see Michael Maclear, *The Ten Thousand Day War: Vietnam 1945-1975* (New York: St. Martin's Press, 1981), pp. 31-37.
31. Maclear, *The Ten Thousand Day War*, p. 37.
32. Undeniably most of the French Troops fought heroically. Virtually all eyewitnesses attest to this as do Vietminh losses. However, there were exceptions. Approximately 3,000 "internal deserters" dug holes along the Nam Yun River and hid there for the duration of the battle. See: Davidson, *Vietnam at War*, p. 225.
33. Maclear, *The Ten Thousand Day War*, p. 43; and Earl H. Tilford, *Setup: What the U.S. Air Force Did in Vietnam and Why* (Maxwell Air Force Base, Alabama: Air University Press, 1991), pp. 22-23.
34. Maclear, *The Ten Thousand Day War*, p. 43.
35. *Ibid.*, p. 45.
36. *Ibid.*, pp. 42-45.
37. *Ibid.*, p. 43.
38. The term "Viet Cong," meaning "Vietnamese Communist," did not arise until 1960. It was short form for the more unwieldy "National Liberation Front for South Vietnam," which Ho had announced the formation of that year. Stanley Karnow, *Vietnam: A History* (New York: Penguin Books USA, Inc., 1997), p. 693.
39. Michael Lind, *Vietnam: The Necessary War* (New York: The Free Press, 1999), p. 35.
40. Maclear, *The Ten Thousand Day War*, pp. 26-27.
41. Davidson, *Vietnam at War*, pp. 287-291.
42. *Ibid.*, p. 290, and Karnow, *Vietnam*, pp. 692-693.
43. Maclear, *The Ten Thousand Day War*, p. 59.
44. Karnow, *Vietnam*, p. 265.
45. *Ibid.*, p. 694.
46. Lieutenant General Phillip B. Davidson, who served as both William Westmoreland's and Creighton Abrams' chief intelligence officer, gives an excellent description of the social and ideological animosities between the uniformed military leaders and their civilian bosses during the Kennedy and Johnson presidencies. He also recounts two statements President Johnson made several years after leaving office: "My greatest mistake was not to have fired ... the holdovers from the Kennedy administration;" and, "I am aware of my main mistake in the war. I would not put enough trust in my military advisors." See: Davidson, *Vietnam at War*, pp. 340-342.
47. Davidson, *Vietnam at War*, pp. 318-320.
48. Johnson's anguished struggle to obtain congressional backing for the Tonkin Gulf Resolution can be traced in: David M. Barrett, ed., *Lyndon B. Johnson's Vietnam Papers* (College Station, Texas: Texas A&M University Press, 1997), pp. 60-79.
49. Davidson, *Vietnam at War*, p. 323.
50. *Ibid.*, pp. 324-325.
51. *Ibid.*, p. 335.
52. Maclear, *The Ten Thousand Day War*, p. 29.
53. Robert A. Doughty and Ira D. Gruber, *American Military History and the Evolution of Warfare in the Western World* (Lexington, Massachusetts: D.C. Heath and Company, 1996), p. 646.

54. Tilford, *Setup: What the Air Force Did in Vietnam and Why*, p. 54.
55. *Ibid.*
56. *Ibid.*, pp. 109-110.
57. *Ibid.*, pp. 215-216.
58. *Ibid.*, p. 176.
59. Robert S. McNamara, *Argument Without End: In Search of Answers to the Vietnam Tragedy* (New York: Public Affairs, 1999), p. 254.
60. Davidson, *Vietnam at War*, p. 359.
61. Karnow, *Vietnam: A History*, p. 553.
62. Center of Military History, *American Military History*, p. 672; and Davidson, *Vietnam at War*, p. 554.
63. Karnow, *Vietnam: A History*, pp. 543-544.
64. Center of Military History, *American Military History*, p. 673.
65. Doughty and Gruber, *American Military History and the Evolution of Warfare in the Western World*, p. 657.
66. Maclear, *The Ten Thousand Day War*, p. 197.
67. Giap has admitted as much in several postwar interviews granted to Western reporters. Whether this was his true conviction or merely a means of rubbing salt in America's wounds is anyone's conjecture.
68. Maclear, *The Ten Thousand Day War*, p. 199.
69. *Ibid.*, pp. 197-199.
70. Karnow, *Vietnam: A History*, p. 697.
71. Tilford, *Setup: What the Air Force Did in Vietnam and Why*, p. 181.
72. *Ibid.*, pp. 171-172.
73. *Ibid.*, p. 221.
74. *Ibid.*, pp. 224-225.
75. *Ibid.*, p. 228.
76. *Ibid.*
77. An excellent analysis of the many factors at work propelling both North Vietnam and the Nixon administration toward a negotiated settlement in the closing months of 1972 can be found in Stanley Karnow's *Vietnam: A History*, pp. 659-669.
78. *Ibid.*, pp. 662-663.
79. *Ibid.*, p. 666.
80. *Ibid.*, p. 667.
81. *Ibid.*
82. *Ibid.*, pp. 667-668.
83. Tilford, *Setup: What the Air Force Did in Vietnam and Why*, p. 264.
84. Center of Military History, *American Military History*, pp. 688-689.
85. Henry Kissinger, *Years of Renewal* (New York: Simon & Schuster, 1999), pp. 484-495.
86. Karnow, *Vietnam: A History*, p. 682.

Bibliography

Personal Interviews

Aguinaga, Reynaldo. Interview with Juan L. Martinez, Brownsville, April 12, 2003.
Barrera, David. Interview with Leo Villarreal, Brownsville, June 10, 2003.
Barrientes, Alonso, Jr. Interview with Erika Longoria, Brownsville, April 6, 2003.
Canant, Willie F., Jr. Interview with Carlos Rodriguez, Brownsville, April 14, 2003.
Casanova, Leonel. Interview with Leonel Casanova, Jr., Los Fresnos, April 14, 2003.
Castillo, Joe. Interview with Leo Villarreal, Brownsville, June 29, 2003.
Cockrill, E.E. Interview with Edith Lizbeth Cano, Brownsville, June 6, 2003.
Cortez, Ben. Interview with Erasmo Chapa, San Benito, April 13, 2003.
Garcia, Roberto. Interview with David Cantu, Brownsville, April 15, 2003.
Ghionzoli, Richard. Interview with Ruben Garcia, Brownsville, April 13, 2003.
Gonzalez, Jose. Interview with Edward J. Garcia, Brownsville, April 16, 2003.
Hanh, Nguyen Duc. Interview with William L. Adams, Hanoi, December 20, 2003.
Hao, Ru. Interview with William L. Adams, Beijing, May 17, 2003.
Hernandez, Alfredo, Jr. Interview with Rodolfo R. Flores, Olmito, June 18, 2003.
Hernandez, Jesus. Interview with Rodolfo R. Flores, Harlingen, June 11, 2003.
Huy, Gen. Nguyen Duc. Interview with William L. Adams, Hanoi, December 17, 2003.
Jin Dinghan. Interview with William L. Adams, Beijing, May 14, 2003.
Khien, Nguyen Van. Interview with William L. Adams, Thanh Ha, Nam Ha, Vietnam, December 19, 2003.
Kornegay, Doss, Jr. Interview with Jorge Pena, Harlingen, April 13, 2003.
Leal, Jose G., Jr. Interview with Arturo Juarez, Brownsville, April 13, 2003.
Leal, Raul J. Interview with Edith Lizbeth Cano, Brownsville, June 4, 2003.
Lin Qingshan. Interview with William L. Adams, Beijing, May 17, 2003.
Lopez, Epitacio. Interview with Carlos Garza, Brownsville, April 15, 2003.
Lopez, Juan. Interview with Santiago Salazar, Jr., Brownsville, June 9, 2003.
Lu Yunkui. Interview with William L. Adams, Beijing, May 17, 2003.
Lucio, Luis. Interview with Rodolfo R. Flores, Brownsville, June 25, 2003.
Martinez, Luis. Interview with Edith Lizbeth Cano, Brownsville, June 24, 2003.
Moore, Col. Edward. Interview with William L. Adams, Brownsville, October 29, 2003.
Murillo, Catarino. Interview with Santiago Salazar, Jr., Brownsville, June 27, 2003.
Ortiz, Ricardo. Interview with Rolando R. Barron, Brownsville, April 16, 2003.

Phuong, Dang Thi. Interview with William L. Adams, Thanh Ha, Nam Ha, Vietnam, December 19, 2003.
Pina, Roberto. Interview with Alfonso Gonzalez, Brownsville, April 13, 2003.
Ramos, Lorenzo, Jr. Interview with Leo Villarreal, Brownsville, June 6, 2003.
Rodriguez, Jesus F. Interview with Jesus F. Rodriguez, Jr., Brownsville, April 12, 2003.
Rodriguez, Roberto Miguel. Interview with Sandra Vargas, Brownsville, April 16, 2003.
Saavedra, Raul. Interview with Edith Lizbeth Cano, Brownville, June 29, 2003.
Saldivar, Feliciano. Interview with Santiago Salazar, Jr., Brownsville, June 26, 2003.
Scanlan, James A. Interview with Billy G. Karavasilis, Brownsville, April 13, 2003.
Serrano, Joe. Interview with Alejandra Sainz, Brownsville, April 19, 2003.
Simonsen, Raymond L. Interview with Carlos Pena, Brownsville, April 3, 2003.
Torres, Juan. Interview with David Rodriguez, Brownsville, April 16, 2003.
Torres, Manuel. Interview with Rodolfo R. Flores, Brownville, June 27, 2003.
Tyra, Garrett. Interview with Joel Rodriguez, Jr., Brownsville, April 17, 2003.
Villarreal, Leonardo. Interview with Leo Villarreal, Brownsville, June 23, 2003.
White, Ralph J., Jr. Interview with Miriam V. Briones, Brownsville, April 16, 2003.
Wilson, Richard. Interview with Justin Lawrence, Brownsville, May 21, 2003.
Wise, Herman. Interview with Santiago Salazar, Jr., Harlingen, June 10, 2003.
Zapata, Ricardo. Interview with Juan Velez, Brownsville, April 14, 2003.

Index

A

A Company, 139
A-4 Skyhawks, 87, 89
A-6 Intruders, 191
A-7 Corsairs, 191
Abuja, Nigeria, 75
AC-130 gunship, 87
Acapulco, Mexico, 193
Acuña, Joe, 40
Adams, Clella, 41
Adams, Harold L., 41-45
Adams, William L., 38-45, 64-65, 67-72, 105-109, 118-120, 122-123, 139-141, 202-213, 214- 231
Adriatic Sea, 3, 228
advanced infantry training (AIT), 143
Aegean Sea, 228
Afghanistan, 130
Agent Orange, 75, 87, 126, 139, 145, 162, 166, 170, 188
Aguinaga, Reynaldo, 116-118
Air-Sea Rescue, 58
Air-Sea Rescue LST, 59
airborne training, 164
aircraft carrier, 79, 85, 193
AK-47s, 96
Alamogordo, 3
Alaska, 4, 61
Alberta, 61
Aleutian Islands, 4
Alpine, Texas, 150

Americal Division, 148, 166, 177
American Airlines, 190
American Civil War, 82
American Legion, 57, 126
American National Guard, 77
American Phase of war in Vietnam, 81, 83, 85
Amral, Korea, 19
An Loc, 133
Anchorage, Alaska, 143
"Anchors Away," 104
Annam Cordillera, 73
Annamites, 80
Annapolis, 222
anti-Mao revisionist, 66
anti-tank mine, 96
anti-war protest, 109, 137, 145, 167, 170
"Arc Lights," 130
Armed Forces Staff College, 114
armistice, 9, 10, 11
ARVN (Army of the Republic of Vietnam), 81, 85, 86, 89, 91, 92, 93
Asian defense perimeter, 4
Atlantic Fleet headquarters, 229
atomic weapons, 3, 4, 25, 79
Audie Murphy Hospital, 49
Austin, Texas, 47
Australia, 5, 85, 93, 189
Australia-New Zealand-United States Treaty (ANZUS), 4

Austria, 25
Avalos, Alberto, 96
Axis Powers, 1

B

B-29s, 79
B-52s (buffs), 87, 89, 91, 92, 96, 124, 130, 146, 157, 182, 201, 204, 211, 225
Babenhausen, Germany, 48
"baby killers," 98, 125, 126, 129, 141, 151, 190
bacteriological agent, 68
Baldwin, Robert B., 222, 223
Baltic, 3
Baltimore, Maryland, 46
Band of Brothers, 61
Bangkok, Thailand, 130
banzai, 47
Barraza, Solomon, 49
Barrera, David, 21-24
Barrientes, Alonso "Tiny," Jr., 172-176
Barron, Rolando R., 190-192
Basic Underwater Demolition Training (BUDS), 101
bastard unit, 22
Bastogne, 7
battle fatigue, 37
Battle of the Bulge, 124
Battleship Row, 223
Bay of Pigs, 82
"Bears," 225

Beijing, 10, 61, 62, 64, 69, 71, 72, 91
Beijing Social Science Institute, 66
Beijing University, 64
Belgium, 5
Ben Hat, 139
Biao, Lin, 72
Bien Hoa Army Base, 84, 117, 119
Big Red One, 165
Binh Dinh province, 84
Black Sea Fleet (USSR), 227
Blankenship, —, 15
Bloody Ridge, 10
Blue House (Seoul), 7
Blum, Sergeant, 18
body bags, 85, 117, 188
booby traps, 52, 106, 115, 116, 160, 178, 179, 186, 187
Booth, Blake B., 42
Borgnine, Ernest, 42
Boston, 217
Boyce, Christopher John, 199
Brady, Texas, 49
brainwash, 59
Braniff Airlines 707, 137
Briones, Miriam V., 176-181
Britain, 1, 3, 80
British, 46, 47, 76, 79
Brooklyn Naval Shipyard Hospital, 231
Browning automatic rifle (B.A.R.), 40
Brownsville Coffee Shop, 45, 48
Brownsville Herald, 145
Brownsville High School, 114, 124
Brownsville ISD, 154, 156
Brownsville, Texas, 21, 27, 28, 29, 32, 41, 48, 55, 57, 96, 97, 105, 106, 109, 110, 111, 116, 124, 125, 127, 131, 136, 137, 138, 139, 141, 142, 144, 146, 152, 154, 156, 160, 163, 172, 176, 184, 190, 191, 194, 196, 197, 200
Brunei, 81, 231
Burma, 81
Bush, George, 65, 118

C
C-130, 100, 111, 146, 160
C-141, 107
C-rations, 34, 95, 108, 154, 189

California, 31, 36, 41, 160, 171
Cam Ranh Bay, Vietnam, 85, 111, 125, 137, 140, 147, 155, 165, 177
Cambodia, 75, 76, 81, 82, 85, 86, 93, 102, 118, 119, 125, 128, 139, 206, 208, 231
Cameron County, 47, 177
camouflage, 206
Camp Aliberry, Indiana, 19
Camp Chaffee, Arkansas, 17, 53
Camp Cook, California, 32, 33
Camp Del Mar, 28
Camp Hogan, 34
Camp Hollaway, Pleiku, Vietnam, 139, 140
Camp McNair, 33, 34
Camp Pendleton, California, 27, 95, 99, 110, 114, 143, 150, 190, 198, 199
Campos, Ignacio, 144
Canada, 5, 93, 145
Canant, Willie F., Jr., 114-116
Cano, Edith Lizbeth, 27-32, 57-60, 124-127, 146-149
Cantu, David, 154-156
Caribbean, 223
carriers, 90, 103, 226
Casanova, Carlos, 192
Casanova, Leo, Jr., 192-194
Casanova, Leonel, 192-194
Casanova, Marcela, 192
Castille, —, 27
Castillo, Joe, 184-190
Castro, Fidel, 202, 203
casualties: Americans in Korea, 11; Chinese, 11; North Korean, 11
Cavazos, —, 17
Cavazos, Richard, 124
CBS Evening News, 88, 90
CCC, 25
ceasefire, 11, 53
Cebu, Philippines, 75
Central Highlands, 73, 85, 86, 93
Central Intelligence Agency (CIA), 82
Central Junior High School, 170
Central Treaty Organization (CENTO), 4
Changjin Reservoir, 28
Chapa, Erasmo, 101-103
Charlie Battery, 155
chemical agent, 68
Chiang Kai-shek, 4, 8

China, 7, 9, 10, 44, 45, 61, 62, 65, 66, 67, 68, 70, 71, 72, 75, 76, 78, 79, 83, 87, 91, 199, 200, 212, 230
China Beach, 174
Chinese, 8, 10, 20, 23, 26, 28, 35, 40, 41, 43, 44, 45, 51, 52, 53, 62, 65, 66, 70, 71, 72, 75, 86, 91, 93, 105, 130, 196, 228
Chinese ships, 96
Chinese soldiers, 37, 69
Chinese-speaking soldiers, 16
Christmas bombing, 92, 201, 212, 201
Chu Lai, 95, 112, 147, 148, 149, 177
Churchill, Winston, 1, 3, 80
Clark Air Base, Philippines, 79, 87, 107
Clinton, Bill, 38
Cloverleaf Hill, 18
CNN-Turk, 118
coalition forces, 5, 8, 9
Cochin-Chinese, 80
Cockrill, E. E. Gene, 27-32
Cockrill, Pat, 27
Cold War, 1, 4, 11, 79, 126, 199, 225, 228, 231
Columbia, 5
combat air patrol (CAP), 226
Combat Infantry Badge, 37
COMIBERLANT (Commander Iberian-Atlantic Area), 230
COMINTERN (Communist International), 76
Communist Party of China, 64
Communist sympathizers, 206, 207
Conklin, Mike, 169
containment policy, 4, 109
Continental Airlines, 119
Convenience of the Government (COG), 27
Corps of Engineers, 22
Corpus Christi, Texas, 33, 142
Cortez, Ben, 101-103
Cotula, Texas, 192
Cronkite, Walter, 88, 89
Cruz, H. Jaime, 24-26
CS gas, 180
"Cuando vienen los Mesicanos con Cartuches y Cañones" (When the Mexicans Come with Guns and Cannons), 28-29

Cuba, 38, 82, 225
Cummings Junior High, 144
CWO (communication watch officer), 229, 230
Czechoslovakia, 25

D
D-Day, 1
Da Lat, 85, 155
Da Nang, Vietnam, 85, 100, 101, 111, 143, 147, 148, 150, 160, 161, 173, 174, 182, 198, 85, 93, 95
Dai Bao, 76
Dak To, 139
Dallas, Texas, 146, 200
Dang Thi Phuong, 209-211
darkened ship, 194, 223
Davidson, Phillip, 88
Davis, Raymond, 205
DD 214, 19
de Gaulle, Charles, 82
de la Rosa, —, 142
de Lattre, Jean de Tassigny, 77, 78
deescalation, 90
Defense Intelligence Agency, 118
delayed enlistment program, 181
Delta, see Mekong River and Delta
Democratic People's Republic of Korea, 3
Department of Food and Grain, 67
Desert Storm, 126
destroyer-radar (DDR), 42
destroyers, 58, 83, 103, 218, 226, 227
détente, 91
Di An, 119
Dienbienphu, 78, 79, 80, 88, 89, 202
discrimination, 153, 193
Distinguished Service Cross, 38, 39, 41
DMZ (demilitarized zone), 11, 73, 85, 88, 90, 92, 95, 101, 102, 128, 143, 146, 161, 206
Do Xa, 211
dogfights, 51
dogtags, 205
domino theory, 81, 109
Dong Ha, 143
"doves," 84
dry monsoon, 75

Duc Pho, 148, 149, 177

E
eagle flights, 180
Easy Company, 29
Edmond, Oklahoma, 221
8th Army Division, 46
8th Infantry Airborne Division, 164
8th Route Army, 66
82nd Airborne Division, 54
802nd Military Police Company, 106
Eisenhower, Dwight D., 10, 79, 80, 81
"Eisenhower Year," 53
El Paso, Texas, 47, 49, 150
El Ranchito, Texas, 139
El Toro Air Base, California, 98, 111, 144, 146, 160
Elbe River, 3
11th Infantry Brigade, 148, 177
Elks Lodge, 150
England, 25
escalation, 82
Espinosa,—, 31
espionage, 199
Ethiopia, 5

F
F-104 Thunderchiefs (Thuds), 87
F-4 Phantom, 87, 100, 147, 191, 194
Falcon, The, 199
Farsi, 228
Field 411, 177
5th Battalion, 155
5th Infantry, 150
5th Marines, 175
5th Regimental Combat Team (RCT), 52
15th Field Artillery, 14
56 (aircraft), 144
532nd Engineering Special Brigade, 25
fifty percent watch, 95
"Fight Against the U.S. War of Destruction in North Vietnam, The," 201
Filipino troops, 85
1st Battalion Headquarters, 110
1st Cavalry, 15, 23, 29, 117, 125, 128, 165
1st Division, 119

1st Infantry, 177
1st Infantry Division, 118, 124
1st Marine Brigade, 29
1st Marine Division, 6, 28, 29, 32, 94, 110
"fire for effect," 35
fire mission, 35
"Five Battles, The," 68
559th Transportation Group, 82
floating battalion, 114
Flores, Rodolfo R., 13-21, 94-99, 141-146
flower children, 98
Flower Village," 201
Fonda, Jane, 96, 108, 141, 152; *also see* Hanoi Jane
40th Infantry Division, 32
Ford, Gerald, 93
Ford Motor Company, 83
Foreign Legionnaires, 79
"Forgotten War," 24, 36
Formosa Strait, 44
Fort Benning, Georgia, 164, 168
Fort Bliss, El Paso, Texas, 117
Fort Brown Resaca, 137
Fort Chaffee, 198
Fort Dix, New Jersey, 171
Fort Gordon, Georgia, 131
Fort Hood, 25, 125
Fort Howard, Maryland, 46
Fort Indian Point, Pennsylvania, 198
Fort Knox, Kentucky, 147
Fort Leonard Wood, Missouri, 106
Fort Lewis, Washington, 13, 17, 18, 22, 116, 147, 155, 164, 177,
Fort Ord, California, 46, 106, 117
Fort Polk, Louisiana, 131, 133, 147, 154, 163, 168, 171
Fort Rucker, Alabama, 153
Fort Sam Houston, Texas, 33, 154, 179
Fort Sill, Oklahoma, 48, 155, 163
Fort Story, Virginia, 49
Fort Walters, Mineral Wells, Texas, 179
forward observer, 48
4-F, 24
44th Medical Brigade, 165
"Fourth Battle, The," 68, 69
"fragging," 122, 181
France, 5, 25, 76, 78
Franceschi, James, 105-109
Frankfurt, Germany, 48

freaking new guy, (FNG), 178, 179
Free-fire zone, 178
French, 77, 79, 80, 81, 85, 88, 97, 201, 202
French colonial forces, 77
French expeditionary corps, 79
French Phase, 77
Friendship Hotel, 63
full court press, 86
Fulton, Missouri, 3

G
G-2 (intelligence), 86
Galaxy Bowling Alley, 127
"Galloping Ghost of the Korean Coast," 42
Garcia, Edward J., 131-133
Garcia, Roberto, 154-156
Garcia, Ruben, 103-105
Garza, Carlos, 136-138
Garza, Juan, Jr., 103
Gearing, 220
general quarters, 225
General Breckenridge, 33
General Offensive, 202
Geneva Convention, 10, 80, 96, 203
germ warfare, 68
Germany, 25, 47, 49, 137, 147, 155, 164, 165, 166, 171, 182
Ghionzoli, Richard, 103-105
GI Bill, 196
Giap, *see* Vo Nguyen Giap
gigs, 217, 218
GIs, 53
Gloor Lumber Company, 176
Goldwater, Barry, 83
Gonzalez, Alfonso, 197-199
Gonzalez, Jose, 131-133
gooks, 111, 112, 174, 223
Grant, U. S., 82
Great Britain, 5
Great Lakes, Illinois, 27, 28, 103
"Great P'ohang Guerrilla Hunt, The," 29
Great Proletarian Cultural Revolution, The, 66
Greece, 5, 164
Green berets, 162
"green" (money), 183
Greene, Colonel, 127
Greenland, 224
Guadalcanal, 38

Guam, 17, 20, 30, 87, 91, 111, 119, 157
Guerra, Carmen, 38
Guerra, Juan, 38-41
guerrillas, 73, 75, 76, 77, 115, 133, 157
Gulf of Tonkin, 143, 191, 193, 200, 221
Gulf War I, 118
Gulf War II, 118
Gullet, Gordon, 96
guns or butter, 78

H
Ha Nam Province, 207
Hai Wang Xing ("God Neptune"), 106
Haiphong, 77, 82, 87, 91, 92, 98, 103, 200
Hamburger Hill, 10, 136, 162
Hamhung, North Korea, 26
Hanoi, 76, 77, 79, 81, 82, 86, 90, 91, 92, 96, 199, 200, 201, 202, 203, 207, 211, 212
Hanoi Hilton, 201, 212
Hanoi Jane, *see* Fonda, Jane, 96
Harlingen, Texas, 17, 27, 28, 32, 57, 139, 159, 167
Hawaii, 6, 111, 119, 147, 159, 160, 174
Heartbreak Ridge, 10
Helena, 42
helicopters: bumblebees, 162; Cobras, 163; hueys, 180; Soviet, 206
Hell Month, 215, 216, 217
Hell Week, 101
Henan Province, 66
Hernandez, Alfredo, Jr., 13-18
Hernandez, Antonia, 20
Hernandez, Jesus, 17-21
Hesseling, Bob, 30
Hesseling, John R. "Rob," 27
Hickam Base, Hawaii, 107
Highland, Captain, 27
Highway 1, 73, 148, 211
Hill 155, 51
Hill 235, 10
Hill 327, 173, 175
Hill 504, 10
Hill 914, 10
Hindi language and people, 64, 228
hippies, 98, 109
Hiroshima, 3, 76, 89, 230

Hispanics, 183
Hitler, Adolf, 72
Ho Chi Minh, 76, 77, 78, 79, 80, 81, 84, 88, 95, 129, 202
Ho Chi Minh Campaign, 92
Ho Chi Minh City, 93, 208; *also see* Saigon
Ho Chi Minh Mausoleum, 201
Ho Chi Minh Trail, 82, 87, 88, 96, 208, 210
Hoa Lo Prison, 201, 202, 212
Holloman Air Force Base, New Mexico, 182
Hondo, Texas, 26
Hong Kong, 6, 194, 200
Honolulu, Hawaii, 42
Hope, Bob, 21, 125, 132
"Horn," of South America, 221
Houston, 200
Hudson Institute, 206
Hue City, Vietnam, 85, 88, 89, 90, 93, 128, 209, 210
"hugging the enemy," 87, 89
human waves, 53
hydrogen bomb, 10

I
I Corps, 85, 128, 130, 143, 147
II Corps, 85, 118, 147
III Corps, 85, 148
IV Corps, 85
Ibarra, Joe, 38, 41
Ibarra, Jose, 139-141
Iceland-Faeroes Gap, 225
illegal drug use, 151
Illinois, 15
immunizations, 127
Inchon, 6, 13, 23, 25, 26, 42, 46, 50
Indian, 196
Indochina, 76, 77, 78
Indochinese Communist Party, 76
Indonesia, 81, 231
interdependent world order, 83
International Dateline, 200
International Talent Monthly, 64
Iowa, 13, 224
Iran, 229
Iraq, 38, 101, 116, 118, 126, 129, 138, 158, 180
Iraq War, 36
"Irish pennant," 217
Iron Curtain, 3
Iron Triangle, 165

Index

IWO (intelligence watch officer), 229, 230
Iwon, 26

J
J. T. Canales Elementary School, 190
Jackson, Mississippi, 171
Jaimez, Juan, 192
Japan, 4, 5, 7, 19, 23, 24, 25, 32, 33, 34, 36, 39, 44, 46, 49, 55, 56, 76, 81, 87, 99, 126, 135, 149, 150, 160, 189, 231
Japanese, 35, 59, 67
Japanese capitulation, 3
Japanese civilians, 49
Japanese homeland, 50
Japanese Occupation medal, 37
Jilin Province, 67
Jin Dinghan, 64-65
John Thompson, 58
Johnson, I. D., 13
Johnson, Lucy Baines, 143
Johnson, Lyndon, 80, 82, 83, 84, 86, 87, 90, 95, 116, 143
"Johnson's War," 84
Joint Chiefs of Staff, 79, 82, 83, 84, 86, 87, 92
Juarez, Arturo, 163-167
jungle bashing, 87
"Jungle Rot PC," 126

K
K-rations, 34
Kahn, Herman, 206
Kansas, 224
Karavasilis, Billy G., 156-158
KC-130, 100
Kearns, Doris, 84
Kenedy Ranch, 19
Kennan, George, 4
Kennedy, John F., 82, 95, 154
Kennedy, Robert, 129
Kent State University, 96
Khe Sanh, 88, 89, 90, 100, 128, 143, 150, 151, 202, 203, 204
Khmer Rouge, 75, 195
KIA, 113
Kim Il Sung, 3, 65
Kim Jong Il, 65
King, Martin Luther, 129, 164
King Ranch, 19
Kingsville, 124
Kissinger, Henry, 91, 92, 93
Kola Peninsula, Russia, 225

Kon Tien, 143
Kontum, 139
Korean "conflict," 26
Korean Battle Citation, 37
Korean Conflict medal, 37
Korean elections, 3
Korean Ribbon, 47
Korean War veterans, 23
Kornegay, Doss, Jr., 167-170
Krugerrands, 228
Kuomintang army, 4, 7, 72

L
"La Cucaracha," (The Cockroach), 28
"La Pulga," 113
Lackland Air Force Base, San Antonio, Texas, 182, 195
Lai Khe, 165, 166
Lake Charles, Louisiana, 105
Lande, Everett, 191
landing zones (LZs), 144, 145, 188
Laos, 76, 78, 80, 81, 82, 85, 86, 88, 128, 162, 195, 206, 210, 231
Las Marianas Islands, 17
Lawrence, Justin, 127-130
Lawton, 54
Le Duc Tho, 91, 92
Leal, Jose G., Jr., 163-167
Leal, Raul J., 57-60
Lee, Andrew Daulton, 199
Leyte, 38
Liaoning Province, 67
"light at the end of the tunnel," 88, 89
limited war, 83, 157
Line Kansas, 9
Line Wyoming, 9
Linebacker II, 92
Lisbon, 230
Littlefield, Texas, 48
Long Binh Army Base, Vietnam, 117, 119, 130
Longoria, Erika, 172-176
Lopez Brothers, 102
Lopez, Epitacio, 136-138
Lopez, Juan, 54-47
Los Fresnos High School, 139
Los Fresnos, Texas, 192
lottery draft, 176
Louisiana, 153, 176
LSD (amphibious landing ship), 193

LST landing ship, 58, 60, 94
Lu Yunkui, 66-67, 69, 71-72
Lucio, Luis, 94-99
"lurps," 118
Luxemburg, 5

M
M.U.S.T., 165
M-tracks, 95
MacArthur, Douglas, 5, 6, 7, 8, 9, 16, 23, 37, 42, 44, 45, 72
magnesium flares, 100
Main Comm, 224
Main Force, 77, 78, 79, 84, 86
Main Line, 88
Mainz, Germany, 164
Malaysia, 81, 231
mamasan, 183
Manchuria, 3, 23
Manhattan Project, 3
Manila, 198
Manitoba, 61
Mao Zedong, 4, 64, 72, 78, 91
Marine Corps, 27
Marine Corps Recruiting Depot (MCRD), 99, 142, 185, 197
MARS station, 177
Marseilles, 231
Martin, Joseph W., 9
Martinez, Juan L., 116-118
Martinez, Luis, 124-127
Martinsville, Virginia, 118
Masan, 29, 30, 31
Massachusetts, 49
Matamoros, Tamaulipas, Mexico, 27, 190, 196
McAllen, Texas, 97
McDill Air Force Base, Tampa, Florida, 195
McDonald, Staff Sergeant, 142
McGovern, George, 91
McNamara, Robert, 83, 88, 95
Med cruise, 227
Mediterranean, 223, 228
medivac, 179
Mekong Delta, 88
Mekong River and Delta, 73, 75, 81, 85, 146
Memphis, Tennessee, 127
Mercedes, 142
mercenaries, 71
Mexicans, 34, 111
Mexican Civil War, 82
Mexican-American, 153
Mexico, 31, 32, 55, 152

Mexico City University, 32
MIAs, 199
Michigan, 41
Midland, Texas, 145
MIGs, *see* Russian MIGs
military prisoners from Puerto Rico, 25
Military Assistance and Advisory Group (MAAG), 81
Military Occupational Specialty (MOS), 28, 198
mines, 58, 59, 91, 106, 144, 160, 179, 208, 219; anti-personnel, 106; anti-tank, 106; claymores, 161
minesweeper, 58
Minh Thu Hotel, 201, 211
Minneapolis, Minnesota, 61
missiles, 91, 92, 130, 226, 230
Montagnard, 181
moon juice, 173
Moore, Edward, 118-120, 122-124
Moorer, Thomas, 92
mooring point, 78
mortars, 100, 111, 112, 113, 115, 117, 118, 139, 140, 144, 161, 198
Moscow, 4, 10, 76
MPC (money), 183
Mr. War," 38
MRE, 34
Mt. Fujiyama, 33
Mullin, Steven, 144
Munich, Germany, 54
Murillo, Catarino, 158-163
Mutual Assured Destruction (MAD), 226, 229, 230
My Lai, 126, 129

N
Nagasaki, 76, 230
Nakhon Phanom (NKP), 195, 196
Nance, James W., 223, 225
napalm, 87, 89, 102, 139, 204
Naples Bay, 221
Naples, Italy, 220
Napoleon, 82, 204
Narragansett Bay, 218
National Chinese army, 8
National Committee of Liberation for Vietnam, 77
National Emergency Command Center, 229
National Front for Liberation, 121
National Guard, 27, 163
Nationalist Chinese troops, 76
Nationalists, 67
Navajo Indians, 123
Naval Air Station Chase Field, 191
Naval Air Station, Cubi Point, Subic Bay, Philippines, 191, 192
Naval Technical Center, Jacksonville, Florida, 190-191
Navarre, Henri, 78, 79
Navy Bureau of Personnel, 229, 230
Navy Day, 84
Nazi Germany, 1, 3, 76, 87
Nazi invasion of France, 76
NECC, 230
Netherlands, 5
Neutral Nations Supervisory Commission, 10
New Guinea, 38
New Guinea campaign, 6
New Jersey, 164
New Mexico, 3
New York, 15, 105, 164, 217
New York Times, 82
New Zealand, 5
New Zealand troops, 85
Newport, Rhode Island, 214, 217, 221
Nguyen Duc Hanh, 207, 211-213
Nguyen Duc Huy, 201-207
Nguyen That Thanh, 76
Nguyen Van Khien, 207-209, 211
Nguyen Van Loi "Nam," 201
Nguyen Van Thieu, 92
Nguyen Viet Bac, 201-202, 207, 209-211
Nha Trang, 85
9th Infantry, 15
9th Marine Expeditionary Brigade, 99
Nixon, Richard Milhouse, 80, 90, 92, 95, 199
No Name Line, 9
Norfolk, Virginia, 53, 114, 220, 221, 223, 229, 230
North Atlantic, 223, 225, 227
North Atlantic Treaty Organization (NATO), 4, 8, 229
North Cape, Norway, 225
North Carolina, 15, 133, 195
North Korean army, 4
North Vietnam Firsters, 81
North Vietnamese sympathizers, 199
North-South Railroad, 73
Northwest Airlines, 61
Norton Air Force Base, 189
NPM (Radio Honolulu), 42
nuclear attack, 230
nuclear bombs, 80, 226
nuclear capable, 222
nuclear inventories, 230
nuclear machinery, 46
NVA (North Vietnamese Army), 77, 87, 89, 90, 119, 120, 140, 145, 200, 202, 206, 210; also *see* Viet Cong

O
Oakland, California, 33, 129, 137
Odessa, 227
Officer Candidate School (OCS), 21, 214, 215, 216, 218, 219
Okinawa, Japan, 5, 46, 51, 61, 111, 114, 116, 130, 143, 174, 186, 189, 194, 198
Oklahoma, 41
Olmito, Texas, 13, 14
Olongapo, Philippines, 103
Olympia, Washington, 22
"1-2-3 Club," 54
101st Airborne Division, 117, 128, 155
101st Screaming Eagles, 61
145th Aviation Battalion, 153
188th Ordnance Battalion, 139
195th Field Artillery, 17
196th Light Infantry Brigade, 168
Operation "Rolling Thunder," 86
Operation Double Eagle, 94
Operation Freedom, 126
Operation Linebacker, 91
Operation Niagara, 89
Operation Vulture, 79
Ops, 48
Orlando, Florida, 192
Ortiz, Marisa, 190
Ortiz, Martina, 190
Ortiz, Ricardo, 190-192

P

P'ohang, 30
Pakistan, 229
palace guard, 178
Panama, 53
Panama Canal, 49, 103, 221
Panmunjon, 10, 53
paper tiger, 84
Paratrooper Infantry Regiment, 54
paratroopers, 55, 56, 79, 107
Paris, 77, 82, 90, 91
Paris Agreement, 92, 93
Paris Peace Talks, 90
Pathet Lao, 78
Paul's Valley, Oklahoma, 15
peace agreement, 91, 92
peace candidate, 83, 84
peace movement, 125
"Peace with Honor," 90
Pearl Harbor, Hawaii, 44, 48, 105, 223
Pena, Carlos, 99-101
Pena, Jorge, 167-170
Peng, General, 69, 72
Pensacola, Florida, 99
Pentagon, 8, 223, 229
People's Liberation Army (PLA), 4, 66, 67
People's Republic of China, 4
Perez, Anthony, 144
Phan Rang, 155
Philadelphia, 105
Philippines, 4, 5, 6, 79, 81, 87, 89, 91, 130, 147, 189, 231
Phu Bai, 128
Pina, Roberto, Sr., 197-199
"Pinkville," 148
Pleiku, 84, 85, 107, 108, 125, 139, 140
Pol Pot, 75
POL (petroleum-oil-lubrication) storage sites, 91
police force, 26
Politburo, 10, 92
political commissar, 66, 67, 68
political officers, 71
Popular Force, 77, 79
Port Isabel, 109, 192
Portland, Oregon, 99
Portugal, 230
Post Traumatic Stress Disorder, 37, 97
Potsdam conference, 3
POWs, 10, 15, 35, 37, 71, 96, 102, 115, 120, 121, 132, 136, 199; Chinese, 53; North Koreans, 53
Presidential Citation, 47
progressive squeeze and talk, 86
promesa, 37
Pueblo, 130
Puerto Rico, 25, 53
"Puff the Magic Dragon," 87, 146
Punch Bowl, The, 10
Purple Heart, 16, 36, 37, 47, 97, 118, 122, 172, 180
Pusan, 5, 6, 13, 15, 17, 23, 25, 28, 29, 36, 40, 46, 50, 59
Pyongyang, 7, 10, 15

Q

Qingshan, Lin, 66-70, 72
"quad fifties," 52, 53
Quang Tri, 85, 92
Querétaro, Mexico, 145
Qui Nhon, 85, 108, 114, 115, 140

R

R-856 (NVA), 208
R&R, 19, 44, 140
RA-5s (reconnaissance aircraft), 228
racial tension, 183
Ramos, Lorenzo, Jr., 45-48
Rantoul Air Force Base, 182
Recio, Felix, 97
Recruit Training Center, Orlando, Florida, 190
Red Army, 1, 3
Red Ball Express, 14
Red Cross, 107, 177
Red River Valley and Delta, 73, 75, 77, 82, 200
refugees, 29, 198, 199
Regional Forces, 77
"REMFs," 122
Republic of Korea (ROK), 3, 4, 5, 6, 11, 59; military police, 53
Reston, James, 82
Rhee, Syngman, 3, 7
Rhine River, 164
Ridgway, Matthew B., 7, 8, 9, 38, 41
Rio Del Sol, 156
Rio Grande City, 124
Robb, Charles, 143
Rocha, Roberto, 96
Rodriguez, Carlos, 114-116
Rodriguez, David, 133-136
Rodriguez, Fernando, 24-26
Rodriguez, Jesus F., Jr., 48-54
Rodriguez, Jesus F., Sr., 48-54
Rodriguez, Joel, Jr., 150-152
Rodriguez, Roberto Miguel, 170-172
Rolling Thunder, 87
Roosevelt, Franklin, 1
Royal Thai Air Force Base, 195
Ru, Hao, 67-72
Rubin, Jerry, 109
rules of engagement, 161
Russia/Russians, 1, 47, 72, 103, 199, 227, 228, 230; MIGs, 23, 87, 192, 228; ships, 87, 96; submarines, 188; weaponry, 102; *also see* Soviet Union
Russian-Chinese border, 3

S

Saavedra, Raul, 146-150
SACLANT (Supreme Allied Commander-Atlantic), 230
Saigon, 75, 81, 84, 85 , 88, 93, 109, 119, 131, 133, 136, 140, 147, 148, 153, 198, 208; *also see* Ho Chi Minh City
Sainz, Alejandra, 152-154
Saipan, 17, 20
Salazar, Santiago, Jr., 32-38, 54-57, 109-113, 158-163
Saldivar, Feliciano, 109-113
SAMs, *see* missiles
San Antonio, Texas, 49, 54, 109, 110, 142, 146, 154, 159, 177, 182, 185, 197
San Benito, Texas, 17, 32, 38, 101, 102, 124, 150, 154, 177
San Benito School District, 124
San Bernardino, California, 143
San Clemente, California, 199
San Diego, California, 28, 42, 57, 105, 142, 150, 185, 193, 197
San Francisco, California, 31, 49, 96, 119, 127
San Jose, California, 67
Sanders, Colonel, 222
Sandy's Restaurant, 21
Santander, Spain, 190
Sarita, Texas, 19
SARS, 62, 66, 200; *also see* "Special Time"

Sasebo, Japan, 44
Saskatchewan, 61
Savanna, Georgia, 153
Scanlan, James, 156-158
Schofield Barracks, Hawaii, 106
Scott, Winfield, 82
Sea of Japan, 43, 45, 58
Seabees, 95, 97
Seals, *see* U.S. Navy Seals
search and destroy, 86, 97, 115, 119, 171
search and rescue, 188
Seattle, Washington, 13, 17, 111, 125
2nd Battalion, 29, 94, 143
2nd Brigade, 119
2nd Gulf War, 103
2nd Infantry Division, 13, 39
2nd Surgical Hospital, 165
Second Battle of the Marne, 124
Second Iraq War, 128, 135, 165
Secret Service, 199
Secretary of Defense, 83
Selective Service, 197
Semmes destroyer, 219
Seoul, Korea, 4, 6, 8, 50
Serrano, Joe, 152-154
Sevastopol, 227
7th Infantry Division, 6, 16, 50
7th Marine Regiment, 29, 94
Seventh Fleet, 6, 72
Shanxi Province, 66
Shepard, Lemuel C., 29
Signal Corps, 22
Simonsen, Joyce, 99
Simonsen, Phyllis, 99
Simonsen, Raymond L., 99-101
Singapore, 231
65th Engineering Battalion (combat), 106
66th Route Army, 67
smallpox, 127
smoke screen, 35
snipers, 29, 46, 136, 140, 144, 161
Snowman, The, 199
Song Be, 117
South Africa, 228
South Carolina, 195
South China Sea, 85
South Korean ambassador to Mexico, 32
South Vietnam Firsters, 81
Southeast Asia, 81, 231

Southeast Asian Treaty Organization (SEATO), 4
Soviet Union, 1, 3, 4, 7, 10, 65, 72, 83, 87, 91, 93, 231; advisors, 102; air force, 225; arsenal, 228; expansion, 8; heartland, 228; Red Army, 4; Soviet-built trucks, 79; territory, 226
"Special Time," 62, 63; *also see* SARS
spies, 97
spy plane, 228
St. Edward's University, 139
St. Joseph Academy, 141, 190
Stalin, Josef, 1, 10
"Stars and Stripes Forever," 49
Stars and Stripes, 113
Stillwater, Minnesota, 21
"Stinking Ninth Category, The," 66
Storekeeper "A" School, 193
strategic target selection, 223
Strategic Integrated Operation Plan (SIOP), 229, 230
Subic Bay, Philippines, 194, 221
submarines, 41, 188, 223, 225, 226
supercarriers, 222
surface-to-air missiles (SAMs), *see* missiles

T

T-34 tanks, 4
Tacoma, Washington, 22, 177
tactical nuclear bombs, 79
Taiwan, 4, 8, 44, 72, 231
Tampa, 105
Tan Son Nhut airport, 88
Task Force Smith, 5
Tay Ninh, 117
Tennessee, 15
Tet Offensive, 88, 89, 119, 122, 128, 137, 155, 157, 164, 204
tetanus, 34, 127
Texas Southmost College (TSC), 27, 131, 154
Thai troops, 85
Thailand, 5, 81, 91, 93, 100, 130, 187, 188, 189, 195, 196, 231
Thanh Ha, Vietnam, 207, 209, 211
3rd Marine Division, 128, 143, 150, 159, 203
Thieu, President, 93

Thieu-Ky dictatorial traitors, 121
38th Field Artillery Battalion, 13, 15
38th Parallel, 3, 4, 7, 8, 9, 23, 35, 51, 59
38th Route Army, 67
Third Battalion, 125
Third Battle, 69
Thompson, Tommy, 27
351st Division (NVA), 202, 204
Three-Five Cavalry, 125
Tiger Beach, 193, 194
Tiger Island, 100, 193
Tilford, Earl H., 87
Tokyo, 38, 39, 41, 50, 61, 62
Toledo (cruiser), 42, 220
Tonkin Gulf, 83, 85, 103
Tonkin Gulf Hunt Club, 223
Tonkin Gulf Resolution, 84
Tonkinese, 80
Torres, Juan, 133-136
Torres, Manuel, 141-146
torture, 71, 102
travel advisory, 62
treaty of mutual assistance, 4
Truman, Harry S., 5, 8, 9, 23, 46
tunnels, 97, 180, 205, 206, 212, 213
Turkey/Turkish, 5, 46, 47, 118, 228, 229
Turner, Ted, 96
23rd Division, 20
23rd Infantry Regiment, 14, 39
24th Infantry, 23
25th U.S. Infantry Division, 23, 106, 121
27th Field Artillery, 155
112th Marines, 143
224th Infantry Regiment, 32
two-front war, 56
Tyra, Garrett, 150-152

U

U.S. Army Intelligence Agency, 128
U.S. Army Security Agency, 127
U.S. Marshal's Service, 114
U.S. Naval Air Station, Sangley Point, Philippines, 198
U.S. Navy Bureau of Personnel, 219
U.S. Navy Seals, 101, 102
U.S. occupation forces, 5
Udorn, Cambodia, 195, 196

Ulsan, 26
United Nations, 3, 8, 9, 10; casualties, 11; coalition army, 7; elections, 3; forces, 5, 7, 8, 72; mandate, 7; Security Council, 5;
United Nations Ribbon, 47
University of Dallas, 190
University of Texas at Brownsville, 27, 99, 118, 124, 137, 141
Uranium City, 61
Urdu, 228
USS *Chevalier*, 42, 44, 45
USS *Shovler*, 58
USS *Alamo*, 193
USS *Forrestal*, 220, 221, 222, 223, 226, 227, 229, 230, 231
USS *Maddox*, 83, 84
USS *Marias*, 227
USS *Midway*, 191
USS *Missouri*, 124
USS *New Jersey*, 225
USS *New Orleans*, 188
USS *Point Defiance*, 193
USS *Rangel Ranier*, 103
USS *Ticonderoga*, 83
USS *Tripoli*, 188
USS *Turner Joy*, 83, 84

V
VA, 179
vaccines, 34, 56
Valley Morning Star, 38
Van Fleet, James A., 9
Vargas, Sandra, 170-172
VC, *see* Viet Cong
Velez, Juan, 194-197
Veterans of Foreign Wars (VFW), 21, 47, 94, 126
Veterans Service Office, 45, 47

Victoria Bar, Pleiku, 108
Vientiane, 78
Viet Bac, 78
Viet Cong (VC), 77, 81, 84, 85, 86, 87, 89, 91, 92, 95, 96, 97, 102, 112, 114, 115, 119, 120, 122, 140, 143, 145, 151, 161, 162, 174, 183, 189, 200, 206, 207, 211; *also see* NVA
Vietminh, 77, 79, 80, 202
Vietnam Military History Museum, 201
Vietnam War phases, 76
Vietnamese Airlines, 200
Vietnamization, 90, 92
"Vigilantes," 228
Villarreal, Leo, 21-24, 45-48, 181-190
Villarreal, Leonardo, 181-184
Vo Nguyen Giap, 77, 78, 79, 80, 84, 87, 88, 89, 90, 202, 204
VT-24, 191
Vung Tan, 140

W
Wake Island, 111
Walker, John, 199
Walker, Walton H., 5, 6, 7
war protesters, 108, 129, 141, 151, 167, 171, 181
Washington (governmental authority), 6, 7, 8, 79, 80, 82, 85, 87, 167, 198
Washington, D.C., 25, 28, 96
Washington, state of, 106
Watergate scandal, 92
Wayne, John, 36
Weslaco, 27
West Coast White House, 199
West Point, 187
West Virginia, 51

Westmoreland, William, 85, 86, 88, 89, 90
Westover Field Hospital, 49
wet monsoon, 75
White, Ralph J., Jr., 176-181
Whitman, Gary, 166
"Whiz kids," 83
Wickham, —, 224
Wiesbaden, Germany, 164
William Beaumont Hospital, 49
Wilson, Richard, 127-131
Wise, Herman, 32-38
Wise, Miguel, 32, 35
Wolmi-do Island, 26
Wonson harbor, 58, 59
World Health Organization, 62, 200
World Trade Center, 154
WWI, 124, 126
World War II, 1, 4, 7, 27, 30, 32, 33, 38, 41, 42, 48, 49, 51, 55, 59, 76, 78, 83, 110, 124, 126, 142, 222
Wright, Dick, 27

X-Y-Z
Xiaoping, Deng, 75
Yalta conference, 3
Yalu River, 7, 16, 23, 39, 58
Yang Hua Jing "Jane," 62-64, 68
Yankee Station, 85, 191, 221
yellow fever, 127
Yellowknife, 61
yippies, 98
Yokohama, Japan, 49
Yokuska, Japan, 194
Yukon, 61
Yung Dun Poo, 13
Zapata, Ricardo, 194-197

About the Author

WILLIAM L. ADAMS was born in New London, Connecticut, in 1946 and spent his childhood traveling in the household of his career navyman father. He was educated at Central State University, Oklahoma (B.A. summa cum laude in English and History); the State College of Victoria, Melbourne, Australia (Grad. Dip. in Ed. Admin.); the State University of New York, Binghamton (M.A. Political Science); and the University of North Dakota (M.A. and D.A. in History).

From 1967 to 1972, he served as a naval officer aboard the aircraft carrier *Forrestal* and as officer-in-charge of the message center at a NATO headquarters in Lisbon, Portugal.

Afterwards he spent twelve years as a lay teacher and administrator in Catholic schools, mainly in Australia and the Solomon Islands. From 1979 to 1983, he was deputy headmaster of Sale Catholic College in Australia. Dr. Adams joined the faculty of Texas Southmost College—(now the University of Texas Brownsville)—in 1987, and is currently an Associate Professor of Government and History. From 1989 to 1992, he chaired the Department of Social Sciences. In 1996, he was awarded an Army R.O.T.C. Military History Fellowship and spent the summer in residence at the U.S. Military Academy at West Point.

Dr. Adams' publications include *Portrait of a Border City: Brownsville, Texas*. He is married to the former Roselyn Grantham of Glasgow, Scotland, and has an adult son and daughter.

www.ingramcontent.com/pod-product-compliance
Lightning Source LLC
Chambersburg PA
CBHW080535170426
43195CB00016B/2573